About This Book

Why is this topic important?

Productive Workplaces Revisited updates the first edition to validate "getting the whole system in the room," a principle that has influenced large scale projects everywhere. The book provides a model, guidelines, and successful methods for improving organizations under conditions of nonstop change. The revised edition may be the only book of its kind, for it includes follow-ups to ten projects done fifteen to thirty years earlier; the author not only reports what happened afterward, but also draws implications for managers and consultants today. With this "glance backward," the book challenges the myth that you can "build in" practices that ensure continuity of new norms when leadership, staff, markets, technology, and ownership are constantly changing. "Each new generation," says Weisbord, "must learn all over again for itself."

What can you achieve with this book?

You can learn how to establish conditions for success before undertaking complex change projects. You will gain a deeper appreciation of key management practices and why some work better than others. The book will lead you to rethink, appreciate, and learn from your own experience and confirm that values matter more than techniques. It will help you become more secure and competent to face unprecedented dilemmas of organizational change.

How is this book organized?

The book contains three parts, and all have been revised to expand the scope and depth of the original. Part One tells key stories from management history, comparing the work of Frederick Taylor, "father of scientific management," to that of several social scientists who came after. Part Two presents cases involving typical managerial dilemmas that illustrate an evolution in practice from expert problem solving toward involving everyone in whole-systems improvement made necessary by conditions of nonstop change. The cases are updated in the 2000s, with implications for today. Two new chapters on seminal workshops in primary medical care and steel production show the benefits of having whole systems study themselves. Part Three presents a practice theory for managing and consulting in the new millennium. It includes key guidelines for success as well as methods by which the theory can be applied, and it shows how one company saved itself using these guidelines. It includes two new chapters on whole-systems improvement and a new summary chapter that answers critical questions about the nature of change and the practice of effective workplace improvement.

To a New Generation, My Grandchildren

Other Books by Marvin R. Weisbord

Organizational Diagnosis: A Workbook of Theory and Practice

Discovering Common Ground (with thirty-one international authors)

Future Search: An Action Guide (with Sandra Janoff)

Contents

---

* Indicates new chapters or includes updates written for this edition.   **vii**

Acknowledgments

First Edition Acknowledgments

This book evolved over twenty years during which I worked with thousands of people as manager, consultant, and learner. Certain colleagues gave of themselves in large ways that call for special thanks. These include Eric Trist and Ronald Lippitt, two friends now gone, who figure prominently in the text. I think too of William J. Schmidt, whose candid reading helped me see the centrality of dignity and meaning in the workplace, and Claudia Chowaniec, the late Robert S. Tannenbaum, Max Elden, Leonard Goodstein, and Edwin C. Nevis, all of whom made valuable suggestions for improving clarity and structure. I am grateful for hours spent talking with the late Richard Beckhard and Fred Emery, and with Edith Whitfield Seashore, all of whom are in my story.

Several others read chapters and made helpful comments, in particular Peter Block, Barbara Benedict Bunker, Douglas Bunker, Per Engelstad, Henry Gautier, Thomas North Gilmore, William S. Hatton, Larry Hirschhorn, Harry Hughes, J. Myron Johnson, Peter Koestenbaum, Jack Sherwood, and Peter Vaill. I'm grateful to Morley Segal for access to his extensive files on Douglas McGregor, and to Merrelyn Emery for an early draft of her book *Searching* and useful materials on Fred Emery's work. Peter Rubin, a practitioner of traditional Chinese medicine, helped me in subtle ways. Many associates of the consulting firm Block Petrella Weisbord had a hand in this book, not just those on the letterhead, but also C. James Maselko, Dominick Volini, John Dupre, Philip Gorsnick,

Jill Janov, Eileen Curtin, Maurice Dubras, Davidson Jones, Carol Meyers, and the late Kathleen Emery. My erstwhile assistant, Gloria Co, put the original manuscript through endless drafts and ran down many obscure references.

Second Edition Acknowledgements

A special thanks is due Sandra Janoff, co-director of Future Search Network and workshop partner for many years, for her good ideas and conversation, insightful questions, and unquestioning support while I was writing this update. I want to thank the many colleagues who read early drafts and made useful suggestions, especially Richard Axelrod, Jean-Pierre Beaulieu, Mary Broad, Claudia Cohen, Drusilla Copeland, Robert Dilworth, Peggy Holman, Ken Hultman, Rick Lent, Kim Martens, Ed Olson, Michael Randel, Donna Singer, and Sandy Weiner. I thank those who provided help with my revisits to workplaces, notably Timothy Althof, Donald Bell, Donald Cooper, Jacqueline Ewer, Connie Fuller, David Kahn, June Klinghoffer, Frank Dodge, David Evans, Phyllis Marciano, Tina Nickerson, William Rathgeber, John Rockstroh, Robert Scarpa, Bernard Sigel, David Vassar, Michael Vogel, Frank Warland, and especially my friend of forty years, David Wagner.

Nobody makes a career of consultation without a considerable boost from others. I received an indispensable lift early on when W. Warner Burke, who hardly knew me, put me on NTL training staffs long years ago. I am fortunate too in having had many fruitful partnerships. I refer to a twenty-plus year consulting practice with Peter Block and Tony Petrella, from whom I learned the business starting in 1971, action research in medical schools and hospitals with Paul Lawrence and Martin Charns from 1971 to 1976, dozens of workshops and consulting projects with Allan Drexler in those same years, an annual NTL Institute Consultation Skills Laboratory with Gail Silverman from 1975 to 1981, the "Men at Work" personal growth laboratories with John Weir and the late

Michael Merrill from 1991 to 1995, Blue Sky Productions with Allan Kobernick from 1987 to 1995, and Future Search Network since 1993 with Sandra Janoff. I would not be doing this work at all were it not for Don Kirchhoffer and Bob Maddox, who started me on self-managing work teams in the 1960s, nor the late Bernard Asbell, who gave me my first consulting job at Ford Foundation.

Friends and colleagues from whom I have gotten inspiration for decades are Billie Alban, Jan Asplind, Håkan Behrendtz, Bapu Deolalikar, Jan Johansson, Bill Lytle, Rolf Lynton, Margaret Wheatley, Larry Porter, Lee Vansina and John and Joyce Weir — master practitioners all — and three other greats no longer with us, the late Gunnar Hjelholt, Mary Beth Peters, and Eva Schindler-Rainman. I am indebted to scores of members, past and present, in NTL Institute, The European Institute for Transnational Studies (eit), and Future Search Network. While I haven't space to name you all, you know who you are. I offer a belated thanks to Steven Piersanti, former president of Jossey-Bass, who got me going on this book in the 1980s and could not be thanked then because of corporate policy. Since there are no strictures now, I am grateful to Leslie Stephen for her insightful editorial help in merging the two editions and to editor Matthew Davis for his encouragement.

I also acknowledge a few of many colleagues who have created ingenious ways to get everyone improving in whole systems. These include Richard Axelrod (2000) with The Conference Model®, David Cooperrider (2001) with Appreciative Inquiry, Kathie Dannemiller (1999) with Whole Scale Change®, Barry Oshry (2000) with the Power and Systems Laboratory®, and Harrison Owen (1997) with Open Space Technology. While this book is about my work, not theirs, I have been influenced by all of them over the years. Their methods and many others are described in Billie Alban and Barbara Bunker's *Large Group Interventions* (1999), and in Peggy Holman and Tom Devane's *The Change Handbook* (2000). That any of us are reducing global uncertainty is arguable. That this journey is worth taking anyway I have no doubt.

Finally, I could not do this work without the love and support of Dorothy Barclay Weisbord, my wife and best friend since 1956. I dedicated the original edition to our fathers, one an entrepreneur, the other a union machinist, both of whom died during the writing of it. At this point in my life I am looking forward, not back, and so dedicate this edition to the next generation, our grandchildren.

M.R.W.

About the Author

Marvin Weisbord is an internationally known consultant and author and co-founder of Future Search Network, involving people worldwide in voluntary social, technological, and economic change. He was for many years a partner in the consulting firm Block Petrella Weisbord and has worked with business firms, government and nonprofit agencies, and medical schools and hospitals. Weisbord serves as a resource faculty member in the Organization and Systems Renewal Program of Antioch University in Seattle and Chicago. He is an elected member of the European Institute for Transnational Studies and of the World Confederation of Productivity Science, and an honorary lifetime member of the Organization Development Network.

Weisbord wrote *Organizational Diagnosis* (Addison-Wesley, 1978), conceived and co-authored *Discovering Common Ground* (Berrett-Koehler, 1992), and is co-author with Sandra Janoff of *Future Search: An Action Guide* (2nd ed.) (Berrett-Koehler, 2000). He also plays piano with the Sunday Jazz Ensemble.

Introduction: How to Get the Most from *Productive Workplaces Revisted*

Welcome to *Productive Workplaces Revisited*. This book is based on a practice theory I devised in the 1980s for improving workplaces in a world of warp speed change. I called it "getting everybody improving whole systems." To me "improving" meant equal commitment to economic viability and enhanced life values — the dignity, meaning, and community wished for by nearly every living person. I came to that conclusion during twenty-five years of managing and consulting. Along the way I found myself studying my own experiences, rethinking theories and methods I had used, and researching key workplace pioneers. All of this I put into the original *Productive Workplaces* (Weisbord, 1987).

Processes for involving everyone in improving whole systems have proliferated like wildflowers since 1987. So too have assaults on dignity, meaning, and community. Few jobs are secure as I write in 2003. The march of technology and globalization has been a mixed blessing for those seeking techniques equal to their aspirations. In consequence, the challenges of workplace improvement have never been greater. Nor have aspirations been higher. In recent years many researchers have confirmed the positive bottom-line impact of encouraging leadership at all levels and attending equally the needs of customers, employees, and stockholders (Kotter and Heskett, 1992), of creating and maintaining community by optimizing people ahead of capital (de Geus, 1997), and of focusing on purpose and values before profits as a key to superior market performance (Collins and Porras, 1994). This evidence ought to be taken seriously by those seeking to reconcile the (illusory) contradiction between honorable ways to make money and the late Philip David Herbst's (1974) memorable assertion that "the product of work is people."

Purpose and Intent

The purpose of *Productive Workplaces Revisited* is to give you a model, guidelines, and successful methods for improving organizations under conditions of nonstop change. At one level, it will guide you to a deeper understanding of key management practices — and why some work better than others — and conditions for success in complex change projects. More, it is my hope that the book will show that values matter more than techniques and lead you to rethink, appreciate, and learn from your own experience. At bottom, this book summarizes what I have learned from mine.

Back in the 1960s, I was executive vice president of a company in which conflict was so bad that co-workers asked to have a wall built down the middle of a large, open office — a bit of cold war Berlin in North Philadelphia. Into this hostile climate I later introduced self-managing work teams. Few precedents existed, and I had no idea what to expect. In the ensuing confusion, output went down at first. Then it shot up like a rocket — 40 percent — as people caught on to this new way of working. Quality improved to levels our industry considered unattainable.

My biggest surprise, though, was the work force. Organized into teams, workers on both sides of the wall surged with energy and commitment. Antagonists eventually became friends. Absenteeism and turnover went to near zero. People built a community of interest around their own learning and business goals. The psychological wall fell, followed by the real one. "I used to hate coming to work in the morning," said Anne, a veteran employee who hadn't smiled in years. "Now I can't wait. I love it." That's when I knew that a productive workplace — based on personal dignity, meaning, and community — was attainable without hoopla or fancy techniques.

Years later I learned to call my project "sociotechnical systems" design, a method for having people plan and control their own work. At the time, lacking any management education beyond Douglas McGregor's writings, I saw self-managing teams as a way to increase business results by acting on my own values. I believed that autonomy and self-control were good for people and businesses. I did not have a vocabulary then for the connections among dignity, meaning, community, and output in work. This book reflects my efforts to create one.

Just before *Productive Workplaces* appeared in 1987, I took a leave of absence from my consulting company and joined Max Elden, an American professor, at the Norwegian Institute of Technology in Trondheim. After Norway I resumed consulting until 1992. That year, having tired of writing proposals, recruiting project staff, and hassling the details of a small firm with a complex tangle of consulting, training, and materials businesses, I called it quits. I thought of an exchange with my friend Gunnar Hjelholt, the late Danish social scientist, just after he gave up his company in Copenhagen for a 14th Century farmhouse in Jutland. Why did he quit? "Well," said Gunnar, "I was no longer lying awake at four in the morning worrying about the clients!" After more than twenty years of worrying about the clients and the business, I too felt like letting go. I had no plans other than to step off the consulting merry-go-round.

In 1993, drawing on principles from *Productive Workplaces* Sandra Janoff and I started Future Search Network, an international nonprofit service agency. By 2003 Network members were assisting with effective strategic planning in every sector of society. During a decade of teaching future search to people around the world, I heard a theme repeated time and again. How can anybody be sure the plans people make are actually carried out? How can we build in enduring, constructive norms and processes? If not for life, at least for a long time?

I have pondered that question for many years. I can tell you one popular practice that works badly — external control by those not directly involved. I also can tell you a no-fail practice with great social and economic benefits: interactive review meetings with "the whole system in the room." This book covers both polarities. I doubt that anybody can "build in" a technical insurance policy for ongoing success that trumps people's willingness to keep revisiting worthy goals and to stay connected with each other. The key leadership policy I advocate is involving those who do the work in planning and coordinating the work. The best methods for doing that tend to be simple.

Why then lust after high-performing work systems through increasingly complicated programs? As I pondered that question, I began wondering what had become of the organizations whose case studies form the core of this book. What actually happened afterwards? What could I learn about turbulence, transformation, stability, follow-up, and continuity by seeking out clients I'd known years back and tracing the lives of organizations I once had sought to make more productive? With 20/20 hindsight and fifteen to thirty years of emotional distance, could I discern patterns now that weren't apparent then?

Productive Workplaces Revisited is the result. This work contains nearly all the text of the first edition plus one hundred pages of new material. Revisiting my earlier work stimulated in me stories, ideas, and tips that did not come up the first time around. Hence the new title.

Who Should Read This Book?

In 1987, I said that I wanted to influence three audiences: managers, consultants, and students and teachers. They are still the main groups this book speaks to.

To managers I suggest that the concept of productive workplaces makes a powerful focus for organizing work — toward purposes, strategies, and structures worthy of human aspiration, cooperation, and sweat. Managing that ideal opens the door — as I will show — to quality and output far beyond what most companies settle for now.

To consultants of every specialty I suggest that we are in the midst of a revolutionary "rethink" of expertise — what it means, what it's good for, and how to use it. Treating every consulting engagement as a potential step toward or away from whole-system improvement is to perform a service desperately needed. Whether or not clients explicity request this, it can be delivered in response to any request.

To students and teachers I suggest that no further research is needed to prove the efficacy of participation in democratic societies. There are no technical alternatives to personal responsibility and cooperation in the workplace. What's needed are more people who will stick their necks out. That means learning as much about ourselves — our impulses, noble and ignoble — as we learn about other major subjects. Theories X and Y are not abstractions invented by Douglas McGregor. They are the parts of us that shape our actions, making of work an adventure and a trial. A "whole system" includes economics, technology, and people — including all of ourselves. I urge students to see the workplace as a "whole brain" adventure involving values, thought, and action. In 1987 I wrote that I would like to see that notion in more academic curricula. In 2003 I am glad to report that I do.

People who might particularly benefit from this new edition include:

- Anyone stimulated by the prospect of creating workplaces that offer economic success *and* satisfying work;
- Managers and consultants curious about what I have learned from more than a decade of community and network development based on principles gleaned from projects in businesses and medical schools;
- People looking for perspectives on helping large, diverse groups work productively;
- Past readers of *Productive Workplaces* who wonder what happened to the organizations I wrote about in 1987;

- Some of the thousands of people who have attended workshops with me and, more likely, with me and Sandra Janoff, since 1987, and the hundreds of members of Future Search Network, who will find their commitments validated here;

- Graduate student cohorts in the Organization and Systems Renewal Program at Antioch-Seattle and Antioch-Chicago, and in the Benedictine University doctoral program who have heard many of these stories since the mid-80s and always asked for more, and their peers in dozens of colleges and universities using *Productive Workplaces* as a text; and

- Readers over the years who have asked me to sign well-thumbed, annotated copies of *Productive Workplaces*. I have received a great deal of job satisfaction from meeting them. They remind me of my life-changing encounter with Douglas McGregor's *Human Side of Enterprise* in 1966 (see Chapter One). That uniquely was the fork in the road that enabled me decades later to write this book.

Three Major Themes

This book has three themes woven into a counterpoint of history, case studies, criticism, and new guidelines for action. My major theme is that we hunger for community in the workplace and are a great deal more productive when we find it. To feed this hunger in ways that preserve democratic values of individual dignity, opportunity for all, and mutual support is to harness energy and productivity beyond imagining.

My second theme is that the world is changing too fast for experts, and old-fashioned "problem solving" no longer works. For more than forty years productive workplaces on several continents have been evolving entirely another way of thinking and acting. First, they have been moving away from problem solving toward whole-systems improvement as the secret for solving great handfuls of problems at once. Second, they have been moving away from getting experts to fix systems toward having experts join everybody else in learning how to make improvements. The chart "Learning Curve," which appears in Chapter 13 illustrates this evolution.

My third theme represents a fresh interpretation of Douglas McGregor's famous dichotomy between Theory X and Theory Y. I believe that these polarities actually represent an inner dialogue between parent and child, hard guy and soft guy, decisive self and passive self within each of us. Managing this dialogue — not techniques, strategies, or models — represents our main dilemma in building more productive workplaces. In his classic management book, *The Human Side of Enterprise*, McGregor classified these opposing voices as theories of human nature, one (X) grounded in assumptions of laziness and incompetence, the other (Y) in assumptions of self-motivation, achievement, and growth. After 100 projects in every imaginable kind of workplace, the only thing I know for sure that I have changed is my own mind about Theories X and Y. They do not describe people with opposing management styles. They describe an inner dialogue within me and within you. This X/Y dialogue energizes our murkier as well as our more enlightened selves, making the search for productive workplaces a risky voyage into the hidden reaches of our own psyches. Changing our workplaces is inevitably bound up with changing ourselves.

These themes mark my journey down a path as old as the Industrial Revolution. Elton Mayo (1945), founder of industrial human relations, noted decades ago how "science and industry put an end to the individual's feeling of identification with his group, of satisfaction in his work" (p. 6). But engineers had noticed the effects of alienation — accidents, low morale, low output — more than half a century before that. I write now as a practitioner committed to involving people in restructuring their own companies, reorganizing and redesigning their own work. I see myself on a road with no end leading toward management practices grounded in dignity, meaning, and community, central to economic success, and also responsive to a sea tide of unprecedented change.

Overview of the Contents

Part One. In Part One I elaborate my first theme — that deep human strivings underlie the search for productive workplaces. Every variety of scientist has pursued that ideal, yet none has ever captured it by purely technical means. I retell stories from management history to support my contention that no good alternatives exist today for employee involvement in reorganizing companies. I offer new interpretations of how the first consulting engineer, Frederick W. Taylor, and four social scientists, Douglas McGregor, Kurt Lewin, Fred Emery, and Eric Trist, translated values into action and on why their innovations are important today.

Chapters in this part explore how Frederick Taylor's "scientific management" lost credibility because it metamorphosed into engineering solutions for what Taylor himself considered people problems. Organization development, a social science of managing change derived from Kurt Lewin, has suffered a similar fate whenever its advocates based solutions on feelings, human relations, or participation unconnected to markets and technology. Likewise, descendants of Emery and Trist — enamored of sociotechnical methods — sometimes lost sight of human processes, feelings, and group skills even as they designed work systems tied to customer needs and technical flexibility. I also show how practitioners of all three traditions have experienced enormous dilemmas in learning to use scientific knowledge while seeking to preserve democratic values and dialogue.

Part Two. Here I take up the practice of management and consultation based on participative methods. I present six cases in which my colleagues and I helped to diagnose and resolve commonplace managerial dilemmas — employee turnover, costs, production, staff-line cooperation — in the 1970s and early 1980s. I then critique this practice against a backdrop of accelerating change. It is here that my second theme — the inadequacy of "expert" management and consulting methods for coping with fast change — takes over. Through these cases I illustrate an evolution of practice from participative problem solving toward whole-systems improvement.

Part Three. The last part starts with a "21st Century practice theory" for managing and consulting now in this new century. It follows from the action steps, values, and thoughts evolved by my five main protagonists, and from the six cases. It is based on simple criteria for assessing the potential for improvement — leadership, a business opportunity, and energized people. I propose three general guidelines for high-risk projects: getting the whole system in the room, focusing on the future, and helping people do it themselves.

I also describe three methods by which my proposed orientations can be applied — the future search conference, team development, and participative work design. Anyone who believes in the value of productive workplaces will find it useful to hone his or her skills in these modes. Finally, I illustrate all the modes in action during an intense year in the life of a company that saved itself from disaster with employment guarantees and employee involvement. This case brings together my themes in one composition. It also leaves me with melodic fragments and unresolved chords that appear in the Epilogue.

Basic Values, Simple Methods

In the first edition I described two methods I found promising for involving everyone in improving whole systems — future search and participative work design. I also noted one, team development, that ought to be in everybody's tool kit. Of these core methods, I have worked only with future search since the early 1990s. So I will not be adding to the technology tool kit this time around. I stand by what I wrote on team building and work redesign. Had I newer examples, I would use them to espouse the same principles and practices. Future search, on the other hand, has been my personal cutting edge for more than twenty years. I consider it my learning laboratory for group-based processes, applicable to most social, technological, and economic dilemmas today. Therefore I devote two comprehensive new chapters to what I have learned from future searching.

Everything I know how to do now grew out of the values, cases, methods, and theories I advocated in 1987. If you are a first-time reader, you will find here a chronicle of the way I and many others practiced organizational change in the latter part of the 20th Century, laying the groundwork for most if not all large-scale participatory methods now in use. My stories were told to illustrate principles and values derived from innovative experiments during and after World War II. If you understand these, you should have no trouble finding appropriate methods for today. The principles for effective workplace improvement, I think, have a timeless quality, independent of the relentless disco beat of technology.

I believe that "getting everybody improving whole systems" remains a worthwhile and elusive purpose if you care about worthy workplaces. Embedded in this prescription are values of ongoing inquiry and widening inclusion. The hard part, in a world of infinite choices, is using techniques equal to our values. Many more methods exist now for involving everyone in the whole than existed in 1987. I have updated the bibliography to include some of them.

You can sail this sea of possibility to uncharted new worlds. You also can drown in it. I can tell you with the confidence born of forty years of chasing rainbows to the far horizon that you will not be able to absorb, let alone use, the proliferating workplace change library. Let go the attractive myth that you will one day learn to choose from the myriad exactly the right process each time. Every method has in it a lifetime of somebody's experience. By the time you master one new trick, people the world over have devised a dozen more. Fortunately, you only need a few good methods to grow on. Seek out the ones that excite *you*. Then look for places where people resonate to what *you* know how to do.

Second Edition Highlights

This edition contains much new material. I have traced my personal cases forward from 1987, bringing all of them up-to-date. I visited, for example, the company that now owns the family business where I learned my trade (see Chapter One). There I saw first-hand what the self-managing work teams of 1966 had metamorphosed into in the computer age. I also researched what happened to AECL Medical Products in the years following the detailed account that appeared here in 1987 in what is now Chapter Nineteen.

I also followed up on the six cases that originally appeared in Part Two. These were the basis for my "learning curve," the evolution of practices for effective workplace improvement during the last century. In this edition you will gain for each case — "Packaging Plant," "Food Services," "Chem Corp," "Medical School," "Printing Inc.," and "Solcorp" — some insight into what came after and implications for today's workplaces.

I also have put in two new tales from earlier times that seem more relevant now with the benefit of hindsight. New Chapter Fourteen, for example, has to do with my work in medical schools in the 1970s. In it I tell how I learned that "training" for medical professionals could be an effective change strategy if done as action research into what people thought would help, rather than as medicine prescribed for organizational malaise. That chapter, useful to anyone concerned with training and/or medical systems, contains ideas for bypassing resistance where it is most likely to be evoked.

New Chapter Fifteen tells a story from Bethlehem Steel that I touched on briefly in 1987 and have fleshed out to include lessons for today. It describes in detail how I learned to get "the whole system in the room" and what the immediate benefits might be. I also have expanded the chapter, once titled "Inventing the Future," into two chapters that reflect my work and concerns of recent years. In Chapters Twenty and Twenty-One you will learn how "future search," an action strategy for involving everyone in improving the whole, came to be used by people on five continents. I also speculate on why this particular method has crossed so many cultural boundaries. Anyone concerned with organizing effective large group meetings in a shrinking world bursting with diversity and fragmentation may benefit from retracing some of the steps I took down that endless road in the last thirty years.

Finally, in Chapter Twenty-Two I sum up what I learned from my cases. *Productive Workplaces Revisited* illustrates something you knew all along and might rather leave unsaid. For every great "cultural change" process destined to last awhile, another will disappear into the void. No one can predict which is which. It doesn't matter how good a leader or consultant you are or how worthy your methods. Like October maple leaves, this season's colorful display will be swept away by a change of owners, new management, a merger, downsizing, market shift, or when the first whiff of the next new thing overwhelms the aftertaste of the last one. If an organization survives, expect a new leafy canopy next year. That is not a problem to be solved. It is a reality to appreciate and live with.

For me the big "take-away" from my revisit to territory I left long ago blends my pessimism about continuity with faith in doing the right things anyway. We need worthy goals to keep going. Whether we can sustain them under conditions of non-stop change remains iffy and unknowable. I think that too much energy goes into fantasizing methods that "guarantee" follow-through, continuity, and that astonishing oxymoron, "sustainable change." We had better spend time doing the best we know how in this meeting. We might do better if we could recognize people committing to useful action *right now* as a stand-in for the elusive follow-up so eagerly chased after.

Thus, a keynote for this new edition:

Anything we do today to enhance dignity, meaning, and community right now while seeking to make workplaces more productive is existentially valuable regardless of how long it remains in use or what people do afterwards.

There are lots of ways to learn how to involve everyone in a workplace in improving the whole. Sustaining people's commitment and energy thereafter requires nothing fancy. The formula is as plain as a Shaker table. Get the right people in the room. Help people design and control their own work. Involving everyone is only half of the story. What the world will permit is the other half. The money, in for-profit and non-profit alike, has to come from somewhere. When the world can no longer pay for goods and services, those who provide them must change what they do or look for other work.

If you — executive, worker, board member, union leader, student, teacher, consultant, elitist and egalitarian alike — want to walk easy in your skin, don't expect eternal life for your beloved methods, norms, and processes *in any given workplace*. The cosmos cares not one whit for your struggle to get "change" accepted. All changes change. *Productive Workplaces Revisited* I hope will confirm that reality and help you walk easy.

What You Will NOT Find in This Edition

Finally, despite my many add-ons, I should tell you why I have left almost all the original text intact. When Jossey-Bass a few years back asked practitioners and college teachers to suggest revisions to *Productive Workplaces*, they proposed several. The book, they pointed out, had "dated references and out-dated examples," a failing, sadly, of any work more than a few years old. Were I able to remedy it here, the fix would last only a couple of eye blinks and the comment would be valid again. One reviewer called for cases reflecting the diversity of today's workplaces, another for attention to cultures not so enmeshed in individualism, a third for chaos theory and more on resistance to change.

Various people hoped I would include B.F. Skinner, Charles Hampden-Turner, Gareth Morgan, W. Edwards Deming on total quality, Peter Senge on the fifth discipline, Chris Argyris and Donald Schön on learning organizations, and Peter Schwartz on scenario planning. One wished for more on Mary Parker Follett, a pioneer whose bold ideas I have admired for thirty years and have in fact cited more than once. Any of these might be relevant, of course. That I have not put them into my update is a choice, not an oversight. This book reflected its author's time, place, and first-hand experiences. So does the revisit.

I never intended a survey of all whose ideas shaped my profession or guidance for cultures other than mine. Rather, I selected people with whom I had a visceral connection. I seized on ideas and methods that resonated with my background, ideals, intuition, and practical bent. This was an idiosyncratic, intensely personal book. I grounded it in a search for my practitioner roots and for processes I could use with confidence to help people work more productively. This new edition likewise reflects my experiences and passions rather than a survey of others'.

A Brief Q&A

Three more thoughts to help you start.

What Else Will You Find? *Productive Workplaces Revisited* represents a journey of discovery into the workplace and into myself. It starts with a 1960s management case (Chapter One) and ends with a summing up of what I have learned from my work — so far — in organizations large and small (Chapter Twenty-Two). If you read those chapters first, you have both ends of my journey.

I expect Chapters Two through Eight in Part One to interest those (like me) who enjoy origins. Every management practice in current use comes from people and precedents. Together these chapters, a series of short biographies, tell a story of enduring values and technological change over the last century, and they have great relevance for management today.

Part Two is for consultants, students, teachers, and managers interested in advancing employee involvement into uncharted territory. It shows why we need to move from problem solving to systems improvement and from expert solutions to involving everybody. Chapter Thirteen, subtitled "Alternatives to the

Report-in-the-Drawer Phenomenon," should interest anyone who has ever received or written a consulting report.

In Part Three, Chapters Seventeen through Twenty-One give how-to-do-it information on team building, work design, and future searching (there's never enough). For the practice theory behind the cases in Parts Two and Three, see Chapter Sixteen. For my speculations about the future of this work, turn to the Epilogue.

Why the Term "Productive Workplaces"? I define productive workplaces as those where people learn and grow as they cooperate to improve an organization's performance. The "bottom line," in this way of looking at things, is people increasing dignity, meaning, and community in work in parallel with good economic results. The tools, both conceptual and practical, exist to build more productive workplaces. The tools are better now than they were when I started consulting. The need for them was never greater. Not everybody can or will use them, though. Their successful application belongs to those who resonate to productive workplaces as a bottom line and who will risk resources to act on their beliefs.

What About Those "Flip Charts"? I deem the flip chart (newsprint or chart pad) a major innovation for communicating with others. Its use is traceable to Kurt Lewin's peculiar way of visualizing problems — a development I tell about in Chapter Five. Many of the charts in this book were first presented for discussion that way. So, in the spirit of a medium congruent with my message, I chose not to typeset the material or have an artist draw it. Instead I have made a set of "flip charts" expressly for this volume, hand-lettered, a bit neater (but not much) than they would be if presented in a meeting. In a few cases, for consistency, I put into flip chart style items published elsewhere. (Source information appears at the bottoms of these.)

One of my favorite jazz pianists, Teddy Wilson, had a knack I have envied since my youth. He had an awesome left hand and could keep many improvised lines going without losing the melody.

I have enjoyed weaving together themes from management history with my own past and current practice in this improvised fugue on productive workplaces. I also have found the lyrics extraordinarily hard to write. I am describing circles, wheels, and spirals in a medium that only permits straight lines.

I hope that what comes through is the music of productive workplaces and that you will find it natural to compose your own words.

Marvin R. Weisbord
Mount Holly, Vermont
November 2003

Chapter One

A Personal Prologue:
Discovering Theories X and Y

Behavior speaks louder than words.
—— The Selected Wisdom of New Jersey, *1975, no. 99*

I had my first experience with significant employee involvement in the mid-1960s. I was executive vice-president of a firm built on printing technology and direct mail marketing. We had achieved national distribution for our more than 200 products. My father had founded the business on the eve of World War II. Like all entrepreneurs, he did everything himself, hiring "pairs of hands" to run machines, keep books, write ad copy, and print and ship, all under his close direction. The late 1950s saw the development of cheap methods for interleaving business forms with carbon paper and crash-printing names and addresses. This led to an explosion of potential markets. Expensive multicopy forms became mass consumer items anyone could afford.

You could hardly invent a more fertile environment for workplace experimentation. When a market expands 25 percent a year, people have secure jobs and plenty of growing room — a fertile arena for productive workplaces. Even in the 1950s my dad, much to his credit, eagerly sought out new technologies. For many years he had worked in a staid Philadelphia brokerage firm. Now, in his own business, he could indulge his inordinate, even naive faith in modern technology. It would make life better, he felt certain, which meant easier, more cost-effective, and above all Depression-proof. This suited my experimental nature perfectly. We quarreled over many decisions, but never whether something new was worth trying. Together we made a lot of mistakes. We also enjoyed a great deal of success.

Long before equal employment opportunity became the law of the land, for example, we accepted the tensions associated with hiring blacks into our office. From lily-white in 1959, our work force became by 1966 one-third minority. We also retained an industrial engineer to do a new plant layout based on the inventory required by rapid growth. We upgraded our advertising as many new competitors entered a market our firm had pioneered.

We were among the early computer users in our industry, starting about 1960 when the state of the art was quite primitive. Our first service bureau was the Franklin Institute, a science museum in Philadelphia that operated an ancient Univac, direct offspring of Eniac, the first computer, developed at the nearby University of Pennsylvania in the mid-1940s. Its massive vacuum tubes required a room the size of a tennis court and forty tons of air conditioning. But it organized our mailing lists and customer records and spit out printed reports that told us a great deal about our business we didn't know before. That it had less computing capacity than the obsolete desktop computer on which I now write astonishes me. It also had the frustrating capacity to shape business policy. Among my indelible memories is the first time a system analyst said of a customer decision I wished to make, "You can't do that. The machine isn't programmed to handle it." In short, while the economics were favorable, we had a full platter of social and technological problems.

Crisis Management. Despite my ignorance of management concepts — I had never been to a workshop or read a management book — I was learning a lot about business. My thoughts focused on crisis, however, not learning. I conceived my work life as "going to war every day" (my dad's metaphor). Each day brought new battles to be fought and won. Would the truckers strike and interrupt our supply lines? Would the employees start a guerrilla operation in the shipping department? Would paper company negotiations break down, causing chaos in the pressroom? Would Congress raise postal rates? What awful crunch would inflation create this week? Could the traffic bear another 4 percent price hike?

I was fighting a war, all right, but only at the level of daily skirmishes. I had never heard of strategy. All I knew were tactics. I had not met up with concepts like management development or supervisory training. Business schools were like the planet Jupiter — remote, inaccessible, vaguely forbidding. Yet by osmosis I had assimilated what social scientists David Bradford and Allan Cohen would later call "the heroic style" of management. "Middle and upper managers," they wrote in a passage that knocked me back twenty years, "are almost invariably preoccupied with control" (1984, p. 28).

In those days I knew nothing about the human relations movement, then washing like a tidal wave over the shores of U.S. industry. The T-group phenomenon, for example, was the subject of intense involvement and research in such companies as TRW Systems, Esso Research and Engineering, and Union Carbide. Thousands of managers were learning in these groups to listen more effectively, take initiative, cooperate, and modify their behavior to have more influence. They also learned that despite formidable improvements in self-awareness and personal skill, they could not alter the policies, procedures, systems, and unwritten rules of behavior at their work sites. Years later I would discover how this research had stimulated many other social innovations — team building, intergroup problem-solving meetings, and other applications of training theory more closely attuned to organizational goals and structures.

None of this did I know in the mid-1960s. My teachers in those years were salespeople, trade journals, competitors, suppliers, my father, who was full of practical wisdom, and our employees, some of whom were mechanical wizards. Jimmie Lee Jones, for example. One day Jimmie Lee showed up on our doorstep from a small North Carolina town, high school diploma neatly folded in his back pocket, looking for a job, any job. I hired him to wrap packages.

Within a year, he was training on printing equipment. Within two years he had suggested a modification to the vaunted Jet Press that the manufacturer declared unequivocally would not work. I insisted the change be made anyway, promising that I would relieve the engineers of responsibility for the (inevitable, to hear them tell it) failure. Not only did the idea work, but the company, without credit to the innovator, incorporated it on future models because it significantly improved output and quality.

Taylor's Legacy. Engineering prejudice against technical problem solving by hourly workers goes back to the turn of the century and Frederick W. Taylor, known as the father of scientific management. Taylor's system called for trained industrial engineers to figure out the one best way to do things. All others — including managers and supervisors — were to keep their hands off. What is not generally recognized today is that Taylor's intent was to increase labor-management cooperation by reducing costs and giving workers greater equity in their output (Chapters Two and Three).

Newer principles that confounded some of Taylor's notions already existed in the mid-1960s but were not widely known until U.S. industry discovered Japanese management and quality circles in the late 1970s. They certainly were not known to me. In the 1960s I was learning the same way Jimmie Lee did — by doing. In short, I muddled through. On one particular day, a significant one for my present career, I became conscious of incentives — not incentives in general, but specific ways to motivate imprinting machine operators to run more jobs each day. I had heard about piecework systems, so I called my friend Don Kirchhoffer, a compensation specialist with a giant corporation, and asked him how they got people to produce more.

Introduction to Theory

Don referred me to compelling research findings: people who work together tend to level off production at a rate that is comfortable for the majority. To most factory workers, the good opinion of fellow employees is as important as money. Even the best individual incentive schemes rarely result in the highest possible output. He referred me to William E Whyte's research (1955), which showed that if you really want high output, you have to consider the operators' many needs besides money. So saying, Don handed me Douglas McGregor's *The Human Side of Enterprise* (1960), the "Theory X, Theory Y" book written half a dozen years before. I devoured it in one weekend. To use language I did not know then but would learn soon enough, it blew my mind.

Management's assumptions, said McGregor, determine management's behavior. McGregor advocated Theory Y — that most people will take responsibility, care about their jobs, wish to grow and achieve, and, if given a chance, do excellent work. What stops them is managerial behavior based on Theory X, which assumes that most people are lazy, irresponsible, passive, and dependent, and must have their work broken into tiny pieces, tightly controlled, and supervised lest they make a mess of things. This was the theory that Taylor's scientific management had reinforced for decades.

Before I finished the first chapter, I knew which assumptions fit my values. Yet when I looked around our company, I saw Theory X everywhere: time clocks, narrow work rules, jobs so subdivided even an idiot would be bored, grown people treated like children, never let in on decisions, having no consequential information about the business or even their own work, expected to deliver for management and not to reason why, all in return for a $5 raise every six months, a turkey at Christmas, and a chance, if they didn't die of boredom in the meantime, to become supervisors. This title, I observed, gave people who had been treated like children the license to make decisions for *other* people. More, it required that they pretend they knew how. After all, that's what their boss did. Taylor's legacy, unbeknownst to me, influenced every aspect of our company.

The Wall. I had inherited "Taylorism" without knowing it. Now, actively stimulated by McGregor, I decided to reorganize order processing into work teams, a task I estimated would take a few weeks. Actually it took many months of anxiety and excitement. Meanwhile the supervisors, encouraged by my new accessibility, requested that a wall be built down the center of the large order processing area.

"A what?" I asked, wondering if I'd heard right.

"A wall," one of them said, "between order entry and billing. We don't care which side credit and mail go on."

"Why?"

"The groups fight a lot. Bad feelings are building up. If they don't have to look at each other they won't fight. We supervisors get along okay, but the people distract each other."

By now I was Theory Y all the way. If people needed a wall to do better work, they would get a wall. I called in the carpenters. Next morning an eight-foot-high partition divided the room, with space at each end to walk around. The place was quiet, people bent over their desks. I thought they looked depressed.

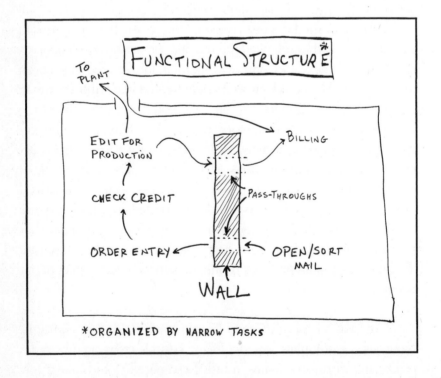

The supervisors were waiting for me. "There's a small detail," one said sheepishly. "We need passthroughs so work can go from one group to the other." That same day openings were cut in the wall, below eye level to minimize contact. The "Functional Structure" sketch shows how the wall functioned to reduce conflict in our order processing department.

Despite a nagging uneasiness, I remembered I had determined to change the way I managed. I believed the wall was a good example of my new management style. After all, it was the employees' idea, not mine. People no longer fought openly. They just flashed hostile glances across the continent that divided them, a vast psychological distance it would take me years to appreciate. The wall was a tangible metaphor for the separation of functional specialties, the passthroughs a symbol of the integration required to make such a divided structure work. In their studies of several industries, Harvard Business School's Paul Lawrence and Jay Lorsch (1967) highlighted the subtle ways in which structure influences behavior. Among other things they showed that avoiding conflict (by building walls, for example) hurts output. I have no doubt that our considerable absenteeism and turnover during this period were directly connected to the narrow jobs, formal and informal status differences, and utter lack of trust embodied in our policies, procedures, and control systems.

Under functional structures it's hard for people to discover one another's capabilities. Narrow jobs diminish all workers, including those sentenced to supervise them. This story also reveals the paradoxes inherent in working on one part of what is after all a whole system. I improved my "management style" by becoming a better "listener," and made a participative decision that did not really solve the problem. Had I been more sophisticated at organization development then, I might have called for an "intergroup confrontation meeting" — solving problems and building trust by getting both sides to put their cards on the table. Fortunately, my ignorance freed me to make an important discovery: the subtle connection between relationships and division of labor and responsibility.

Hiring Consultants. At about this time Don Kirchhoffer, who had given me McGregor's book, offered to moonlight as my personnel consultant. He and Bob Maddocks, a training specialist with the same company, met with us each Saturday morning to teach us how to implement Theory Y. For several months it was nonstop anxiety and excitement — the most intense learning laboratory of my life. At one of these sessions Maddocks introduced me to systems thinking. He suggested I stop building long lists of undifferentiated problems and instead think of myself as managing three related systems, which he wrote on a flip chart with "Human System" at the top.

This introduction to conceptual thinking enormously expanded my ability to manage. For the first time I could see which problems I was likely to solve with, say, a new conveyor system in the factory, and which problems I was likely to increase.

The Initial Project: Multiskilled Teams

At one of these Saturday meetings it struck me that our major business problem was not in printing production. It was in order processing, the department with the wall. There was a very practical reason for starting there: the department was extremely vulnerable to absenteeism. Picture this situation: four or five people staffed each of five narrow functions through which orders flowed on their way to production. One group did nothing but sort mail and send out samples. Another group entered orders, a third checked credit, a fourth made up production orders. A fifth typed and mailed invoices and matched incoming checks with unpaid bills. Each person had a few, simple, specialized tasks, little discretion, and no knowledge of the whole.

About 200 to 300 orders arrived each day by mail or phone. They could become bottlenecked at any point. One absentee in any function could put the whole system down 20 percent. Two people absent from, say, order entry, cut order flow nearly in half, even though 90 percent of the work force was present! This cost overtime dollars and hurt morale because people hate to fall behind in their work.

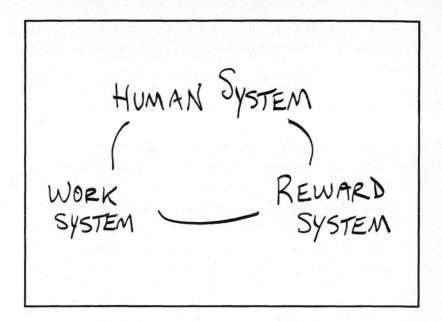

Reading McGregor on teamwork, talking with Don and Bob, I had an insight. If order processing were reorganized into *teams* of four or five, each with its own customers, a few absentees would hardly matter. People could acquire many skills. Teams could set their own goals and priorities, based on total work load. The entire work force would develop greater flexibility and become more productive. How much more would prove extraordinary — 40 percent, it turned out (a number not unusual, I have since learned, in sociotechnical design projects).

But how to do it? I needed help. Again I approached my friend Don. After twenty years with an international giant, he was excited at the prospect of total systems change in a small company, and he quit his job and joined us. Determined to institute work teams, we called in the supervisors and enlisted their help. Two out of five were enthusiastic, two thought it wouldn't work, and one was neutral. We charged ahead. New teams were formed that included people from each of the five functions with experience in each specialty. The enthusiastic supervisors became floating coordinators and coaches. They did tasks in support of the entire office — linking with production, for example, buying supplies, interviewing potential new-hires. The reluctant ones chose to work on a team together.

Our model was Non-Linear Systems, a California maker of electronic voltmeters mentioned by McGregor in one of his books (McGregor, Bennis, and McGregor, 1967). At Non-Linear, teams made the entire product and team members put their names on it — so the customer could call them if something went wrong. In our adaptation we gave each team its own customers — about 17,000 of them, arranged geographically — and its own typewriters and telephones. My instructions were succinct, encompassing everything I knew about team management and training. "Teach each other your jobs," I said.

Endless Problems. It soon became apparent this simple dictate wasn't enough. We had problems, endless problems. Team A didn't know what to do when Carrier B shipped to the wrong city. Team D misunderstood the production order sequence. Team C's samples person, three weeks on the job, didn't know all the products. I was appalled at the number of problems we had that previously could be solved only by supervisors or, more frequently, me.

I realized that the flow of crises to my desk resulted from the fact that most employees didn't know what needed to be done or why. For years we had played "blind men and the elephant." Each of us saw a tiny piece of the puzzle — a payment record to be checked, a number to be corrected. Few pictured a customer on the other end wanting fast service and quality products.

I was blind, too. I could picture the customer, but I hadn't the least inkling why it was so hard to reduce our error rate and improve our service. None of us was stupid. We were just ignorant of how many moving parts a business has and how impossible it is for any one person to track them all. With more than 200 inventory items, tens of thousands of customers, and 25 order processors — each of whom had a good working knowledge of only one-fifth of the order processing stream — there was a great deal that could go wrong.

What the Boss Doesn't Know

What I experienced accidentally as a manager in the 1960s has since been demonstrated systematically. Max Elden (1983a, 1983b) in his participative research projects in Norway has shown that people at the bottom have a much deeper appreciation of the range and origin of operating problems than do middle or upper managers. In a bank where a new on-line computer system was being installed, Elden found that top management thought its peak load problem was related to uneven distribution of work and too few backup people. People lower down could relate the problem to organizational structure and practice — overload on the vice-president, centralized decisions, too little flexibility in the work force. In work-design projects this is a predictable phenomenon: top managers sit in on a design team that includes staff and workers. Invariably they are taken aback at their own ignorance of how the system actually works and how little operator knowledge is being used.

The Meetings. At Don's urging, we instituted a radical innovation — meetings. I knew nothing about meetings. My academic training had been in journalism and the social sciences. Before McGregor I had never read a management book. Don, however, understood meetings. Large corporations, he assured me, held them all the time. There was nothing in them I couldn't learn to do. How, I asked naively, did people make up the enormous time lost? (I believed that if you weren't producing something tangible, you weren't working.) They didn't, Don said soothingly; meetings were a part of the job.

Each team would save up its problems and send one member to a weekly meeting. The problems piled up and poured out. The meetings dragged on interminably. I could not believe that such a little business could generate such a long list of problems, or that so many people knew so little about what they were doing — including me. I realized with a pang that the supervisors, now eliminated, had for years been making every decision. Every one, that is, except those (and I suddenly was appalled by the number) that they used to delegate upward to me.

The hourly employees had been what the computer people call peripherals, hooked up like accessories to the phones, typewriters, and copy machines. Now I thought I saw why. They simply didn't have the brains or experience to solve the endless parade of problems. Old Fred Taylor understood this a lot better than I did. After four weeks I was ready to quit. The work team experiment had fizzled. Theory Y was okay in principle but not in the workplace. Maybe business school graduates or psychologists could implement these far-out notions. Not me. I had a war to win. Don was disappointed. Give it more time, he pleaded.

Frustrated, we held our fifth and (I planned to reveal) final meeting. I sat at one end of the table, palms cold and wet. Don sat at the other end. The troops filed in and sat down. Nobody said anything. I still recall that scene: the square office, the small rectangular table with the walnut-grain laminate top, the high ceilings, the tiny windows at one end of the room, the eerie white fluorescent bulbs throwing a shadowless pallor over a depressing tableau.

"Where," I asked, halfheartedly, "are the problems?" I would build the case that the work teams were not time-efficient. My voice wavered at the thought of the speech I must deliver. We had blown it.

"We don't have any this week," one woman said sheepishly.

"What do you mean you don't have any?" I asked.

"Well," said another bravely, sensing my surprise, "nothing new came up. We knew how to handle all the problems from our other meetings." She looked crestfallen, as if wondering what sort of screwup *that* could be.

From our other meetings! (Those long, unproductive, time-wasting meetings?) I could hardly believe my ears. Suddenly I thought of the words of flight instructor Wolfgang Langewiesche (1944), whose writings had comforted me when, as a fledgling pilot, I had convinced myself I would never master three-point landings. "When you really understand something," he wrote, "a little spark jumps. Watch for it!" In that moment, in the fifth meeting, a little spark jumped for me.

Discovering Learning. I understood, really understood, that the essence of effective organization was learning, not coercing and controlling output. I realized that it took time; required real problems to be solved; involved trial, error, give, take, and experimentation. Above all, it generated tremendous anxiety. I also had my first hint of what good managers do instinctively: involve people in setting important goals, structure the chance to learn, offer feedback and support, provide tools and ideas, and stay out of the way.

With a shock I realized that the way we had been running our business was anti-learning. We had no tolerance for mistakes. I wanted everything done right the first time, including solving problems nobody had ever faced before. Naturally, only I could handle such problems. Naturally, only I knew what a fraud I was, appearing to be the only one who invariably knew the right answers. Instead of giving people learning time, I leaped to solutions. I did not understand the subtle connections among learning, self-esteem, and productivity. I thought the work team was simply a structure, another "solution." Suddenly I had a glimmer of the link between structure and process. Team members had learned — almost by accident — how to be self-correcting. But until they knew that was what they had learned, it was not really usable knowledge. In short, we had stumbled on a *process* essential to the success of our structure.

When I attended my first T-group a few years later and heard the expression "learning how to learn," I understood it because of the work teams. For most managers this concept remains very abstract until linked to something they consider important. Without Don and Bob's help I could not have conceived the notion of stopping the movie in the middle of the best part to ask, "Now what — really — did we learn from that?" Instead of dropping the work teams, we decided to cut out meetings unless something affected the whole department.

Within a week the teams called an ad hoc meeting. "We want the wall taken down," said one person.

"Why?" I asked.

"Easy," replied another. I waited. "We don't need it anymore. We like talking to each other." Back came the carpenters; down came the wall.

Successes

In a learning organization, of course, you don't need walls. When everybody has a chance to learn, grow, and achieve, when mistakes become okay, when a lot of people get in on the action, there is a great deal more control in the system. It's called self-control. It's the strongest kind, and it can't be bought, legislated, or behavioral-scienced in.

I learned a great deal more about these dynamics in T-groups in the early 1970s, especially the extent to which I liked to do it all myself — and how this kept others dependent, blind, and unskilled — though these outcomes were far from my intentions.

"Pay for Knowledge." "Team Structure" shows our new department layout with the wall gone. Now each team had its own customers, typewriters, and telephones. All team members had a chance to learn every job. Teams began to interview and hire new members. Inevitably, compensation came up. How would we administer wages when people were no longer functional specialists? A committee was formed to recommend a new compensation scheme. The group deliberated for several weeks, helped by Don, who had been a compensation expert. At last they presented a matrix. Increases, they said, should be given for new skills. "Pay for Skills" illustrates the plan.

They noted skills required at each level in each function. Raises, they said, should be granted for movement in any direction — broad knowledge across functions, or in-depth knowledge of any one. The highest-paid people should be those who could do everything. "You mean," I said, a bit taken aback, "that if everybody learns all the skills, everybody gets the highest rate?"

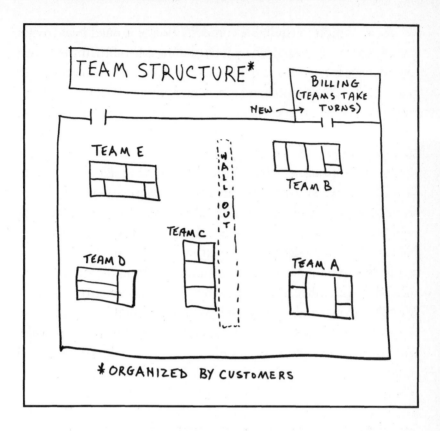

"Right," said a committee member.

"How can we afford that?"

"Well," said another, "we figure when we all know how to do everything we can handle a lot more work without adding people."

Nowadays, it's called a pay-for-knowledge plan. In the early 1970s the former General Foods pet food plant at Topeka, Kansas, installed a widely publicized example with help from the Harvard Business School. Reading that tickled me because I knew the scheme was dreamed up by a handful of high school graduates, assisted by Don Kirchhoffer, in a North Philadelphia printing plant in 1967. Who knows how it got to Harvard? (Later I found out. It came by way of Norway, where it was first used in the pioneer design of Norsk Hydro's new fertilizer plant in the 1960s.)

As a solution to equitable compensation, you can't beat pay for knowledge in any system where multiskilling is feasible. Yet relatively few managers have been willing to try it. It strongly contradicts traditional compensation and job evaluation schemes. Of course, as the lady said, when everybody does everything, you don't need so many people — including direct supervisors, middle managers, and staff specialists.

In his seminal writings on sociotechnical design, Fred Emery (1967) pointed out that there are essentially only two work-design strategies: redundant parts or redundant skills. In the first strategy, people are treated as interchangeable cogs, in the second as capable learners. This astounding breakthrough in human thought had somehow got from Norway to Non-Linear Systems to McGregor to me. I did not realize at the time that I was implementing an idea literally inconceivable only a few years earlier. Pay for knowledge is a way of compensating under Emery's second design principle. Individuals earn more because they are more productive and require less supervision.

SKILL LEVEL	TASKS				
	OPEN/SORT MAIL	ENTER ORDER	CHECK CREDIT	EDIT ORDER	SEND BILL
1	[ENTRY - SIMPLEST TASK IN EACH FUNCTION]				
2	[KNOWS 2 OR 3 SIMPLE TASKS]				
3	[CAN DEAL WITH CUSTOMERS, KNOWS FILES]				
4	[CAN DO ALL BUT UNUSUAL EXCEPTIONS]				
5	[INDEPENDENT DECISIONS ON 99% OF ORDERS]				

PAY-FOR-SKILLS PLAN

Good News and Bad News. Another task force took on the computer. Working with a systems analyst, they revised order processing procedures to fit the work teams, integrating a new computer billing machine to be run by volunteer team members. We had changed the office structure significantly. What I could not envision were the significant changes in behavior to follow. Our social system slowly, invisibly, informally altered in dramatic ways. People spent more time together. Spontaneous parties sprang up at lunch and after work. People began celebrating co-workers' birthdays during coffee breaks. They started visiting one another's homes. We had become productive. Now we were becoming a community.

We were not without casualties, however. Two former supervisors, looking miserable, stuck it out for three months in a team, complaining bitterly that "this system will never work." Meanwhile, not fifteen feet away, another team, made up mainly of recent hires, put out more orders than the most results-driven supervisor could have imagined a year earlier. Indeed, the newcomers performed tasks that the old unwritten status rules, zealously enforced by supervision, would not have allowed them to do for months, and maybe never.

The reluctant former supervisors soon left for traditional places they could understand. At the time I hated that outcome. Now I know it was unavoidable. Both morality and practicality dictate that all those involved in this kind of change be offered jobs at their former pay. What cannot be offered are jobs that are no longer needed. I also believe strongly in a point made by Marshall Sashkin (1984). It is irresponsible for managers to knowingly maintain work systems that punish, diminish, and may even injure many of the work force simply to preserve status and perks for a handful who, it often turns out, don't get much job satisfaction anyway.

Nor could I get much going in the shipping department. Our best shipper, Sidney, a world-class miracle of efficient distribution, had about as much interest in participation as a gourmet chef would have in a fast-food joint. Sid liked time clocks and had no need to influence policy. "I don't want more responsibility," he said.

"Why can't I just pack orders?" When it was pointed out that he couldn't expect to advance very far in the kind of place we were becoming, he pointed right back to the fact that he already had advanced as far as he wanted to. He never missed a day, and as long as I had my job, Sid's was secure too. I thought I would find a way to reach him. Of course I never did.

A High-Performing System. Our order processing operation, however, boomed. The literature called it high motivation or commitment. My friend Peter Vaill (1982) called it a "high-performing system." I didn't know what to call it then, but it looked very good to me. McGregor, I decided, was a pretty sharp fellow after all. Without any training, without any official team building, without any social technology except flip charts, we had gotten remarkable results. Our order processing capability went from under 300 to more than 400 orders a day. Absenteeism and turnover, with the exceptions noted, went down nearly to zero. Teams finished work early and prowled the office looking for new things to do. We commissioned them to test photocopiers and select the best one for us.

Our first formal training program was a free offer from the telephone company to coach people in collecting overdue accounts by phone. This led to reductions in past-due receivables and bad debts, and higher self-esteem for some former "clerks" who found they could make significant contributions to the business. (It's hard to overrate the symbolism here. In the old days, calling up large past-due accounts had been my father's personal province. He hated to let go of it — until he saw the checks roll in.)

The Transformation of a Family Enterprise (2003)

I left the direct mail printing business in 1968, having decided that I needed to be on my own. Rare is a family business passed on smoothly down the generations. Fathers and sons have conflicting agendas, one desperately wanting power, the other desperately holding onto it. Four years later my dad invited me to lunch one day and announced that he was selling his business. He offered it first to me, a gesture of reconciliation that earned my respect and gratitude. By then I had a solid consulting practice and said "no."

In 1972 my father sold to a venture capital group. The company grew more than tenfold under its new owners. They in turn sold it in the 1990s to a mail order conglomerate making forms, greeting cards, stationery, and work clothes. In 2000 I found the phone number from a website and called a vice president who sent me the latest catalogs. The collective businesses now filled more than 100,000 orders a week for 2.5 million customers. What had been a 32-page business forms catalog in 1968 was now a 148-page wish book of office specialties. Buried inside I even found a few business forms that I had designed forty years earlier!

I arranged for a tour and soon found myself in a rental car with my son Dano in rural Massachusetts. I was curious to see how customer service functioned all these years later in the face of the computer revolution. What had become of the work teams who had among them all the skills needed to do the whole job? We were ushered into a large, brightly lit space in which perhaps 150 people sat in their own cubicles. Plants and greenery hung in baskets from the ceiling and filled planters near the door. Each cubicle reflected its owner. Some had family photos, children's art, or favorite cartoons.

I met Bill, a service rep, who pulled a second chair up to his desk. Would I like to hear what happens when customers call? Most orders now came in by phone, fax, or the Internet. Relatively few people ordered by mail. Bill gave me headphones and patched me into his line. He pointed out a large display board hanging high over the middle of the room. It showed the number of incoming calls waiting, and the longest wait time. A light flashed and the numbers changed with each call.

Because all had access to the same database, any service person could serve any customer. They had no reason to organize teams by geography or customer groups. Bill took the next call. As the incoming phone number appeared on his screen, he hit a button.

Instantly, he had the customer's buying history in front of him. It was a small retailer in Baton Rouge, Louisiana. When he picked up the phone and heard a woman's voice, he said, "Hi, this is Bill. Am I speaking to Marie?" For a second there was silence, then a laugh, followed by "Yes! And I need to reorder invoices."

Bill went on to review with Marie her buying practices, offer her savings on larger quantities, check to see whether she needed envelopes, and remind her to fax the exact wording for her imprint. He asked for her billing information and checked her credit history. Then he thanked her for the business. The exchange took ten minutes. I looked up at the board. There were six calls in the queue, the longest on hold for less than a minute.

From Work Team to Team of One

I was impressed by Bill's product knowledge and phone presence. In the 1960s it would have taken a skilled person half a year or more to achieve his capability. Many never did. He was at once salesperson, order taker, credit checker, customer relations' manager, and data base updater. I was watching a one-person multi-skilled work team. "How long have you been doing this?" I asked, expecting to hear about the extended learning curve. "About a month," said Bill. "It took a couple of weeks to learn the system. Now it's a piece of cake." This was technology undreamed of in the 1960s, friendly to employees and customers alike.

People were organized in teams, Bill said. It seemed to me this was largely an administrative convenience. The teams met mainly to share information. Each person did the whole job. Supervisors were available for troubleshooting and training. Mostly, they left people alone. Customer service reps spent their time on the phone, interacting mainly with customers.

What could I recognize from my 1960s experience? The most obvious thing was that paperwork was largely a thing of the past. The keyboard was king, the terminal a form of empowerment nonexistent during my tenure. I also noted that the company promised that they would do whatever you wanted if you weren't satisfied with an order.

In the 21st Century the customer was king or queen, and "delighting" royalty had become an inviolable norm for direct marketing firms. (While writing this, I called a credit card company and was asked, "How may I delight you today?" I laughed aloud, delighted by this zany inanity.)

The forms company office seemed to me relaxed, orderly, and effective, a good place to work. Computers gave people feedback so they could control their own work. In electronic sweatshops I had seen computers used to monitor bathroom breaks, personal phone calls, and emails. Here I saw computers in service of employees and customers rather than the other way around. Old cynic that I had become, I felt reassured that my father's legacy was in good hands.

The visit stirred up all sorts of memories in me. Those years in the forms business started me on a learning trip from which I have never recovered. Without my dad's technology bug and Don Kirchoffer's interest in humane work structures and Jimmie Lee Jones's persistence with printing machinery and Bob Maddock's three systems and the incredible adventure with the wall, I would not appreciate the utter simplicity and astonishing economic benefits of involving employees in designing their own work. Nor would I appreciate how much patience and hard work it takes. You can't write anybody off in productive workplaces. Even Sidney the shipper taught me something important: every management theory has its limits; not one of them fits everybody.

Part One

THE SEARCH FOR PRODUCTIVE WORKPLACES

Communities, in the sense which we are using the term, have a history in an important sense — they are constituted by their past — and for this reason we can speak of a real community as a "community of memory," one that does not forget its past. In order not to forget that past, a community is involved in retelling its story. . . and in so doing, it offers examples of the men and women who have embodied and exemplified the meaning of the community. These stories of collective history and exemplary individuals are an important part of the tradition that is so central to a community of memory.

—— *Bellah and others,* Habits of the Heart,
1985, p. 153

In this section I reinterpret the stories of some "exemplary individuals" in management history. Each one has strongly influenced me toward dignity, meaning, and community as the bottom line of change. I have, for example, traced one of my own client projects back 100 years to Frederick Taylor, to demonstrate the pervasiveness of cooperative values in industry and the limitations of expertise. The "labor problem" — meaning managerial obtuseness about what motivates output — was not the creation of 20th-Century psychologists. It was first identified by engineers installing new machinery in 19th-Century factories. They fashioned the earliest solutions, which survive as work measurement, piece rates, external control systems, narrow jobs, fragmented expertise — all intended to motivate people to produce more through cooperative effort.

I have been reinforced in my conviction that most of us want dignity, meaning, and community from work through my study of five innovators whose stories make up Chapters Two through Nine. Who are: Taylor, Lewin, McGregor, Emery, and Trist? The short answer is that they are four social scientists and an industrial engineer. What have they in common? They are all reformers and managerial innovators, antiauthoritarian in the extreme, all on the record for important values widely shared today. These include labor-management cooperation, personal fulfillment in work, rationality, experimentation, commitment, problem solving, and cooperation across barriers of status and hierarchy. Each has added immeasurably to our understanding of what it takes to manage productive workplaces.

Frederick W. Taylor, the father of scientific management, was a proper Philadelphian who swore like a sailor. He started a new profession in 1893 — "consulting engineer" — because he saw that captains of industry, caught in a swirl of change, did not know how to untangle cost, productivity, and motivational problems. Taylor was a systems thinker of sorts, the first person to realize that workplace problems must be solved together, not piecemeal, although he never figured out to anyone's satisfaction how to do that. I tell his story, with my own twist on his contradictory personalities, in Chapters Two and Three.

Kurt Lewin, a legendary social scientist who died in 1947, is my second exemplar. He provided the conceptual tools needed to bring change to the workplace in ways both practical and ethical. Seeking to apply Lewin's methods to industries where Taylor had once worked, I discovered the many commonalities between technically and socially based change efforts. Lewin provided a process for any form of content that is unusually well suited to the changing needs of democratic societies. His insights underlie all successful large-scale efforts, no matter what you call them or which experts are involved. They are absent, or badly applied, in all failed change efforts, even those with trendy labels. In Chapters Four and Five I tell about Lewin, his interest in Taylor, his connections with McGregor and Trist, and his major contributions to management.

Douglas McGregor, a gifted professor, wrote *The Human Side of Enterprise* (1960) and changed forever the way managers view their own assumptions and behavior. From his writings I first learned how I acted to reinforce the conditions I hated most. That painful insight put me on the path to this book. McGregor identified two contrasting sets of assumptions about people, which he characterized as Theories X and Y. He made the point that the only way to win the tug of war between them is to figure out which end of the rope you want to pull on. In Chapter Six, I describe his influence on the organization development profession, and in Chapter Seven show how similar his values were to Taylor's, how their ideas were misused in roughly the same way, and why I think X and Y exist in all of us.

Fred Emery, an Australian disciple of Lewin, and Eric Trist, a British social scientist, friend of Lewin and McGregor, and spiritual progenitor of the notion of quality of working life (QWL), achieved the conceptual breakthroughs needed to bring systems thinking to the workplace and undo Taylorism. Their work remains an inspiration to people the world over who are committed to productive workplaces. Trist invented a way of thinking about management more grounded in the way businesses really run. He called it "finding the best match between social and technical systems." Emery, perhaps the first to apply open systems thinking to social change, pointed out that optimal results could be achieved only when social systems, which obey the laws of biology, psychology, and sociology, are designed integratively with technical systems following the laws of physics, chemistry, and engineering. The sociotechnical approach required that those who do the work get a great deal more authority, control, skills, and information than is customary under scientific management.

Years ago Trist (1974) pointed out that Japan, whose main natural resource is curious people, leapfrogged the world economically in the 1970s in part because the Japanese Union of Scientists and Engineers gave away its expertise to workers and supervisors — the real secret of Japanese management. They did not collect input the way managers had done for decades and then go off and solve the problems for others. They gave *their* input away so that people could solve problems for themselves. In Chapters Eight and Nine I tell of the exploits of Emery and Trist and liken their achievement in rethinking work from observing coal miners to the Wright brothers figuring out the secrets of flight by watching birds.

Chapter Two

Scientific Management Revisited:
A Tale of Two Taylors

The relations between employers and men form
without question the most important part of
this art.
—— F . W. Taylor, Shop Management, 1911, p. 21

If ever a reformer fought for labor-management cooperation, it was
the engineer Frederick Winslow Taylor, called the father of scientific management. For me the most striking thing about him is how
much his life and work paralleled Douglas McGregor's — the person whose writings changed my own. Indeed, he has stimulated all
the social scientists whose lives I sketch in the next several chapters. I first became aware of Taylor's pervasive influence in 1980
while consulting to the Bethlehem Steel Corporation. There, at
the turn of the century, Taylor installed the most highly rationalized individual incentive wage schemes industry had ever seen.
Nonetheless, when the imperious financier Charles M. Schwab
bought Bethlehem in 1901, he went on a cost-cutting spree and
threw out Taylorism.

Within a month, output in what was probably the world's most
productive machine shop fell 50 percent. To stem the losses, a con-
scientious manager secretly set up a skunk-works of slide rules and
time-study manuals in a kitchen Schwab never visited. When the
kitchen burned years later, the incentive paraphernalia and records
were lost. Production fell so much that Schwab fired the shop managers for incompetence. His subordinates finally told him the truth.
Time study thereafter was practiced openly at Bethlehem Steel

(Copley, 1923, vol. 2). When Tony Petrella and I showed up eighty years later, there were 3,400 wage incentive plans and 400 industrial engineers setting rates in plants across the United States.

Even so, the U.S. steel industry in the early 1980s yielded only about 70 percent good steel while Japan, helped by modern technology, was turning out 95 percent. Taylor's solution, a cornerstone of steel manufacture, had now become a serious problem. Jobs were so narrow it took enormous staffs to support them. Incentive bonuses were paid for good steel and bad. In consequence the steel workers' union and management had turned to a social experiment — labor-management participation teams hoping to close an economic gap too wide for existing technologies and unmanageable under Taylorism.

I started reading Taylor's treatise on scientific management and had hardly got past the introduction when I made a startling discovery. It is, first and foremost, a treatise on human resource management. Taylor's overriding objective was productive labor-management cooperation — the same purposes that had brought Block Petrella Weisbord to Bethlehem eighty years later (see Chapter Fifteen).

Today Taylor's name conjures up dehumanized, inefficient, and conflicted work methods. His purposes were exactly the reverse. No consultant in history ever had so much impact on the workplace as Taylor. The road toward productive workplaces is fraught with many pitfalls. Taylor, the first productivity consultant, encountered all of them. I determined to learn as much as I could from his experience.

My search took me back 100 years, to Taylor's life, his writings, biographies old and new, scholarly studies, research papers, strident attacks, passionate defenses. Few men ever were such powerful magnets for both admiration and revulsion. There exist, I discovered, two Taylors. One is a mechanistic engineer, dedicated to counting, rigid control, and the rationalization of work, an unfeeling authoritarian who turned his own neurosis into repressive methods anathema to working people. This Taylor became the living incarnation of Theory X. The other was a humanitarian social reformer, who believed workers could produce more with less stress, achieve greater equity in their output, and cooperate with management for the good of society. This Taylor has hardly been recognized publicly since 1925.

The first Taylor, obsessed with self-control, invented a harness at age twelve to keep himself sleeping on his back, hoping to avoid recurrent nightmares (Copley, 1923, vol. 1). This Taylor also was a brilliant inventor, holder of many patents, and discoverer, through thousands of experiments, of high-speed steel, a major technological breakthrough of the 20th Century. The second Taylor was a devoted husband who put his wife's severe illness ahead of his own fame, who adopted three children late in life, who identified with working people and invited them to his home.

One historian labeled him a reactionary, "indifferent, even ruthless, in his relations with workers" (Nelson, 1980, p. x). His biographer noted that retirees who had worked for Taylor described him "with admiration and affection running on into reverence and worship"; many kept his photograph on the mantelpiece (Copley, 1923, vol. 2, p. 170). By all reports Taylor was an abrasive cuss, honest, plainspoken, stubborn as hell. But his scorn was directed mainly at financiers and managers. On the shop floor he was a sympathetic listener who tempered his perfectionism with "a touch of human nature and feeling," encouraging workers to unburden their personal problems. He was quick to admit his shortcomings. "I never saw a man," said one of his former employees, "who had a greater courage of his convictions . . . willing to rise or fall by his own actions and not blame any mistakes on other people" (Copley, 1923, vol. 1, p. 176).

Though rank-and-file workers under his system did not share the judgment, early union leaders denounced Taylor as exploitive of labor. They hounded him at the end of his life, sparking an acrimonious congressional investigation of his system that sapped his energy and debilitated his spirit. Organized labor's jaundiced viewpoint, which was "a myth . . . of popular magazine writers" (Mathewson, 1931, p. 151), is favored today in human resource management circles. When I pointed out similarities between

Taylor and psychologist Douglas McGregor to an executive conference, a veteran staffer of the human relations wars angrily
accused me of "de-Stalinizing Taylor," whom he characterized as a
"first-class p —" (impolite epithet).

That was not what his liberal contemporaries saw. Muckraking
journalist Ida Tarbell (1924) and social reformer Stuart Chase
(1924) supported Taylor's attempts to create rational, humane
management systems. Taylorism became a cornerstone of the
Harvard Business School when it was founded in 1908 and of
the Amos Tuck Business School at Dartmouth in 1910. Taylor's
book *The Principles of Scientific Management* (1915) was greeted
with critical acclaim by the liberals and progressive thinkers of his
day. The title was coined by social activist Louis Brandeis, later a
Supreme Court justice, who used Taylor's work to argue against a
rate increase for inefficiently run railroads. The case catapulted
Taylor to fame. He became a public figure, in demand as a speaker,
adviser, and university lecturer. In his later years he metamorphosed into a social philosopher, espousing ideas, theories, and
practices more idealistic and comprehensive than those he had
implemented as manager or consultant (Nelson, 1980).

The debate rages on today. One academic detective discredited
Taylor as a fraud and a cheat who plagiarized or made up much of
his great book (Wrege and Perroni, 1974; Wrege and Stotka,
1978). Another concluded that "most of his insights are still valid"
and his practices widely accepted now (Locke, 1982, p. 23). Peter
Drucker, our leading contrarian philosopher of management,
ranked Taylor with Marx and Freud for his impact on the modern
world. Taylor above all, said he (1976), deserves to be called a
humanist.

I find Taylor a perfect projection screen for the dialogue in each
of us between social and technological impulses, external control
and self-control, freedom and constraint, authority and dependency — the tension that Douglas McGregor vividly immortalized
as Theories X and Y. Indeed, so similar were Taylor's values to Douglas McGregor's that many of their sentences cannot be told apart.

(If you doubt this, see Chapter Seven.) Taylor's story deserves to be better known by those who aspire to productive workplaces — a cautionary tale for all who believe they have *the* answer.

Taylor's career spanned four decades. It can be divided into three phases: his years as worker, engineer, and manager (1878–1893); his stint as consulting engineer (1893–1901), a new profession he invented because he believed entrepreneurs did not understand how to use capital and people productively; and a stormy period as proselytizer for scientific management, when, during his final fourteen years, he refused money, even travel expenses, for his services.

Throughout he was the experimenter, tinkerer, and inventor, with a knack for collaboration. Henry Gantt, of Gantt Chart fame, a major figure in the democratization of work, and Frank Gilbreth, hero of the film *Cheaper by the Dozen*, were among his disciples. Uninterested in politics, Taylor was adopted by the Progressive political movement. His principles influenced the organization of work everywhere. They have affected the lives of practically every person in the industrial world.

Taylor the Quaker Pacifist

Origins: Social Consciousness and Wealth

Taylor was born on March 20, 1856, into a liberal, upperclass Philadelphia family. His Quaker father, a Princeton graduate and lawyer, earned enough money from mortgages to make regular work unnecessary. He served — noblesse oblige — as trustee for a retarded children's school. His mother, a spirited Quaker abolitionist, feminist, and friend of Lucretia Mott, was rumored to have run an Underground Railroad station for runaway slaves.

True to their Quaker roots, the Taylors espoused plain living and high thinking. Parental authority in the 19th Century was considered sacrosanct and children thought to be "depraved, willful, and intensely selfish" (Kakar, 1970, p. 16). In the Taylor household children were seen, not heard, and family members addressed each other with "thee" and "thy." Taylor learned self-control at an early age. He internalized Quaker pacifist values, hated war games, and sought to avoid or resolve conflicts among his playmates.

He also was a compulsive kid, always measuring, counting, figuring out better ways to do things. Other croquet players lined up their shots and smacked away; Taylor plotted the angles. Others watched the scenery when they walked; Taylor counted steps to find the most efficient stride. When the Taylors toured Europe (1869–1872) to give their children an appreciation of art and culture, their son tolerated the experience without enthusiasm (Copley, 1923, vol. 1). Fred excelled at sports and math. He graduated from exclusive Phillips Exeter Academy in 1874 and easily passed the Harvard entrance exams, but never attended because of severe eyestrain. He could have had a soft bank job or stayed home and tinkered. Instead, he apprenticed as a pattern maker and machinist at the Enterprise Hydraulic Works in Philadelphia.

Blue-Collar Aristocrat. From the start there were two Taylors. On weekdays he worked a noisy ten-hour shift at Enterprise, inhaling the stink of oil fumes and burning metal. A nonsmoker and nondrinker, not even coffee or tea, he cultivated a salty vocabulary to accentuate his blue-collar egalitarianism. Yet he could not hide his origins. "Mr. Taylor," said the journalist Ida Tarbell, "never seemed more of a gentleman to me than when he was swearing" (Copley, 1923, vol. 1, p. 91). On weekends he played tennis at the Young America Cricket Club, sang with a choral society, and sported a wig and long gown playing female roles in amateur theater. He became a superb tennis player, a sparkling social companion, and an excellent machinist — Philadelphia's most urbane factory worker.

At the end of his apprenticeship he used family connections to become a common laborer at the Midvale Steel Company. William Sellers, Midvale's president, a scholarly ex-machinist, engineer, and inventor, believed in methodical experimentation. He had enormous influence on Taylor. When other workers made fun of

Taylor's zeal, calling him "Speedy" or "Monkey Mind," Sellers's support sustained him (Copley, 1923, vol. 1, p. 130). Mentored by Sellers, Taylor rose rapidly to shop clerk, machinist, gang boss, foreman, maintenance foreman, and chief draftsman. Within six years he was research director, then chief engineer.

Earning an Engineering Degree. At age twenty-five Taylor enrolled in Stevens Institute of Technology in Hoboken, New Jersey, where he showed up mainly for exams. Because of his travels and elite education, he easily passed tests in French, German, and history. He was the only Stevens student to earn an engineering degree in two years while holding a full-time job; that record still stands. And he became a star athlete. In 1881, his first year at Stevens, he and his brother-in-law won the U.S. Lawn Tennis Association doubles championship, using a patented spoon-shaped racket of his own design.

Taylor's graduation picture shows a long, unsmiling face framed by short straight hair parted just right of center, a firm, dimpled chin, a straight, full-lipped mouth topped by a wispy moustache, prominent nose turned up at the end, eyes set deep under a high forehead. He is looking off into the distance (in control of the situation, I fancy), oblivious of the photographer. Shortly after this picture was taken he married socialite Louise Spooner, who became his lifelong companion.

Young Taylor was appalled at the wasted effort, exhausting work, long hours, petty dictators, arbitrary rules, inefficient methods, and goofing off he observed at Midvale Steel. He understood, having been one, why skilled workers rarely gave their best. Still, when he became a supervisor, he sought to dictate compliance, using the stick-and-carrot "driving" methods of traditional supervision.

Taylor already was ambivalent about authority because of his upbringing. He abhorred conflict and now had more than his share. Alone among his peers he owned up to an obvious conclusion: driving was ineffective with workers who understood the exquisite subtleties of passive resistance. "It's a horrid life for any man to

Frederick Winslow Taylor as a Stevens Institute of Technology graduate, 1873.
(Williams Library, Stevens Institute of Technology)

live," he would write, "not being able to look any workman in the face without seeing hostility there, and a feeling that every man around you is your virtual enemy" (Kakar, 1970, p. 62). Long before McGregor invented Theory X, Taylor decided coercion simply did not work. It was a waste of time and effort. He wanted a new way to assure output without the ongoing war between managers and workers.

Unprecedented Management Problems of the 1880s

It is useful to view Taylor's work in this period against a backdrop of dramatic industrial change after the Civil War. Small factories became large plants. Local trades — glass, steel, textiles, shoes — became national industries. Mass production meant enormous wealth for the owners of capital. Workers, in comparison, received only a trickle. Machines also deprived craftspeople of manual skills and forced alien work patterns on ex-farmers and immigrant peasants. The widely discussed labor problem — increasing conflict between owners and workers — sparked the rise of unionism.

Employers had no idea how to manage all this. They had unprecedented problems: inefficiencies, careless safety, arbitrary supervision. One obvious symptom was soldiering — worker foot-dragging — on the job. It was widely observed that working people resisted producing as much as they could. They were thought lazy at best, uncooperative at worst, dumb in any case.

The first to recognize the labor problem were 19th-Century engineers installing new technology in factories. The American Society of Mechanical Engineers, founded in 1880 at Stevens Institute, worked out the first factory incentive wage schemes long before there were business schools or personnel staffs. These schemes have been continually "beaten" by labor. "We have a good understanding with management," I once heard a union member say. "They pretend they pay well, and we pretend we're working."

Taylor, the ex-machinist turned engineer, sought to get past the pretense. He knew that incentive bonuses were futile unless all parties benefited. The work itself had to be redesigned to remove oppressive supervision. That required management initiative. More, 19th-Century management methods made it *impossible* for workers to do their best (Tead, 1924). Workers could make much more money *and* management could cut costs dramatically *only if* they could cooperate on goals, work methods, and quality. The concept remains a contemporary challenge; see "Steel Industry Innovation."

Innovating at Midvale

Taylor's thinking evolved rapidly after he became Midvale's machine shop foreman. He concluded that incentive wages were no solution unless coupled with efficient tasks that were carefully planned and easily learned. Management, he reasoned, existed to *support* workers with whatever tools, equipment, and training were required. This required cooperation. Trained engineers would identify the tasks and the best way to do them. They would select what Taylor called a "first-class man," for whom the assigned task represented optimum ability. The secret of productivity was finding the right challenge for each person, then paying well for increased output. The right pace was something a first-class man could keep up month after month without stress. A variation on this theme would surface decades later in Abraham Maslow's "self-actualizing" people, and Frederick Herzberg's job enrichment theories.

The supervisory equivalent of a first-class man was the well-rounded foreman. The latter had brains, education, technical knowledge, strength or manual dexterity, tact, energy, grit, honesty, common sense, and good health. Taylor (1911, p. 96) could not imagine all these traits in one person. So he chopped the supervisory role into eight discrete tasks, and invented functional foremanship, a radical innovation. It was first implemented in Midvale's machine shop in 1882–1883. A gang boss set up jobs and kept material flowing; a speed boss picked cutting tools and machine speeds; a quality control inspector set standards; a repair boss maintained equipment; an order-of-work and route clerk wrote out production lists; an instruction card clerk tracked job specs and rates; a time and cost clerk kept score; and a disciplinarian handled insubordination or impudence.

In short, because he believed specialists would learn faster and do a more thorough job, Taylor invented matrix management. He did something quite contrary to what many people think. He systematically undercut centralized, authoritarian supervision. He did it by contradicting a central tenet of bureaucracy: one person, one boss. In his system bosses became "servants of the workmen." They did not order people around. They implemented a rational system, based on discovering the one best way to work. Mary Parker Follett, an early-day humanizer of bureaucratic systems, would call it "the law of the situation." Its great virtue was that "it tends to depersonalize orders" (Metcalf and Urwick, 1940, p. 59).

Steel Industry Innovation.

A great deal of Taylor's 19th-Century vision is embodied in a trailblazing agreement between National Steel Corporation and the United Steel Workers of America (1986). Union and management agreed to cooperate in reorganizing the steel mills, reducing the labor force, merging jobs and functions, and jointly planning production. To protect labor's central interest and gain commitment, National guaranteed employment security for the existing work force. Labor costs would be reduced through attrition, retraining, and voluntary termination rather than layoffs. The company also guaranteed workers a share of profits. The latter guarantee could not mitigate the economic decline of the 1990s. In 2002 National filed for voluntary reorganization under Chapter Eleven of the Bankruptcy Code, becoming the 25th steel company to do so since 1997. Employment guarantees, however, remained in place.

Tayor and T-Groups. Thus Taylor broke up supervision into small pieces as well, reducing the long lead time needed to hire and train superbosses. Since his system was based on the authority of knowledge, not position, he saw no conflict in each functional foreman taking leadership. I am amused to note that the group dynamics people also discovered this principle in quite another way. The role we now call human relations group trainer began in the 1950s as a leader who refused to lead, creating a vacuum to be filled by the group members. Once members confronted their unrealistic expectations and dependency on the leader, they made an interesting discovery: a leaderless group could, if members trusted each other, rotate leadership based on relevant skills and knowledge. It was a structure both efficient and functional in the absence of hierarchy. Where Taylor relied on external motivation and control, the T-group — a learning system — shifted control to its members. In Taylor's system success hinged on the engineer's ability to get the tasks organized right in the first place.

Taylor, the erstwhile pacifist, was also mindful of conflict. To promote harmony he set up over-foremen to coach the bosses and resolve disputes among them or, as a last resort, to call in the assistant superintendent, guardian of the unwritten rules governing the shop. In modern jargon he set up constructive conflict management ground rules. He advocated four modes of discipline: lowering wages, temporary layoff, fines, and "bad marks" leading to the other remedies. He preferred fines, insisting they be impartial and that every cent be returned to the workers' mutual benefit association. At Midvale he demonstrated impartiality by fining himself.

Rethinking Wage Incentives. The cornerstone of Taylorism, however, was a novel incentive wage system. In the 1880s many engineers proposed profit-sharing or bonus plans to split gains between workers and management. Taylor shrewdly observed three factors that led these schemes to fail. One, people work first for themselves; the general welfare is not a primary motivator (a conclusion McGregor later shared). Two, people respond to immediate feedback, not "a profit six months or a year away." Three, only costs and output are controllable by workers. Both profit and loss "may be due in great part to causes entirely beyond their influence or control, and to which they do not contribute" (Copley, 1923, vol. 1, p. 407). Today this concept is the key to successful gain-sharing plans — group bonuses of a kind Taylor opposed. Finally, Taylor held in contempt management's tendency to cut incentive rates each time people increased their daily output — a practice that made the worker, in Irving Fisher's words, "a donkey following an ever receding bundle of hay" (1925, p. 55). Under these conditions, said Taylor, workers "become imbued with a grim determination to have no more cuts if soldiering can prevent it" (Taylor, 1915, p. 23).

Paying the Person, Not the Job. Taylor improved on a method so old the Egyptians had used it to build the pyramids: breaking tasks into their smallest components. He set daily production quotas based on time study. Workers received an instruction card each morning. Those who made the daily goal received much higher pay than the old hourly wage — 60 to 100 percent more. Those failing got much lower pay, the differential piece rate. If, after repeated coaching, willing workers failed, they were assigned other work. Those considered able but unwilling were fired. In short, Taylor paid the person, not the job. At Midvale Steel in the 1880s Taylor doubled productivity using systematic tools and controls, functional foremanship, time study, and his new wage scheme (Drury, 1915). He knew he had hit on an uncommonly effective work system and was eager to prove it in other factories.

A Failed General Manager

Taylor left Midvale in 1890 to become general manager of Manufacturing Investment Company (MIC), a firm set up to capitalize on a new papermaking process. Through time study and piecework he cut cost per ton to less than half and doubled production in one plant. To his chagrin, he ran into problems he could not control: weak patent protection, poor plant location, flaws in mill design, and finally the Panic of 1893. Pressured for a quick fix, Taylor short-circuited his systems, quarreled with the financiers, and finally quit, losing $25,000 of his own capital.

The experience was not a total loss. He had been impressed, before he left MIC, by a former railroad accountant who reduced paperwork and provided quick feedback on results through new financial controls. Taylor realized how neatly these procedures dovetailed with his own. He determined to make cost controls an integral part of his system and hired the railroad accountant to teach him how (Wren, 1979). Factory managers, Taylor concluded, could benefit enormously from a system that integrated planning and goal setting with the right tools, techniques, and rewards — a powerful form of economic and social control to reduce conflict and increase output. (Some years later a Chicago University professor named James O. McKinsey picked up on Taylor's notion that accounting information should be a management tool, not a score sheet. The consulting company that bears his name is testimony to the power of that idea.)

So, in 1893 at age thirty-seven, during a business turndown, with little money and no prospects, Taylor quit his job and printed up a business card:

FRED W. TAYLOR, M.E.
Ross Street, Germantown, Philadelphia
Consulting Engineer
Systematizing Shop Management and
Manufacturing Costs a Specialty

His assets were fifteen years of factory experience, contacts from his Midvale days, and a personal vision of the connections among standardized tools, tasks, financial controls, wage incentives, and labor-management cooperation. "I believe," Taylor later wrote, "I was the first man in this country to undertake this work as a profession" (Copley, 1923, vol. 2, p. 345).

Taylor the Pioneer Consultant

Taylor's consulting practice integrated cost accounting and planning with standardized tools, forms, and methods. His core procedure was time and motion study, supported by piece-rate wage incentives. He believed all were required by an efficient, unified business. Since Taylor, consultation has expanded to include every imaginable aspect of economics, technology, and people — from short interval scheduling to cosmic cultural transformation. Consultants will advise on everything from what to wear to what to say, to acquiring new technology, getting into new markets, going international, or making over corporate cultures. Yet the dilemmas of implementation — building understanding and commitment to act — have changed not at all.

A New Profession

Taylor was inventing a new professional practice neither he nor his clients fully understood. He quickly found that there is no correlation between the quality of the solution and the likelihood of its implementation. When all else fails, managers use fire power — the authority to get rid of those who oppose them. Taylor, the ex-manager turned consultant, sought to retain this power. He often would take over and operate the client's factory, threatening to leave if management balked at implementing his ideas down to the last detail.

Consulting Dilemmas. He knew enough to get total support at the top. He spoke the workers' language and was patient with those at the bottom. He was very shrewd about how long change takes and understood the need for experimentation and learning. His consultancy came apart on two issues that are better understood today (though not always better handled). He was baffled by resistance from middle managers and supervisors, the ones most threatened by his system. He also was single-mindedly focused on productivity, so he did his damnedest even where the market was evaporating, cutting costs when in fact the problem called for new products or customers.

Taylor's clients came from personal contacts made during his Midvale and Manufacturing Investment days and his family's ties to old-line Philadelphia Quakers. Between 1893 and 1901 — his entire paid career — he installed systems in such firms as William Deering & Company, Northern Electrical Company, the Steel Motor Works division of the Johnson Company, Cramp's Shipyard, and Simonds Roller Bearing Company, which had given him stock for his forging patent in the 1880s.

He took charge of the Simonds plant in 1896 and increased output from five million to seventeen million balls a month. Over workers' protests, he cut the workday from ten and a half to eight and a half hours in the inspection department, physically separated people, inserted four breaks to provide a chance for socializing previously done on the job, and raised wages more than 80 percent with differential piece rates. Accuracy and speed improved dramatically.

He required new support roles: clerks, teachers, time-study experts, supervisors. However, the added cost was trivial because now 35 women, selected for "quick perception," did the work of 120 (Taylor, 1915). One critic used Simonds to argue that Taylor in practice "took a harsh, often ruthless approach" to chopping heads rather than saving jobs (Nelson, 1980, p. 75). Taylor's preference was to find all people work where they could be "first class."

The problem at Simonds was that the market fell apart. Bicycle makers sprouted like weeds in the 1890s, and dozens of competitors sliced Simonds' market share to ribbons. Ball-bearing prices fell from $3 to $.75 per thousand in less than a year. Even by reducing the work force Taylor could not stave off disaster. Simonds shut down in the summer of 1898, a victim of market conditions that could not be cured by productivity.

Taylor Appreciated Unions. Taylor's stand on unions in that period drew harsh criticism from employers, not labor. In 1895, he challenged the common view that unions hurt everybody, noting that they "have rendered a great service not only to their members, but to the world, in shortening the hours of labor and in modifying the hardships and improving the conditions of wage workers" (Copley, 1923, vol. 1, p. 406). Workers were driven to collective bargaining by mismanagement, argued Taylor. Unions would be unnecessary if employers subscribed "to the plan of stimulating each workman's ambition by paying him according to his individual worth, and without limiting him to the rate of work or pay of the average of his class" (Copley, 1923, vol. 1, p. 406).

Both labor and management, said Taylor, assumed that wages came from a fixed pie. He believed that the pie could be enlarged by greater efficiencies. Thus the paradox of high wages and low costs was resolved by finding the one best way to do the job. First-class men would attain the high rate without extra effort or bargaining. The ideal rate would be one that a first-class man "can keep up for a long term of years without injury to his health. It is a pace under which men become happier and thrive" (Wren, 1979, p. 131). Under this scheme Taylor was sure unions would not be needed. Taylor never understood groups, social needs, or the divisive potential of incentive wage differentials for a close-knit shop. He could not see that unions also fulfilled a powerful communal need most employers were not aware of.

Taylor's Consulting Methods. Taylor expected top management to back any steps he proposed. "Before starting to make any radical changes leading toward an improvement in the system of management," he said, "it is desirable, and for ultimate success in most cases necessary, that the directors and the important owners understand what is involved in the change." He insisted on a vote of support before entering. Once in, he expected resistance. "I have found that any improvement is not only opposed but aggressively and bitterly opposed by the majority of men," he later reflected, "and the reformer must usually tread a thorny path." If management can't wait "two to four years, they had better leave things just as they are, since a change of system involves a change in the ideas, point of view and habits of many men with strong convictions and prejudices." Moreover, "they should be prepared to lose some of their valuable men who cannot stand the change and also for the continued indignant protest of many of their old and trusted employees who can see nothing but extravagance in the new ways and ruin ahead" (Copley, 1923, vol. 1, p. 416).

Sometimes Taylor engineered the demotion or removal of opponents, a risky business that contributed to his downfall at Bethlehem Steel. He did not understand that the way to get past resistance is to encourage its expression. He wished to control his clients. "I always personally insist," he wrote, "that in all essential matters relating to the management the company. . ., must do as I tell them, and the only way . . ., to enforce this is that I hold myself free to withdraw from the work at any time. I have therefore not made contracts extending beyond two or three months" (Copley, 1923, vol. 1, p. 417). That practice is common among many process consultants today, who will terminate on twenty-four hours' notice as long as reasons can be discussed with the clients face to face. Taylor shared the risks too, in his fashion. He offered to reimburse clients for economic losses resulting from his unilateral decisions.

He was at his best with hourly workers. Fearful of groups, which he perceived only as potential organized opposition, he would divide and conquer, winning converts with his empathic swearing, his mastery of materials, his skill with lathe and drill press. He changed one person's job at a time, finding willing volunteers, studying the job, upping the wage, allowing the person to experience success, then moving on. He stressed quality standards and careful inspection first, observing that more output usually means lower quality, a lesson rediscovered in the United States as a result of Japanese competition.

He would upgrade skilled people but never move a person until a successor had been trained. Workers, Taylor said, must come to see that the previously antagonistic management is now working alongside them to upgrade quality, reduce conflict, cut costs, and raise wages.

Systematizing Bethlehem Steel

Taylor's most important client was Bethlehem Iron Company, a major armaments contractor that, in the wake of Navy contracts for all-steel ships, was renamed Bethlehem Steel in 1899. The president, Robert Linderman, wanted to cut costs in Machine Shop Number 2, the company's biggest bottleneck. Bethlehem manager Russell Davenport, Taylor's former boss at Midvale, brought Taylor and Linderman together. The necessary steps, Taylor wrote, "will undoubtedly be strenuously opposed by the workmen. . ., and probably also by most of your foremen and superintendents" (Copley, 1923, vol. 2, p. 12). To succeed, he required:

- A shop head who believed in piece work and had the authority to reverse or fire those who would not cooperate
- A promotions policy based on merit, not "whose friend a man may be or what influence he has"
- Wage rate increases up to 50 percent for increased production

The job would take nine months to two years, added Taylor, which would "very greatly depend upon the tractability of your men and upon the energy of the foreman and assistants" (Copley, 1923, vol. 2, p. 12). Joseph Wharton, company chairman, soon to endow a famous business school, balked at higher wages until

Taylor showed how much higher output would be. True to his policy, Taylor fully discussed his approach with Bethlehem managers and built support among superintendents and foremen. When they made him welcome, he rented a house in Bethlehem and went to work full time.

The honeymoon ended within a year. Taylor forced the removal of the general superintendent's brother as head of Machine Shop Number 2 and split the top plant job in half, giving manufacturing to the loyal Davenport (a sort of reverse nepotism). Using Henry Gantt, another Stevens graduate, he installed functional foremanship, production planning, and differential piece rates in 1899, making Machine Shop Number 2 by 1901 "the world's most modern factory and potentially a prototype for manufacturers and engineers in other industries" (Nelson, 1980, p. 85).

Henry Gantt, developer of the Gantt Chart and early advocate of learning and democratic work methods. (*Williams Library, Stevens Institute of Technology*)

Early Participative Management. Indeed, the real innovator at
Bethlehem might have been Gantt and his assistant, C. H. Buckley,
who straightened out the disorderly shop. Today Gantt's name stands
for a form of planning chart. He also was one of the more interesting
figures in the evolution of participative management. At Bethlehem,
for example, he used instruction cards, a Midvale innovation, coupled with a bonus. Like Taylor, he did not attempt to overcome
worker skepticism, but simply had machinists experiment with new
methods until they discovered how easy it was to earn a bonus.

Gantt went further. He allowed workers to ignore the cards and
attempt to improve the way the assigned tasks were done. If they
succeeded, the cards were revised — an early example of workers
being consulted and having influence over how the job was done.
"Whatever we do," wrote Gantt, "must be in accord with human
nature. We cannot drive people; we must direct their development" (Wren, 1979, p. 162).

Gantt appreciated the importance of learning. He instituted a
foreman bonus if all workers in a team made their individual
bonuses. The extra bonus was for "bringing the inferior workmen up
to the standard [and] made him devote his energies to those men
who most needed them." It is probably the first recorded effort to
reward management for sharing its expertise and teaching people
the right way to do things — a cornerstone of innovative change
projects today. "The next and most obvious step," he wrote, "is to
make it to the interest of the *men to learn more than their cards can
teach them.*" He considered rewarding new ideas and new techniques
developed by the men, anticipating modern gain-sharing plans
(Nelson, 1980, p. 100).

Gantt believed that autocratic management threatened free
enterprise. "In order to resume our advance toward the development of an unconquerable democratic civilization," he wrote, "we
must purge our economic system of all autocratic practices . . . and
return to the democratic principle of rendering service, which was
the basis of its wonderful growth" (Wren, 1979, pp. 167–168).

The Pig-Iron Loading Experiments. The Bethlehem experiments Taylor exploited, however, were related not to technology but rather heavy yard work like shoveling ore and loading iron. In later years his basic speech featured "Schmidt," a prodigious pig-iron loader whose tale became the most memorable, and curiously damaging, example of Taylorism.

For years Taylor had sought to find the law governing hard physical labor. There was no connection between human energy expended and output. Shortly after he arrived in Bethlehem, the firm sold a large quantity of pig iron, which had to be hand-loaded onto railway cars. Taylor seized the opportunity to continue his heavy labor studies. An iron "pig" weighed ninety-two pounds. The loader picked it up, walked an inclined plank, and deposited it on a rail car. The job required strong leg, arm, and back muscles. An average man could move twelve and a half tons a day. Taylor's theory was that physical stress caused deterioration of the muscles, which needed recovery time. Using a stopwatch and varying loading times, researchers decided a first-class man could load forty-five tons a day as long as he was paced properly (Copley, 1923, vol. 2).

Volunteers were offered $1.68 a day if they hit this goal, against the old rate of $1.15, a 46 percent increase. This much is roughly supported by the evidence, although there is doubt about how scientific the rate setting was. (Wages, Taylor readily admitted, were set through trial and error at an amount high enough to encourage optimum productivity but not so high as to support frequent absences. The figure had to be rediscovered in each new situation — exactly the practice now; not science exactly, but not haphazard either.)

Recruiting "Schmidt." In Taylor's oft-told story, the Spanish-American War presented Bethlehem a chance to sell 80,000 tons of pig iron rusting in the yard. A hardworking Pennsylvania Dutchman he called Schmidt, whose dialect he mimicked, was recruited to prove the standard could be obtained. Taylor's version of the discussion is embarrassing to read today.

"Schmidt, are you a high-priced man?"

"Veil, I don't know vat you mean."

"Oh, come now, you answer my questions. What I want to find out is whether you are a high-priced man or one of those cheap fellows here . . . whether you want to earn $1.85 a day or . . . are satisfied with $1.15, just the same as all those cheap fellows."

"Did I vant $1.85 a day? Vos dot a high-priced man? Veil, yes, I vas a high-priced man."

"Oh, you're aggravating me. Of course you want $1.85 . . . everyone wants it. You know perfectly well that has little to do with your being a high-priced man. . . . Now come over here. You see that pile of pig iron?"

"Yes."

"You see that car?"

"Yes."

"Well, if you are a high-priced man, you will load that pig iron on that car tomorrow for $1.85. Now do wake up and answer my question. . . . Tell me whether you are a high-priced man or not."

After Schmidt decided that he was indeed high-priced, he was told how high-priced men perform: they walk, lift, and rest on cue, and don't answer back. Such rough talk, noted Taylor, "is appropriate and not unkind," for it fixes attention on high wages "and away from what . . . he probably would consider impossibly hard work" (Copley, 1928, vol. 2, p. 45). So motivated, Schmidt, the John Henry of pig-iron handlers, proceeded to load forty-seven and a half tons a day. Only one in eight — "a man of the type of the ox" — was capable of such sustained work, said Taylor. Schmidt he characterized, with unconscious bigotry, as little more than an "intelligent gorilla."

What Really Happened. In point of fact there were only 10,000 tons of pig iron to load, not 80,000. The lot was sold in 1899, some months after the war with Spain ended. Taylor's recruiting dialogue with Schmidt was imaginary. The offer was made to the whole work crew. There was considerable resistance to piece rates, even high ones. Taylor had the rate wrong; it was $1.68, not $1.85. One gang, mostly Hungarian, threatened to strike and were initially discharged. The remaining men, Irish and Pennsylvania Dutch, were told that if they fell below the goal they would be given easier work until they were rested enough to return. Seven volunteered, two lasting only a day. Others came and went, including some of the recalcitrant Hungarians. Only three first-class men, able to load forty-five tons a day for days on end, turned up. About ten others earned more than the old day rate by averaging about thirty tons.

Bethlehem records show that Schmidt, whose real name was Henry Noll, far from an ox, was five feet seven and weighed 135 pounds — the smallest man on the crew. Yet he had extraordinary strength and endurance. He was the only one who showed up daily for two months, running to and from work, using the found money to build a new house on nights and weekends. During one two-week period Noll averaged 49.9 tons a day, 2.4 more than in Taylor's story.

But two workers exceeded him. One named Conrad averaged 55.1 tons, lifting an incredible 70.9 on one occasion, earning more than twice the old wage (233 percent) for more than six times the output (Wrege and Perroni, 1974). This prompted the socialist Upton Sinclair to point out the discrepancy between increased output and wages under Taylorism. Taylor countered that a person could earn more only because management had invested in figuring out and teaching workers how to do it, a social benefit leading to higher wages, lower costs, higher profits, and lower consumer prices. This outcome would not occur under Sinclair's proposal that workers "take possession. . . of the means of production" (Copley, 1923, vol. 2, pp. 50–51).

The "law of heavy laboring" was not found until months later, when Carl Barth recruited two "extraordinary laborers" expressly for this purpose and reduced their efforts to curves and graphs. He determined that the law governing iron pigs was that the arms must be free from load 57 percent of the day for a man to do his maximum work (Wrege and Perroni, 1974).

Why Fake It? Why would Taylor embellish facts and understate actual tonnages that would have made his story even more persuasive? A plausible answer is that he recited it from memory, using it to illustrate his principles, not his practice. It is a fact that much of *Scientific Management* was written from transcripts of talks Taylor gave at his estate years after he stopped working for money. It reflects evangelism more than documented facts. Hardly a public speaker ever lived who was above embellishing a good story to make a point.

There is a contemporary explanation for this phenomenon that I like very much. Harrison Owen, writing of transforming organizations, says, "From the point of view of the function of mythos it makes little difference *when* something happened, *where* something happened, or indeed if it ever happened at all. The single important factor is the existence of the myth in the culture and the way that myth functions by itself and in concert with all other present myths to create the field of meaning which images the spirit and guides its activity" (1984, p. 318).

The Inadvertent Myth. There is a second, related question that I find, from the standpoint of "mythos," even more intriguing. Why would Taylor report with pride a phony dialogue that makes him sound like a slavedriver and a bigot? We can only speculate that he didn't see it that way, and neither did his progressive friends. Racism in Taylor's factories was vastly more manifest and accepted than now. Rivalries among Hungarians, Irish, Poles, and Pennsylvania Dutch in the steel mills were intense. Managers played immigrant groups against one another, as the pig-iron story shows. Taylor never discussed this facet of factory life. It's a good bet that the workers he invited to dinner were skilled machinists, not yard laborers.

Taylor's own contribution to his tarnished reputation in human relations circles, I'm convinced, stems from his constant repetition of a story that reveals his bigoted side, offending modern sensibilities. In 1911 even progressive liberals accepted this apocryphal dialogue and mimicked accent in another spirit. Few true-blue Americans saw anything wrong with calling muscular immigrants who spoke broken English oxes and gorillas.

Today it is difficult to infer from this example the cooperative spirit between management and labor that Taylor valued. He was oblivious to the myth he was creating for posterity. It is hard to stomach Taylor's public racism now because it surfaces universal feelings we are seeking to resolve in more constructive ways. I would rather not look at that side of Taylor because I wish to restrain it in me. Each of us, I suspect, regardless of race, creed, color, or gender, has a "them" buried somewhere, unconsciously experienced as odd, scary, or inferior.

Long after Noll's retirement, Taylor's detractors spread rumors that he had been worked to death at Bethlehem. Taylor dispatched two old friends to pose for a picture with Noll. "Schmidt" stands between them in a bowler hat and overcoat, tie and rounded collar half covered by a scarf, his moustachioed face looking tired. He outlived Taylor by almost a decade. Anybody can view him today in *The Stevens Indicator* (Spring 1980), alumni magazine of Taylor's alma mater.

Taylor's Swan Song

By 1901 Taylor had given Bethlehem a modern cost accounting system, a real-time analysis of daily output and costs. He had doubled stamping mill production, reduced yard workers' ranks from 500 to 140, and lowered cost per ton of materials handled from eight cents to four cents, even after adding clerks, time-study engineers, teachers, a telephone system, labor office, implement room, supervision, and staff support.

He had raised hourly wages by 60 percent and the company was saving $78,000 a year in 1901 dollars. He and Manusel White also discovered high-speed tool steel, building on Taylor's Midvale work. They found that tools made from steel heated 300 to 400 degrees higher than recommended performed at twice the speed of conventional tools. Bethlehem paid the inventors $50,000 and licensed the process around the world. This discovery, after twenty-five years of dogged experiments, probably advanced Taylor's international reputation most of all.

Despite impressive achievements, he also made enemies. His reduction in the yard force, said some managers who also were landlords, would "depopulate South Bethlehem" (Nelson, 1980, p. 97). That, said Taylor, is essentially what they had hired him to do. His critics replied that they did not expect he would actually do it — a sobering reminder to modern consultants to mistrust their own too-ready acceptance by any client. In fact, given Bethlehem's growth rate, displaced workers were moved to other jobs and did not lose employment.

By 1899, demoted executives were thwarting Taylor's plans by controlling the engineering department. They delayed changes requiring new plant layout, pleading economy. Taylor constantly went over their heads and often won. However, when he sought more people for his staff and higher pay for others, President Linderman drew the line. In May 1901 Linderman, himself soon to be fired by Bethlehem's new owner, Schwab, forced Taylor out. Taylor's self-esteem was injured, but not his pocketbook. His response to this setback was to adopt three orphaned children, concentrate on his home and his hobbies, and begin a missionary campaign that would make scientific management a worldwide phenomenon. He had been born rich, and wise investments plus patent royalties made him even richer. After leaving Bethlehem Steel he never worked for money again.

The "other" Taylor, a family man, with wife, Louise, and the three children they adopted in 1901. (*Williams Library, Stevens Institute of Technology*)

Chapter Three

The Consulting Engineer: Taylor Invents a New Profession

> It would seem to me a farce to devote one's whole life
> and money merely to secure an increase in dividends
> for a whole lot of manufacturing companies.
> —— *Frederick Taylor, in F. B. Copley*, Frederick W. Taylor,
> *1923, vol. 2, p. 238*

Between 1880 and 1910 the United States "underwent the most rapid economic expansion of any industrialized country for a comparable period of time" (Bendix, 1956, p. 254). Getting rich from new technologies, cheap labor, and untaxed capital was dignified by a new term, social Darwinism, meaning that only the fittest survived the jungles of commerce. The labor problem was considered genetic. What did you expect from ex-farmers and immigrants working for $1.15 a day?

Management theory and methods always reflect the time and place. Taylor's scientific management became an excellent tool for quickly making productive workers out of hundreds of thousands of semiskilled European immigrants. It enabled them to earn more than they might have, and hastened their assimilation into American society. Taylor, the erstwhile factory hand, realized that immigrants, many of them experienced only at farming, could hardly be expected to understand new technology. He blamed *management* for unmotivated workers. He argued that most piecework pay systems were badly conceived, poorly administered, based on folk wisdom. Management controlled the playing field. But workers controlled quality, quantity, and costs. Their innate ingenuity convinced Taylor that workers had a great deal to offer if they could get something in return. Douglas McGregor later called that notion management by integration — finding a fit between personal and organizational needs.

Preaching cooperation between labor and capital, Taylor helped bury social Darwinism for good. He also undermined the arbitrary use of authority in factories. Taylor said what everybody knew but could not articulate: people who have power don't necessarily know what to do with it. In an economic enterprise they could hurt all interests, even their own. Only experts could bring reason, order, high output, and high wages to industry. It was not a message to warm the hearts of management. If Taylor was right, what were managers being paid for? Taylor did not see technology as *the* fix, just one factor in an equation. Machines could be speeded up, tools improved without achieving gains. "A good organization with a poor plant," he wrote in words that might come from any modern organizational psychologist, "will give better results than the best plant with a poor organization" (Taylor, 1915, p. 62).

Key to a good organization was a productivity expert, roughly analogous to third-party facilitator. It is important to see that Taylor, reared as a pacifist, disliked conflict and sought to depersonalize it. The trained engineer would collect the data, gain agreement on easier methods, higher output, and higher pay, and then install the system. Managers were not there to improve it, just to see that it ran right. It was the way reasonable people should want to solve problems and make money, better than fighting, better than forcing. Taylor put the work itself, not labor-management conflict, at the center of the analysis. That the work did not always stay put is more a commentary on human fallibility than Taylor's values.

Extending Taylorism

From 1901 on Taylor worked tirelessly, extending and defending his system. He wrote his major books and papers, delivered many speeches, became president of the American Society of Mechanical Engineers (ASME). He developed a cadre of disciples whose services he sold in a unique way. He would regularly invite groups of potential clients to Boxly, his Germantown estate. They would hear a two-hour lecture ("Schmidt" was always included), then tour the Link Belt Company or Tabor Manufacturing, two local firms run on the Taylor system.

Those who liked what they saw were introduced to trained consultants like Gantt or Morris Cooke, a brilliant young engineer who had worked at ASME. Taylor "supplied advice and moral support to both the employer and disciple, acted as conciliator in the event of disputes, and, above all, guaranteed the expert's competence and professionalism" (Nelson, 1980, p. 124). At first he was an absolutist — his ideas had to be used *in toto* or not at all. He softened his message when Cooke, whom he respected, pointed out that many businessmen were not ready to grant consultants authority to do whatever they wished.

Cooke became Taylor's alter ego. He transcribed the Boxly lecture and used much of it in an unpublished manuscript called "Industrial Management," begun in 1907. By mutual agreement this later became a major segment of Taylor's book (Wrege and Stotka, 1978). One biographer, disparaging the effectiveness of Taylor's speeches, said that "no more than 10% of the businessmen who listened to the lecture subsequently employed one of Taylor's select corps of scientific management practitioners" (Nelson, 1980, p. 124). That would mean two new clients from every twenty-person seminar, the consultant's equivalent to a baseball player getting "only" three hits for each ten times at bat.

Unpaid Consultant

Taylor performed his brokerage and monitoring services free. He also acted as unpaid consultant to the U.S. Army ordnance department and Navy shipyards, and to many business and engineering schools. He became a popular speaker on college campuses — Toronto, Penn State, Penn, Dartmouth, Wisconsin, Chicago, and of course Harvard. Yet he became increasingly anti-academic, criticizing business schools for not imposing more discipline on their curricula and urging that every student be made to work six months in a factory. He thought the best scientific management consultants would be ordinary working people, not college graduates.

Many Taylor imitators were more opportunistic than he and did not live up to his standards. A typical trial for him was Harrington Emerson, an ex-professor of modern languages, who set up the Emerson Company in 1907 and got as a client the Union Pacific Railroad. Emerson, a promoter and salesman, left the actual work to assistants less competent than Taylor's. Emerson lacked system, methods, or sequence of work. He did whatever the client would pay for. Like most consultants of the time, Emerson admired Taylor, writing to him, "I would rather have your approval of what I am trying to do than any other man living or dead" (Kakar, 1970, p. 179). It was a case of love unrequited. Taylor thought Emerson's work tainted scientific management.

Union Troubles

The Railroad Rates Case. Taylor first achieved public notoriety through a lawsuit brought by Louis Brandeis on behalf of manufacturing trade associations fighting a railroad rate increase. Brandeis argued that more efficient work methods would cut costs $1 million a day. He called Emerson, Gilbreth, and Gantt as witnesses to prove it. Taylor declined to appear, saying that he knew too little about railroads. His work was cited so often, however, that Ray Stannard Baker, editor of the *American Magazine*, offered to serialize *The Principles of Scientific Management*. Until then Taylor's preferred publisher, ASME, had declined to act, feeling that the book was not scholarly enough.

It was during the rate case planning sessions that Brandeis coined the term *scientific management*. That is how Taylor came to be identified with Progressive politics. Progressives loved the idea that rationalizing work could make it more humane and eliminate class conflict. Taylor's philosophy fit their faith that science would improve every area of society — law, government, public welfare.

Taylor "made efficiency synonymous with morality and social order," an industrial complement to Progressive reforms like women's suffrage, direct election of senators, workman's compensation, a minimum wage, aid to low-income people, and the income tax (Wren, 1979, p. 284).

Trouble at Watertown. The installation of Taylor's system by a disciple at Watertown Arsenal in Massachusetts in 1911 finally stirred up organized labor. Taylor had insisted that worker sentiment be checked in every department before starting time studies. Molders at Watertown were not consulted, nor did they get briefings on time study's goals and advantages. In a test of power, one molder, following orders from union leaders, refused to participate. He was summarily fired. The others walked out, the first strike against scientific management. The workers did not oppose time study and production bonuses, but rather the method of introducing the change (Nadworny, 1955, p. 80).

When Renault workers similarly struck in France in 1913, Taylor wrote, "If a man deliberately goes against the experience of men who know what they are talking about, and refuses to follow advice given in a kind but unmistakable way, it seems to me that he deserves to get into trouble" (Nelson, 1980, p. 179). Indeed, at the Frankford Arsenal in Philadelphia, where Taylor's system had been installed smoothly, several hundred rank-and-file members petitioned to continue it against their own leaders' advice (Drury, 1915).

One contemporary study performed in response to the hubbub showed that by 1912 there were 60 Taylor and 200 Emerson systems in use, that production went up 100 percent at Midvale, 50 to 75 percent at Bethlehem and on the Santa Fe Railroad, 250 percent at Tabor, and 200 percent at Link Belt. All this happened without widespread turmoil or displaced workers and was seen as beneficial by management and labor alike (Drury, 1915).

Congressional Hearings. Nevertheless, organized union opposition mounted. Taylorism became a lightning rod for one of the great social struggles of all time. The Watertown strike attracted so much attention that Congress at the end of 1911 ordered an investigation of charges (in the spirit of today's OSHA and EPA) that workers were mistreated under scientific management. Union leaders badgered Taylor mercilessly during his four days as a witness. The pro-union committee chairman refused to let him define what he meant by first-class man, insisting on the implication that only a few exceptional people could ever hold jobs under his system.

The panel concluded that there was no evidence that scientific management abused workers. It added that it was too soon to evaluate effects on health, pay, and labor costs. It proposed no legislation. Still, anti-Taylor forces used the hearings as a lever to prohibit the Army or Navy from spending money on systematizing. Thus ended the first attempt, quite successful until then, to make government agencies more efficient (Wren, 1979).

Portrait of Taylor late in life, after many battles. (*Williams Library, Stevens Institute of Technology*)

In his running battle with labor leaders, Taylor repeatedly invited Samuel Gompers, president of the American Federation of Labor (AFL), and John Mitchell of the United Mine Workers to talk with workers in plants operating under his system. Both refused. Gompers denied the existence of soldiering. Unions observed an informal truce during World War I and did an about-face during the 1920s, when a recession thinned their ranks. Both clothing workers and railroad unions adopted joint committees to address work issues. The AFL under William Green hired its own consulting engineer, and other unions did research on job design. Union acceptance of Taylorism lasted until 1932 when, at the bottom of the Depression, the AFL gave up on cooperation and started lobbying for survival (Wren, 1979). Eventually unions institutionalized the subdivision of jobs as a way to protect employment, and workers continued to find ingenious ways to defeat time-and-motion studies.

The Bitter End

Taylor's last years were marked by bitterness and resignation. A portrait painted about this time has him staring at the artist, self-possessed, belligerent, hair and moustache gone gray, face fuller than in his college graduation picture, straight mouth thinner and more tight-lipped. He is unsmiling, challenging. Widely admired by political reformers, still he felt misunderstood by zealous unionists and quick-fix managers, and wronged by consultant-imitators. More, his energy was drained by constant attention to his wife's periodic illnesses. The Taylors moved regularly — Atlantic City, the Poconos, New England, Europe, Philadelphia — seeking quiet, a pleasant climate, a change of scenery that would lift Louise Taylor's spirits.

On a speaking tour in the Midwest early in 1915, an exhausted Taylor contracted influenza. He entered a hospital in Philadelphia, where on March 20 he celebrated his fifty-ninth birthday. The next morning a nurse heard him winding his elegant Swiss watch somewhat earlier than usual. When she looked in at 5:00 A.M., he was dead.

Learning from Taylorism

I have been a long time arriving at an appreciation of Frederick Taylor that makes sense today. His is a sort of wall-sized color projection screen on which every scenario comes across larger than life. It is not generally appreciated how modern Frederick Taylor's core values were. He knew the importance of productive workplaces. He was working on the right problems — social, technical, economic — even when he did not have the right solutions. The tension between the two Taylors is the tug of war in all of us between what we believe and what we do. We have a great deal to learn from Taylor about productive workplaces.

He was not an "open systems" thinker by any stretch. More than anyone, he believed every effect had a cause. At the same time he had an intuitive appreciation for how things fit together that went far beyond most people in his day. He created a unique role — the industrial engineer — as a sort of third-party facilitator to bring reason and impartiality to labor-management relations.

Today many productivity programs rely on third-party facilitation for the same reasons. Unionized places (some auto and steel plants are typical) pair facilitators, one from labor, one from management. Instead of a stopwatch, their main tools are patience, trust, and group problem-solving techniques derived from Kurt Lewin. They seek to bring about, from a much wider perspective, the sort of cooperation between management and labor that Taylor envisioned. Still the methods are widely mistaken for the goals, which was and is *the* psychological dilemma of the Industrial Revolution. The quotes in "Every New Idea" are a sobering reminder of how mixed up we become between form and substance when we try to program a new way of looking at things.

Resistance from middle managers cut out of the action is as pervasive today as it once was to scientific management. The reasons are the same. How can you claim to make life at work better if you exclude a significant segment of the work force? We have a hard time accepting and using policies and procedures we did not help to select or invent. It does not matter how good they are.

Taylor's Contemporary Values

Disdaining Taylor's contributions, human resource experts embraced his core values: labor-management cooperation, higher output, improved quality, lower costs, higher wages, the rule of reason, questioning old habits, experimentation, clear tasks and goals, feedback, training, mutual help and support, stress reduction, and careful selection and development of people. Taylor thought people should be trained to succeed, not thrown into the water to sink or swim. He standardized tools and equipment to match human capability. What is now called ergonomics was an integral part of Taylorism. He was the first to consider a systematic study of the interactions among job requirements, methods, tools, and human skill, to fit people to jobs both physically and psychologically, and to let facts and data do the talking rather than prejudice, opinions, or egomania.

Taylor saw restriction of output as a consequence of poor management, not worker inferiority — a radical idea in his day. He believed in giving people feedback on their performance, a central tenet of participative management. He thought that labor strife was not inevitable — extraordinary in light of the bitter, sometimes murderous relations between employers and employees at the time. He argued that raising output and cutting costs would make possible higher wages, a view embodied in labor-management cooperation in many industries now. He was sure that money was the major motivator, certainly true in 19th-Century factories and still true for many people low down on the economic ladder — a conclusion Abraham Maslow would applaud.

Considering the time and place, Taylor's version of applied science was not so different from our own. There was a great deal of judgment in time study. Taylor, like every consultant, did not look only at "what is." He searched for the gap between "what is" and "what ought to be." The *ought* is a statement of future intent, not prediction or probability, but aspiration based on reasonable judgment derived from existing data and experiments, tempered by social values. Scientific time study for Taylor was the discovery of

The Every-New-Idea-Has-Nomenclature-Problems Department

What Scientific Management Is Not . . . (1912)

"Not an efficiency device . . . not a device of any kind for securing efficiency . . . nor any bunch or group of efficiency devices . . . not a system of figuring costs . . . not a new scheme of paying men . . . not a bonus system . . . not a premium system . . . not a stopwatch on a man and writing things down about him . . . not time study . . . not motion study or an analysis of the movements of men . . . not divided foremanship or functional foremanship . . . not any of the devices which the average man calls to mind when scientific management is spoken of.

"In essence, scientific management involves a complete mental revolution on the part of the working men – and on the part of those on the management side, the foreman, the superintendent, the owner of the business, the board of directors – as to their duties towards their fellow workers in the management, toward their workmen and toward all of their problems."

— Frederick W. Taylor, testimony to a special committee, U.S. House of Representatives, January 25-30, 1912, Washington, D.C.

What Quality of Work Life Is Not . . . (1978)

"Not a single, specific notion . . . not a soft, touchy-feely approach to working . . . not a vague, imprecise kind of notion . . . not a threat to power – management's or union's . . . not quick . . . not easy . . . not a panacea . . . not a closed system, not an end . . . not job enrichment, not a productivity gimmick . . . not imposable . . . not manipulative . . . not an ideology . . . not a passing fad . . . not elitist.

"The cluster of notions it sucks into itself combine to suggest something simple, operationally feasible, intensely human and even more intensely cost-effective . . . That something is to provide people at work (managers, supervisors, rank-and-file workers) with structured opportunities to become actively involved in a new interpersonal process of problem solving toward both a better way of working and a more efficient work organization, the payoff from which includes the best interests of employees and employers in equal measure."

— Ted Mills, Director, American Center for the Quality of Worklife, speech entitled "The Name That Isn't There," to Centre international de Recherches et d'Etudes en Management, June 8, 1978, Montreal, Canada.

how a job *should* be done. When jobs were broken down into their smallest parts, it was possible to discard waste motions, and through trial, error, and observation to find out what worked best — meaning most accurately, most efficiently, with the least stress. Taylor added factors for delay and interruption, newness of worker to job, and rest periods. These additions were based on the observer's experience, since the scientifically correct figure was bound to vary from job to job, place to place, and situation to situation, not to mention worker to worker (Wren, 1979, p. 126).

In summary, Taylor wanted a more humane and sensible solution to the degradation of work, which, like smog and pollution, was an early byproduct of the Industrial Revolution. We were not a society of innocent artisans before Taylor. We were a society of growing inequity, sweatshops, brutal working conditions; and he wanted, with all the tools of science and engineering, to do something about it.

Despite resistance, Taylor's ideas, embraced at last by organized labor, spread after his death to the public sector, office management, and marketing arenas. Germany, Sweden, Great Britain, and the Soviet Union all adopted scientific management in the 1920s. Lenin called it, with exquisite ambivalence, "a combination of the refined brutality of bourgeois exploitation and a number of the greatest scientific achievements. . . . We must organize in Russia the study and teaching of the Taylor system and systematically try it out and adapt it to our ends" (Simmons and Mares, 1983, p. 26). Hugo Munsterberg, called the father of industrial psychology, built directly on Taylor, seeking to discover "the men whose mental qualities make them best fitted for the work which they have to do." He too asked "under what psychological conditions we can secure the greatest and most satisfactory output from every man." He sought through psychological means to "produce most completely the influences on human minds which are desired in the interest of business" (Wren, 1979, p. 212). The field of personnel management is directly traceable to the integration between industrial social work, once called welfare, which Taylor disdained, and scientific management. "No man in the history of American industry," wrote Ida Tarbell, "has made a larger contribution to genuine cooperation and juster human relations than did Frederick Winslow Taylor. . . . He is one of the few — very few — creative geniuses of our times" (1925, p. 81). No wonder Peter Drucker credits Taylor with as much influence on the modern world as Karl Marx or Sigmund Freud.

Lessons to Remember

But that is not the whole story of Fred Taylor. So attractive were his ideas, so dramatic his results, that his descendants simply divorced his values and married his techniques. Greedy managers coveted the quick fix of time study without staff-line cooperation, and without paying workers a fair share of increased productivity. A modern analogy might be reducing the larger notion of a new corporate culture to task forces, attitude surveys, or flex time while leaving narrow jobs and hierarchical structures intact. Taylor hated that his integrated system was trivialized by 1912 into measured piecework, the wage differential treated as a rate to be cut each time high output levels were reached or exceeded.

Lessons for Management. In time Taylorism became synonymous with speedups, employer insensitivity, people turned into robots, doing more work for the same pay instead of working smarter, producing more, and taking home fatter paychecks. This last gasp of social Darwinism fanned the flames of unionism. Between 1897 and 1904 American trade unionists increased from 487,000 to more than 2,000,000. Technocratic engineers mastered the method and forgot the intent.

"The stopwatch and time study are baseball bats to clobber workers to get more," said industrial engineer Mitchell Fein at a seminar I attended in 1982. "I'm a high priest of time study. It won't work any more." Gain-sharing plans like the Scanlon Plan and Fein's Improshare symbolize a constructive return to Taylor's original intent: to give workers equity in increased productivity. These plans are based on a design principle that turns Taylorism upside down — to promote *group* control of results, a form of accountability unimaginable in 1911.

Lessons for Labor. Organized labor, after an uneasy truce in World War I, by 1930 largely accepted Taylorism. In the Depression unions turned toward bread-and-butter issues, especially job security. They rejected Taylorism in one way but tacitly embraced it in another. Narrow specialization could enhance job security. Many unions made a deal with the devil: jobs might be dumb but they would be safe. Each specialty would protect its own turf with restrictive work rules.

Decades later Chrysler's manufacturing vice-president described what happened when an engine block angled out of place on the assembly line. The line stopped. A foreman came from the other end of the plant and called in a toolmaker assistant, who straightened the block. In the process, he noticed a bent switch. He called for an electrician. Half an hour of production was lost. In Japan, he noted, workers took care of the same problems in a minute or two. "We have a stock chaser and a stock counter and a high-low man who moves the stock. Why can't the man who moves the stock be the chaser or the counter?" (Flint, 1984, p. 94). The practice made no sense — economically, technically, socially.

Perhaps the most historic clause in the 1984 agreement between General Motors and the United Auto Workers was the provision to protect employment in return for job flexibility. Without employment security it is an uphill battle to alter the system Taylor created. There is as much resistance to dismantling Taylorism as there was to installing it in the first place. "None of GM's ambitious plans to automate factories will be worth much," noted one writer, "if in the 21st Century plants are run under systems rooted in the 19th Century. Like other American manufacturers, GM has to overcome inefficient practices built up by both management and labor that stand in the way of high output and high quality" (Flax, 1984, p. 228).

Lessons for Operations. For Taylor, subdividing tasks was an essential but minor part of a much grander integrating scheme. Unfortunately, the form survived without the spirit or substance. Companies have staff experts for anything you can think of — pay, benefits, safety, hours, forms design, machinery, plant layout, schedules, inventory, quality control, public relations, law, maintenance, planning, safety, training, organization development, you name it. None of it guarantees anything except overhead. You can't simply break jobs down indefinitely without spending pots of money to put everything back together. So more line managers and supervisors are needed to integrate the system — the reason some steel companies developed fourteen layers of management in the 1970s. "Who should I listen to?" asks a manager. "Me first!" answers every staff specialist within earshot. Managers drown in a sea of conflicting staff pressures. Because they are not visible like a pile of pig iron, these pressures — which are the intangibles that determine whether people will cooperate — cannot be managed according to scientific principles as Taylor conceived them.

What were Taylor's "scientific principles" anyway? They are so simple as to be laughable: simplify each task; reduce conflict; cooperate; increase output; develop people to their highest capabilities. Who could argue with any of that? See "Scientific Principles" for Taylor's own words.

Scientific Principles

Science, not rule of thumb.
Harmony, not discord.
Cooperation, not individualism.
Maximum output, not restricted output.
Development of each man to his greatest efficiency
and prosperity.

—— Taylor, 1915, p. 140

Taylor Mythology

There are other reasons why Taylor became an ogre and a bogey-man. One is that his "scientific" task simplification violates social systems thinking and psychological knowledge. One Taylor precept was that "brainwork" should be taken from the shop floor and put in the planning department. This deprived workers of learning and growth, shifting expertise and control to staff departments — industrial engineering, personnel, maintenance, quality control — that became repositories of enormous technical skill and conflict-ing objectives as they sought to tread the fine line between being cops and coaches.

Another Taylor dogma was that management must gather in "all of the great masses of traditional knowledge, which in the past has been in the heads of the workmen, and in the physical skill and knack of the workmen," and reduce it "to rules, laws, and formu-lae" (Copley, 1923, vol. 1, p. 13). His intent was to accumulate the best knowledge available and ensure its quick transfer.

That is still our intent. Productive workplaces require it. Yet we know for certain now that optimum productivity and human satis-faction can't be reduced to rules and formulas, whether grounded in economics, engineering, or human relations. Indeed, high-quality work requires a creative interaction of all three perspectives. In successful workplaces workers, managers, and staff specialists achieve a partnership, learning together, bringing skills, expertise, information, and mutual support to economic and technical prob-lems. There will always be a certain class of "real-time" information and expertise among workers, specialists, and managers that can be accessed *only* through joint discussion and mutual learning. This is notably evident under conditions of uncertainty and fast change.

Taylor insisted late in life that his main goal was a degree of "intimate, friendly cooperation" between workers and managers impossible under the management practices of his day (Copley, 1923, vol. 1, p. 18). What he could not envision (in the years before Lewin and Maslow) were the more dramatic forms such cooperation might take — work teams without supervisors, management through self-control, multiple skills in each person, including planning, scheduling, and support functions. Taylor worked out the economic and technical sides of the equation. It remained for post-Freudian social scientists and open-systems thinkers to achieve a different philosophical and practical integration, one more suited to late 21st-Century technologies.

New technologies, more than anything, have made Taylorism obsolete. Ironically, in deskilling individual jobs Taylor removed skill and discretion from managers, supervisors, and staff people too. It became very difficult to introduce new knowledge into a system, even for the industrial engineers whose job it became. The "law of the situation," as Mary Parker Follett called it, became the law of past precedent. It could not regulate continuous process plants, microchip technologies, automation, robotics — even when pert-charted down to the last detail.

Taylor was not interested in democratizing work. He stood for rational control, not shared influence. He opposed group tasks and group incentives, arguing (with reason, in the case of narrow one-person tasks) that they reduced accountability. He had no concept of the power of multiskilled work teams, joint decision making, or worker participation. Such matters would not be studied systematically — the way Taylor studied shoveling — for many decades. No theories existed in 1900 for harnessing the peculiar and unpredictable synergy of well-motivated workers. Despite a growing emphasis on its importance, we still do not know how to bring democracy fully alive in the workplace. Moreover, we simply do not know enough about the complex process of working to make a true science of figuring out the right balance among people, economics, and technology. In each place it will be different.

We come at last to the inadvertent myth. What obscures Taylor's values more than anything, I think, like mists swirling across a dark road at night, are shadows of "Schmidt" and harnesses used to control nightmares, battles with organized labor, battles with middle managers, battles with the owners of capital, battles with the government, battles with the university, battles with other consultants who could not meet his standards. Taylor, like many pacifists, fought endlessly for a more rational, objective way to manage agreement. If his results fell short of his aspirations, that is more a commentary on human limitation than on what he stood for and what he accomplished.

Taylor's Main Contributions

Taylor made three kinds of contributions. First, he was an enormously creative technical engineer in the spirit of Thomas Edison. His patents alone — he had more than forty — assure him enduring fame. Second, he pioneered concepts of organization and management — the integration of methods, policies, planning, people — that were light-years ahead of his time. Finally, he spoke eloquently for labor-management cooperation — an ideal that his techniques, without significant alteration, could not support. A letter written just ten days before his death — and reproduced here — leaves no doubt of his sentiments.

Management accepted Taylor's organizing principles to a much greater degree than is generally recognized today. But neither operating managers nor factory workers have been entirely happy with the results. "What is resisted and criticized," wrote Peter Drucker, "is a misapplication of work analysis rather than work analysis itself. . . . The fact remains that scientific management or industrial engineering has been content to stop where Taylor stopped" (1974, p. 202).

Taylor cannot be blamed for not anticipating that development. Companies are learning, just as mine did in the 1960s, that they can get along with a great deal less management and supervision when workers are involved in designing their own work. This changes the system in a qualitative way, making possible product quality and productivity previously thought impossible. The important thing to see is that three realities — social, technical, and economic — must be simultaneously worked with if we wish to achieve productive workplaces. More, none of the three bailiwicks can be left to experts. Information from and about all three must be freely available to everybody, so that an organization develops through mutual influence, knowledge, and commitment, rather than coercion, whimsy, or unilateral action.

Lessons for Consultants

Taylor understood the inevitability of resistance, the virtue of support, understanding, and experimentation. Yet he could not act as constructively as he would have liked because he did not know how. As a consultant his track record was mediocre by modern standards. Taylorism as a total system was attempted in no more than two or three factories during his lifetime. Not only was it complicated, it also worked against the development of management generalists, people who could see a meaningful whole in the work. To make up for this lack, Taylor invented a gimmick still popular today: the exception principle, which says that managers should deal only with those few matters that fall outside established guidelines. The rest of the time they should focus on larger issues of planning, coordination, and resources. The agony is in trying to establish guidelines that stay put.

The system Taylor described in his famous book was in fact a composite of everything he had learned from trying bits and pieces in many companies. In no workplace was the whole system implemented exactly as conceived. I find this oddly reassuring. Taylor did what he could in each situation, fitting as much of his thinking as he could to his client's motives and problems. That, by and large, is what consultants do now. We can conceptualize processes — large systems change, cultural change, transformation — far beyond our capacity to implement them. Progress on any front (social, technical, or economic) seems a lot less rational and programmable in practice than our models of it — an entirely appropriate phenomenon, which in no way depreciates the models.

Out of many projects have come grand designs for planned change, cultural change, organization development, corporate excellence, total quality control, organizational transformation.

FREDERICK W. TAYLOR
CONSULTING ENGINEER
NEAR
HIGHLAND STATION
CHESTNUT HILL
PHILADELPHIA

Hotel Brighton, Atlantic City, N.J.

March 11th, 1915.
(Dictated March 9th)

Mr. Richard A. Feiss,
c/o Clothcraft Shops,
Cleveland, Ohio.

My dear Richard:

I am still thinking of the two most delightful and instructive days that I spent in your shops. What you have accomplished there is certainly magnificient and I am sure is destined to be even better yet. You can hardly improve, however, on your main feature, i.e. the fine relations which exist between the management and the working people.

I wish that every honest trade unionist in the country would go there and stay long enough to fully appreciate what you are doing so that it may be borne home to him that true co-operation and friendship is better than war.

Will you not knidly remember me to all of the friends at the shop who were so attentive to me.

Please tell Mrs. Feiss that I regret exceedingly not having see her.

I succeededing in staving off the grippe until after my address at Youngstown. The following morning, however, I was so hoarse with a bronchial cough that I was almost unable to speak and the fever and grippe still continue. I consider this a great piece of luck.

With kindest regards, believe me,

Very sincerely yours,

Fred. W. Taylor
M.

Pinpointing cases — the megabuck, all-out, everybody-in-it-until-the-job-is-done, honest-to-goodness, full commitment, synergistic, use-everything-we-know, culture change effort — is a lot like hoping to meet somebody who has rowed across the Atlantic Ocean. I can assure you that. It has been done, but you probably don't know anybody who did it.

The "Other" Taylor — Take Your Pick

Those who think this way about change — that the job can be done once and for all through a particular program — share the least universal aspects of Taylor's thinking: that every effect has a cause; every problem has a solution; big problems have big solutions; organizational change is largely a matter of the right machinery, the right program, or the right expert. If it takes social science machinery, let's get the best. That is one form of contemporary Taylorism. It is also one side of the dialogue in all of us, the yearning for control, the wish to be seen as competent and successful, the desire to influence others, the fear that we are too lazy, too irresponsible, too incompetent, too humorless, or too frivolous, too unworthy, too . . . (fill in your own most pessimistic worry) to ever measure up.

In his first Harvard lecture, Taylor attributed the withholding of output to two different sources. One was the "natural" tendency to laziness, which only money could overcome. Another, more systemic, which presaged Kurt Lewin's work, was a form of social collusion, "association with other men, with the deliberate object of keeping their employers ignorant of how fast work can be done" (Simmons and Mares, 1983, p. 26). That was a very shrewd observation of what is now called a "group norm." Taylor understood the existence of norms, even though he believed that worker needs began and ended with money. He could not see the social need behind the norm.

Yet, in his efforts to integrate and manage his own inner dialogue, Taylor was more holistic than either his direct descendants, the efficiency experts, or the human relations experts who disowned him. Turn the prism just a little bit and it is not so hard to view Taylor as the original QWL pioneer. He was the first person in history to make a systematic attempt to improve both output and work life in factories. He argued, as McGregor would eighty years later, that the big gains would come through the development of effective human systems.

Taylor erred in believing *his* system was the only game in town. "Throughout his life," wrote his admiring official biographer, "he was inclined to take too much upon himself, to assume and to feel too great a responsibility. He did not leave enough up to God" (Copley, 1923, vol. 2, p. 438). It remained for a later mental revolution to implement Taylor's more radical values. What new technologies have made essential has become possible only because of a new social science. To understand that, we have to investigate action research and Kurt Lewin.

Chapter Four

Lewin: The Practical Theorist

> When the intellectual history of the twentieth
> century is written, Kurt Lewin will surely be
> counted as one of those few men whose work
> changed fundamentally the course of social
> science.
> —— *Dorwin Cartwright, editor, introduction to Lewin,* Field
> Theory in Social Science, *1951, p. vii*

I first heard the name Kurt Lewin at a management conference in 1969 when Bill Dyer, later dean of Brigham Young University's School of Management, echoed Lewin's famous line, "There's nothing so practical as a good theory." Dyer went on to prove it by demonstrating force field analysis, Lewin's unique problem-solving tool. Lewin's ideas — especially "action research" — soon formed the core of my consulting practice. Yet for years I knew little about how he came to think up so many ingenious alternatives to Taylorism.

Frederick Taylor had seen only the shadow side of group life. He viewed work groups through a narrow filter, the high-control, Theory X side of his own nature. He knew that dissatisfied people soldiered on the job — an indisputable observation. What he did not know was how to use this social fact constructively, how to help people achieve self-control. Instead, he designed a system in which each individual's daily achievements would be precisely specified in advance. It remained for Kurt Lewin to build a rationale and a methodology for cooperative social problem solving as an antidote to individualism and expertise separated from people.

He also developed a theory of organizational change that enormously attracted me to consultating when I left my family business in the late 1960s.

Some years ago I began a systematic search for Lewin, for what would be my professional roots. I devoured Alfred Marrow's biography (1969), and began hounding friends and colleagues who also had been Lewin's colleagues — notably Ronald Lippitt and Eric Trist. In the library I found a curious parallel between Lewin and Taylor. In 1912 the American Society of Mechanical Engineers had observed that Taylor's revolution was built on "an attitude of questioning, of research, of careful investigation. . . of seeking for exact knowledge and then shaping action on discovered facts" (Nelson, 1980, p. 198). That describes Lewin's approach exactly — if you add one important concept: full participation of the research subjects.

Lewin's Contributions to Management

Lewin's life, like Taylor's, was marked by a passion for experimentation and faith in science. As Taylor sought to rid workplaces of authoritarianism and conflict through scientific management, so Lewin strove to free the world from prejudice, ignorance, and self-hate through social science. In Part Two I propose that to honor Lewin and his values today we must update his theory in practice. That requires an appreciation of how important his values and practice theory have been.

What struck me first about Kurt Lewin is how much modern management owes him and how rarely the debt is acknowledged. Peter Drucker, in his "big" book (1974), for example, does not mention Kurt Lewin at all. Neither does Edward Lawler in his thorough review of participative practices (1986). Yet Lewin's stamp is everywhere in contemporary management: running meetings, work design, training, team development, systems change, cultural change, leadership styles, participative methods, minority-majority relationships, survey feedback methods, consultation skills.

Lewin conceived a novel form of problem solving that might be called "doing by learning" — a core method for helping people find meaning in work. His theory for turning research into action and vice versa enabled a merger of Taylor's vision of labor-management cooperation with systematic social experiments. I was tickled to find that one of Lewin's early research interests was Taylor and scientific management, a fact known only to Lewin scholars and (now) you and me.

Lewin wed scientific thinking to democratic values and gave birth to participative management. And he did much more. He taught that to understand a system you must seek to change it. This led to one of the most important managerial insights of the last century: diagnosis does not mean just finding the problem, but doing it in such a way as to build commitment for action. Lewin's twin emphases on science and democracy form the philosophical base for participative work design and reorganization.

His was an unprecedented idea. Not only could you solve the problem, you could simultaneously study your own process and thereby refine the theory and practice of change. In contrast to Taylor, who believed only trained engineers could improve work, Lewin believed any well-motivated person could "learn how to learn" from everyday situations, improving general as well as specific skills. Hardly a corporate training department exists today that does not build on his ideas.

He also pointed the way toward collaborative consultation — a radical departure from the mode pioneered by Taylor in the 1890s. Lewin showed that all problems, even technical and economic, have social consequences that include people's feelings, perceptions of reality, sense of self-worth, motivation, and commitment. It is not given to consultants, for example, to sow the seeds of change (a screwy notion that gets us into trouble), but to discover what seeds are already present and whether they can be grown. We owe that priceless insight to Lewin. As it becomes better understood, fewer consulting reports will be filed in bottom drawers. The practice of organization development — adapted by corporations, government agencies (notably the U.S. Army), colleges, universities, hospitals, nonprofit institutions of all kinds — is Lewin's living monument. "I have come to believe," wrote Warren Bennis, a major shaper of organization development practice, "that we have so carefully disguised our identification to ourselves that we forget we are all Lewinians" (Marrow, 1969, p. 234).

Kurt Lewin was an experimental social psychologist whose career overlapped both Taylor's and Freud's. He lived on the fringes of establishment psychology. He was an odd duck, trained in Germany by class-conscious "Herr Professors." Unlike them, he was egalitarian with students, an eager collaborator with anybody who had energy and ideas. He was an inspired teacher and a loyal friend, quick and full of nervous energy, juggling so many projects his colleagues could hardly keep up. He lived, ate, breathed psychology, often losing track of time, forgetting to eat. Instead of specializing, he studied everything — child behavior, industrial psychology, social services, war research, education, community development. Instead of guarding his concepts, he freely offered them to all.

Psychologist Edward C. Tolman linked Lewin, the great experimentalist, with Freud, the great clinician, "the two men whose names will stand out before all others in the history of our psychological era. For it is their contrasting but complementary insights which first made psychology a science applicable to real human beings and to real human society" (Marrow, 1969, p. ix). Lewin saw unsolved problems frozen in a field of forces — people, institutions, motives, perceptions, wishes — that pushed toward good solutions or away from them. In Lewin's youth that notion was considered kooky psychology, a pseudoscience of factors nobody could see or touch. Its tangibility now is a tribute to Lewin's faith that science could advance only outside the laboratory, that real-time experiments were required to make breakthroughs in theory and practice.

Like Taylor in management, Lewin aspired to make psychology a science based on formal principles that account for human behavior. Lewin knew that psychology could never be as precise as physical science. Yet, like Taylor, he had faith in experimental procedures and believed they could bring a great deal more predictability to human affairs. Lewin "was singular in that he was one of the few psychologists who could transpose a life problem into controllable experimental form," wrote Alfred Marrow

(1969, p. x). As Taylor's passion had been work measurement, Lewin's was the accurate measurement of psychological forces. For thirty years he used a mathematical system he called "topological psychology," based on a geometry of relationships between points rather than sizes or shapes. He applied it to every class of human problem. The "Topological Map" is an example. The circle in the middle represents the marriage space. Each partner's family of origin — the large ovals — affects the marriage. Lewin believed the forces holding the pair together and those pushing them apart could be delineated in a force field analysis.

"The drawings," said psychologist Norman Maier, "convinced me that Lewin and his students were trying to communicate concepts that were entirely new, and they suggested the need to explore forces that went beyond psychological processes" (Marrow,

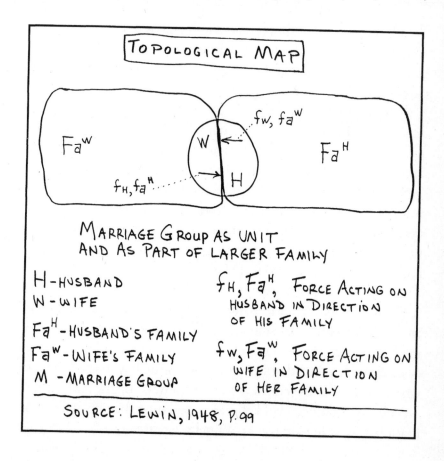

1969, p. 37). Maier based his famous group exercises emphasizing both quality solutions and commitment on this insight.

Lewin related to psychology not unlike Taylor to management. A nonconformist member of the "club," he put burrs under complacent saddles, agitating people to question assumptions, use common sense, and find out what works by *trying it*. Like Taylor he turned what others saw as his marginality toward the creation of novel methods for getting people more deeply involved in their own lives and work. Lewin's thinking made possible the evolution of an orderly method for dealing with events that are irrational, unmanageable, and — but for this way of doing things — out of control.

From East Prussia to Iowa

Kurt Lewin was born, the second of four children, into a close-knit, middle-class Jewish family in the Prussian province of Posen (now in Poland) on September 9, 1890. (In that year, thirty-four-year-old Frederick Taylor left Midvale Steel to become general manager of a wood pulp business.) Lewin's parents ran a general store. His mother had high aspirations for her son. When he was fifteen she moved the family to Berlin where he could get a classical education and become a country doctor. Instead young Lewin enrolled in Berlin University in 1910 to study an offshoot of philosophy called psychology. He was sociable, popular, a good dancer, a lover of the outdoors, whose conversation tended toward topics like "democratizing Germany and liberating women from the conventional restrictions of their freedom" (Marrow, 1969, p. 6).

His psychological interests were equally radical. He wanted to study human will, emotions, and sentiments, considered in 1910 the stuff of poetry, not science. Who could see a motivation or measure a feeling? Lewin was already as out of place as a Martian in academia. He joked that he felt like the little boy in the fairy tale who shouted that the emperor had no clothes. Still, he set his heart on college teaching, a bold choice considering the public discrimination against Jews in Kaiser Wilhelm's Germany.

Lewin volunteered for the German Army in World War I, advanced from private to lieutenant, sustained battle wounds, and won the Iron Cross. Convalescing, he wrote an article on "The War Landscape," in which he observed that soldiers' reality depends on whether they are behind the lines or in battle, when everyday objects — a haystack, for example — become survival tools (Marrow, 1969). The interplay between environment and behavior was a theme that would echo throughout his life.

Lewin married while on furlough in 1917. When the war ended he and his wife, also a teacher, settled down to academic life in Berlin. From the start he was attracted to the psychology of work. In 1919 he wrote a paper contrasting farm and factory labor, driven, his daughter speculated, by a "romantic attachment to the small farm his parents owned" when he was a child (Papanek, 1973, p. 318). Farm work, he pointed out, required the whole person. It was not specialized, like mill work. However, new farm technology, he speculated, would lead to new problems. Written many decades ago, this paper contains the seeds of open-systems thinking and the first glimmers of what would be called "action research." Nothing could have seemed more farfetched in German academia than Lewin's proposal that psychologists leave the laboratory and team up with farmers to improve work methods. A simple tool like the hoe, he wrote, might be the focus for systematic joint experiments to find less strenuous procedures for all tools and tasks.

Lewin Discovers Taylor

If these ideas sound familiar, Lewin's follow-up essay (1920) leaves little doubt of their origin. In "Humanization of the Taylor System: An Inquiry into the Fundamental Psychology of Work and Vocation," Lewin accepted the idea that scientific management raised output, cut costs, increased wages, and reduced stress and working hours. But that was not the whole story. Work, he insisted, had "life value." It gave meaning to a person's existence. To the extent Taylor's methods reinforced boredom and reduced learning, they exacted a cost in life value.

"The worker," wrote Lewin, "wants his work to be rich, wide, and protean, not crippling and narrow. Work should not limit personal potential but develop it. Work can involve love, beauty, and the soaring joy of creating. Progress, in that case, does not mean shortening the work day, but an increase in the human value of work." Commented his second wife, Gertrud Lewin, after his death, "You cannot help realizing that this is how Lewin actually felt about his own chosen work and how he lived" (Papanek, 1973, p. 318).

Among the Berlin psychologists who established the Gestalt school, Lewin alone had an interest in industrial management. Taylor knew before 1900 (and before anybody else) that less stress and more equity were critical to improved labor-management relations, more humane workplaces, and higher output. By 1920 Lewin understood (before anybody else) what would later be called job satisfaction. Psychologists and efficiency experts, he suggested in a foreshadowing of early work-design practice, should team up to enhance *both* productivity and satisfaction.

One example of Lewin's out-of-sync conceptualizing was his theory of psychic tension, a state of readiness for action, caused by an outside stimulus — a desire, a goal, or an unfinished activity. He saw this tension as a contest between strong and weak forces in a person's "life space." Achieving a goal temporarily balances the forces. A combination of tension systems in each of us is the source of energy for action. Dormant unfinished business might be activated by a word, gesture, sight, or sound.

Lewin's psychology differed radically from beliefs that all behavior is motivated by past influences (Freud) or future goals (Skinner). Lewin saw motivation as an interaction of a specific person in a specific situation, like the soldier in battle. Lewin's field theory holds that we act to resolve tensions that impinge upon our life space, which is defined as our subjective experience of situations. Invisible it might be, yet we *should* be able to measure it as precisely as weighing a stone. Lewin translated this insight into a formula. Behavior (B) is a function (f) of person (p) and environment (e), or

$$B = f(p,e)$$

He applied this formula to every kind of problem. It lives on today in force field analysis, which allows managers to analyze and act more confidently on problems that cannot be measured in ordinary ways. In the simplified "Force Field Analysis" drawing, for example, the behavior (B) of the smoker (p) results from all the forces (f) both in the environment (e) and the smoker (p). Briefly, the forces driving toward and those restraining problem resolution reach an equilibrium, the status quo line. Arrow length indicates the intensity of forces. You "move" a problem by increasing drives or reducing restraints. Lewin

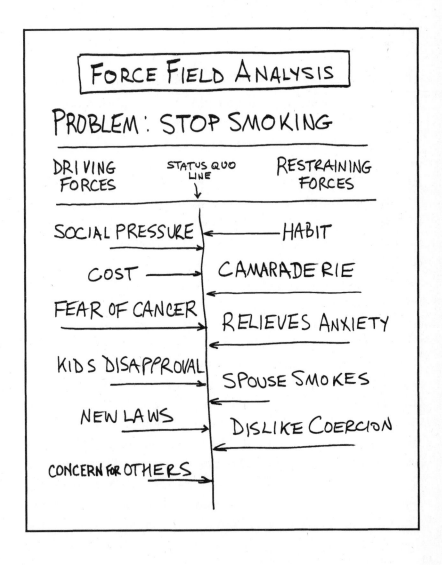

believed the latter was better. Driving forces attract more restraints while reducing restraints permits existing drives to prevail.

Lewin combined abstract thinking with great personal warmth. He had an unusual knack for turning everyday events and observations into useful theories. Like a benevolent sponge, he sucked people into his pet projects. His biographer Alfred Marrow (1969), for example, while a graduate student, visited Lewin in the early 1930s and was quickly involved in his studies. They became lifelong friends, and Marrow's family business, Harwood Manufacturing Company, sponsored the first industrial action-research projects in the United States.

1920s Origins of Management Practices

But Lewin's influence goes further still. As a young professor in the 1920s he attracted a legion of mavericks to Berlin. Their novel research significantly affected not only psychology but management training, organization development, and job design decades later. Strikingly, most were women in a field dominated by men.

Tamara Dembo, for example, had read Taylor in her native Russia and became interested in "making machines more suitable to human beings" (Marrow, 1969, p. 21). Her Berlin experiments confirmed that reactions to frustration — working harder, running away, fighting the researcher — were a function of the situation, not just individual style. She coined the term *level of aspiration* to describe a person's assessment of the difficulty of reaching a goal — the basis for the concept of "stretch" in setting business objectives.

Bluma Zeigarnik, also Russian, discovered a phenomenon that now bears her name. She was among the students Lewin met regularly at a Berlin coffeehouse. The waiter tracked the bill accurately in his head for hours. One day Lewin, a half hour after paying, asked for a repeat of the total. The waiter could not remember it because, he said, the bill had been paid. Lewin instantly formed a new concept: the waiter's memory was erased by completion. Zeigarnik went on to prove experimentally that people tend to remember interrupted tasks better than completed ones — the famous Zeigarnik effect.

Another Russian student, Maria Ovsiankina, showed that interrupted tasks are almost always resumed. Unfinished business cries out for completion. These discoveries underlie the design of conferences today. Merrelyn Emery (1983), for example, a modern practitioner, points out that starting a long meeting with a group task after dinner, with results to be reported the next morning, is a sure way to keep momentum. Anybody who has struggled to warm up a new group at 8:30 A.M. can appreciate the value of the Zeigarnik/ Ovsiankina research.

Still another student, Anita Karsten, proved that simple tasks, repeated until the subject tired and stopped (called "satiation") would be picked up easily later only if seen as part of some larger, personally meaningful whole. That discovery was the forerunner of job enrichment and a central tenet of work redesign. When Ford assembly-line workers called up car buyers at night to ask them how they liked their cars, they were enacting Karsten's discovery — a quantum leap beyond Taylor's concept of what workers needed to know. One reason the psychoanalytically oriented Tavistock Institute (see Chapter Eight) later adopted Lewin's ideas was his experimental proof that people continued to deal with unresolved issues — a demonstration of the theory that childhood conflicts carry over into adult life.

By 1928, Lewin was deeply into the development of field theory. He studied the "life space" and "boundaries" of Silesian textile workers, noting that the successful ones organized their total work flow to cope with disruptions like broken threads and empty spools. It was not just dexterity but a feeling for the whole — systems thinking, we call it now — that allowed them to be effective. Even Lewin's procedure foreshadowed the notion of interactive systems: one researcher followed the machines, another the people (Papanek, 1973, p. 319).

Lewin showed how textile workers' behavior resulted from many simultaneous forces inside and outside the person. His finding that manual dexterity tests for mill workers were not relevant to *total job* demands was a significant revision of Taylor's scientific selection based on narrow competence. Yet in these early explorations Lewin, like Taylor, still focused on individuals. It remained for his American colleagues — notably Ronald Lippitt — to draw his attention to the power of groups.

Lewin in America

By 1930 Lewin's work was known throughout the psychological world. Yet, being Jewish, he could not get a permanent teaching job. In 1933, when Hitler became chancellor, Lewin resigned from Berlin University, declaring he would not teach where his children could not study. He took a two-year appointment at the Cornell University Home Economics School and left Germany a few months later, never to return. On his way to the United States he stopped in Cambridge, England, and was given a sightseeing tour by

Kurt Lewin, a primary shaper of ideas and methods for democratic leadership and social change. (*Miriam Lewin*)

a young graduate student named Eric Trist. In the chapel of Trinity College, standing in front of Isaac Newton's statue, Lewin gestured wildly at the swirls in the ceiling and told Trist they reminded him of the topological diagrams in a book he was writing. Trist was so taken with Lewin's thinking he reoriented his own career from literature to psychology and later became Lewin's leading exponent in Great Britain (E. Trist, memo to author, January 1987).

Lewin never became a full professor. Instead, he held a string of non-tenured jobs in American outposts of psychology. (In the United States he Americanized the sound of his name, but many who knew him still say "Lahveen.") In 1935 he became a child psychologist at the University of Iowa's Child Welfare Research Station. There began his most fertile period, as he shifted interests toward the use of the social sciences to solve social problems.

Photos taken about this time show a slender man of forty, on the short side, balding in front, straight black hair combed back from a high-domed forehead. Large rimless glasses, set firm on a long, broad nose, frame intense dark eyes with laugh wrinkles in the corners. He is clean-shaven, with a straight mouth, thin upper lip set back on a broad lower one, above a large, square jaw. He looks pleasant, not smiling exactly but benevolent; and there is something else, a tenseness, like a coiled spring.

Studying Groups

Lewin was the quintessential collaborator. He had the rare gift to seed new ideas with warm enthusiasm and dispassionate critique. "It was a common experience," wrote Dorwin Cartwright, "when coming to him with some vaguely conceived notion to have him react enthusiastically, and then to discover that from the conversation a new view of the problem had emerged, hardly recognizable as the original notion but incomparably better" (1947, p. 97). Nowhere was this unique alchemy more evident than in his relationship with Ronald Lippitt, a former Boy Scout leader and recreation major from Springfield College, who came to Iowa City as a graduate student in the fall of 1938.

Lippitt had led and studied neighborhood youth street clubs in college. When he saw the word "group" on Professor Lewin's suggested theses list, Lippitt told me, he went to visit "this funny little man with the German accent" (comment to author, August 1982). He proposed to research his observation that the way leaders managed camping trips, outings, and hikes affected a group's experience and achievements. Lewin immediately saw the implications: that leader behavior could shape culture. He had already perceived grim echoes of Nazism in American colleges establishing quota systems and resort hotels banning Jews. His attraction to Lippitt's ideas was intensely personal. Together they conceived a comparative study of how autocratic and democratic leadership affected children's groups.

In early dialogues between Lewin and Lippitt the term *group dynamics*, used by Lewin in a 1939 article, was coined. Ironically, Lewin's group theories were triggered by a misunderstanding. Years later he confided that until that first conversation with Lippitt he had seen "group" in topological terms — an interaction between parts of any kind of system, rather than interdependent people who develop unwritten rules for their joint behavior.

Discovering Management Styles

Lippitt and teacher Ralph White designed experiments with volunteer boys' clubs doing typical activities like arts and crafts. Each researcher led a group democratically for several sessions, then autocratically for several more, observing the impact of different styles on group climate and output. Acting as authoritarians, White or Lippitt dominated, set goals, issued instructions, interrupted, made all decisions, and criticized the work. Their followers argued more, showed more hostility, fought, damaged play materials, lost initiative, became restless, showed no concern for group goals or others' interests. They scape-goated the weaker members (an analogue to Hitler's Germany not lost on the researchers). Then, as democratic leaders, the researchers encouraged groups to set goals, make decisions, and mutually critique one another's work. These groups stuck to the task and developed more friendliness, group spirit, and cooperation.

Lewin, running a movie camera behind a screen, soon observed White, an inexperienced group leader, using a third variation: letting the boys do what they wanted. The team called this style "laissez-faire" and made it part of the experiment (Marrow, 1969). Groups led in laissez-faire style showed less task focus than either of the others. Lack of direction frustrated the boys, who felt vaguely inadequate and blamed their unhappiness on less able members.

Climate and results followed style, no matter which leader exhibited it. The extraordinary thing was how fast group behavior changed when leaders changed their styles. The chart "Aggression in Boys' Groups" plots these changes over time.

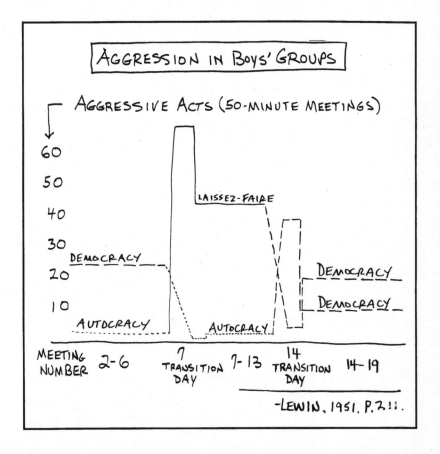

Watching Lewin's film in my office (you can rent it for a few dollars), I was struck by the marked differences in behavior when the leader left the room (a deliberate act). In the autocratic group, the boys picked on weaker members, goofed off, even destroyed their work. In the democratic group, the boys hardly noticed the leader's absence and kept right on working. In laissez-faire, boredom quickly surfaced. Some boys quit doing anything and wandered around the room.

The last one reminded me of a company where I had once consulted. The boss, a self-professed democrat, allowed people to do what they wanted. His people, hungry for leadership, wandered around uncertain of what to do, while the boss seethed silently at their "childish" behavior. "I thought that's how democratic leaders get results," he said. It had not occurred to him that democracy has always required goal focus and active leadership.

"I think there is ample proof," wrote Lewin, "that the difference in behavior. . . is not a result of differences in individuals. There have been few experiences for me as impressive as seeing the expression on children's faces during the first day under an autocratic leader. The group that had formerly been friendly, open, cooperative, and full of life, became within a short half-hour a rather apathetic-looking gathering without initiative" (1948, pp. 81–82). He also noted that it took much longer to adjust from autocratic to democratic leadership. Lewin's inference will be instantly recognized by those who have sought to modify their own management styles. "Autocracy is imposed on the individual," he wrote (pp. 81–82). "Democracy he has to learn!" Thus unfolded in a 1938 student project on child behavior — the foundations for a core technology of management development — the impact of management styles on output and climate in work groups.

Change Efforts Are Group-Based

The transplanted Iowans were now on the verge of discoveries that would usher in a new form of applied social science. "In our discussions with Margaret Mead," Lippitt told me of those days, "the importance of the small face-to-face group as the linker between person and 'macro' system became a basic rationale for group dynamics." The group, Lewin would assert, was a powerful shaper of individual behavior. From this practical theory came a core tenet of management and organization development: a group's behavior changes with the conditions operating in and upon it. Nowhere is this more evident than in the leader's behavior. If you want to be an effective leader, you need to do more than study group dynamics. You also need to learn more about yourself.

Reading Lewin, I suddenly had a new appreciation of the "personal style" exercises so important to my own group training in the early 1970s: paper-and-pencil instruments like Atkin's and Katcher's Life Interpersonal Orientation Survey (LIFO), Strength Deployment Inventory, Will Schutz's FIRO-B, the Myers-Briggs Type Indicator, and so on. Each highlighted aspects of my behavior, attitudes, and preferred actions under different conditions. They taught me how my style augments or conflicts with other people's styles, how I help myself or dig my own hole deeper. They gave me another way of seeing my own X and Y parts and the many other selves inside that determine how effectively I work with others.

I also saw that personal styles were only part of the story. Group forces could *not* be understood by looking only at individuals. Lewin's field theory suggested that my style and yours interact in a particular way, depending on the situation. We might behave differently with different others or in different groups. For that reason, in each situation learning anew our own and others' styles could be a powerful form of team development. Validating one another's styles could lead to acceptance and commitment to build on one another's strengths and to minimize weaknesses.

Nor could large numbers of people be helped to change through one-to-one counseling. Positive group experiences, based on mutual tasks, could alter the attitudes and actions of all those in a particular social system more quickly than individual awareness exercises. There are solid reasons, then, why groups, rather than individuals, became the focus for organizational change strategies. Many aspects of behavior simply cannot be understood or modified in any other way. (During World War II Wilfred R. Bion, of Tavistock Institute, also initiated a group dynamics tradition based on similar insights; see Chapter Eight. In Part Three I trace how Lewin and Bion converged in current practice.)

American individualism abhors herd behavior. A group can be a pressure cooker for mindless action. It can also promote personal identity and lead to acceptance of diversity. Most people, unless they grew up playing team sports, acquire group skills (if ever) only as adults. Few secondary schools or colleges offer training in meetings as basic skills, like reading and writing. As a result, many people remain suspicious of group problem solving and teamwork. That is too bad, because one critical piece of learning possible in groups is how all of us exacerbate our own problems. Another is that each group member has unique contributions to make. A third is that we are more likely to modify our behavior with group support than without it. Yet it takes democratically led groups to learn the considerable skills needed to resist group pressure toward conformity. To have a productive workplace we need self-knowledge *and* group skills.

If it is possible to have too much of a good thing, from ice cream to football, we Americans always manage to have it. In the 1950s and 1960s consultants sprouted like dandelions in the meadows of group dynamics. Applied social scientists, like consulting engineers enamored of piece rates, packaged Lewin's insights in every conceivable format — books, instruments, tapes, and films. Group exercises, committees, task forces came to be prescribed for everything that ails you, from low motivation and morale to lower back pain and gout. That is no fault of Kurt Lewin. It is an example of a universal phenomenon. Some of Lewin's descendants mistook techniques for values the same way Taylor's did.

Chapter Five

The Learning Organization: Lewin's Legacy to Management

> Today, more than ever before, democracy depends
> upon the development of efficient forms of
> democratic social management and upon the
> spreading of the skill in such management to the
> common man.
>
> —— *Kurt Lewin, "Frontiers in Group Dynamics,"*
> *1947, p. 153*

Lewin's action research on leadership and participation rank with the 20th-Century's great social achievements. As Taylor's discovery of high-speed steel made possible better machine tools, Lewin's group discoveries enacted social values Taylor reached for and could not grasp. His work heightened the tension portrayed so vividly by Bellah and associates in *Habits of the Heart* (1985). He challenged rugged individualists to consider life's other dimension — the need for community.

Group Decisions

Participative management had an improbable origin. It evolved during World War II from a collaboration between Lewin and anthropologist Margaret Mead to reduce civilian consumption of rationed foods. It was discovered through experiments with Iowa housewives, helping them decide — given facts about nutrition and scarcity — what to feed their families. Lewin's method was simple. He would identify the "gatekeepers" who control a situation, then he would reduce the resisting forces by involving them in studying and planning the change. Mead pointed out that husbands, contrary to belief, ate foods their *wives* liked. Lewin charted the flow of meats from store to table the way a systems analyst follows a shipping order from office to loading dock. It was obvious that Mead was right. The homemakers bought, stored, prepared, and served the food.

The resistance to nonscarce meats must be reduced. If gatekeepers were given new information and participated in deciding what to do, it should be possible to get more nonrationed meats on the table. He set up a comparative experiment. An expert nutritionist lectured housewives on what they "should" do — a traditional, reasoned exhortation to change. Women in comparison groups were given the facts and invited to decide together what to do. With 20/20 hindsight it's easy to guess what happened. Groups that reached consensus through discussion changed their food habits much more than those given expert advice.

Lewin had found a core principle: *we are likely to modify our own behavior when we participate in problem analysis and solution and likely to carry out decisions we have helped make.*

This finding was value-based, a fact largely lost in debates about participative management. "Kurt's special gift for understanding American ideals of democracy," said Margaret Mead, "led him to include in these first research plans his clear recognition that you cannot do things to people but only with them" ([1954] 1983, p. 164). One striking aspect of Lewin's gatekeeper theory decades later is that he always had the emphasis right in deciding who to include — those who directly controlled the situation. He was never an ideologue of mindless participation any more than Taylor was an ideologue of mindless time study.

After the war the Iowans extended participative action research to industry. Harwood Manufacturing, Alfred Marrow's garment company, had opened a new pajama factory in rural Virginia. The local women, even with training, produced only half as much as Northerners. Alex Bevalas, an Iowa graduate student, sought to change the situation by involving people in setting their own goals and controlling output. He discovered again a fact on which Taylor had based his whole system — that people use many methods for the same job. Instead of engineering "one best way," Bevalas conducted weekly discussions between high and low producers on the pros and cons of various techniques. Not only did people learn efficient practices from one another, they removed the barriers to change by deciding together what to do.

One experimental group, for instance, voted to go from seventy-five to eighty-seven units a day within five days — once an unimaginable goal. They then raised output to ninety units, greatly increasing piecework wages over what they would have earned had industrial engineers set the rates. No other groups increased at all (Marrow, 1969). Harwood experienced productivity improvements as dramatic as Taylor's, the first experimental evidence of the impact of group decision making, self-management, and democratic leadership training in industry.

The Motivational Force Field.   Lewin compared social change to altering a river's course not by damming it but by digging a new channel, taking advantage of the flow instead of fighting it. Discussion alone did not reduce forces in the field tending toward lower production. Motivation was closely tied to ability to have a direct influence on results. Lewin showed through force field analysis why this happened. Harwood's status quo was low output, almost but not quite stable. One force keeping down production was the stress of hard, fast work. Increasing pay would not reduce it. "There is an upper ceiling for human activity," observed Lewin, echoing Taylor. "The common belief views the desire to make more money as the most important force toward higher production levels" (1947, p. 25). Pay, he went on, means different things to people. Rural women, earning more than ever at Harwood, had upped their living standards enough, and would not work harder.

Thus Lewin reinforced Taylor's observation that there is an optimum wage rate that encourages production. Set the rate too high or too low, and forces enter the field to cancel out potential gains. Again, he added a crucial social factor opaque to Taylor: "general living standards of the group." Pressures of stress, fatigue, aggressiveness, anxiety, and variation in output were based in part on *group norms*, not just individual capability. Lewin suggested self-management as a way to optimize results. It is a practical theory that today underlies work redesign, innovative factories, and labor-management cooperation in hundreds of U.S. and European firms. Force field analysis is one of many widely used tools.

Extending Harwood. Personnel manager Lester Coch and social scientist John R. P. French (1948) extended Bavelas's pioneering work to Harwood's managers and supervisors. They used role plays and group problem solving to build confidence in democratic supervision based on openness and feedback. Instead of lectures, they helped supervisors learn from their own experience — an innovative form of management education.

French also broke new ground in his efforts to cut down manager stereotyping of workers. Harwood supervisors refused to hire women over thirty for machine jobs, insisting they were less productive. French knew from the food studies that giving them facts would not change their minds. He suggested that *they* test their assumptions and find out how much it cost to keep older women — hardship cases, widows, long-term employees — on the payroll. Supervisors chose to measure output, turnover, absenteeism, and learning speed. They collected and analyzed their own data, concluding that women older than thirty did as well as or better than younger ones on all measures. Imagine their chagrin when they fed back these facts and found their management sponsors — the gatekeepers, who had not participated — unwilling to change hiring practices.

No research finding in management history was ever more relevant. If you want *any* change to succeed, get the gatekeepers in on it early. Otherwise, you will start over again with every new stakeholder group. The field is strewn with the skeletons of quality circles and other change programs that used all the right training techniques but had the politics of involvement wrong. It is a mistake to charge ahead with a project just because some manager blesses it from Mount Olympus.

Gatekeepers are found in all functions at all levels. Getting them on board is a principle, not a technique. How to do it in *this* situation is exactly the action-research problem. We may exclude people for reasons of "efficiency" and find that that is not always the efficient thing to do.

Reducing Resistance to Change

Coch and French illustrated this principle another way at Harwood. Pajama-making jobs changed with the seasons and styles. When people's jobs changed, they could not get back to previous output levels. The usual procedure was to have an industrial engineer describe the new basis for piece rates. The usual outcomes were long relearning time, more absenteeism, grievances, and turnover. The researchers tested this traditional approach against two others: (1) work group representatives discussed changes with management; (2) the work group recommended and planned its own changes.

Production of the traditional group, as usual, dropped 20 percent and never came back; morale was low; many complained to the union; one in ten quit. Both other groups remained intact and cooperative. The representative group recovered output in two weeks. The direct involvement group, however, did something extraordinary. They regained productivity in two days and steadily increased it to 14 percent above old levels! Output went up and turnover down in direct proportion to participation (Marrow, 1969). Lewin, the believer in measurement, thought production figures *exactly* calibrated the strength of driving forces for output. External job changes *increased* restraints on output for nonparticipating groups. Direct participation removed restraints. Workers then broke through to higher productivity, an option inconceivable to Taylor.

Resistance dissolved when you "got through the gate" and with it old assumptions dissolved — a discovery I repeated for myself in the 1960s when I found that involving people in building their own work teams led to 40 percent more output, a level I had assumed impossible. Unavoidable change can be a hassle or a breakthrough. *All* untested assumptions are probably false.

W. Edwards Deming (1982), the statistical guru who introduced quality circles into Japan, went further, showing that emphasizing quality instead of setting production targets leads to much higher output. This is one of the most startling insights in management history. It goes against the textbooks. It is part of a new mental revolution that I believe started with Lewin. It is a mistake to assume we know any system's productive capacity before we involve people in shaking out the bugs.

Harwood and Hawthorne: A Modern Perspective. To understand what really happened at Harwood, contrast that research with the controversial Hawthorne studies (Roethlisberger and Dickson, 1939). The latter varied conditions like light levels to find the effects of environment on output. These studies started in the Taylor tradition. Researchers, not workers, planned and made the changes. The most noted finding, the famous "Hawthorne effect," was discovered by accident: output went up regardless of changes, a result attributed to special attention paid to the people. That had nothing to do with participative problem solving or decision making.

The Harwood experiments from 1940 through 1947 represented a different sort of thinking entirely. They were *action research*, intended both to solve problems and create useful knowledge about the processes of change itself. Subjects and researchers teamed up to create change. Bevalas, Coch, and French brought to life Lewin's vision when, as a young man in Germany, he had proposed that psychologists and farmers improve hay loading jointly. The Harwood pajama factory, as best I can tell, represents the first recorded attempts at participative systems change.

The method had worked for Lippitt and White, wearing their "democratic leader" hats with the Iowa boys' clubs. It worked in the wartime Lewin-Mead food habits experiments. It was the only experimental condition that led to effective job changes at Harwood. It is one of the best-researched practices, and one of the least used. Most managers think they do it already. Only a handful know what "it" looks like at its best — a serious effort to maintain community by involving people in the economics and technology of the business. It means high stakes, high anxiety, and high payoff, not (as some cynics would have it) people sitting around a flip chart asking each other how they feel.

Kurt Lewin saw no panacea in participation. "Managers rushing into a factory to raise production by group decisions," he wrote, "are likely to encounter failure. There are no patent medicines, and each case demands careful diagnosis" (1947, p. 36). To Lewin each change project was a new frontier. No two force fields are the same, no two solutions identical. Involving people was not a "technique." It was the bedrock of social learning, requiring goal focus, feedback, leadership, and participation by all the relevant actors.

"Unfreezing" as a Key to Change. From many such studies, Lewin (1946) conceptualized his famous theory of how change takes place. He described it as a three-phase process: "unfreezing, moving, and refreezing." Unfreezing means reducing the negative forces through new or disconfirming information — new data on nutrition for Iowa housewives, new understandings about productivity for Virginia factory workers. That is the function of diagnosis. Moving means changes in attitude, values, structure, feelings, behaviors — what happens when people discuss and plan new actions. Refreezing means reaching a new status quo with support mechanisms to maintain the desired behavior.

From this formulation came an action-research model of consultation, which I describe in Chapter Ten. Briefly, it involved contracting for joint study, diagnosis, and action. The consultant's role was to provide the data that would unfreeze the system, reduce the resisting forces, and alter the status quo. Of all Lewin's ideas, I find this the one most in need of rethinking if we wish to achieve productive workplaces today. The concept falls apart as the rate of change in markets and technologies becomes a state of perpetual transition, rather than the "quasi-stationary equilibrium" Lewin described. The cycles tumble on so fast that whatever is refrozen lasts only weeks or months instead of years.

Change can be painful or exhilarating, but it cannot be avoided. For decades now we have been discovering that technical, economic, and social change is a mirror for our own values. One promising new management perspective is the growing realization that the future is shaped by present responses, that we make our future dreams come true by acting on our own values today. Treating action that way is infinitely more satisfying and efficient than turning the problems over to experts to be solved in light of *their* values. In Part Two I propose a new theory for doing that in places where "moving" has become a way of life.

Action Research Today

Lewin's standing offer was to trade help with the solution in exchange for the advancement of knowledge, a win-win use of scientific thinking never surpassed. He advanced applied social science simply because he insisted ("the emperor has no clothes") that laboratory experiments are not enough. In real life you cannot control all the variables, especially other people, so you do the scientific thing — you involve them in learning how to do the experiment. That is what works.

Lewin's major contribution to management was his way of thinking: every change requires a new participative experiment. That is *the* central tenet behind the concept of a learning organization. It's also the hardest principle to master if you have been trained, in the Taylor tradition, as an "expert." It applies not only for labor-intensive textile factories, but also high-tech projects, installation of robots, automated production, electronic offices. It does not matter what a machine is rated to do. It does only what those who run it are willing for it to do. There are no totally failsafe technologies, as we will see in Chapter Nine. The best insurance policy is having all workers know what they're doing, which requires their direct involvement.

Lewin realized in 1920 that scientific management was incomplete. The old manager formula — planning, measuring, controlling, leading (a Frederick Taylor derivative) — sounds good. It is very hard to apply today unless you include everybody. It takes wisdom to see that no one person knows enough to do it all and courage to involve those who have the information and control the change. Note how similar Lewin's and Taylor's goals were: raise output, reduce stress, improve labor-management relations, increase wages. But Lewin added another value and an expanded list of scientific factors influencing the objectives. The new value was democracy. It called for exceedingly novel, and for managers, anxiety-provoking, techniques. The enlarged view of "scientific" called for considering a worker's entire life space, not simply the relationship with the tools and the task.

Taylor was always ambivalent about lecturing business students on his system. He believed that education without firsthand experience was futile. So did Lewin. Neither mistook methods for values. Reading Lewin, I realized that he had devised experiments that proved what Taylor knew intuitively: that the authoritarian in all of us is ineffectual when faced with modern technology and skilled co-workers. Taylor hated conflict so much, yet had so much need to control, that he devised impersonal, technical systems to humanize industry.

Lewin, abhorring Nazism and fearful of the shadowy side of democracy too, added social systems to Taylor's thinking. He expanded the concept of workplace to include the life space of each person, and the unwritten rules that govern action. Lewin helped develop the knowledge needed to break through the frustrating paradox faced by every expert: knowing the right answer and not being able to get others to act on it. "Lewinian methods," wrote Marrow, "helped shift the focus of industrial management from mechanistic engineering approaches to social-psychological concepts. The great interest in recent years in the humanization of industry stems in large measure from Lewin's emphasis on the dynamics of groups at work" (1969, pp. 151–152). "Lewin's Practical Theories" demonstrates the accuracy of that assessment.

From Research to Real Life

By 1945 Kurt Lewin had determined to use social science to alter systems, not just to describe them. He saw changing individual behavior as a weak, even futile strategy for intractable social problems. Productive workplaces were a community responsibility. From his wartime experiments, he concluded that managing participation required skilled leadership. Someone had to fertilize the soil for effective groups to take root. Developing such group leaders called for an applied social science far outside academic psychology.

A New Kind of Research Center

Lewin's ideas attracted Douglas McGregor, a young psychology professor at the Massachusetts Institute of Technology (MIT). McGregor, whose story I will tell in Chapters Six and Seven, had spent the war years as an industrial relations manager in industry. He believed that Lewinian thinking could solve many labor-management problems. In 1946 McGregor helped Lewin launch the Research Center for Group Dynamics (RCGD) at MIT. (By establishing the new center at an engineering school, Lewin preserved his unblemished record for avoiding the mainstream of academic psychology.) Thus began a revolution — still in progress — that will one day be seen as being as far-reaching as Taylor's.

The center sought to do something wholly new: train leaders to become skilled at improving group relations and managing change. Group experiments, insisted Lewin, must be governed by a code of ethics — no manipulation, only honest, above-board

Lewin's Practical Theories.

Theory	*Management Implications*
You can understand behavior only in relation to all forces acting on a person at a given moment.	To change a system, you must take into account economics, technology, and the people who are stakeholders.
The best way to advance knowledge is having experts and workers study together the relations among person, tools, job, and situation.	Successful work design requires teams of engineers, managers, supervisors, and workers starting together from scratch.
Only freely chosen work has the meaning and life value needed to motivate high performance.	People should have as much elbow room as possible in doing their own jobs.
Democratic leadership leads to higher achievement and better relationships than hands-off authoritarian behavior.	Leading people to set goals, choose methods, and make decisions is learned. Nobody is born knowing participative management.
It is easier to change behavior in a group than one-on-one because norms (unwritten rules) strongly affect individual actions.	Talking over important decisions in groups before implementation leads to higher commitment to change.
People are more committed to solutions they have helped to design than to carrying out "expert" advice.	It is better to give people a few boundary conditions and let them solve the problem than to hand them ready-made solutions.
Every unsolved problem represents forces pushing for and against resolution. Easier and effective solutions come by reducing restraints rather than adding pressure.	Force field analysis quickly identifies restraints to be reduced. It is effective as a group exercise because it helps people see all at once what can be done, and builds group support for followthrough.
No two force fields or problem diagnoses will ever be the same. Every situation is different.	The solution, package, design, policy, or system that worked well for someone else may not work for you.

objectives and socially acceptable procedures. Involving those whose attitudes were to be studied and altered was a bedrock principle.

Decades later group methods would be criticized, even by practitioners, as "soft" on the realities of human nature, like power. Lewin had no illusions. Leaders must learn to see themselves as part of both the problem and the solution. "There is no individual," he wrote, "who does not try to influence his family, friends, occupational group. Management is one of the most important functions in every aspect of social life. Few aspects are as much befogged as the problems of leadership and of power in a democracy. We have to realize that power itself is an essential aspect of any and every group. Not the least service which social research can do for society is to attain better insight into the legitimate and non-legitimate aspects of power" (Marrow, 1969, p. 172).

Nor did he stop there. He had suffered anti-Semitism since childhood. Now he envisioned action research used against bigotry, which he considered an aberration of democracy. In 1946, backed by the American Jewish Congress, he started the Commission on Community Interrelations (CCI). (Another founder, coincidentally, was Supreme Court Justice Louis Brandeis, Frederick Taylor's advocate decades earlier.) In the late 1940s CCI did fifty community-based action-research projects, studying prejudice against black store clerks, vandalism of synagogues, juvenile gang wars. CCI staffers developed an action-research repertoire that later would be adapted to the managerial problems of large organizations (Marrow, 1969).

Origins of NTL Institute

Lewin also was central to the founding of a world-famous adult education organization, National Training Laboratories (NTL Institute). NTL pioneered the T-group, a generic name for a training group that studies its own "here and now" behavior. The T-group, curiously enough, resulted from a Lewinian action-research experiment — when the researchers discovered more than they were looking for.

In 1946 the Connecticut State Inter-Racial Commission sought Lewin's help in training leaders to combat racial and religious prejudice. He saw a chance to design new methods, built on previous work like the Lippitt-White and Harwood projects. He tapped Lippitt, then at MIT, as project director, and Lippitt recruited Lee Bradford of the National Education Association and Kenneth Benne of Boston University. They planned a research and training event to observe and measure how people transfer leadership skills from workshop to workplace — to what my partner Peter Block called "realife" (as in, "Yeah, that's fine for a workshop, but what happens if you try it in realife?"). The T in T-group was short for BST or Basic Skills Training. The forty-one participants, mainly teachers and social workers, about half of them black or Jewish, said they wanted more skill in changing attitudes, understanding prejudice, and dealing with resistance to change. They were offered a chance to study these processes in themselves, using group techniques like role playing and problem solving.

Discovering the Power of Feedback. This conference became a management milestone. In it the enormous learning potential of personal feedback — trading perceptions of self and others — was first discovered, almost by accident. Training groups were observed by researchers, who reviewed interactions with the staff each night. One evening three trainees asked to sit in. "Sometime during the evening," Lippitt recalled, "an observer made some remarks about the behavior of one of the three. For a while there was quite an active dialogue between the research observer, the trainer and the trainee about the interpretation of the event, with Kurt an active prober, obviously enjoying the different source of data that had to be coped with and integrated" (Marrow, 1969, p. 212).

Next night half the group showed up. This interchange on what "really" happened proved to be the most exciting session. Bradford recalled "a tremendous electric charge as people reacted to data about their own behavior" (Marrow, 1969, p. 212). None had fully appreciated the learning potential of feedback until that summer evening in 1946. People became aware that we always attend, in my former colleague Jim Maselko's words, "the same different meeting together." The discovery created some anxiety — and enormous energy for learning. Groups observed changes in their daytime productivity after the evening discussions of the process. A set of effective feedback rules evolved: be specific, nonjudgmental, express your own feelings, don't "psych out" the other person, don't give advice. Such premises today underlie performance reviews, goal setting, even the praises and reprimands of one-minute managers.

The 1946 conference also marked the first use of newsprint, antecedent of flip charts, traceable to Lewin's habit of drawing topological force fields on butcher paper taped to the wall. That summer Lippitt secured newsprint from the end of the press rolls at a local newspaper; it was cut into manageable pieces and everybody started using it. (For decades after NTL bought newsprint from local papers for its Bethel summer workshops.)

Transferring Skills. Follow-up interviews confirmed the Connecticut workshop's hypothesis, People told of using new techniques, especially role playing, at work. About 75 percent said they had gained group skills, become more optimistic and more sensitive to others' feelings, and worked better with people. The research also revealed that teams of two or more were more likely to use what they learned than those who came alone. This important finding got lost in the enthusiasm to spread T-groups everywhere. It took many years to confirm beyond a doubt what was suspected from the start: individual training, no matter how powerful, cannot by itself be a strategy for organizational change.

Supporting the Use of New Knowledge. Despite this knowledge, there remains extraordinary faith in many business firms of the organizational change potential of individual training, uncoupled from efforts to alter structures, policies, procedures, and rewards. That strategy is wholly refuted by research and experience clear back to Frederick Taylor. Organizational voodoo abounds in management seminars where people hear all the right noises, derived directly from Lewin, about unfreezing and refreezing and dealing with resistance to change and why employee participation is more likely to build commitment than "kicking ass." What they do not always learn are the right moves. Managers are cynical about such activity unless they see it linked to action, to a serious effort to promote needed change.

Each time people are sent to classes without vehicles for participating in policy, procedure, strategy, goal setting, and work design, they rightfully feel conned. This is an abuse of Lewin's work as egregious as the abuses (by upping quotas) of Taylor's efforts to give workers more equity in their output. It is using Lewin's words divorced from his music, which can be heard only when we seek to involve people in pushing beyond a system's assumed design limits to new levels of output and satisfaction.

The Road to Bethel and NTL

In 1947 Lewin obtained a grant from the Office of Naval Research to establish summer workshops at a private boarding school in Bethel, Maine. It was a cultural island (translation: small town, hard to reach), picked because it was thought people would unfreeze faster outside the office. T-groups opened a new window on human consciousness. Suddenly, dynamics that were always there — Taylor knew about some of them — became manageable through learning.

We take organizational structure for granted. Remove it (or, more accurately, substitute an unfamiliar form) and we shake up perceptions of reality. People find themselves puzzled, anxious, excited, vying for leadership — behaving in ways we rarely stop to examine. The T-group made possible the study of general phenomena present in all meetings that *cannot* be studied in any other way. It also delivered on Robert Burns's longing "to see ourselves as others see us," a valuable gift not always pleasant to receive.

Tens of thousands have attended NTL laboratories in group processes, personal growth, consulting skills, organizational change — all outgrowths of the summer of 1946. Hundreds of training and consulting organizations have adapted experience-based methods. "Sensitivity training," wrote Carl Rogers, "is perhaps the most significant social invention of this century" (Marrow, 1969, p. 214). (NTL's founders, Benne, Bradford, and Lippitt, it should be noted, were influenced by many others, such as John Dewey, the philosopher of education, and Mary Parker Follett, one of the most interesting figures in management history. Jacob Moreno, the innovator who created sociodrama and psychodrama, was the source of the role-playing techniques used at Harwood and later in NTL.)

Experience-based learning and social systems thinking have been put to ingenious uses. To cite just one example, the Danish social psychologist Gunnar Hjelholt, who had worked in Bethel in 1958, adapted T-group methods to the outfitting of new Danish merchant ships with crews of forty-two rather than the traditional sixty. In parallel with early sociotechnical projects, Hjelholt organized conferences of officers, engineers, mates, stewards, administrators, and shipowners. Together they examined the new technologies and made innovative decisions about food service, location of quarters, leisure time, and use of alcohol. More important, they created a seagoing planning system that gave more influence to mid-level officers and crews. The training led to significantly fewer disciplinary problems, less sickness and accidents, vastly more employee suggestions. After a year at sea, the captain, a skeptic at first, said, "It's the best ship I ever had — and I mean the crew" (Hjelholt, 1968, p. 16).

Limits of Sensitivity Training

Lewin's insights, like Taylor's, also were diverted early on by some of his disciples swept up in the headiness of group encounter. Inevitably the realization dawned in T-groups that organization life reinforced the tendency (mainly male) to repress feelings. People began to use T-groups for the intense study of emotions, a frontier linked to goals, roles, and rational problem solving in ways not obvious at first. The T-group became a laboratory for the recognition and expression of feelings — joy, sadness, confidence, anxiety, fear, anger, appreciation, guilt, excitement.

Because T-groups engendered intimacy and support — "together this group can lick the world" — many concluded that organizations would be transformed if groups were run in-house. Some business firms experimented with this proposition in the 1960s. People soon learned that the impulse to be open sometimes backfired. Reframing leadership skills as increased sensitivity could trigger powerful emotions, often negative, in people unsure of other feelings. An authoritarian norm could evolve in which people were pressured to express undifferentiated feelings about one another that they would later regret. Yet, most people had overwhelmingly positive experiences, which they could not describe very well. At the same time, they found they had little leverage on company goals, tasks, policies, and procedures — a proposition supported by much research (Dunnette, 1969). This was a major disappointment. It also stimulated innovative workplace applications (see Chapter Seventeen).

Lewin did not live to see NTL Institute born. In his last years he was like a top, spinning faster and faster, driven, like Taylor, to extend his ideas widely. He felt compelled to accelerate social science, as he wrote, "to that level of practical usefulness which society needs for winning the race against the destructive capacities set free by man's use of the natural sciences" (1947, p. 5). Lewin organized a research fund to aid residents of World War II displaced persons' camps. He grew deeply worried about black-white relations, believing that "every minority problem is, in fact, a majority problem." He saw democracy threatened by self-rejection and advocated positive group experiences to alter negative black self-image, which, he inferred from anti-Semitism, could damage a person as much as prejudice. An important source of self-esteem was strong group identity, an insight on which consciousness-raising and black-power groups later were built.

In 1946 Lewin linked with Eric Trist (Chapters Eight and Nine), of the Tavistock Institute of Human Relations in London, to found a distinguished journal, *Human Relations*. His planned sabbatical at Tavistock never materialized. "Something profound and extraordinary would have happened had Lewin come to us that year," laments Trist, who had known and admired Lewin since the early 1930s (interview with author, February 19, 1985).

Toward the end of his life Lewin focused on conflict, tension, crises, and change. If action-research projects have seemed overly focused on group tensions, the reason is easy to locate. The originator of this major organization development strategy was motivated, like Taylor before him, to alleviate, with all the tools that science and good sense could muster, humankind's self-made travail. In that respect, he was very much in the tradition of his adopted land. After a hectic February day in 1947, Lewin, then fifty-six, spent a quiet evening with his wife. That night he died unexpectedly of a heart attack.

Ronald Lippitt, a pioneer of leadership theories, group dynamics, and future-oriented planning. (*Peggy Lippitt*)

"Lewin," said psychologist Donald MacKinnon of his former teacher, "took on much more than any human being should have taken on; he was too generous of his time and energy, too busy, too involved with too many projects, too many people. It is almost surprising that he lived as long as he did" (Marrow, 1969, p. 225).

On the last day of his life Lewin talked by phone with Ronald Lippitt about how unfortunate was "the American cultural ideal of the 'self-made man,' and everyone 'standing on his own feet,'" a notion "as tragic as the initiative-destroying dependence on a benevolent despot." To Lippitt he said what might be a benediction for leaders everywhere, especially in a time of fast change and dramatic new technologies. "We all need continuous help from each other. Interdependence is the greatest challenge" (Marrow, 1969, p. 226).

Chapter Six

McGregor and the Roots of Organization Development

The essence of [McGregor's] message is that people
react not to an objective world, but to a world
fashioned out of their own perceptions,
assumptions and theories about what the world is
like. . . . McGregor wished passionately to release
all of us from this trap, by getting us to be aware of
how each of our worlds is of our own making. Once
we become aware we can choose —and it was the
process of free choice that we believe was Doug's
ultimate value.

—— *Edgar Schein, quoted in McGregor, Bennis, and
McGregor,* The Professional Manager, *1967, p. xii*

It was Douglas McGregor, author of the management classic
that changed my life, who brought Kurt Lewin to MIT in 1946.
Until his death eighteen years later, McGregor built upon Lewin at
every turn. I have used Lewin's story to illustrate my second theme:
that the world is changing too fast for experts. In this chapter and
the next, I want to use McGregor's story to illustrate my third
theme: how and why social change starts deep inside each of us,
and what the implications for action are.

To do that I must draw connections between the "two Taylors"
and McGregor's controversial Theories X and Y, which have now
stirred up generations of managers. In particular I will illustrate my
belief that X and Y represent the "hard guy, soft guy" dialogue in

each of us, and why accepting both is the likely path to integrated management solutions under conditions of relentless change. In the next chapter I also will show that both X and Y have positive and negative aspects. There are good guys and bad guys on both sides of the fence. I came to that conclusion through an odd turn of events.

McGregor and Taylor

Paging through *The Human Side of Enterprise* a few years ago, I came across a sentence about doubling productivity that read just like *Principles of Scientific Management.* Comparing the two books, I made a startling discovery. The Harvard-trained psychologist and the self-taught engineer, writing half a century apart, had come to remarkably parallel conclusions (see "Management According to Taylor and McGregor," p. 108). Not that they advocated the same methods. What struck me were the notes of sincerity, commitment, passion for rational problem solving, antiauthoritarianism, and faith in science as a solution. Taylor's "mental revolution" and McGregor's "theoretical assumptions" both supported greater management-labor cooperation, more satisfying work for each person, greater equity, more stable and successful businesses—the bedrock of productive workplaces.

Later I would realize that Taylor and McGregor were only two of many reformers who sought an integrated approach to enterprise. Harvard's Elton Mayo was another. Contemporaries in this tradition include statistician W. Edwards Deming and industrial engineer Joseph Juran, quality improvement gurus, both heroes in Japan before winning notoriety in the United States, both convinced that quality problems are systemic and result largely from myopic management (Main, 1986). The issues they have raised are much broader than business. They have to do with what Tolstoy called the tension between the personal and the general. Or what organization development consultants call "the fit between the individual and the organization" or the "public good versus private good."

Management According to Taylor and McGregor.

Taylor (1915)	*McGregor (1960)*
"The best management is a true science, resting upon clearly defined laws, rules, and principles as a foundation" (p. 7).	"Progress in any profession is associated with the ability to predict and control, and this is true also of industrial management. To insist that management is an art is . . . a denial of the relevance of systematic, tested knowledge" (pp. 3, 8).
"The general adoption of scientific management would readily in the future double the productivity of the average man in industrial work" (p.142).	"Many mangers would agree that the effectiveness of their organizations would be at least doubled if they could discover how to tap the unrealized potential present in their human resources" (p. 4).
"The time is fast going by for the great personal or individual achievement of any one man alone without the help of those around him" (p. 140).	"We cannot hope much longer to operate the complex, interdependent, collaborative enterprise which is the modern industrial company on the completely unrealistic premise that it consists of individual relationships" (p. 42).
"The universal prejudice in favor of the management of 'initiative and incentive' is so strong that no mere theoretical advantages which can be pointed out will be likely to convince the average manager that any other system is better" (p. 35).	"The philosophy of management by direction and control — whether it is hard or soft — is inadequate to motivate because the human needs on which this approach relies are relatively unimportant motivators of behavior in our society today" (p. 42).
"The first object of any good system must be that of developing first-class men. No great man can hope to compete with a number of ordinary men who have been properly organized so as efficiently to cooperate" (p. 6–7).	"Management should have as a goal the development of the unique capacities and potentialities of each individual rather than common objectives for all participants" (p. 187).

Given so many common values, how did Taylor come to be associated with Theory X assumptions and McGregor with Theory Y? The reason is in McGregor's definitions. Theory X assumptions seem to come from a punitive, judgmental measuring rod in the sky. It is not hard to see Taylor's external work measurements as an expression of that assumption. Theory Y seems rooted in another place entirely, one firmly on the side of each person as a forgiving, learning self-judge with huge potential for self-development and responsibility. I think both exist in each of us — in you, in me, in Taylor, and in McGregor too. McGregor's life story reveals many clues as to why he saw the polarity between people rather than within.

A Family with a Mission

McGregor was born into a strict Scotch Presbyterian family in Detroit, Michigan, on September 16, 1906. In the year of his birth Frederick Taylor, president of the American Society of Mechanical Engineers, received an honorary doctorate from the University of Pennsylvania. And Kurt Lewin, who would cross his path more than thirty-five years later, was a sixteen-year-old philosophy student in Berlin. Ministry and mission were McGregor's heritage. His great-grandfather was a preacher. His grandfather, a piano and organ vendor, organized McGregor Institute, a shelter for homeless laborers in Detroit; he died of pneumonia contracted while digging the foundations. Douglas's father, a Bible scholar and lay preacher, became director of the shelter in 1915.

At its peak the mission fed and housed 700 men. They were, in the words of Douglas's wife, Caroline, "low on the totem pole of human dignity" (McGregor, Bennis, and McGregor, 1967, p. xi). The elder McGregor conducted daily services, and played the organ behind his wife's hymns. Young Doug worked in the office after school and sometimes accompanied on piano, becoming an accomplished gospel keyboard performer. Management professor Jerry Harvey, a graduate student in the 1950s, once recalled a meeting of social scientists where, during the break, "all the biggies like Argyris, Likert, and Blake suddenly disappeared. I peeked through the door to the next room and saw them huddled around the piano singing gospel songs, accompanied by Doug McGregor" (interview with author, 1981).

Like Taylor, McGregor had a strong, energetic mother, deeply imbued with the Protestant ethic. She was forthright and optimistic in her belief in the salvation of productive work. His father, by contrast, was weighed down by the social pathology of the men he sought to save. Douglas shared his father's compassion but rejected his gloomy outlook. Later, he chose to work with successful leaders, not failures. He often pointed out how many of those befriended by the McGregors later repaid the debts, *prima facie* proof of Theory Y.

McGregor was a hardworking student. After two years at Detroit City College (later Wayne State University), he spent a semester at Oberlin College, thinking to become a minister. Not knowing what he really wanted, he answered an ad for a gas station manager in Buffalo, New York. It was 1927. At age twenty-one McGregor had his first management job. The following year he married Caroline Ferris, moved with her back to Detroit, reentered college, and worked nights in the mission to finance his education.

In 1932, at age twenty-six, he decided on graduate training in psychology, choosing his school by tossing a coin. When it came up Stanford (heads), he knew from his reaction that Harvard (tails) was where he really wanted to go. Most tough decisions, he told his friends, could be made that way; the heart's desire emerged the moment the coin landed. With financial help from his wealthy Uncle Tracy, he earned a doctorate in social psychology in 1935 and became a Harvard instructor. When he asked professor Gordon Allport for advice, Allport suggested he stop jingling keys and coins in his pockets and keep his feet off the lecture desk. He also observed that "the trouble you will have next year is to get a theoretical framework into which to put things" (McGregor, Bennis, and McGregor, 1967, p. xiii).

Two years later McGregor went to Massachusetts Institute of Technology, where he helped found its noted Industrial Relations Section. In the 1930s and 1940s he did considerable research and consulting in labor-management relations. After 1948 he put many of his theories into action as president of Antioch College. Except for six years at Antioch, he taught at MIT from 1937 until his death in 1964.

McGregor's Influence

McGregor had an enormous impact on those he met. Eric Trist, a major figure in the quality of working life movement (see Chapter Eight), was a frequent visitor to McGregor's country home in Acton, Massachusetts. "He was one of the most wonderful people I've ever known," Trist told me. "He had the art of being both gentle and confrontational at the same time. He was a maternal person, a nurturer, and it's characteristic of him that when he became famous he went to live in the country where he could tend his garden and reflect on his basic ideas without being imposed upon as he was while living near MIT" (February 25, 1985, interview). He wrote *The Human Side of Enterprise* sitting in a chaise lounge beside the garden pond.

Organization development professionals are indebted to him not only for his ideas and exemplary practice but for the people he encouraged and inspired. McGregor helped Kurt Lewin found the Research Center for Group Dynamics at MIT. He was one of the earliest appliers of Lewin's ideas in academia, encouraging the Antioch College community to use itself as a learning laboratory in democratic education and self-management. McGregor recruited the extraordinary MIT organization group — Richard Beckhard, Warren Bennis, Mason Haire, Joseph Scanlon, Edgar Schein — who played major roles in setting the boundaries, practices, and values behind systematic organizational change.

Edith Whitfield Seashore, consultant and former president of NTL Institute, recalled McGregor's inaugural address as Antioch College president when she was a student in 1949. "Two minutes before he started to speak," she told me, "I had no idea what I wanted to do with my life. At the end of his talk, I knew" (August 11, 1985, interview). Seashore, at McGregor's urging, attended NTL Institute and became a trailblazing woman in what had been a wholly male profession.

McGregor encouraged Richard Beckhard, among this generation's most influential consultants. The two became lifelong friends. "When I started in the management consulting field in the early 1950s," Beckhard told me, "he helped me learn to use the knowledge from the behavioral sciences as a way of working with clients (interview August 11, 1985). Later McGregor recruited Beckhard for the MIT faculty, one of the few social science professors to come from practice to academia rather than the other way around. "Doug was a gardener with people," Beckhard said. "He just grew people the way he grew plants. He was the most meaningful person in my life." Consulting together at General Mills in the 1950s, the two coined the term *organization development* (OD) to describe an innovative bottoms-up change effort that fit no traditional consulting categories.

Pioneer Consultant. McGregor was perhaps the first psychologist to emphasize the strategic importance of personnel policies, such as congruent values, cultures, procedures, systems, and training. Bell of Pennsylvania, Standard Oil of New Jersey, and ICI in Great Britain were among the many companies he helped. As a consultant he built deep personal relationships with his clients, inviting them to his home in Acton, visiting them frequently, always available as a trouble-shooter. He acted more like a concerned friend than a professional expert or a stereotyped professor. "If you walked in in the middle you couldn't tell the players without a program," said Beckhard. "He was gentle in his criticism. But he could also be very piercing. And he was a great integrator."

Change at Union Carbide. Stories abound of the way he influenced large systems-change projects at a time when the idea was not widely understood. In the early 1960s, for example, Union Carbide's industrial relations manager, John Paul Jones, set up a pioneer OD department. Jones was especially mindful of McGregor's prediction that using full human potential in organizations would stand or fall on the ability to work successfully with groups.

He introduced team management into what had been a seriously disunited company, based on "leveling" and collaborative problem solving. "Organization development's group programs offer no panacea," reported *Fortune* magazine at the time. "Everybody can't be in on everything. . . you can't make a town meeting out of a stock-option plan . . . some executives are still indifferent or skeptical. But O.D. finds itself with more work than ever, and even if it never took on another job its residual influence would be immense. Practically everybody of consequence in the company is tolerably familiar with Jones's ideas" (Burck, 1965, p. 149).

Affectionate Memories. People found McGregor engaging and attractive. He had large features and a high forehead topped by a burr haircut. His brow was furrowed by worry lines, deepened, his friend Warren Bennis (1972) would speculate, by a persistent guilt that he could never measure up to his own ideals. He often sported just the trace of a moustache. "He had an enormously interesting face," recalled Seashore. "It was a mobile face, very warm and boyish." Trist described a tall, slightly bent figure, with a long "bloodhound face, a hanging face," relaxed, soft-spoken, with a wry wit likely to pop up at any moment. Once Trist asked him what he was doing in England with a large corporate client. "Cleaning up after — — ," said McGregor with a laugh, mentioning a large consulting firm whose recommendations had led to "regressions to an older, authoritarian, bureaucratic culture." The assignment deeply upset McGregor, said Trist, yet he could laugh at the absurdity. Lack of trust at all levels had curtailed innovation and market opportunities. "McGregor," Trist recalled, "reversed this disastrous trend" (interview with author, February 19, 1985).

McGregor's sudden death of a heart attack on October 13, 1964, was a shock to his family and friends; at age fifty-eight he had

seemed in good health and good spirits. Edith Seashore was astonished at hearing the news by telephone. "I remember standing
there in the kitchen, saying, 'That's not possible. He didn't say
goodbye. Doug would never leave that way, he wouldn't be that
inconsiderate.'" In a memorial service a colleague said he would
always "remember Doug bending over slightly, a quizzical look in
his eyes, followed by a probing question in a soft voice. ., always
designed to make the other person grow." His friend Warren Bennis missed "his warmth, directness, immediacy, and spontaneity,"
others his responsiveness and sense of fun. An outpouring of calls,
wires, commentary, reminiscence, admiration, respect, love, affection, and, above all, loss, followed his death ("Memorial to Douglas
McGregor," 1964, p. 2).

Douglas McGregor, author of a major management book on how assumptions affect
behavior. (*The MIT Museum*)

Theories X and Y

All his life McGregor and his father exchanged letters on their opposing philosophies of life. In them could be seen two theories of human behavior, each informed by compassion, one based on essential sinfulness, the other in the potential goodness and strength of each person (Bennis, 1966). No wonder I had found McGregor's writings contrasting Theories X and Y so confirming in the 1960s. The dialogue Bennis described is one I had had repeatedly with my own father during the time I was experimenting with self-managing work teams. The emotional hook in me was, of course, a wish to stand on my own feet. There was another note too, a nagging inner voice saying, "And suppose the old man is right?" X and Y were descriptions of my struggle for independence, an internal tug-of-war between freedom and constraint.

So I was not surprised to learn that McGregor once told Trist that he thought Theory Y might be "an avoidance mechanism" for his own rebellion. Trist once pointed out to McGregor that he sounded a lot like the late Wilfred Lord Brown, whose own problems with managerial authority had led to the famous Glacier Project in a manufacturing company he controlled (Jacques, 1951). Whatever its source, McGregor used his own dilemma creatively as a lightning rod for the central dilemma of the Industrial Revolution. He put into a boss-subordinate context the age-old struggle between authority and dependency, master and servant, father and son. He converted a philosophical, and at bottom a religious, issue into a metaphor for managing large organizations.

In so doing he reached an audience hungry to find alternatives to bureaucracy, authoritarianism, alienation, and the mechanization of relationships that accompanied the mechanization of work. It was not simply ideology. For me at least it was (and is) an expression of life's purposes — affirming dignity in every person, finding meaning in valued work, achieving community through mutual support and accomplishment.

By which assumptions, McGregor asked, are large industrial enterprises managed? He could as well have asked by which assumptions is a homeless laborers' shelter run, or is a life best lived. X and Y were not just symbolic of McGregor's personal dilemma. They were metaphors for a tension in each of us, in Trist's words "a profound cultural diagnosis of our time." (See "Trist on McGregor.") McGregor's ability to express this universal theme in managerial language accounts for the great success of *The Human Side of Enterprise*.

He posed the question in a context that troubled a great many people, and still does. The spectre of unemployment haunts us in smokestack and high-tech industries alike. It is never far away for those who came of age in manufacturing. My guess — pure speculation — is that McGregor believed that if he could reach people whose hands moved the levers of industry, he could change conditions that led to degrading unemployment, the lot of those who sought shelter in his family's mission. A sympathetic psychologist has observed that an important appeal for executives in McGregor's message was "the subtle way it addresses itself to the underlying guilt which plagues men who exercise power in modern organizations" (Zaleznik, 1967, p. 68).

McGregor refined his ideas in a series of papers and speeches between 1937 and 1949. From his earliest writings we see him observing the same phenomena Taylor did, often in the same words, then arriving at new solutions by applying psychological knowledge. With his friend Irving Knickerbocker, for example, he speculated on ways to enhance labor-management cooperation and achieve "superefficient production" during World War II (Knickerbocker and McGregor, 1942). The pair attacked traditional labor relations methods as based on "conflicting opinions and unverified beliefs" (p. 50), a charge McGregor later leveled at management thinking in general. They also tagged management with responsibility for worker resistance to change, just as Taylor had done. It is one of the earliest attempts to build on Lewin's belief that change itself is a phenomenon subject to systematic research (action research) as much as machine tools or shovels.

"It is not the fact of change but the method of bringing it about which is important if we are going to achieve a greater degree of cooperation

Trist on McGregor

"He was very keen on organizational learning and that you have to *learn*, the organization has to learn and so do the people in it, to keep up with the times. It wasn't a sentimental concept. It was a bedrock concept, that the human being is a learning individual, and when he wasn't allowed to go on learning he was dehumanized.

"The last time I saw Douglas was on a golden early September afternoon sauntering in the London sunlight down the narrow side street leading from the Strand to the Savoy, which is on an embankment overlooking the Thames. I had just driven him in from my house after several hours of absorbing discussion. When he got out of the car, I just sat and watched, unwilling to turn away. Eight days later he was dead. I don't think we'd heard the last of him. We'd only heard the first.

"X and Y were a profound cultural diagnosis of our times. McGregor understood that a far-reaching reversal was taking place in contemporary values — a reversal of superior-subordinate relationship, not only in bureaucracies but deeper in Western and other cultures as well. This contemporary shifting of values was also *necessary*, in his view, for the effective management of large, complex organizations. He was a profoundly democratic man. I talked with him far into the night the last time I stayed with him in Acton. His concern was that modern industry was on the wrong path and that there has got to be a very profound change in relationships throughout organizations to permit participation and learning" [conversation with the author, February 19, 1985].

between management and labor," the authors wrote, underlining the text (pp. 53–54). (Taylor said something similar, though probably less printable, after his associate rushed things at Watertown Arsenal and brought down the wrath of organized labor.) Like Taylor, the authors traced resistance to reorganizing production methods without informing workers, much less consulting them. Money, they pointed out, is not the only motivator. When wages are adequate, other things become important: equity, recognition, a chance to contribute. "Factory workers would strive less desperately to express their uniqueness and importance if this expression were not denied them by the increasing regimentation of industrial life" (p. 54).

A New Prescription

McGregor's prescription came from research on group norms and personal needs. Taylor understood these phenomena only as potential restrictors of output. He could not conceive that group pressure might work the other way. Undoubtedly Taylor's narrow outlook contributed to union rejection of his concepts, for group solidarity, emotional support, and the self-esteem inherent in belonging were important underpinnings of unionization, which Taylor threatened when he declared unions unnecessary. (After Taylor's death, unions embraced narrow jobs, time study, and work measurement as a way of increasing wages and protecting employment — exactly Taylor's intent — without, however, that spirit of "friendly cooperation" he thought inevitable.) "We want to develop the morale of the working force," said McGregor and Knickerbocker (1941, p. 57). "We want to encourage enthusiastic cooperative effort, we want to increase efficiency to the utmost. *These things we can accomplish only if the changes which are made in technical processes are perceived as necessary and reasonable by those whom the changes affect.*"

To build a constructive group dynamic, however, requires a degree of worker participation greater than McGregor could then visualize. The way to dissolve resistance to change, the authors vaguely said, is to understand employee perspectives by talking with foremen and shop stewards and using counselors (now called ombudspersons) to sound out employee sentiment. The authors could not yet invoke the power of group decision making, for it was only just then being discovered by Lewin among Iowa housewives.

Still, the authors were very shrewd in their political analysis. They identified excellent first-line supervision as the key to good union relations. That observation has so far not been improved upon, except in those few innovative places that have eliminated such supervision altogether.

Becoming More Practical. Building on these insights, McGregor and Knickerbocker (1942) also devised a three-stage model of the rocky road to mature union-management relations. The first stage, they said, was usually aggressive antagonism during union organizing. It would be followed by a bureaucratic consolidation in bargaining and contract enforcement. Eventually, in rare cases, there emerged mature, mutual problem solving.

Retrogression might occur any time for seemingly trivial reasons. Building trust and close cooperation on major issues can be agonizingly slow. There are key differences between management and labor. Unions, for example, are run by elected officials. Members think short range, want specific gains, are quick to grieve and slow to forgive. Union members need to express past resentments and be heard before they can let go of them. The union's toughest problem is that the rank and file tend to support rebellious leaders at first, while mature relations await the election of confident and steady people. Even so, the union rank and file "always lags behind their leaders in understanding and in willingness to accept broad policies and long-range aims" (1942, p. 528).

Management has to change too. "Many firms have faced a real problem in the re-education of a group of 'unenlightened' old line foremen after a union has been organized in the plant," pointed out McGregor and Knickerbocker (1942, p. 528). Union members tend to judge management's intention from their experiences with foremen. Good union relations require training in close cooperation among managers and supervisors too.

Using the Past in the Present. What struck me forcefully in 1985 about their 1942 concept was its relevance to a current project of mine. "We can't get too far ahead of our people," a union local president confided to me, "even when they're wrong." The day I read the McGregor-Knickerbocker article I was called to an emergency meeting: two union officials had walked out on a steering committee, having decided, when managers posed ideas different from their own, that "management isn't serious about participation."

McGregor and Knickerbocker also showed how workers use their creativity to beat wage incentives. They proposed group gain-sharing plans and intangible rewards like prestige, recognition, job security. Workers and managers, they said, all want to be treated the same way. That was radical stuff in the 1940s. In the 1980s such egalitarian practices as open parking, a single cafeteria, informal dress codes, identical offices regardless of rank were a feature of such diverse settings as "new design" Honda and GM auto plants and Union Carbide's corporate headquarters.

Labor Relations Manager: Dewey and Almy

During World War II McGregor got a rare chance to test his theories in action. He became temporary labor relations manager at Dewey and Almy Chemical Company, a progressive firm founded in 1919 on a bedrock of benevolent paternalism. It employed 1,500 people and ran two plants near MIT, making such diverse products as container sealants, shoe cement, football blad-ders, and organic chemicals (McGregor and Scanlon, 1948, p. 42).

The idealistic president accepted his employees' vote for union-ization in 1939 because he trusted the American Federation of Labor's regional director. Yet paternalism continued, as the presi-dent personally handled contracts and grievances. When he left for war work in Washington, he hired McGregor, the firm's consultant, to manage labor relations.

McGregor later wrote a monograph with Joseph Scanlon applying his theory of labor-management maturity to Dewey and Almy. It is a gold mine of practical how-to information as well as a preview of his famous book. When the company, for example, adopted a wartime policy of no work stoppages, middle managers and supervisors, left out of the decision, interpreted this as "give the union whatever it wants." It was typical of McGregor to collaborate with Scanlon, a former labor leader, on this important paper. Years later McGregor would compare Scanlon with Kurt Lewin and Charles Kettering, General Motors's erstwhile research director, three men who believed in risk and experimentation, who "wanted to look ahead and see what could come next," who "were always emphasizing the chance of success" (Bennis and Schein, 1966, p. 115). In the late 1930s Scanlon, a steelworkers' organizer, conceived a cost-reduction-sharing plan that helped save an on-the-skids steel company. McGregor brought him to MIT as a teacher, and later gave the Scanlon Plan worldwide visibility in his book. Scanlon Plans are a popular form of gain-sharing today, and an association of companies engaged in them meets annually to trade experiences (Moore and Ross, 1978).

Involving Middle Management.   McGregor realized the futility of buying labor peace while alienating middle managers. So he redefined the personnel function as advisory, establishing a principle now widely recognized if not always practiced. He turned labor relations over to operating managers, requiring that they become involved in negotiating and carrying out the contract. He also installed human relations training for foremen. Those who continued unfair or inept supervision were transferred or forced to resign.

Ideas the old Dewey and Almy personnel department had sponsored without success now were refined and implemented by line management. These included weekly management policy and company-union leader meetings, a looseleaf labor policy manual based on joint discussions, and union consultation on nonbargaining issues like job evaluations and promotions. These were enormous strides toward dignity, meaning, and community, for they gave managers and workers alike direct influence over key policies affecting everybody.

There were failures, too. Labor-management cooperation extended largely to policy and procedural matters. Despite a desperate need for wartime production, it was impossible to get joint action on major technical and economic decisions involving methods, systems, and plant problems — the essence of mutual survival and growth.

Union members, as I would rediscover years later, would cooperate on productivity, cost reduction, and equipment improvement under conditions of mutual trust. However, the attempt at Dewey and Almy in 1943 "failed miserably, quite probably because the management representatives . . . were defensive and somewhat antagonistic. Worker suggestions were accepted but not carried out. Committee meetings involved a great deal of petty bickering" (McGregor and Scanlon, 1948, p. 42). Manager prejudice against worker competence, subtly reinforced by decades of Taylorism, was too strong to overcome even in Dewey and Almy's rare climate.

Early Visions of QWL Principles. McGregor's creative personnel work at Dewey and Almy anticipated by more than thirty years the principles of the quality of working life (QWL) movement. He and Scanlon summed up the contributing factors. First (then, now, always) was leadership — a president who "believed in the possibilities of successful union-management relations" (McGregor and Scanlon, 1948, p. 42). Next was acceptance by middle managers and supervisors of their unique responsibility for labor relations and their willingness to learn how to become good at it. A third was good communication within management and between management and the union.

Finally, the union local's capacity to stand on its own feet as a secure, independent bargaining force was essential. Today these principles underlie every cooperative union-management effort. They spotlight McGregor's groundbreaking creativity, and his exceptional ability to team with diverse people in building productive workplaces.

Chapter Seven

The Human Side of Enterprise Revisited: A New Look at Theories X and Y

I believed . . . that a leader could operate
successfully as a kind of adviser to his organization.
I thought I could avoid being a "boss."
Unconsciously, I suspect, I hoped to duck the
unpleasant necessity of making difficult decisions,
of taking the responsibility for one course of action
among many uncertain alternatives, of making
mistakes and taking the consequences. I thought
that maybe I could operate so that everyone would
like me. . . . I couldn't have been more wrong. It
took a couple of years, but I finally began to realize
that a leader cannot avoid the exercise of authority
any more than he can avoid responsibility for what
happens to his organization.
—— *Douglas McGregor, "On Leadership," 1954, pp. 2–3*

McGregor had most of *The Human Side of Enterprise* thought out before going to Antioch. Had he written it then, it would have been a good book. However, his six years as a college president gave him insights into leadership that led him to write a great one. Reading it as an uneducated manager in the 1960s, I felt from page one that this man had been there and knew what he was talking about. I experienced awe, empathy, support, challenge, anxiety, and excitement that I have gained from no other nonfiction work. McGregor expressed ideas I did not know it was possible to think.

The book touched thousands of managers the same way. First published in 1960, it remained in print for decades.

The event that delayed and enriched publication of this work occurred in 1948. McGregor was asked to recommend candidates for the presidency of Antioch, a unique college in Ohio where students divided each year between academic study and paid employment. He showed so much enthusiasm for Antioch's goals that he was offered the job.

McGregor at Antioch

Antioch's faculty were skeptical of this "human relations expert," an alien from the worlds of engineering and business. His insistence on his friend Irving Knickerbocker as chief assistant, rather than an Antioch veteran, didn't help. In fact he needed Knickerbocker's toughness and political judgment to counterbalance his own deep wish to be liked.

Influenced by Lewin and the enormous educational potential of groups, McGregor visualized Antioch as a learning laboratory for "a genuine program of research, with ourselves as subjects." His objective was to "discover why the things we try work, or why they fail to work." The meaning of a college went beyond its curriculum and faculty competence to the very means used to understand and to change itself. His goal, said McGregor, was "to resolve the major paradox of our culture by making educational institutions a democratic way of living, rather than a democratic way of talking" (1949, p. 7).

A Learning Laboratory. McGregor started what he called an "Antioch Goals Discussion," involving secretaries and janitors with students and faculty. Skeptical teachers said that Antioch already was a model democracy. It had students on admissions, curriculum, and discipline committees — a great rarity in the 1940s. Representative democracy, McGregor insisted, was not enough. Everybody must help explore the college's future. "We know pathetically little about how to make democracy work," he insisted. "The list is long of problems that baffle us and frustrate us" (McGregor, 1950, p. 4).

Some faculty called the goals exercise "Madison Avenue manipulations." The criticism stung. In a typical response, McGregor wrote openly of his loneliness and nostalgia for MIT when he felt misunderstood and insecure in this unfamiliar and challenging job (McGregor, 1949). Persistence paid off. Eventually "his warmth and gift of laughter and respect for the convictions of others" won over many faculty critics, recalled Antioch's dean of faculty ("Memorial to Douglas McGregor," 1964). A consensus emerged for a smaller student body, a revised curriculum, greater integration across fields of study, new methods of teaching and learning, closer connections between academia and the workplace. "Skeptics grumbled at first that the idea was a gimmick, but they were soon amazed at the new sense of purpose that resulted" ("Memorial to Douglas McGregor," 1964).

By his second year, McGregor had facilitated major changes in the college's operations. Students chose their own newspaper editors, managed the publications budget, ran the fire company, oriented freshmen. An honor system was implemented. In student meetings "he was likely to be found sitting on the floor as an alert listener and participant," said Dean Keeton in his eulogy. "The dormitories were open to him at all times, and so was his home to students. He never lost sight of a college's primary function — the education of young people. For him the way to do this was to be with them in person" ("Memorial to Douglas McGregor," 1964).

Keeton recalled McGregor as "a man of utter candor and courage. ., his own most astute and insightful critic." When a rich donor cut off Antioch because of "malicious rumors," McGregor invited him to visit and see for himself. The man "became Douglas McGregor's admirer for life." At the height of the McCarthy hearings in the early 1950s, when superpatriots cast suspicion on academics everywhere, McGregor took the offensive in a speech to the Cleveland Rotary Club, defying charges that his faculty were anything but loyal Americans.

An Exciting Place to Be. McGregor and Knickerbocker became campus fixtures. Their Christmas shopping foray was a legendary afternoon of drinking, followed by a splurge on gifts for family and friends. Indeed, Knickerbocker was McGregor's alter ego. Edith Whitfield Seashore, student community manager in 1950, recalled for me the first time Knickerbocker sat in on her meetings. "Knick began to make comments that were, I thought, enormously disruptive — but terribly interesting and insightful — about what was going on. I didn't have the foggiest idea about process. 'I'm coming in to sabotage your meetings,' he told me, 'because you're running very bad meetings and don't know what's going on in the room.' I said, 'This is the most fascinating thing that's ever happened to me in my whole college career'" (August 11, 1985, interview).

Irving Knickerbocker, McGregor's unsung collaborator and alter ego at Antioch. (*The MIT Museum*)

So McGregor's Antioch became a spawning ground for what would later be called organization development. A student group began meeting regularly to study group dynamics with Knicker-bocker. One member was a twenty-two-year-old freshman named Warren Bennis, recently discharged from the Army. Later he would join McGregor at MIT, become his close friend and confidant, and achieve prominence himself as a management professor, college president, and authority on leadership. Another was Matt Miles, destined to be a noted writer, teacher, researcher, and consultant on social change. Antioch students also took up race relations problems and invited the director of the Lewin-founded Commit-tee on Community Interrelations to consult with them. They put on an exhibit of what they had learned from their action research on participation in campus governance.

Antioch, in short, was an exciting place to be in the early 1950s. "We are pioneering a method about which nobody knows very much," wrote President McGregor and community manager Whitfield in a joint report. "Widespread participation in setting direction and determining organizational policies is rare, and we have a lot to learn" (1950, p. 15).

After six years, though, McGregor grew weary of administra-tion. He especially disliked a role that put him at odds with other faculty. He wanted everyone to like him, impossible for an effective college president. He told Keeton that he "preferred the role of col-league and student to the role of boss." With typical candor he wrote in his valedictory (quoted at this chapter's start) that he had changed his mind about leadership, that its essence was the courage to decide.

Creating a Classic

McGregor wrote *The Human Side of Enterprise* in the late 1950s, targeting it for those who manage "the production and sale of goods and services at a profit." His theme was that managers base their actions on theory, conscious or not. He attributed the failure of "stick and carrot" management to faulty assumptions about human motivation that induce the behavior they predict. External controls demotivate, requiring more controls. Many organizational practices seem based on the belief that people dislike work, and "must be coerced, controlled, directed, threatened" to produce (McGregor, 1960, p. 34). Indeed, many would *rather* be directed, since a worker's main motivation is security, not growth. That, by deduction, is Theory X.

In most union environments around 1950 that was an easy conclusion to come by. The average union worker, having spent decades adapting to Taylorism — meaning external control of tools, work methods, pacing, output — had opted for security over growth. Look behind that stuff about "our people" in the annual report, said McGregor (1960), at what is actually done — time clocks, work rules, reorganizations dictated from the top, manipulatively "making people feel involved" by asking opinions on decisions already made, one-way performance appraisal, and goal-setting. All this, he wrote, "*could only have been derived from assumptions such as those of Theory X*" (1960, p. 35).

Taylor and Theory X

From this perspective, Taylor's ideas too looked as if they derived from Theory X. Taylor himself started with quite different (conscious) assumptions. He believed in workers' initiative, "their hard work, their good will, and their ingenuity" (1915, p. 36) when treated fairly. He wanted all persons in jobs tapping their maximum abilities, an idea not so far from Maslow's self-actualization.

Close supervision was needed, said Taylor, not because workers were lazy but because they were ignorant of the best methods. So was management, for that matter. So Taylor's system, built to backstop the uneducated laborers and ignorant managers of his time, broke jobs into small pieces, enforcing uniformity through standard procedures and high wages. In the hands of people less scrupulous than Taylor, his methods contributed to conditions he deplored: alienation of labor from management, staff from line, and workers from work itself.

Peter Drucker (1976) has argued that Taylor, because he believed every person was "first class" at something, actually held Theory Y assumptions. I think this stretches Taylor's understanding too far. He certainly believed workers should work to the limit of their ability; but in his eyes no worker could ever define tools, tasks, goals, systems, methods, and procedures. The point of breaking jobs down was to make them easy for uneducated workers to learn.

It was inconceivable to Taylor that higher productivity would one day be achieved by combining fragmented jobs to make a coherent whole. The idea of multiple skills, conceptualized by Emery and Trist in the 1950s (see Chapter Eight), exactly contradicts Taylor's thinking. It has become the modern solution — at a new level of technology — to the same problems Taylor set out to solve a century ago.

Moreover, Taylor's view of teamwork meant a rigid, nonoverlapping division of labor among staff experts, managers, and workers, all minding their own business as defined by the engineers, not solving mutual problems together. His methods are implementable today only in the simplest work. Where markets, technologies, and systems change rapidly, people *must* interact across levels and functions constantly to do anything right.

In a funny way Taylorism proved McGregor's self-fulfilling prophecy. By assuming workers' ignorance as a starting place, scientific management sets up systems that keep them that way. For Taylor took up these issues in a pre-Freudian age when psychology was even more primitive than industrial engineering. He had rejected social workers in industry for their lack of appreciation for productivity, contending that the right work system would take care of much social pathology. He was right in one way, as well as narrow-minded about what the "right" system meant. Like many reformers, he could not see that his system had its limits too.

One curious consequence of his rejecting social initiatives was the splitting off of personnel from engineering. While Taylor's system was being adopted worldwide, labor reformers successfully established personnel management as a specialty. Hardly had the engineers wrested job descriptions and people selection from management than a new breed of "employment managers" stole them from engineering. By 1920 there were between 4,000 and 5,000 personnel professionals.

"The last bastion of the 19th Century foreman's power had been breached, and a new relationship, based on managerial control of the worker, became the basis of personnel work" (Nelson, 1980, p. 201). This was the staff role that McGregor had played and then abandoned at Dewey and Almy in the 1940s. *The Human Side of Enterprise* argued that expert staff specialization was a mistake, that first-line supervisors, armed with 20th Century human relations skills, were the right people to select, train, and evaluate workers.

Theory Y

McGregor's thinking matured at a time of significant new developments in the social and behavioral sciences. It was he, after all, who had brought Kurt Lewin to MIT, and Lewin had by the late 1950s influenced a whole generation with his "practical theories," the most important of which was that people are more committed to implement action steps they have helped plan. Abraham Maslow recently had described his famous "needs hierarchy" (Maslow and Murphy, 1954). As security and safety needs are satisfied, said Maslow, we require more intangible rewards — status, recognition, responsibility — to perform at our best. Frederick Herzberg, studying accountants and engineers, discovered that job "satisfiers" — pay, benefits, working conditions — don't motivate. They only *dissatisfy* if inadequate. "Motivators" are items on Maslow's list — recognition, achievement, responsibility — and must be built into the work itself (Herzberg, Mausner, and Snyderman, 1959).

McGregor was deeply committed to the ideas of Maslow and Herzberg. He pinpointed the source of bad quality years before Japan raised our consciousness. Separating producing and inspecting (Taylor's legacy), he observed, encourages workers knowingly to pass mistakes down the line to those whose job is to find them. Motivation and quality, he believed, could be achieved only by redesigning work systems to make quality everybody's business and infuse dignity, meaning, and community into work.

Curiously, of Theory Y's six assumptions, four incorporate echoes of Taylor; only numbers 3 and 5, based on a changed society and modern psychology, directly challenge scientific management. See "A Comparison of Theory Y and Scientific Management."

A New View of Staff-Line Relations. McGregor especially challenged staff-line relations. In the decades between Taylor and McGregor, staff expertise flowered. After World War II corporations scrambled to build state-of-the-art resources in planning, engineering, finance, personnel, management information systems, training. Too many CEOs, said McGregor, delegated control, not responsibility. They built big staffs to monitor exceptions, driving line managers to become as ingenious as hourly workers in defeating home-office policies that compromise their judgment. Paradoxically, the more in-depth knowledge a staff person has, the harder it is to transfer. Every form of expertise tugs against every other, competing for manager attention. So McGregor came to a paradoxical conclusion: for staff expertise to be fully used, it can't be mandated. That "process" reality is independent of the technical correctness of staff solutions.

Effective Staff Work. Staff, said McGregor, should be coaches, not cops, giving managers data for controlling themselves, not others. They should consult on managerial problems, not coerce compliance with corporate directives. Staff should "devote a great deal of time to exploring 'client' needs directly, and to helping the client find solutions which satisfy him. Often the most effective strategy. ., is one in which the client develops his own solution with professional help"

A Comparison of Theory Y and Scientific Management.

Theory Y Assumptions	*Today's Analogy*
1. Work is as natural as play. People like or dislike it based on conditions management can control.	Soldiering on the job is management's fault, not the fault of lazy workers. Management is arbitrary as long as nobody has figured out the best tools, methods, incentives, and required talents for each job.
2. External control is not the only way to achieve organizational goals. People will exercise self-control toward objectives they feel committed to.	People will be committed to methods that clearly have been found, through trial and error, to be the best, least stressful, most productive, and most suitable for them. The incentive is greater success, higher pay, easier work, and less conflict.
3. Commitment comes from rewards based on satisfying people's needs for status, recognition, and growth.	*No Taylor analogy.* He believed in feedback, but did not understand social needs like status, recognition, and community.
4. Under the right conditions the average person will seek and accept responsibility rather than avoid it.	All workers, supervisors, and staff experts have a role to play in making a workplace successful, and all will readily do it if they believe the system is the best possible and they are paid well for their efforts.
5. Many people have the ingenuity and creativity needed to solve organizational problems. These qualities are not the rare province of a gifted few.	*No Taylor analogy.* He believed the contrary: only those trained in specific functions should be allowed to carry them out.
6. Modern industry uses only a part of the ability, talent, and potential brainpower of the average person.	Every person is "first class" at something. The best work system is one where every job is filled by the person for whom first-class performance represents that person's highest level of functioning.

(McGregor, 1960, p. 169). One powerful enactment of this theory is Peter Block's popular workshop "Staff Consulting Skills," where technical experts discover how to transfer their knowledge when they have no formal authority.

Leadership and Teamwork. McGregor also concluded, contrary to Taylor, that there is no one best way to manage. No particular style has proved universally satisfactory in every situation; successful managers tend to have a clear sense of direction and a flexible repertoire of behavior. They are able both to listen, delegate, involve and to decide and direct. These are not contradictory behaviors, McGregor learned at Antioch. They are equally needed, the same way a carpenter needs a hammer and a saw.

McGregor made a compelling case for teamwork. No discovery in social science history has challenged and threatened managers more than group dynamics. The subtle potential of groups directly opposed a sacred American myth: the manager as Lone Ranger, heroically and single-handedly cutting costs, innovating, and motivating people. McGregor, influenced by Lewin and his own T-group experiences in Bethel, by the Antioch Goals Discussion, by his joint consultations with Beckhard, by John Paul Jones's work at Union Carbide, by Elton Mayo's writings (1945), confronted the myth.

Most management "teams," McGregor observed, are really collections of individuals vying for the boss's favor. Unity of purpose can't be achieved that way. Managers misuse groups because they have low expectations and few group skills, and put too much burden on leaders. Properly used, groups can only improve decision making and problem solving. Effective teamwork requires informality, give and take, openness, frank criticism, self-examination of team effectiveness, shared responsibility for work and outcomes. These skills are best learned, he thought, through team building, which I take up in Chapter Seventeen. Moreover, McGregor emphasized that "groups" and "participation" are not synonymous. Those who think Theory Y means "everybody participates in everything" obviously have not read his work.

McGregor also rejected fitting people to jobs. He thought the best strategy "is to provide a heterogeneous supply of human resources from which individuals can be selected to fill a variety of unpredictable needs" (McGregor, 1966, p. 76). We cannot tell what a firm will need tomorrow. Therefore, we must encourage diversity. More, we must design human resource systems that give people control over their own development and career moves.

It is not important that management accept Theory Y, McGregor said. Its assumptions surely will be revised by new knowledge. What we must do is abandon practices we *know* don't work, "so that future inventions with respect to the human side of enterprise will be more than minor changes in already obsolescent conceptions of organized human effort" (1960, p. 245).

Perhaps the most far-reaching difference between Taylor and McGregor was this: their views of control. Taylor, who made a harness for himself as a youth to prevent nightmares, sought to create *external* conditions to optimize work. McGregor, the missionary who believed that even the worst among us were capable of self-help, sought to build on *internal* needs. He taught that the best control is self-control. That radical idea has caused a managerial revolution wherever it is applied. The bottom-line performance of social systems managed to maximize technical capability and economy through each person's self-motivated efforts is incalculable.

Worldwide Acclaim

The Human Side of Enterprise was met by a worldwide outpouring of praise, excitement, letters, reviews, awards, invitations to speak. McGregor, more clearly than anybody, had taken Lewin's work, married it to Maslow's, and created personnel, labor relations, performance appraisal, goal setting, and compensation methods that all could apply if they really wanted to. He also accented the big *if:* leader behavior. He gave analogy after analogy and example after example, drawing on his experience as manager and consultant. He was widely praised and, sad to say, still misunderstood. Criticism came mainly from fellow academics, grumbling, harumphh . . . that McGregor, uh . . . er . . . did not cite specific research to support his ideas. Indeed, the book's great weakness is lack of an index and bibliography. Yet McGregor wanted a book managers would read, understand, and identify with; as little like a textbook as possible. Academic quibbling only accented how well he had succeeded.

Three kinds of charges were leveled at the book. The most direct came from those who said Theory X comes closer to the truth than Y, that a combination of paying well and "kicking ass" is the only sensible way to motivate people. A second charge, more sorrowful than angry, came from people who shared McGregor's wish for a Theory Y managerial world, but saw it as idealistic, impractical, and futile. Notable among these was the same Abraham Maslow whose theories underpinned McGregor's. Maslow, during his year as a scholarly gadfly-in-residence at Non-Linear Systems (the firm on whose self-managing work teams I had modeled my own in the 1960s), repeatedly questioned and qualified the application of Theory Y (Maslow, 1965). There was, he said, too little evidence (his own included) for this view of human potential. It required hothouse conditions and astute selection of rare, self-motivated people. It "assumes good conditions, good luck and good fortune" (Picker, 1968, p. 51).

Indeed, Maslow made so much of the issue precisely because he wished to believe. Yet, as a psychologist who had studied human pathology, he doubted — like Douglas McGregor's real father — that the darker forces of human nature could be overcome. (A contemporary advocate of that view is John Weir, the creator with his wife Joyce of intense workshops in "self-differentiation." He cites the enormous work it takes for any one of us to experience and eliminate the negative consequences of life's "shadow" side.)

Another sympathetic critic saw too much zero-sum conflict (if you win, I lose), too few shared goals, too many power differences, and too much boring, routine work negating Theory Y assumptions. "In sum," he wrote, "there do not appear to be enough influential advocates for the redesign of work according to 'theory y' principles to stimulate the allocation of scarce resources to this goal" (Nord, 1978, p. 65).

The statement illustrates one of McGregor's major themes: how an assumption leads to the belief that "the facts" support it. My own contrary evidence comes from countless projects, some described in Part Two, to which many corporations, medical centers, hospitals, and government agencies have allocated enormous resources since 1969. Indeed, one of the positive outcomes of the 1980s recession was the investment by General Motors (Saturn auto plant), Nissan (Smyrna, Tennessee, truck plant), Diversified Printing (Attie, Tennessee, printing plant), and a hundred others in "new design" factories in which Theory Y assumptions play a central role.

Systems, Not Formulas

Nevertheless, McGregor, despite his best efforts, could not envision a management practice embodying all his ideals. Not that he didn't try. It must have hurt him most that his many vivid analogies, examples, and illustrations did not satisfy the critics who *still* demanded more "how-to" stuff. McGregor was busily writing it into *The Professional Manager* when he died. In that book, published posthumously, he strongly argued, as did Frederick Taylor in his later years, that Theory Y implied a *system* of management, and that no single technique could ever embody the philosophical implications of a manager's mental map of reality. Systems change involved "costs and risks," might take "three to five years," and required as much investment as new product research and development. Anything less, said McGregor, left managers with "recipes, fads, and other 'instant cures'" (McGregor, Bennis, and McGregor, 1967, pp. 95–96).

Nobody criticized, and few even observed, the central theme of McGregor's life and work: that the actualization of management practices — at once efficient, humane, and democratic — was not a function of any particular formula, but rather the basis for a continual search for dignity, meaning, and community. McGregor above all advocated an experimental style of change, finding out what works in each new situation. His pragmatism was grounded in a faith in democracy and human potential, which Western science has only recently linked to effective management through the medium of open systems thinking (see Chapter Nine).

Unlike Taylor, who thought that only trained engineers could find one best way to do anything, McGregor put the burden on each person. One paradox is that Taylor's motivation formula — concrete goals, tied to a bonus — has been shown to increase output in routine jobs 40 percent or more in studies cited by Edwin Locke (1982). It is equally true that work systems embodying principles McGregor advocated also have improved output up to 40 percent over traditional systems. My own case from the 1960s (see Chapter One) is one of many examples. Such systems have also registered important social gains — better jobs, less absenteeism and turnover, more mutual support, personal growth, and higher morale. They also have cut overhead, mainly by moving supervision and staff expertise outside and skills and knowledge inside the boundaries of work teams — a reversal of Taylor's way (Lawler, 1986). That, I'm convinced, is what makes managers and supervisors so skeptical. If people can plan and ensure their own output, why do they need supervision? McGregor's vision threatens status and power everywhere in middle management.

More, there is an organizational version of "Gresham's Law" (bad money drives out good), which says that technology tends to drive out other values in the workplace. Unfortunately, some Taylor techniques, especially narrow tasks and control by experts, not workers, proved very attractive to managers holding Theory X assumptions (though few embraced his value that workers should share significantly in productivity gains). McGregor believed that X assumptions were dated by education, experience, and modern social science. For a good part of the population they were false — but if acted upon could be made to come true.

A New Look at X and Y: Two Selves in Each of Us

Here's the rub with X and Y, given 20/20 hindsight. How can a false theory come true, unless there's a grain of truth in it already? From Jungian psychology comes a profound possibility McGregor's writings elude. That is the presence in each of us of both X and Y assumptions — a polarity of the human spirit within, not just between, persons. But there is more. Here is the possibility that boggles me: X and Y *each* have positive and negative aspects.

To tell you how I know that requires a short digression. Some years ago in Sweden, through my friend Jan Boström, I met a social psychologist named Claes Janssen. Janssen (1982) had worked out a powerful group exercise to surface our projections on others. (A projection is seeing in someone else traits we admire or deny in ourselves.) He created a simple, twenty-four item yes/no questionnaire. Those answering most questions "yes" he called "yes-sayers"; those answering most "no" were "no-sayers." If you ask these two groups to write adjectives about themselves and the other group, you get the chart in "Yes/No Observations" — a result I have repeated many times.

"Yes-sayers" see themselves through a Theory Y lens — optimistic, creative, independent. They give "no-sayers" Theory X traits — repressive, authoritarian, fearful. "No-sayers," on the contrary, cite their own positive traits — dependability, loyalty, and cooperativeness. They see "yes-sayers" as confused, anxious, and self-centered — far from self-control and responsibility.

Projecting Our Own "Shadow." Janssen's theory is that each
list of descriptors represents a projection of what we value in ourselves and what we fear. The feared side — our "shadow," the human
impulses we disown — may appear on the Yes or No side of the
dialogue. More, he shows that in any life crises we are likely — each

one of us — to move through the four positions, experiencing (or running from) all the states described as we face up to our situation. (In Chapter Sixteen I show how Janssen's theory also can be used to assess an organization's potential for change, depending upon which position people take at any particular time.)

The reason McGregor's powerful notions stirred such strong feelings, I believe, is that he unintentionally set up a good guys/bad guys scenario that left people on both sides in an uncomfortable box. I can't change my assumptions the way I change undershirts. To do that is to surrender part of my own identity. McGregor — the passionate optimist of human potential — was tuned in only on the negative aspects of his No side, which came through strongly in his father, and on the positive aspects of his own Yes.

Yet both sides exist in each of us. Edwin C. Nevis, a consultant and applier of Gestalt theories to organizations, surveyed 5,000 managers between 1970 and 1979. Consistently they opted on the average for 56 percent of the Theory X statements on the survey *and* 67 percent of those based on Theory Y (personal memo to author, January 1987).

So I know I am not alone. I was propelled by McGregor's vision to initiate change in the 1960s because of my urgent need for an outside voice granting relief from the incongruities I experienced. It was company policy and procedure that needed changing. I soon learned that the hardest work would not be the work system. It would be myself — to find my own integrated side, to accept and let go my negative No, which led me to want constant (although unconscious) control in a striving for unattainable perfection.

To act on constructive assumptions — X or Y — is to accept that not everybody wants to grow, and that we must not take it personally when our good intentions fall short. Most of all it means accepting our own tendency, when we are denied what we had hoped for, to jump to the negative Theory X conclusion that people are no damn good after all. Shocked at our primitive impulse, we may (like McGregor) repress the feelings, thus deepening our own guilt and anguish. I believe now that I need both sides of my X and Y, to hear my inner dialogue as a creative but not always harmonious discourse on my own growth and learning. I can foster conditions for my own learning, but I cannot expect that everyone else will want to take my trip.

One critic imagined that McGregor intended for his theme to relieve the guilty consciences of people in authority. "It is as though leaders listen for the voices outside themselves," wrote psychoanalyst Abraham Zaleznik, "which will testify to their humanity in opposition to the disquieting inner voices that disapprove, depreciate, accuse" (1967, p. 67). That certainly describes part of my experience.

But there is more. Years ago his close friend Warren Bennis observed that McGregor's conception of Theory Y also created an intolerable burden for leaders — accepting responsibility for the growth, nurturance, and success of subordinates. "When," asked Bennis, "do the boss's needs, growth, defenses, distortions, 'hang-ups,' disappointments, narcissism, sufferings, come into play?" (1972, p. 142). Unless we accept good/bad X *and* good/bad Y in ourselves, we cannot become fully human.

Values Over Techniques. Taylor lamented that managers embraced his methods without understanding his principles. He was furious with greedy employers who raised quotas instead of sharing gains and with ignorant consultants who put in systems without proving their value to workers. McGregor was disappointed that so many managers thought he wrote a Theory Y cookbook when his intent was more ambitious: to show that wrong assumptions lead to ineffective management. We must resist the temptation, then, to see either Taylor or McGregor as pioneering techniques — time study and work measurement, on one hand; work teams, gain sharing, participative management on the other — rather than experimental styles of introducing change. If ever two vastly different people had a common objective, it was the application of science, the spirit of inquiry, to the workplace.

Every technique described by Taylor or McGregor has worked. And — this is why social science can never be a science — every technique also has failed. We can specify the right conditions until the moon becomes an Earth colony. Unlike high school chemistry, we can never repeat one another's experiments. The problem with "searching for excellence" is not that the cases are overdramatized. The fact is that Hewlett and Packard started working side by side in a garage with certain values of human dignity. As their company grew, they invented policies and methods to embody their values. They did not, could not "create a culture" that was not already indigenous to their lives; they would consider it ridiculous even to try.

If we wish to find out what works, we must start with our own values and personal situation. Management is best conceived as constructive self-fulfilling prophecies, acting in ways to make happen what we most believe in. It is at bottom an exercise of moral imagination. I fancy Taylor, Lewin, and McGregor would readily have agreed to that.

Chapter Eight

Undoing Taylorism: Emery, Trist, and the Sociotechnical Revolution

> Information technologies, especially those concerned
> with the microprocessor and telecommunication,
> give immense scope for solving many current
> problems — if the right value choices can be made.
> —— *Eric Trist*, The Evolution of Socio-Technical
> Systems, *1981, p. 59*

Douglas McGregor was writing a how-to book for managers when he died suddenly in 1964. *The Professional Manager,* edited by McGregor's wife, Caroline, and his friend Warren Bennis (1967), was the closest thing to a cookbook he ever wrote. It contains the earliest accounts in manager's language of workplaces designed as whole systems. I patterned my multiskilled work-team experiments from McGregor's account of Non-Linear Systems. I did not know then that only a few experiments had been tried in the United States. Because I thought everybody was doing it, I cut out direct supervision. More than any other step, that one fed my vision of the potential of productive workplaces. It was not until the early 1980s, revisiting management history for this book, that I came to appreciate the origins of experiments like mine. They can be traced precisely to a revolutionary discovery in Great Britain in 1949 in a South Yorkshire coal mine.

Sociotechnical Systems: Choice, Not Chance

Now, with 20/20 hindsight, let's look at the genesis of sociotechnical systems (STS) design. Because of this remarkable innovation, many companies have revolutionized the division of labor among managers, workers, and experts quite differently from both Taylorism and participative management. I owe my enriched understanding of this trend to the work of two remarkable social scientists, Eric Trist, an Englishman living in the United States, and his frequent collaborator, the Australian Fred Emery, who figure prominently in chapters to come.

Trist coined the phrase *sociotechnical system* to underscore his observation that the interaction of people (a social system) with tools and techniques (a technical system) results from choice, not chance. Our choices are dictated by economic, technological, and human values. Emery enlarged the concept in major ways and created the practice theories necessary to modern work-redesign efforts. He also was the driving force behind a significant "permanent whitewater" innovation, the large group conference that I describe in Chapter Twenty. It is made necessary by a world trend that Emery and Trist (1963) flagged together long ago — unceasing "turbulence" in society. It is that trend, more than any other, that has impelled me to rethink Lewinian methods.

Trist, an unpretentious man in his late sixties when I last met him, had a lean, benevolent face, thinning hair, and a small moustache still showing traces of red. His dark eyes, somewhere between blue and brown, peered out from silver-rimmed bifocals. He disdained photographs, and the severe portrait here gives no hint of the engaging pixie smile that often lighted his face and lightened his conversation. Small-boned, physically delicate, tough in mind and spirit, Trist influenced two generations of practitioners to value learning, caring, and collaboration as quintessential ingredients of social change. William Westley, former head of McGill University's Quality of Work Life Centre, once said in a meeting I attended that "Trist is to QWL what Sigmund Freud was to psychoanalysis." What makes Trist an innovator is the way he derived various organizational choices and showed, in social, technical, and environmental terms, the consequences of each. He also organized many early field studies that led to new work designs, and has been a sparkplug for major macro system change efforts in cities and communities.

Eric Trist, a shaper of modern thought and action for improving work and community life. (*Beulah Trist*)

Emery, younger than his sometime-collaborator, was a lanky, rawboned, sandy-haired Australian, with blue eyes set in a lined, world-weary face. Antiauthoritarian in the extreme, he disliked sitting at the head table in a seminar or being introduced as an expert. His erudition and extraordinary ability to synthesize obscure sources, research, theories, and practical experience into new concepts and methods made him a leading social innovator of this or any era. His concept (1967), for example, that developing "redundant skills" in each person irrevocably transforms work systems, was, in Trist's words, "a major breakthrough that has affected everything that has happened since in the enlightened practice of sociotechnical theory" (memo to author, December 3, 1986). Hans van Beinum, director of the Ontario Quality of Work Life Centre, characterized Emery as "someone who is inclined to go for the dark corners," those parts of social reality "which are a bit foggy, misty; the twilight areas" (1985).

Emery was born on August 27, 1925, into a working-class family (his father was a sheep shearer and drover) in Narrogin, a tiny town in the rugged frontier outback of Western Australia. A "wild, independent bush kid" (his wife's words), he quit school at fourteen, went back later to night school, finished Fremantle Boys High School, and had two degrees from the University of Western Australia by age twenty-one. In 1953 he earned a doctorate in psychology from the University of Melbourne, where he became a senior lecturer (associate professor) while still in his twenties.

Emery met Trist at the Tavistock Institute in London while on a UNESCO research fellowship in 1951–52. For a decade starting in 1958, Emery was a senior Tavistock staff member, doing major projects in England and Norway and devising important new theories of action. He worked mainly from Australia after 1969, traveling the world as an independent researcher and consultant, except for two years each at the Center for Advanced Study in the Behavioral Sciences at Palo Alto, and as a visiting professor at the University of Pennsylvania. For many years he was also connected with the Centre for Continuing Education in the Australian National University in Canberra.

Trist was born, "totally a Celt," to a Cornish father and Highland Scottish mother near the white cliffs of Dover in Kent, England, on September 11, 1909. A sea captain's son, he was the first male in that line since Elizabethan times to turn down a life at sea. Instead, he studied English literature and psychology at Cambridge and moved decisively toward the latter after meeting Kurt Lewin. He attended Yale on a fellowship, mentored by anthropologist Edward Sapir. After World War II he was a founder of the Tavistock Institute of Human Relations. After 1967 Trist lived mainly in the United States, teaching at the University of California, Los Angeles, the Wharton School of the University of Pennsylvania, and at York University in Ontario, Canada, and directing or consulting to some of the more ambitious social change projects of our time.

Tavistock Institute

For the full story of Taylorism's undoing, we must turn back the clock and visit London's Tavistock Institute of Human Relations just after World War II. The institute was incorporated separately from its parent, the Tavistock Clinic, a mental health treatment and training facility, when the clinic joined Britain's National Health Service. The institute's purpose was teaming with client-sponsors to use social science knowledge for a wide spectrum of human problems, intending along the way to make new theories about what works (Gray, 1970).

If these twin goals — solve the problem and learn more about how to solve future ones — sounds like Lewinian action research, the reason is not far to seek. Trist had admired Lewin's work since the early 1930s. As a graduate student he became noticeably excited over a Lewin paper in the Cambridge library, and "received a bad mark for that, because no Briton should be guilty of enthusiasm" (Sashkin, 1980, p. 145). He avidly read Lewin's Berlin experiments. When Lewin visited Cambridge on his flight from Germany, Trist, the starry-eyed student, showed him around. They remained friends until Lewin's death. As Lewin had read Taylor, the better to use psychology in the workplace, so Trist would read Lewin, the better to undo Taylorism and give Taylor's values — labor-management cooperation, optimum use of each person's talents — a new lease on life.

Like Lewin in the United States, Tavistock's founders sharpened their ideas through wartime action projects. Trist, for example, had worked as a clinical psychologist in the Maudsley Hospital, Britain's premier national psychiatric hospital. He quickly realized the futility of one-at-a-time treatment compared with the enormous wartime need, finding it impossible to accept that only the hour with the doctor could be therapeutic. Imbued with Lewinian thinking, he sought support for the idea that the social institution, the hospital community, could be a powerful rehabilitator.

Bion's Group Theory

His search led him to Major Wilfred R. Bion, a much-decorated former World War I tank commander, who was an extraordinary innovator. Trist was immediately attracted to this physically imposing "psychiatrist who looked like a general" (Trist, 1985, p. 6). He especially liked Bion's private memorandum on using everyday hospital events and relationships as treatment — the first notion of a therapeutic community (later applied in a British military hospital and in the resettlement of repatriated war prisoners). Trist became an Army psychologist in 1942, rose to lieutenant-colonel, and won the Order of the British Empire. He also joined Bion and his colleague J.D. Sutherland in a collaboration that would have far-reaching consequences for the workplace.

Bion devised a leaderless group method for front-line officer selection, facing candidates with the dilemma of competing in a test that required cooperation for success. Bion observed that tension between cooperation and self-centeredness under stress was the officer's core battle dilemma. Selection became a therapeutic learning experience for soldiers and psychologists both, reducing dependence on psychiatrists and increasing the military's confidence in its ability to pick good officers. It was based on the concept of "handing back power from the technical to the military side," a tenet of later consultancy (Trist, 1985, p. 9).

From experiments like these Bion, a psychoanalyst, evolved another version of group dynamics in parallel with Lewin's. He imagined a group's dilemmas as an interplay between the task (its stated purposes) and the process, contained in three unconscious basic assumptions people make to contain anxiety. One, "fight-flight," is the tendency to battle others or withdraw. A second, "dependency," is the predilection to let the leader do everything. A third, "pairing," describes the inclination to pair up. Bion (1961) thought that exclusive pairs symbolized a sexual purpose — the unborn leader or messiah who guaranteed group survival — and also raised defensiveness. Each assumption required different leader behavior to be worked with creatively.

In 1957 Tavistock Institute pioneered a form of laboratory education on Bion's ideas. The "Tavi" groups emphasized structure, boundaries, and collective behavior when presented with responsibility for self-learning by an impassive authority, the trainer. In contrast to NTL Institute's T-groups, Tavistock trainers refused interaction with group members. Instead, they delivered infrequent, impersonal, and sometimes cryptic analytic interpretations of group behavior. ("This consultant believes that the group collectively avoids action and refuses to know that is what it does." Period. End quote. What did *that* mean? No comment.) People projected on the trainer every feeling they ever had about parents, teachers, or bosses. Acting as if the trainer really were these other characters, they lived out Bion's basic assumptions in the meeting room. Tavistock groups, like those of NTL Institute, became rich learning laboratories. (Later they were developed in the United States by the A. K. Rice Institute.)

Wilfred R. Bion, a pioneer of leadership and group behavior and a major force in the Tavistock Institute of Human Relations. (*Francesca Bion*)

You can see obvious analogies between these learning groups and the workplace. Feelings about authority indiscriminately control our behavior in many situations when we least realize it. Work group conflicts, passivity, demoralization, withdrawal are traceable to group feelings about authority. What may not be so obvious are the uses of this insight. Perhaps the most practical derivative is this: when people fight, run away from the task, pair up defensively, or depend on a leader to solve their problems, they become childish, immature, and unable to grow. They cannot use their creativity or commit to joint action. The constructive course, in a group or a large organization, is to join with others in purposefully defining and carrying out mutual tasks. So what else is new? It's the sort of thing everybody knows. And it is far from the easy path.

Keeping people working together instead of fighting or fleeing, seeking to reduce dependency on expert authority and bosses, pushing people to join each other in tasks of mutual importance — these are major consultant contributions to clients buffeted by high-anxiety change. They are, in my opinion, at least as important as the "right answer," since people who are running away, fighting, abdicating, or waiting for a new leader to be born cannot do anything with right answers, even when they have them. This knowledge later became a cornerstone of work design based on sociotechnical ideas. When the task was determined, it became essential to remove blockages that kept people from carrying it out.

Industrial Action Research in a Yorkshire Coal Mine

Like the T-group a few years earlier, sociotechnical practice did not result from armchair analysis. It was discovered in real time, turned into concepts and methods, and tried out in many settings. More, it was stimulated — like group dynamics in both the United States and Britain — by a social crisis. After World War II investment capital was a scarce commodity in Britain. So Tavistock researchers devised an industrial action research program to find examples of quantum leaps in output based on human skill and brainpower rather than money.

In 1949 Tavistock student Kenneth Bamforth, a former coal miner and trade union member for eighteen years, visited the South Yorkshire colliery where he had once worked. He made a startling discovery. There were now self-regulating work teams sharing jobs, shifts, and responsibilities in a new seam. He returned to London very excited and in Trist's living room described what he had seen. Trist went down into the mine with Bamforth. "I came up a different man," he said (Sashkin, 1980, p. 151). Later he wrote Fred Emery, "It was both moving and exciting to talk to the men about the value they placed on their experience in the newly formed autonomous groups. The older miners remembered the very small self-regulating groups of pre-mechanized days and how these had been broken up with bad consequences for them when semi-mechanized long-walls had come in" (Emery, 1978, p. 6).

Improved roof control had made feasible short-wall mining in a rich coal seam near the surface not accessible by long-wall methods. To complement the new roof-control methods, miners on each shift did all tasks, making possible three shifts a day, or continuous mining. "I was certain that the things I observed were of major significance as I experienced the two methods in parallel," Trist recalled. "It was the same sort of discovery that we had made with Bion in studying leaderless groups. All of the work on therapeutic communities that led to group work at Tavistock and all of Lewin's work on group dynamics came together in my mind as I was seeing it happen" (Sashkin, 1980, p. 151).

Two features struck Trist. First, the catalyst for change was a new technology. Long-wall miners had done one narrow task, under close supervision — an ugly way to make a living underground. Imagine a factory, damp, dark, and dangerous, in which workers move their machines daily, extract an ever-changing raw material, transport supplies, equipment, and product through two narrow tunnels, and spend much of each day keeping the walls and ceiling from falling in. Add repetitious, stressful jobs — drilling, cutting, hewing, and building roof supports — and a coercive supervisor: *voila*, you have a work force marked by 20 percent absenteeism, high attrition, frequent accidents, and low productivity.

Despite an infusion of capital in mechanization, output in the mines was dropping.

In pick-and-shovel days the miners' fathers had worked in small, mutually supportive teams. Each team, doing whole groups of tasks, acknowledged its dependence on the others for safety and output. Years later, advanced roof-control technology had led a new generation back to the teamwork and self-control lost years before. Significantly, Trist and colleagues (1963) titled their landmark study of coal mining under changing technologies *Organizational Choice: The Loss, Re-discovery, and Transformation of a Work Tradition*.

The second important feature, not fully appreciated at first, was how the teams came into existence. The general manager and miners, with union support, had jointly carried out the change. The miners showed they could make wise decisions about their own work. Bamforth and Trist called it "responsible autonomy." Extraordinary social and economic consequences accompanied this adaptation to new technology. "In marked contrast to most mines," Trist wrote, "cooperation between task groups was everywhere in evidence; personal commitment was obvious, absenteeism low, accidents infrequent, productivity high" (1981, p. 8).

Could others apply the underlying principles and get the same dramatic results? Experimental sites were hard to come by, but Trist and A.T.M. Wilson ([1951] 1983) managed to team up with a general manager of an area containing twenty collieries that had more advanced equipment. The manager had created "a new basic pattern" of continuous mining without being fully aware of the great social importance of what he had done.

It should be noted that both the initial innovations were stopped when they ran afoul of Coal Board politics. But the cat was out of the bag. Another way of working was possible, one that defied beliefs about the primacy of technology that went clear back to Taylor. This way depended on finding what Trist called "the best match" among customer needs, the producers, and their equipment. Separate attempts to improve human relations alone fell short because they left the work structure intact. A new unit of analysis was needed, the sociotechnical system that included technology and people both.

The researchers soon found another mine in the north of England using the group method (called "composite" mining) with long-wall technology, a feat mining experts had assured them was impossible. Now they could do a meticulous comparison of identical long-wall mines with different work organizations. They showed the decisive superiority of composite methods in output, costs, absenteeism, turnover, health, and safety. Tavistock confirmed the impact of teamwork in several field studies in other industries undergoing technological change in the 1950s.

A Paradigm Shift

What was learned from these studies between 1949 and 1958 Trist and Emery later called a "paradigm shift," a wholly new view of workplace reality. "I never would have seen the old paradigm for what it was," Trist wrote Emery, "had I not experienced the reality of the new" (1977, p. 6). The new principles sharply contradicted those of that other QWL pioneer, Frederick Taylor, who sought the same results by other means. That this was a perceptual breakthrough can be seen in an early chart drawn by Trist for use by A.T.M. Wilson ([1951] 1983) in the first public presentation of their organizational studies when the Tavistock Group won the Kurt Lewin Memorial Award; see "Comparing Mining Methods."

The new systems, based on values similar to Taylor's, differed in practice on every particular. This was not simply an improvement; it was a revolution. Taylor had sought to rationalize jobs, using a primitive stick-and-carrot psychology. He had no constructive concept of social systems, so he had approached work design empirically. How much could a "high-priced" man do in a day? Using a stopwatch, he broke jobs into tiny pieces — scoop a shovel full of coal, swing it in an arc, dump it in a car — each motion timed to be done as quickly as humanly (and, he believed, humanely) possible.

COMPARING MINING METHODS	LONGWALL	CONTINUOUS
WORK ROLES	FIXED	INTERCHANGEABLE
TASK ORDER	RIGID	FLEXIBLE
INDIVIDUAL SKILLS	SPECIALIZED	ALL-ROUND
RESPONSIBILITIES	OWN TASK	GROUP TASK
STATUS	DIFFERENCES	EQUAL
PAYMENT	PIECE-RATE	FLAT-RATE
SUPERVISION	EXTERNAL INSPECTION	INTERNAL LEADERSHIP
INTRA-SHIFT STRUCTURE	SEGMENTED	INTEGRATED
INTER-SHIFT RELATIONS	DEPENDENT	INDEPENDENT
COMMUNITY EFFORT	SPLITTING	COHESIVE

—A.T.M. WILSON, 1951

Taylor, remember, was a careful observer of human energy and stress at a time when few managers took these matters seriously. Because his ideas worked, they had enormous influence. He offered the ablest people the carrot of a large bonus for higher output. He also removed all discretion from jobs. Engineers designed the tasks. Supervisors enforced standards and discipline. Workers did as instructed. Old long-wall mining methods came straight from Taylor.

Turning Taylor Upside Down. As students of Freud and colleagues of Bion, the Tavistock researchers went into the mines with a sophisticated view of individual and group dynamics. They viewed tools and technology in a way not possible a half-century earlier. Although armed with new social knowledge, they still started where Taylor did — with an analysis of the work itself. As Trist later wrote, "appropriate structural settings had to be created before desirable social climates and positive interpersonal relations would develop" (1981, p. 23).

There is a significant difference between Taylor's concept of structure and Tavistock's. Taylor worked backward from the obvious task. He reduced discretion at each step, reasoning that scientifically designed jobs would be learned fast and carried out accurately, and would yield more. This led to "dumber" jobs and a reduction in required skill at every level of work, including, ironically, managers and specialists. Taylor's system evolved inexorably to deprive *everybody* of a whole view of what was being done. Engineers rationalized task efficiency but lost sight of the customer. Supervisors enforced output but had no criteria to judge whether engineers had done the job right. And workers, who knew a great deal that could not be put on a slide rule about their own nine square feet of space, were considered too ignorant to be consulted on anything that mattered. So they passed others' mistakes down the line, not caring if they added their own, investing creative energy in beating the rate system and not getting caught.

Sociotechnical designers worked in the opposite direction: seeking to broaden each person's knowledge of social and economic consequences, and to encourage each worker in developing a range of skills needed to get results. They treated the work system, rather than discrete tasks, as the unit of analysis. The work group, not each person, became the focus for change. Sociotechnical principles called for internal regulation, each person monitoring and helping achieve group goals. The housewives in Lewin's food habit experiments had performed the same way. The best nutritionists in Iowa could not get them to serve foods in support of the war effort. They had to assess the importance for themselves (see Chapter Five). It's obvious why McGregor saw these methods as exemplary Theory Y in action.

Now the Tavistock researchers made a complementary discovery. Autonomous work groups could develop a capacity for self-regulation far beyond the best supervisor's powers of control. Both Lewin and Bion had caught the essence of processes as old as the species. Groups could be self-regulating if dedicated to a common task. What Taylor conceived as an adversarial herd instinct might also be a constructive force for mutual benefit. The question was not whether such behavior was possible; that had been proved conclusively. The tantalizing question — we still ask it — was *under what conditions* it could happen.

People as Skilled Resources, Not Spare Parts. There were clues in the mines. Each miner, instead of specializing, learned several skills, not all of which were used every day. The group in a sense stored excess capacity. Together they could do a lot more of any one thing than was needed at the moment. They could cover for each other if somebody got sick. If work backlogged in one spot, they could unblock it quickly by putting more people on it.

Taylor's system relied on excess bodies — people not needed just now were standing around or, if aroused, making mischief — a setup for Theory X in action. If the excess continued for a few days, they went on layoff. If work methods changed, they never returned. However — get *this* — *too much* work in process could idle people too. A blockage at one end of the line stemmed the flow. None of the other "spare parts" had anything to do until one set of specialists (overworked specialists) finished. Everybody took a mini-holiday even though under failure conditions there was more work to do than when things went smoothly. Put that way, it's a nutty way to work, neither economic nor humane.

Instead of one person/one task, the new principle became one person/many skills. That enormously increased team flexibility. (My first work-team experiment, remember, grew out of my frustration that two absentees in one function could reduce output 40 percent in a twenty-five-person department because nobody else knew how to do their special, albeit simple, tasks.) Taylor improved productivity by squeezing out of jobs human variability, managerial whim, and personal control, at a time of relatively certain markets, simple technologies, uneducated labor, and capricious management. By reducing variability he increased safety, output, quality, and wages.

The world moved. Markets shifted, technology evolved, workers became better educated, and management information improved. Yet Taylor's descendants had hardly passed "Go." Fifty years later the short-wall miners put the discretion back into jobs. Why? To restore the balance between technology and people that Taylor had sought to improve by removing discretion in the first place! The miners had organized around the need to make frequent independent decisions that could not be captured in job descriptions. They discovered a design principle more suited to fast-changing technologies and unpredictable market pressures: increased variety for each person and department. The miners made a technical breakthrough. They enormously stepped up system control and flexibility. Imagine a system so versatile that it can be used at a moment's notice to do any job required of it. They made an economic breakthrough. They reduced costs not controllable by technical means — absenteeism, turnover, safety, and quality. Most of all they achieved a social breakthrough. They proved more graphically than a thousand texts an age-old value: the enormous power of cooperation for personal and mutual benefit. Taylor had known this, of course. He simply did not know how to build it into work groups and sustain it in the face of labor union dynamics, market swings, and changing technologies. His techniques were too narrow for his vision.

The miners not only found a superior way to dig coal. They conjured up an opposing organizational philosophy to scientific management. They enacted values of learning, social cooperation, and self-control in their methods. No wonder McGregor quickly picked up on this example. He was a frequent visitor to Tavistock in the 1950s, comparing notes on consultation and change projects. "He became part of the Tavistock tradition," Trist recalled.

Fred Emery, voracious reader, writer, conceptualizer, and translator of theory into democratic practices. *(Merrelyn Emery)*

"We made connections between Theory X and the Taylor tradition going back to the 1890s — all that parent-child stuff" (December 23, 1986, interview). The coal studies vividly illustrated McGregor's belief that the most effective control systems were self-induced and knowledge-based. They were found where you'd least expect them — inside all people caught up in their own work and committed to a common task.

Enter Emery and Open Systems

The person who developed the vast potential of the mining discoveries, sharpening many of the insights just described, was Fred Emery, an assertive young activist who came to Tavistock in 1951. Two men could hardly differ more in temperament and demeanor than the small, patient, diffident Trist and the tall, brusque, supremely confident Emery. Trist constantly questioned his own ideas, listening closely, receptive to input, seeking the nub of the other person's reality. Emery was output-focused, deeply committed to opinions about which he had given a lot of thought. He conversed through a barrage of citations — of theories, studies, concepts, and experiences — and would ignore questions he did not choose to answer. A born protagonist, he thrived on opposition.

Still, the two developed an affinity for one another. Then twenty-six years old, Emery found Trist, fifteen years his senior, a willing mentor. "Fred had a vast, incredible erudition," Trist recalled. "None of us had time for reading during the war. Fred had read and digested everything" (December 23, 1986, interview). To Trist's delight, Emery also was an avid student of Kurt Lewin's work. Later Emery would say that Trist was the first person who fully recognized his ability. And Emery, growing up among working people, having labored some months in an Australian mine, gravitated toward the real-world flavor of the coal mine studies. He wanted to do more than be a passive observer of social systems. So intertwined did the two names become that when they were invited to a conference in the United States in the 1960s, one confused young participant asked, "Which one of you is really Emery Trist?"

Emery introduced into Tavistock a new concept that would influence all subsequent work — the "open systems" thinking of biologist Ludwig von Bertalanffy (1950). Emery, Trist told me, "was the first social scientist who fully appreciated the significance of von Bertalanffy's ideas for psychology and the social sciences" (December 23, 1986, interview). The open systems idea, simple to state but radical if acted on, is that all things, somehow, some way, link up and influence one another in all directions. Cause and effect is not the only possible relationship between force and object. Indeed, the effect might be the cause. An amusing example is the observation that psychologists don't train pigeons to ring bells by giving them food. Instead pigeons, by ringing bells, train psychologists to feed them. The pigeon reinforces the researcher. Cause and effect become an illusion, a sleight-of-hand trick made possible by linear thinking.

Taylor assumed that any system could be isolated, rationalized, and its living parts taught their unvarying responses. That led him to "systematize" a ball-bearing company even while its market was drying up (see Chapter Three). He had no concept of environment as a source of renewal. The Tavistock researchers noted that closed systems are forever closed to the energy they need for survival. The people in them cannot learn anything new from outside, which is where major changes originate.

Emery and Trist posed a more workable description of reality: systems import stuff — ideas, raw materials, money — convert them into something else, and export goods, services, and ideas back to whoever will pay for them. All those who touch the process add value, the economic concept that makes possible income, jobs, and security. The exchange renews a system, for it provides feedback on effects. If this is so, the most useful way to understand technology and people within a system is to understand their relationship to the larger whole they serve.

It's not enough to know how the technology works. It's not enough to know what makes people tick. It's not enough to understand sales, manufacturing, and cost accounting. To make a system hum, you need feedback from customers, suppliers, regulators, local communities — outsiders who make demands for service, products, compliance, support. They spark innovation and change. Lewin had said that you can't understand a person's behavior if you look only inward at personality. You also need to know the context of the here-and-now situation. In an open system there is traffic in both directions. Everything counts.

The most deceptive of all open systems notions was von Bertalanffy's concept of "equifinality," meaning equal paths to the same place, or, roughly speaking, lots of ways to skin a cat. So profoundly simple is the idea, in contrast to the obscure word, that I could not grasp equifinality until I read a symposium in a woodworking magazine on how to sharpen chisels. Some twenty experts swore by water stones or oil stones, artificial or natural, from the quarries of Arkansas or the factories of Japan. One expert said rub the chisel back and forth on the stone, another said side to side, a third in small arcs, a fourth in large circles, a fifth in figure eights. Each asserted his combination worked best, some with elaborate scientific rationales backed up by diagrams.

"This is no help at all," I said to my wife, a ceramic sculptor. "Every one of these guys says their way is the only right way. I still don't know what I should do."

"The answer is obvious," she said. "They *all* work."

Equifinality! Nature arrives at the same place from many directions, and people, being part of nature, can do the same thing. That scientific observation never occurred to Taylor, who was convinced that only "one best way" existed to do anything. In the mid-1950s in one field experiment and many descriptive studies, the Tavistock researchers documented several variations on composite mining teams that got roughly the same results. The signs all pointed the same way. "Equifinality," Trist told me, "was the end of the one best way. The full implications are still not grasped" (December 23, 1986, interview).

After the 1950s, any person who internalized the ideas posed by Trist and enlarged by Emery could never again make sense out of workplaces conceived in Taylor's terms.

Chapter Nine

Open Systems and the New Paradigm: How Emery and Trist Redefined the Workplace

If we survey the various fields of modern science, we note a dramatic and amazing evolution. Similar conceptions and principles have arisen in quite different realms . . . and the workers in the individual fields are hardly aware of the common trend. Thus, the principles of wholeness, or organization, and of the dynamic conception of reality become apparent in all fields of science.

—— *Ludwig von Bertalanffy*, Problems of Life, *1952, p. 176*

I had my first lesson in systems thinking on a windswept North Carolina beach long before I knew of von Bertalanffy. It was a clear winter day at Kitty Hawk; and there was I, an enthusiastic pilot, living out my Walter Mitty fantasy of the first powered airplane flight in 1903. Surely you've seen the famous photo of the brothers Wright dressed as if for a formal picnic, with coats, ties, and peaked caps, Orville lying prone over the "flyer's" lower wing, Wilbur leaning into the wind.

Aviation pioneers — notably Otto Lilienthal, on whose calculations the science of flight was said to rest in 1900 — had figured out how to get planes into the air. They did not know how to control them. Indeed, Lilienthal was killed flying a glider, which he got aloft but could not steer. The Wrights, self-taught bicycle mechanics, took a different tack. Birds do it, bees do it, even fleas do it; why couldn't engineers do it?

In 1900 Wilbur, the philosophical brother, wrote to his mentor Octave Chanute, "What is chiefly needed is skill rather than machinery. It is possible to fly without motors, but not without knowledge and skill. This I conceive to be fortunate, for man, by reason of his greater intellect, can more reasonably hope to equal birds in knowledge, than to equal nature in the perfection of her machinery" (McFarland, 1953, vol. 1, p. 15).

How did two young tinkerers from Ohio succeed where better-educated contemporaries had failed? You can find the answer in the museum display at Kitty Hawk. They alone were systems thinkers. They alone identified three *interconnected* facts of flight demonstrated by birds without motors. Before you could hang wings on a bicycle and ride it through the sky, you had to figure out how to:

1. Get it into the air.

2. Keep it in the air.

3. Make it go where you want.

Not a bad management model, huh?

The Wrights repeated Lilienthal's calculations, tried them out in a primitive wind tunnel, and reached a startling conclusion. The whole "science" of flight was wrong! You could get killed flying a wing designed on Lilienthal's principles, a hypothesis that brave pioneer already had proved. (He may have been the prototype for my flight instructor's admonition, "There are old pilots and bold pilots but no old, bold pilots.") Birds twisted their wing tips to control direction. Watching this, the Wrights figured out the aileron. Next time you sit over a wing, notice the slight movement of one segment of the trailing edge each time the plane turns. That is how you and I, lacking perfect machinery, use skill and knowledge to imitate birds.

The Wrights turned to the other problems: an engine light enough to lift a wing, powerful enough to overcome gravity, durable enough to run a long time between overhauls. When they got those, there was still another problem: a modification of the controls to compensate for engine torque, the tendency of a prop turning in one direction to push the nose in the other. For smooth control they had to counteract the tail's wanting to skid in a turn, which meant coordinating aileron and rudder. They worked that one out, too, leaning the craft into the wind like a bicycle, instead of steering it like a car.

The flyer was an unstable machine in an unstable medium. Brute force made no difference; the birds flew effortlessly. To maintain control in unstable conditions required exquisite balance among the system's many elements. Eventually the Wrights threw out all the "scientific" knowledge of flying accumulated up to then (Westcott and Degen, 1983). They invented their own wing, elevator, rudder, engine, and propeller. The Wrights had to rethink how each part of the system affected the other parts before they could fly like birds. They used wires to hold the plane together and to link the controls. The first flight lasted twelve seconds. Within two years they could keep their flyer aloft for half an hour. After that even a natural dodo bird like me could become an eagle in ten hours.

Work As a Systems Problem

What Eric Trist and Fred Emery did with work design after studying coal miners ranks with the Wrights' rethinking of flight from observing buzzards. Like that older discovery, we are not anywhere near finished with it. Taylor's old solution was like Lilienthar's, incomplete and unscientific. The Tavistock researchers set out to discover, as the Wrights did at Kitty Hawk, whether their new seminal principles — notably adaptation to technology through unspecialized teamwork — were applicable elsewhere. Could skills and knowledge be applied with people who had not spontaneously invented them? Was it possible to design change so that workers could fly like birds? They had repeated the South Yorkshire results in one field experiment and had observed viable variations elsewhere (Trist and others, 1963). Were these early results a fluke? To be valid, a new paradigm had to be repeatable in all kinds of workplaces.

Indian Looms. During the 1950s one important work-redesign opportunity emerged outside the British mines — in the loom sheds of the Calico Mills at Ahmedabad in India. (Trist happened to sit next to the owner, husband of a Tavistock student, at a party and heard his many complaints about installing new machinery.) Trist proposed the services of a former colonial service officer named A. K. Rice, also a former department store manager and personnel executive.

Rice went to India in 1953. Through a translator he suggested to workers, supervisors, and the manager that individual specialties be replaced by worker groups responsible for all tasks on several looms. His proposal derived from all that was then known, especially Lewin's and Bion's group concepts, von Bertalanffy's open systems thinking, and the tantalizing coal-mine studies. The workers came back next day with an action plan. Workers and managers then implemented their own changes — a common theme of many workplace innovations. Rice had used his expertise to be a catalyst, not a designer. It was a dramatic shift in the use of specialized knowledge.

Backed up by phone calls to Trist, his shadow consultant in London, Rice also stimulated benchmark changes in supervisory roles for innovative work systems. Taylor had been on the right track when he sought to remove authoritarian behavior. His solution, however, was to centralize skills and knowledge, fragment supervision, and enforce standard procedures from outside. The method could not stand up to new technology and fast change. The British miners had reversed the game, decentralizing, broadening skills, and systematizing self-control. Rice's adaptation made supervisors resources to, not leaders of, worker teams redesigning the loom sheds. They became teachers, not doers, managing the boundaries rather than the work itself, linking with other departments. As predicted, output, quality, and work satisfaction all improved (Rice, 1958).

So far, this adaptation of 1935 Lewinian thinking — manage the boundaries and help people learn self-correction — has not been improved upon. I have on my desk a half-dozen case studies of changing supervisory roles in new design work sites. The conclusion is always the same. Managers and supervisors do best guarding the goals and values — the input. Workers control the output. Where more self-control is wanted *inside* a system, the leaders must stay *outside*, working on it, not in it. The staff experts, fewer in number as workers take on more skills, seek continually to transfer what they are learning. Where this does not happen, we get high error rates, unexplainable failures, dissatisfied customers, and a demoralized work force. (I happened to be present at a seminar in the early 1980s when somebody asked Fred Emery, for the umpteenth time, to define "quality of working life." Said he with a snort, "It means get the foreman out of the system!")

In India Rice also built upon Bion's concept of group task. Every work system, said Rice, has a "primary task," its central purpose or core mission (Miller, 1975). If you can define the primary task, and get people to analyze the social, technical, and economic assumptions surrounding it, you can invent an organization more flexible, adaptable, dynamic, and self-renewing than the ones Taylor created. To get it into the air, you need a primary task. To keep it in the air, you need a new form of first-line leadership. To make it go where you want, you need self-control, based on feedback from *outside* the work system.

Norwegian Industrial Democracy Projects. Now there were two examples from two industries in two cultures. Still, it was hard to get these new ideas diffused. The next great leap was made in Norway, a strongly egalitarian nation with traditions of stable labor relations, social welfare, and work reform. A joint national committee of trade union and business leaders had been formed to support local industrial democracy initiatives. Its members had fought together in the Norwegian underground during World War II. Now they teamed up again to promote cooperative improvements in working life as an antidote to a lagging national economy. They set up a research institute at the Technical University in Trondheim. As their sparkplug they picked another former Resistance fighter, Einar Thorsrud, a young social scientist who had become a personnel manager. Thorsrud had been a regular visitor to Tavistock in the 1950s. In 1962 he invited Emery and Trist to participate in a study to discover how to "change work itself in such a way that new economic, technological, and social needs are met" (Thorsrud, 1984, p. 344).

The joint committee sponsored four field projects: work redesigns in a wire-drawing plant, a pulp and paper mill, a panel heater assembly operation, and a fertilizer plant. In each case productivity and quality increased for varying lengths of time. But the researchers quickly found how intertwined were history, economics, technology, politics, and people in starting and sustaining change. Trust was a long time building among workers, management, and the researchers. It took significant political skill to maintain support nationally and locally. Changes in the work itself posed unprecedented threats to supervisors and engineers. Wrote Thorsrud, "Specialists were shocked to see how their models and measurements were inadequate or even irrelevant when workers were given a chance to use something more than their hands . . . the very concept of controlled experimentation was open to doubt" (1984, p. 346).

Deep anxieties surfaced when status differences among supervisors, industrial engineers, and workers were changing. The change to self-managing teams was fragile unless managers at the top and middle appreciated how a simple design principle — multiple skills — irrevocably altered their roles. Nor did the innovations spread. Even when results could be shown beyond doubt, other departments and companies, as in British mining, did not adopt the new methods. There was something deep in the human psyche that clung to familiar patterns, even obsolescent ones. Curiously, the Norwegian results had significant impact in Sweden, where hundreds of adaptations occurred in the 1970s, including the famous Volvo project (Trist, 1971).

Norwegians associated with Oslo's Work Research Institutes kept the research tradition going for decades after. In the mid-1980s significant new labor-management initiatives were underway in several industries to put methods of inquiry, search, and democratic dialogue into the equation for creating more productive workplaces (Gustavsen, 1985).

Major New Concepts

Kurt Lewin had said that if you want to understand a system, you have to change it. Now Emery, his close student, produced from live change efforts in Norway a series of conceptual *ah-ha's* that took more than twenty years to seep into American workplaces. He expanded on Trist's notion of an ideal fit between social and technical systems. The two systems, pointed out Emery, follow different logics, one derived from physics, the other from social relations. Either system maximized alone might *reduce* the output of the whole. Thus the requirements for each must be considered iteratively and together whenever work is redesigned. What we need is joint optimization.

This insight is still widely ignored. It's common for sociotechnical consultants, after engineers have the "one best" technological solution, to be asked to graft on an "ideal" social system. Yet quality of output and work life both require involving people in rethinking the whole process, giving rise to a common fallacy that sociotechnical design "takes too long."

The Second Design Principle. Emery (1967), consciously refuting Taylor, also contributed the insight that workers with multiple skills embody a wholly contrary design principle. It cannot be emphasized too strongly that every work system requires *redundancy* — a way of storing excess capacity so that it can cover fluctuating demands for goods or services. Emery showed that redundancy comes in two forms. From Taylor we get redundant parts — one person, one task, all interchangeable within specialties, but not between them. From sociotechnical studies we derive redundant functions — multiple skills for all, allowing flexible work loads within and between.

Only redundant functions support the flexibility and innovation needed to deal with rapid shifts in markets, technologies, lifestyles, and jobs. Emery, an even more militant antiauthoritarian than Taylor, saw multiskilling as the real key to removing parent-child-type supervisory relationships.

Key Factors for Designing Work. Using knowledge from Lewin, Bion, and the Norwegian field projects, Emery (1964) also drew up a list of six intrinsic factors that make work satisfying:

1. Variety and challenge
2. Elbow room for decision making
3. Feedback and learning
4. Mutual support and respect
5. Wholeness and meaning
6. Room to grow — a bright future

The first three must be optimal — not too much, which adds stress and anxiety, nor too little, which produces stultifying tedium. The second trio are open-ended. No one can have too much respect, growing room, or "wholeness" — meaning a view of both the origin and the customer's use of your work. Social design means jobs with optimal variety, discretion, and feedback, and as much respect, growth, and wholeness as technology, the environment, and ingenuity will allow (Emery, 1959).

Emery and Trist also drew on work by Louis E. Davis, a mechanical engineer who spent a year at Tavistock in the mid-1950s. Davis had shown that "scientific" engineers routinely impoverished job content and reduced motivation. Personnel people then sought to put motivation back by improving working conditions, selection, training, and wage incentives — none of which gave workers control, growth, or social meaning (Davis, Canter, and Hoffman, 1955). It was a battle dating to Taylor's time. Personnel was mistaking satisfiers, to use Herzberg's term (Herzberg, Mausner, and Snyderman,

1959), for the motivators the engineers had taken away. New work design specs must include both.

The list of intrinsic factors embodied the motivators. Now Emery and Trist added the satisfiers, a list of six extrinsic conditions of employment. These are:

1. Fair and adequate pay
2. Job security
3. Benefits
4. Safety
5. Health
6. Due process

Emery (1978) later created simple do-it-yourself work redesign methods embodying these formulations. His model is replacing Taylor's as the core work-design concept today. It is worth noting that the satisfiers are what unions have always fought for, while the motivators are central to management's wish for quality and output. Only in workplaces embodying both lists can the century-old dreams of labor-management cooperation ever come true.

An Ethical Imperative. Researchers regularly find evidence to support these principles. Studies of Swedish and American men, for example, show that the more influence people have over their jobs, the less likely they are to get heart disease. Taylorism and traditional middle management perpetuate low job influence (Nelson, 1983). Marshall Sashkin (1984, p. 4) has gone so far as to argue that "participative management is an ethical imperative." Low control of their own work hurts people physically and emotionally, wrote Sashkin. Therefore, ethical managers should not knowingly reduce people's control by excluding them from important matters that affect them.

Sashkin's view has been strongly challenged by those who consider participation and work design optional management techniques

EFFECTIVE ORGANIZATIONS	
OLD PARADIGM [EARLY 20th CENTURY]	NEW PARADIGM [LATE 20th CENTURY]
• TECHNOLOGY FIRST	• SOCIAL/TECHNICAL SYSTEMS OPTIMIZED TOGETHER
• PEOPLE AS MACHINE EXTENSION	• PEOPLE COMPLEMENT MACHINE
• PEOPLE AS SPARE PARTS	• PEOPLE AS SCARCE RESOURCES
• NARROW TASKS, SIMPLE SKILLS	• MULTIPLE, BROAD SKILLS
• EXTERNAL CONTROL: PROCEDURES BOOK	• SELF-CONTROL: TEAMS AND DEPARTMENTS
• MANY LEVELS, AUTOCRATIC STYLE	• FLAT ORGANIZATION PARTICIPATIVE STYLE
• COMPETITIVE	• COOPERATIVE
• ORGANIZATION'S PURPOSES ONLY	• INDIVIDUAL AND SOCIAL PURPOSES INCLUDED
• ALIENATION: "IT'S ONLY A JOB"	• COMMITMENT: "IT'S MY JOB"
• LOW RISK-TAKING	• INNOVATION

— ADAPTED FROM ERIC TRIST, 1978, p. 17

rather than new-paradigm values evoked by fast-changing technologies in democratic societies. Their eloquent argument testifies that the old paradigm is alive and well in academia (Locke and others, 1986). That worker participation in work design constitutes a radical open-systems breakthrough, altering all past concepts of effective work, is still not as widely appreciated as it should be.

As work becomes more complicated and uncertain, I believe the values of dignity, meaning, and community will increasingly serve democratic societies as anchor points, bedrock concepts underlying quantum leaps in output, product quality, and the quality of life itself. What Trist and Emery dubbed a paradigm shift is now the major countervailing force to Taylor's "mental revolution" in the workplace. Note how the modern version, described in "Effective Organizations," expands upon Wilson's coal-mine example in Chapter Eight.

Representation vs. Involvement. Sociotechnical design evolved as a way to extend democratic and humane values into the workplace. Many European nations have taken a bolder step: worker or union participation on boards of directors and in national policy making. Both modes embody democratic values. However, there is no necessary connection among participation, democracy, and productive work; no guarantee that if each group is represented, a company can, or will, create more whole jobs and a learning-focused climate. This observation has been confirmed in many organization development projects in the United States. It is possible to build trust and openness at the top without gains in output or quality at the bottom.

Conversely, it is possible for people at the bottom to be represented on task forces and committees without altering the worst features of their work, the factors that induce alienation and low quality. Representation in management is not the same as solving deep-rooted structural problems associated with mindless jobs and tight supervision. Therefore, both increased influence at the top and more control of the work itself are the signposts for change in productive workplaces. This point has been confirmed in Norway, where industrial democracy has taken many forms besides joint labor-management work-design experiments. Researchers, for example, tracked what happened in five major government-owned companies required by law to have workers on their boards. Contrary to expectation, neither rank-and-file participation nor productivity went up, and worker alienation did not decline.

Only when the sociotechnical work-design principles derived from the coal mines were applied did major changes show up. In the wire-drawing plant redesign, for example, production went up so much that the workers took home more money than the most skilled people in other operations. The situation became so anomalous that the union withdrew because of pay differentials among its members. This is perhaps the most puzzling and disturbing aspect of new-paradigm change. Taylor was right when he said the pie could be made larger. He was wrong in thinking that is what labor leaders, or managers, always want. See "Economic Paradox in the Workplace" for a contemporary example.

The early Norwegian experience showed how hard it is to untangle traditional work cultures and rewards after years of operating differently. In a funny way this discovery also was the real beginning of the end of Taylorism. It showed how much old and new paradigms were in conflict. Unless a whole system could be switched over, innovation was bound to be swallowed up. Old norms are so deeply entrenched that they cannot be changed incrementally. That's one reason pilot projects don't spread.

Economic Paradox in the Workplace.

Firms still reduce good economic results to control employees' ability to share more of the fruits of their efforts, a phenomenon that threatens free enterprise and democracy now just as it did in Taylor's time. I know of a company that was acquired in the 1970s by a conglomerate. Its managers allocated work loads between plants to achieve maximum profits on each job. Because all shared in bonuses, there was no competition for profitable jobs. One plant, by design, showed higher profits than the others, but all managers shared a third of total net profits as bonuses. The parent firm considered this sum too high, even though the company was two and a half times more profitable than its competition.

First the parent (apt term) reduced the total bonus pot, then put a cap on individual bonuses. Next it sought to allocate bonuses by plant instead of companywide, insisting that fragmented incentives would make all plants as profitable as the top one. Since the managers knew this was impossible, they were demoralized, cynical, and "resistant to change." It's this version of capitalism that keeps Marxism alive.

Enlarging the pie requires a vision of how much interdependence exists in an open system, the exquisite, indefinable connections among the many moving pieces, the degree of good will, trust, and cooperation needed to find out that what is best for each party is what is best for all. Is it ignorance or the "shadow" side of our natures that keeps us from making and sharing more? We still have a great deal to learn about the politics of effective work systems. The game is deeply rooted in our own inner dialogues about freedom and control, initiative and dependence.

To become more aware of these dialogues is to stop saying "bottom line" as if systems generate money apart from the willingness of people to produce. The bottom line on bottom lines is dignity, meaning, and community. It delights me that W. Edwards Deming (1982), the quality expert, made quantum leaps in productivity by *removing* production goals and substituting an orientation toward quality. Top executives as interested in money as they are reported to be should take that idea more seriously. That many don't is a commentary on the human need to hold on, to keep control, to make others behave so that we will not have to do anything new ourselves.

The Knowledge Revolution

Two notable changes have occurred in industry since open-systems ideas were first advanced. Both drive us toward increased awareness of ourselves in relation to our larger world.

First, the march of technology has taken workers *outside* the technology. In Taylor's factories workers truly were extensions of machines. Now, machines do physical work better, more precisely, and faster. However, people have to be smarter about using them. Instead of adding energy, factory workers increasingly add intelligence and judgment.

Second, knowledge work is replacing physical work in offices and service businesses. What is the "output" of an airline reservation service, or a bank's telephone customer service? The output is

information and customer satisfaction, not paperwork or products —
although the Taylorized solution to output even now is to have the
computer count how long people stay on the phone and how many
calls they take per hour. That use of technology serves neither customers nor workers.

The worker, Trist pointed out, had became "a fact-finder, inter-
preter, diagnostician, judge, adjuster, and change agent; whatever
else he does is secondary" (1981, p. 88). In fact, workers do many
tasks once reserved for managers, exercising judgment and discretion exactly of the sort Taylor once identified as dysfunctional.
Because of the change from physical to knowledge work, from
hands to brains, from running a machine to controlling its information center, workers *must* take more responsibility. If they don't
we face serious accidents, foul-ups, poor service, high costs — all
the things Taylor once sought to eliminate.

In chemical plants, nuclear power plants, paper manufacturing,
continuous casting and steel finishing, ideas like time and motion
study, individual incentives, and piece rates become irrelevant.
Control systems are based on constant feedback and course correction. Work means hand, eye, brain. Workers control the controls,
not the machines. They must make decisions based on understanding the whole process, a Gestalt of what's happening, rather
than reasoning from cause to effect.

In a powerful book, Larry Hirschhorn dissects the Three Mile
Island nuclear accident to prove his point that "machine systems
inevitably fail, given the realities of materials and human behavior" (1984, p. 86). Nuclear power workers misread their gauges, and
worked on wrong assumptions taught to them by engineers who
had figured out in advance what to do in every emergency except
the one that actually occurred. Cause-effect training made failure
inevitable. The workers turned off vibrating pumps, for example,
although the vibration meant the pumps had never gone on. Their
training consisted of "If this happens, do that." So operators failed
to diagnose what was happening, "relying too much on first impres-
sions, the victims of their own tunnel vision" (Hirschhorn, 1984,
p. 89). What they needed was knowledge and conceptual skill, the

kind talented auto mechanics use to rule out causes of unwanted vibrations by building a Gestalt of the whole problem.

"External supervision may correct errors," says Trist, "but only internal supervision can prevent their occurrence." When change is rapid and continuous, even an automated plant is in a constant state of redesign. It cannot be left to function automatically day in and day out. It puts people who work there on a continual "expedition of learning and innovation from which there is no return" (1981, p. 89).

The "Turbulent" Environment

I cannot leave this discussion of open-systems thinking in the workplace without visiting the most dramatic implication of all. It had been evident in the coal mine and other Tavistock studies by 1960 that no workplace could be isolated for long from changes in society. Even as managers developed better long-range planning tools, their use was mocked by rapid, unpredictable, and discontinuous changes on the world scene. "The rate of change was picking up so much," Trist told me, "that neither we nor our clients knew what was happening to us" (January 9, 1987, interview).

From this observation came Emery and Trist's most widely cited joint paper. It is titled, in language that has taken me a long time to digest, "The Causal Texture of Organizational Environments" (1963). It describes how outside events interact to produce conditions organizations can neither control nor ignore. Emery and Trist identified four types of causal textures, each calling for a different sort of organizational response. The names are a mouthful: "placid, randomized," "placid, clustered," "disturbed-reactive" for the first three. The first mode needs only local tactics, the second more strategic action, the third a campaign of planned tactics to enhance competitive advantage. Terminology to the contrary, the situations correspond to well-known business conditions in the 1960s.

The fourth — what I have called (borrowing from Peter Vaill) "permanent whitewater" — is the one most relevant to my purposes. It is the world created by accelerating change, growing uncertainty, increasingly unpredictable global connections of economics, technology, and people. This environment was producing "irreversible general change" (p. 24), requiring companies to alter course or face serious disruption. This world, Trist told Emery while they were working together in Norway, felt to him like a recent airplane flight he had taken through extremely rough air. He was upset by the turbulence. Emery sparked to the word. So was born the concept of the turbulent field — relentless, unpredictable swings in communities, governments, markets, and technologies. This is the central fact of life for organizations throughout the world today, one requiring the invention of unprecedented forms of data collecting, problem solving, and planning (Emery and Trist, 1963).

This insight, perhaps more than any other, was the beginning of the end of unfreezing, moving, and refreezing as a viable model of the change process. (In 1987 Trist was describing the world as a mix of the third and fourth environments.) In Chapter Sixteen I propose a new practice theory for managing turbulence. In Chapters Seventeen through Twenty I describe three modes of action, two of which build upon pioneering work by Emery and Trist.

Communities, States, Nations

It does not take much imagination to see that turbulent environments and open-systems thinking push us to think about society at large as the context for effective work design — or effective anything. Employment security, for example, one extrinsic essential, is at least a regional, certainly a national, and probably a global concern. All three levels now play a role in every business decision. Both Emery and Trist extended their thinking over many years, to whole industries, communities, societies, and global networks. The noted Jamestown (New York) Area Labor Management Committee, for example, was an extension of sociotechnical thinking to a region (Trist, 1985). From 1972 on, this effort to increase employment through community cooperation resulted in more than forty workplace innovations, attracted a new Cummins Engine plant, and influenced the renewal of downtown Jamestown. This same spirit infused the twenty-year-old Craigmillar Festival Society, an annual community music and drama event, which brought hope to an economic-disaster area near Edinburgh, Scotland (Trist, 1985).

In 1987, Trist went into semi-retirement, living in Gainesville, Florida, with Beulah, for twenty-seven years his wife, friend, companion, secretary, and administrative assistant in numerous projects. Chief among these was a book with Howard V. Perlmutter on the meaning of new-paradigm thinking for a dozen major social institutions, such as nations, cities, corporations, and families. Their position is one of diversity and balance, a mix of large and small institutions, local and central initiatives, and not either/or battles between proponents of "small is beautiful" and "centralize everything."

Emery, except for his two years at the University of Pennsylvania, worked tirelessly after 1969 in Australia to institutionalize new-paradigm thinking. In the mode of "barefoot social scientists" he and his wife Merrelyn Emery stimulated hundreds of projects and conferences with people in every sector. One result was that by 1985 every department in the Australian government had an industrial democracy officer and was drawing up plans for workplace democratization. Australia's Public Service Board had proposed what is probably the most far-reaching restructuring ever envisaged by a democratic government agency. It would affect more than a third of 200,000 civil servant jobs, reducing forty-eight categories of office work to only five through multiskilling. Government workers would alternate filing, word processing, memo writing, and public contact to provide variety, learning, and better client service (Castle, 1986).

The board's head said he intended that citizens from all walks of life by the year 2001 "will be looking toward a period in the public service as part of their career progression" (Wilenski, 1986, p. 3). He envisioned women in 30 percent of public executive jobs, more ethnic minorities in all positions, multiskilling at every level, fewer levels, and other innovations — all established by law or public policy.

On several continents, then, we were in a quantum leap into a workplace equivalent of what Star Trekkies know as "hyperspace" and worlds where no person has gone before. It was a workplace shifting from physical manipulation to machine-controlled processes, from doing the work to making sure machines do it right, from routine and predictable sequences to "anything can happen." It was a global society awakening to the interdependence of every living thing.

The new paradigm is only a snapshot, a still picture, of what future productive workplaces might look like. But how about the movie from which the picture was taken? Enacting a new paradigm raises an interesting paradox. To get there, an organization needs to act as if it has already arrived. It is not possible to design innovative work systems by using the methods, procedures, assumptions, or time frames derived from Taylorism, Theory X, and placid environments.

Making the movie — taking the jump into hyper-space — requires that those whose lives will change be involved in figuring out the changes. The community of memory can help us there too. The South Yorkshire miners not only showed what is possible — flatter, self-managed organizations — they also showed how to get there. Workers and superintendents revamped the system together. It was not done for them by outside experts or coal board bureaucrats. It was done at the coal face by those with the biggest stake in getting it right because their lives depended on it.

Three lessons came roaring through for me as I delved into this history and compared it with my own experience. First, we have real choices to make, not trivial ones, about who controls what and who ought to. The future doesn't just happen; we carve it out of what we do today. Second, none of us is expert enough to supply somebody else's answer. If we delude ourselves that we do, we can only make change problems worse.

Finally, we have to learn effective participation. We cannot expect to do that with buzzwords, hoopla, and videotapes *unless* we are prepared also to make significant changes in policy, procedure, structure, and division of work; sweating it out together, labor and management, sales and production, supervisors and workers, middle managers and staff. No one group is competent to figure out what constitutes quality and output, what the customers really want, how to measure that, and what it takes to get it to them.

To sum up, informed self-control, not close supervision, is the only way to operate new technologies without making mistakes so bad we might not live to say "I'm sorry." Knowledge and skill can't be pumped into people the way traditional schools have done it. They can be mastered only by applying theory directly on the job, to real problems, here and now. That requires the learner's direct involvement. Even Taylor knew that. Moreover, the future of democratic values — dignity and worth of each person, free choice and free expression, social responsibility coupled to personal opportunity — depends on what we do today. Lewin understood that, and the sociotechnical thinkers, led by Trist and Emery, provided us with tools to implement these values. If we want to create a society worth fighting for, we had better fight for the integration of social, technical, and economic change. Otherwise, we surely will put ourselves on the losing side of the knowledge revolution.

Remembering Eric Trist and Fred Emery (2003)

Eric Trist died June 4, 1993, in Carmel, California, at age 83. He had lost a leg to diabetes a year earlier and had a stroke two weeks before his death. Eric was my friend, colleague, mentor, gentlest collaborator, and toughest critic. For fifteen years I had enjoyed his calm presence, dry wit, boundless compassion, and intellectual rigor. Eric had a quality shared with his mentor Kurt Lewin. That was the ability to find a kernel of truth in every statement, a seed of constructive possibility in every experiment, no matter how outlandish. I had seen Eric many times take a novel idea, turn it this way and that, and hand it back to its originator richer, fuller, and more insightful.

When I showed him the cases that appear in Part Two of this book, he said, "Fine, so far as you've gone, but what do they all *mean*? What you need," he went on, "is a *conceptual emboldening*." Until then I did not know that people could embolden conceptually. Willing to try, I grabbed a scratch pad and listed the cases, showing Eric how each was an advance over the others in certain ways — from . . . for instance, expert problem solving to, uh, er, what you might call . . . uh . . . "involving everybody in improving the whole system." So the Learning Curve on page 329 became the core framework for this book.

Eric, modest in the extreme, had a hard time accepting that his concepts had influenced so many people. He was uncomfortable if praise for his work did not include his collaborator Fred Emery. I marveled at the way these two polar opposites had produced so much together. Their relationship surely validated the cliché about the creative use of differences.

I visited Eric often over the years — in Swarthmore when he taught at the University of Pennsylvania, later when he retired to Florida, then at Denman Island in British Columbia, his happy summer retreat. When we met I would tell him of my latest experiments with work redesigns involving the "whole system in the room" and a future search model based on confronting chaos rather than rigorous analysis. Eric would listen intently, reflect a while, and unfailingly hand me back the same gift — the courage of my convictions. I always came from a talk with him believing that whether something was "practical" was secondary to whether I believed it was the right thing to do.

Eric often would describe the ups and downs of the trilogy he was editing on the work of the Tavistock Institute (Trist and Murray, 1990–1997). Progress always varied with his iffy health. I saw him for the last time a few months before his death in the Carmel, California, apartment where he had moved so that he could watch the Pacific Ocean from his window. In an intimate moment, he told me that for years he had stifled intense feelings of vulnerability certain to well up in anybody whose passion was changing the world. He was sure that "stiff upper lip syndrome" had contributed to his medical crises, including heart surgery.

At the end he grew more introspective, studying Eastern philosophies in counterpoint to Western science and wondering whether there was still time to change himself. On good days, he read, wrote, edited, and answered his mail. The unflappable Beulah Trist — his wife, business manager, secretary, cook, chauffeur, and best friend — energetically organized their lives to make work and good times with friends doable. On bad days, he fretted and slept.

A fact of his biography haunts me. Earlier I wrote that he had descended from a long line of British sea captains. He alone chose Cambridge. The course he charted irrevocably changed the way we encounter the world. Having turned his back on the sea, still he needed to be near it and walked the beach whenever he could. Eric's spirit was large, generous, and timeless as his beloved ocean. He had a great head for ideas, as I have amply shown. It was his great heart I missed most when he was gone.

A Collaboration Resumed

Emery and Trist, after a hiatus of some years, resumed their collaboration in the 1990s. Fred assisted Eric with his Tavistock trilogy, writing key articles and picking up the editing of the sociotechnical volume after Eric's death. Fred died at age 71 at his home in Canberra, Australia, on April 10, 1997, four years after Eric. I met Fred through Eric, and while we never became close, I found him a stimulating person to know. Fred had a tremendous capacity for synthesizing and seeing the big picture. He was generous with his time and his papers when I was writing this book. Fred was a better theorist than consultant. He never became much of a group facilitator, nor, I suspect, did he wish to.

Fred had little patience for meetings. I recall him several times sitting in back, outside the circle, listening, letting people muck around, then coming in with a definitive statement that rendered further conversation unnecessary. Merrelyn Emery was the practitioner, designing and leading hundreds of groups during the development of the Search Conference and Participative Redesign methods. Still it was Fred who suggested that a dialogue among practitioners was the way to test whether there was the basis for the book that became *Discovering Common Ground* (Weisbord et al., 1992). And both Emerys' insights in that book helped many others crystallize their thinking and improve their practices.

Eric Trist, self-effacing and open to anything, had enormous curiosity. Fred Emery, a blustery character, had a hard time with ideas that did not fit his frameworks. I was conscious in writing *Productive Workplaces Revisited* of my debt to Fred for his awesome intellectual creativity, to Eric for his unfailing support, and to both for their remarkable insights and collaborative writings.

Part Two

TRANSFORMING THEORY INTO PRACTICE AND PRACTICE INTO THEORY

> The transformation of our culture and our society
> would have to happen at a number of levels. If it
> occurred only in the minds of individuals (as to
> some degree it already has), it would be powerless.
> If it came only from the initiative of the state, it
> would be tyrannical. Personal transformation
> among large numbers is essential, and it must not
> only be a transformation of consciousness but must
> also involve individual action. But individuals
> need the nurture of groups that carry a moral
> tradition reinforcing their own aspirations.
>
> —— *Bellah and others*, Habits of the Heart,
> *1985, p. 286*

I retold in Part One the stories of the pioneers who shaped my vision of productive workplaces. I showed how three diverse traditions — scientific management, organization development, and socio-technical systems design — evolved to restore social values eroded by the Industrial Revolution. The change targets — author-itarian supervision, irrational work, unproductive conflict — were derived from widely shared values in our society.

Taylor proposed a technical fix, McGregor a psychological one. Lewin provided an all-purpose process, action research, that could be used with any form of content in changing large systems. Taylor understood the need for cooperation between labor and manage-ment. He sought new work systems to make cooperation attractive. Lewin added the social context of group participation, and the insight that all of us are potential gatekeepers of change. McGregor showed how our assumptions become self-fulfilling prophecies. Emery and Trist altered our concept of work systems, illustrating the unity of work, life, and human institutions. All added to our action repertoire, each making possible constructive activities not previously imagined. And each could be misapplied as well.

If I have learned anything from my time trip it is this: those who set sail to improve innovation and stability, work and working life, quality and output, always come up short if they focus only on technology, only on costs or profits, only on human resources. Pro-ductive workplaces require that people — you, me, everybody — be deeply engaged in understanding and working with economic and technological matters. The only sensible way to make real a commitment to "our people" is to have our people work together in rethinking their own work — as captured in the flip chart "Productive Workplaces." Figuring out how to do that has been a dominant theme for workplace improvers for two decades now.

Today I see many managers and consultants moving toward a more open-ended merger of organizational maps and change theo-ries. The *direction* of movement can't be emphasized too strongly. It is toward broader, more systemic forms of assessment and action, looking at how whole systems function when we want to improve any one part. It is toward including in the assessment as many stakeholders as can be got together at one time. That we don't know exactly how to do all that is not a problem; it's an ongoing agenda for learning.

Now I want to revisit my own groundwork, reconstruct the audit trail, and propose a direction for this learning. Part Two of this second edition contains six chapters. In Chapter Ten I describe how management and consultation evolved away from Taylor's way of approaching problems toward Lewin's, including people and situation both. In Chapter Eleven I illustrate this movement with my own action-research cases, and analyze second-generation applications of Lewin's work. The cases represent a transitional form of management activity unknown in Taylor's day, involving many more people in the problem solving than he did.

The world keeps moving, however, and so must we. In Chapter Twelve I critique my 1970s cases and advocate an evolution beyond Lewin's original model to a new mode of action more suited to fast change. In Chapter Thirteen I speculate on two "whole system" cases that changed my approach toward consultation. For this edition, I also bring all cases up to date.

Historically speaking, this work is still in its infancy. My cases represent baby steps down the road toward productive workplaces, bare hints at the vehicles needed to make the journey suggested in

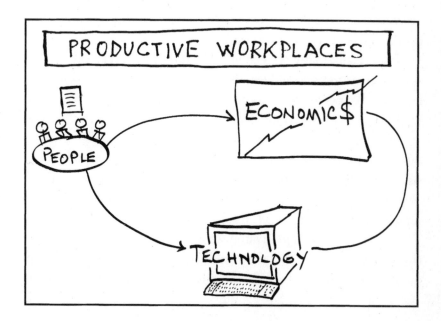

In Search of Excellence (Peters and Waterman, 1982) or *Good to Great* (Collins, 2001) plausible for people who had not thought it up spontaneously. They are, to use an aerospace analogy, like the early DC-3 airliners — bigger, safer, more comfortable, and faster than open-cockpit Jennies, but not big enough, comfortable enough, or fast enough to suit our new expectations.

We are evolving new vehicles for creating more cohesive and more satisfying workplaces. We can't reach the moon yet. We don't have the moral or logistical booster power. Nobody yet knows how to involve everyone in planning and changing large systems. We don't understand entirely how improving a system makes many problems go away. But we're doing a lot better than Taylor did. We are in the midst of what will certainly be seen one day as another revolution. Not only is the world changing, we are changing irrevocably our ways of thinking and working. In fifty years, if we take seriously our aspirations, Taylor's fragmentation of work will be an artifact schoolchildren study in museums.

Part Two of this edition contains two new chapters, Fourteen and Fifteen. With the distance of years I am aware of how much the projects they describe influenced the way I learned to practice what I preached: getting everyone improving the whole. Both cases, paradoxically, involved training workshops, one in a hospital, the other in a steel mill.

For decades many of us believed that training everybody in new skills and attitudes would lead to a revolution in organizations. We assumed that people were not ready, willing, or able to improve their workplaces without training in — pick your diagnostic lens — conflict management, communications, negotiation skills, group dynamics, problem solving, cultural sensitivity, Transactional Analysis, assertiveness, sociotechnical analysis, statistical process control, or (fill in your favorite). Needs analysis ruled, and training aimed to remedy people's deficiencies, the better to enable collective action.

A cultural change strategy consisted of putting everyone through workshops. We theorized that when every person, top, middle, and bottom, had the same inputs and practiced the same skills, they would act to transform an organization's culture. That turned out to be an iffy proposition. Many of us discovered something we already knew from having worked assiduously on our own personal growth. Even when we could change our own behavior, we had a much harder time changing organizational policies, procedures, and systems.

Alas, individual education did not lead to systems improvement. People improved themselves more than they improved their organizations. The reason was not far to seek. Individual training mainly took place in peer groups. Many of us in the 1970s thought it risky business to have people from different hierarchical levels learn together. Neither bosses nor subordinates wished to reveal their vulnerabilities. Yet, nobody gained influence on the whole attending peer-group workshops.

Still, the fantasy persisted. Training could level the barriers to better systems. Hence "flavor of the month" programs came and went like songbirds with the seasons. We were always getting people ready to do something they never got to do. They acquired skills to be open, confront conflict, appreciate differences, value positive experiences, diagnose negative ones, set goals, and assert truth. What they did not acquire in workshops was influence, let alone power — over policy, procedure, system, and structure.

Changing Systems Without Prior Training

Still, education is independently valuable. You can't have too much interpersonal and group skill or cross-cultural awareness. Learning ought to be a lifelong quest, and people need technical skills on the job. Yet, training up to change an organization's culture year after year without playing a real game was a recipe for cynicism. Little by little, some of us began to think differently about the role of training in systems change. Suppose we could come together just the way we were, with whatever nature had dealt us genetically, behaviorally, ethnically, and hierarchically? Rather than train in peer groups to learn skills we might never use effectively, we could join together in diverse groups that collectively had their arms around the whole system and go right to work on consequential systemic matters rather than our personal shortcomings. Accepting ourselves as is — without having to be fixed first — could be a good starting place. We could change systems in ways no one had thought possible, using the knowledge and experiences we already had if . . . now here comes the big IF . . . if we had access *all at once* to resources, authority, expertise, and information.

This concept did not negate the value of training, nor of coaching or individual therapy. It suggested other forms of activity entirely. Assume for a moment that a high percentage of systemic organizational problems are structural, meaning who is allowed to do what. If you asked, workers everywhere would tell you what the Indiana farmer told the tractor salesman: "Sonny, I ain't farmin' now as well as I know how." When people cannot use at work the capabilities they already have, then bad behavior becomes a symptom, not a cause. Bad structures and bad behavior are mutually reinforcing, to be sure. However, the way to make significant systems change is to set it up so that people can use what they are learning to alter the systems they work in right away, if not in a workshop, than shortly after.

This means empowering in real time, not learning concepts of empowerment for future use. The quickest way to empower people in real time, I learned, was to "get the whole system in the room" and create a relatively level playing field. Now more paradox. I was greatly reinforced in this conclusion because of two remarkable *training* experiences. In both cases we violated a critical norm. Instead of homogeneous peer groups, we trained people from many levels and functions at once.

Chapter Fourteen describes a workshop to develop a curriculum for doctors, nurse practitioners, and pharmacists learning primary care program management together. Chapter Fifteen, a story from the steel industry, tells how I learned that systems thinking, to be of use in workplaces, needed to be translated into experiences anyone, conceptual thinkers or not, could have for themselves.

Chapter Ten

Adding Action to Research: Lewin's Practice Theory Road Map

Now they wanted . . . *manual control of the rocket!*
They weren't kidding! . . . How could they be
serious! — the engineers would say. Any chance of
a man being able to guide a rocket from inside a
ballistic vehicle, a projectile, was so remote as to be
laughable. This proposal was so radical the engineers
knew they would be able to block it. It was no
laughing matter to the seven pilots, however.
—— *Tom Wolfe*, The Right Stuff, *1980, p. 161*

In one memorable scene in Tom Wolfe's astronaut fable, the Apollo pilots force engineers to modify the first capsule, adding a window, an escape hatch, and manual controls. They renamed it a spacecraft. When an engineer cites high costs, one astronaut says, "No bucks, no Buck Rogers!" The dialogue crackles with tension between designers and pilots. Engineers and astronauts enact a high-tech version of omniscient parent and dependent child — Theory X comes to outer space. It is an exact replay of the process Taylor elevated to a high art. (In 1986 a similar organizational disconnect and narrow cost focus led to the space shuttle *Challenger* disaster.) Also known as the medical, or doctor-patient, model, it's typical of our transactions with authority figures, from schoolteachers and psychologists to plumbers and electricians.

The Wright brothers designed, built, and flew the first airplane themselves. Theirs was a triumph of systems thinking, a wedding of experimentation, intuition, cooperation, and persistence. They would not risk their lives until they had worked through all the details. The first astronauts had little to say about the design of the first space vehicle. Far from collaborators, they were considered research subjects. Chimpanzees took the same tests as pilots, and a chimp imported from West Africa became the first "American" in space. The astronauts refused the chimp's contract. Unless they could control the spacecraft, they wouldn't fly.

The engineers' assumptions came right from the "Expert/Medical/Taylor Consulting" model. Here was the traditional scenario, enacted not with uneducated laborers but with sophisticated pilots, most of them trained as engineers themselves.

Going Beyond Taylor

Taylor's model assumed perfect rationality of all actors in the drama. The expert could get all the right data to solve the problem, a triumph of left-brain thought before the right brain was discovered.

A step-by-step tool evolved for rational problem solvers. It was considered the essence of scientific method. "Expert Problem Solving" assumes that every result is traceable to a cause, which only the expert can pinpoint. This model still fits many problems (such as trouble-shooting mechanical breakdowns) and is widely applied in all walks of life, both appropriately and not. Both model and tool omit an astonishing key variable: whether other actors will play their assigned roles. It matters very much *who* gets to apply the model.

The Taylor model is more likely to succeed the simpler the problem, the more the cause and effect correspond, and the less others' motivation matters. Emergencies are classic examples. If clear-air turbulence puts your plane in a dive, rely on the pilot to pull out of it. If peritonitis sets in, trust the surgeon to remove your appendix. And yet I find even these examples unsatisfying. The way a pilot handles emergencies influences whether people fly with that airline again. A surgical patient's mental attitude, influenced by what the surgeon says and does, may be critical to the patient's

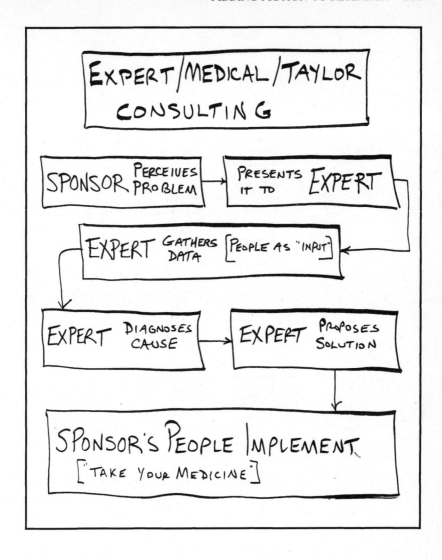

recovery. How the pilot and surgeon are *seen* to act — not just what they accomplish, becomes, in science jargon, a "key variable." Over time the process makes as much difference as technical skill. Norman Cousins (1984), the magazine editor who cured himself of an incurable disease with laughter, has cited many examples of physical changes not explainable by the medical model. They point toward variables beyond traditional problem-solving models. The main *ah-ha* of open-systems thinking is that *everything* counts.

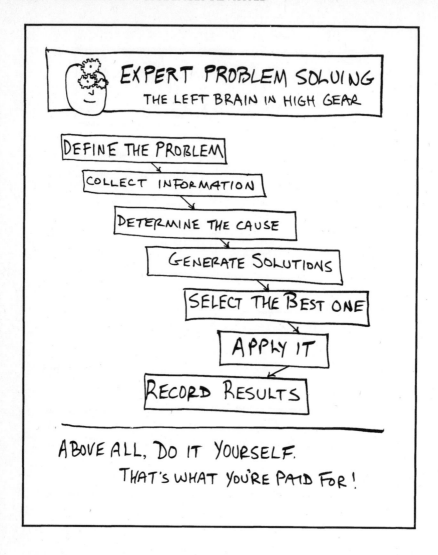

Taylor knew early on that a system to increase cooperation required cooperative people. The more work the expert did alone, the less cooperation could be expected. Indeed, union outrage was a response to the arbitrary way industrial engineers acted, not to the systems themselves. This is hardly surprising in a society where people believe opportunity, free expression, and self-governance are birthrights. The Industrial Revolution pushed people toward passive dependence on the assembly line, the engineer, and the supervisor.

Democratic aspirations pulled them toward more influence over their work.

Yet the tendency of experts to assume knowledge they could not have, or to discount any that did not fit their model, grew in direct proportion to the explosion of technical expertise in the 20th Century. The clouds from that explosion still hang over every workplace. Lewin saw that segmenting knowledge into discrete packages subtly undermined science and democracy as much as breaking work into little pieces. People interact not only with one another but with their environments — the stuff of their work. It is both antidemocratic and unscientific to imagine astronauts would risk their lives in vehicles they could not control. Key variables had been left out.

Adding Action to Research

It was this dilemma that Lewin in the 1940s sought to resolve through action research. His process evolved from his speculations on Taylor's system. He had imagined in the early 1920s that better use of farm implements was more likely to follow from psychologists and farmers teaming up in the field than from laboratory experiments on animals, even the human variety (see Chapter Four). Facing problems that cannot be isolated to a single cause, his descendants have been experimenting ever since with his generic road map for getting from here to there. Lewin intended his enhanced problem-solving model to preserve democratic values, build commitment to act, and motivate learning — all at once. Indeed, some people have renamed the process "action learning" to more accurately indicate its nature (Revans, 1982).

Few concepts have ever been so simple or so powerful. Yet this road map is not the kind you buy from Rand McNally. There are no visual keys for cities, airports, or interchanges, no measuring scales in miles or kilometers. Indeed, our perceptions of the terrain keep changing as we involve more people and learn more about each new situation. The vice-president sees costs going up and blames it on poor motivation in the factory. The workers know they could produce more, but for oppressive supervision. They are both right. It is the systematic relationship between these views that action research addresses.

Every action-research project is different. You can't expect to repeat my procedures and get my results. Why? First; my procedures are not repeatable — exactly. They change with the people, facilities, history, local traditions, unique problems. Real life is not a chemistry lab where all the beakers are the same. Second, you may change the sequence in which you approach a problem, or involve other people, or collect information. Since you can't just change one thing, the first change changes everything. Third, the itch you scratch will always be your own. If you try to scratch my itch, nobody will believe you. In action research, you are part of the action. You cannot stand outside as an objective observer, telling people what's going on and what to do.

A New Look at Expert Problem Solving

Building on Lewin, social scientists by the 1960s evolved in the workplace a significant modification to doctor-patient problem solving. They refined group and interpersonal dynamics, adding wrinkles to alter situations Taylor considered immutable. Resistance, instead of a force to be ignored or wiped out, was seen as a source of energy needing constructive outlets. The emerging model (see "Lewinian Consulting") took account of feelings, attitudes, perceptions. It required that all the people who are key to implementation wrestle with the data together and arrive at a mutually acceptable action plan. What made this a significant advance over earlier problem-solving maps was the shift in relationship between expert and sponsor. Now the expert sought to bring those experiencing the problem into the diagnosis and solution, to treat their reservations and insights as "data," and to consider *their relationships with one another* the key to implementation.

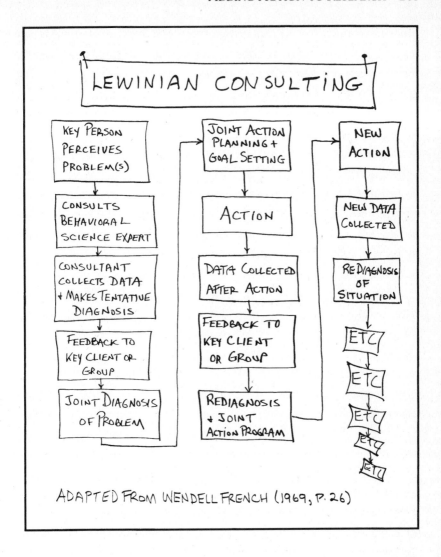

LEWINIAN CONSULTING

KEY PERSON PERCEIVES PROBLEM(S)

CONSULTS BEHAVIORAL SCIENCE EXPERT

CONSULTANT COLLECTS DATA + MAKES TENTATIVE DIAGNOSIS

FEEDBACK TO KEY CLIENT OR GROUP

JOINT DIAGNOSIS OF PROBLEM

JOINT ACTION PLANNING + GOAL SETTING

ACTION

DATA COLLECTED AFTER ACTION

FEEDBACK TO KEY CLIENT OR GROUP

REDIAGNOSIS + JOINT ACTION PROGRAM

NEW ACTION

NEW DATA COLLECTED

REDIAGNOSIS OF SITUATION

ETC

ETC

ETC

ETC

ETC

ADAPTED FROM WENDELL FRENCH (1969, P. 26)

There are no practical reasons why this model should be wholly owned by behavioral science consultants, any more than new work methods only by industrial engineers. The reasons are mainly historical. Taylor early on disdained to join with "industrial social workers" blazing trails parallel to his own. Lewin, alone among his contemporaries, recognized the commonalities. He influenced educators and social scientists to follow the path. Follow it they did, quite separately from engineering types until Trist's coal-mine studies. We have been a long time bringing the two modes of thought back together again. All the modes of action, consultation, and group dynamics I have described in Part One — Lippitt's famous authority-democracy leadership experiments, World War II food studies by Lewin and Margaret Mead, the work of Bion, Sutherland, and Trist in officer selection, Coch and French's change experiments at Harwood, the T-group, sociotechnical work design, community action projects — were milestones in evolving this generic practice theory. But the biggest progress is being made (as in the AECL Medical case; see Chapter Nineteen) where workers, managers, engineers, physical scientists, and accountants cooperate to do valued tasks.

What makes action research unique is the concept that those with a stake in the problem help define and solve it. It becomes a joint venture of clients and consultants, so that everybody learns. Each step involves multiple realities, the views of several people, not simply those of the experts, or top management, or supervisors, or workers, or customers, or suppliers, but all those whose information is relevant. From 100 years of experience, repeating the same patterns over and over again, we can predict social consequences for *any* improvement project: the less involvement of those affected, the less likely will be an implementable solution.

The uses of this insight have proved literally infinite: team development, task forces, training course design, technology transfer, planning cities and towns, rethinking corporate strategies, reorganizing offices and factories, devising futures for states and nations. Had they known how, the first space-vehicle designers might have spared themselves much travail by treating the astronauts as full partners, not just appendages to the capsule.

The Middle of the Movie. The expert always arrives in the middle of somebody else's movie and leaves before the end. Experts unschooled in Lewin's ideas — the Apollo engineers, for example — come to believe they *are* the movie, that only one reality counts.

They assume that past, present, and future dynamics quickly yield to superb technical or economic analysis. Lewin showed why this will not work. Social behavior is *always* a function of the situation in which we find ourselves and vice versa.

So action research became the opposite of scientific research, on which protocol it originally was based. Instead of standing outside the experiment, watching what happens and writing up your findings, you become a learner in a situation you helped devise. You develop a stake. You assume responsibility. A hypothesis (unproved theory) is not a neutral statement of possibility; it is a statement for or against a preferred discovery.

That mental gyration goes down hard in some academic bastions of science. Many social scientists, management scientists, other kinds of scientists, still attempt to get themselves outside the boundaries of experiments, including social experiments, to discover how people behave. The main thing that has been learned from this activity — other than that it makes a safer graduate thesis than narrative or anecdote — is that nobody really gets outside. It's a pretense. "Our findings," to quote management professor Peter Vaill, "follow our lookings" (1979, p. 4).

Lewin saw the process as never-ending, based on trial, error, feedback, learning. He was especially scathing about managers who delegate one-shot change projects. He likened this to a ship's captain ordering a course correction to the right, then going to dinner while the ship sails in circles. What is missing is the feedback loop, which steers the action by its effect outside the vessel rather than its impact within.

This understanding opened the door to a generic form of consultation quite different from that Taylor had pioneered. A new set of personal process skills evolved for relating to individuals, groups, and whole systems in dynamic ways that made constructive change more likely. These skills included testing commitment, making solid working agreements, involving clients in their own problem solving. These skills could be learned independent of other technical, economic, or psychological expertise. They could enhance expertise in marketing, finance, personnel, production, or research. They could be acquired and used by anybody if — a big if — they had the will to learn and the ego strength to fail while doing it.

After Lewin's death, many people began studying and describing a new form of third-party behavior needed to make action learning methods accessible to users through the medium of consultation. NTL Institute (see Chapter Five) has run laboratories in this form of consultation for years. Peter Block (1981) has successfully integrated many perspectives in "Staff Consulting Skills" workshops, where those with technical skill and no formal authority learn practical ways to transfer their knowledge to operating managers.

Survey Feedback. Lewin's way of seeing things stimulated a great many social innovations. The most elaborate spin-off on action research was survey data feedback, invented at the University of Michigan's Institute for Social Research (ISR), where Lewin's Research Center for Group Dynamics moved after his death. ISR's Floyd Mann invented survey data feedback while surveying supervision, promotion, and job satisfaction among 8,000 Detroit Edison employees. Mann fed back his findings in an "interlocking chain of conferences." Departments that discussed their data made more significant changes than those that heard nothing or received feedback only. Face-to-face discussion, not the survey technique, was the key to constructive change. This discovery became the benchmark for effective surveys (Mann, 1957).

Likert's Refinements

While Mann worked on change processes, ISR's Rensis Likert (1961) collected numerous leadership and motivation studies and related them to results. He identified four prototype organizations, named Systems 1, 2, 3, and 4, defined by the degree to which they were open, participative, and satisfying to work in (see "Likert's Systems"). He flagged the boss's behavior as the key variable. Likert

LIKERT'S SYSTEMS				
	1	**2**	**3**	**4**
MOTIVA-TION	SECURITY MONEY	STATUS	GROWTH RECOGNITION	IDENTITY ACHIEVEMENT INFLUENCE
ATTITUDES	HOSTILE	MIXED(−)	MIXED (+)	FAVORABLE
COMMUN-ICATION	DOWN ONLY ↓	MOSTLY DOWN ↓	DOWN AND UP ↓↑	UP, DOWN ↓ ⇄ SIDEWAYS ↑
TEAMWORK	NONE	LITTLE	SOME	MUCH
GOALS SET	TOP DOWN	TOP DOWN	TOP, WITH DISCUSSION	GROUP PARTICIPATION
OUTPUT	MEDIOCRE	FAIR TO GOOD	GOOD	EXCELLENT

ADAPTED FROM NEW PATTERNS OF MANAGEMENT, 1961.

showed that as systems moved toward 4 on his scales, they had lower costs and higher output than those tending toward 1, a finding I have repeated in several factories.

Likert created a diagnostic model, a survey form, and analytical tools for interpreting data (Bowers and Franklin, 1977). Combining his survey with Mann's feedback procedures produced a method for inducing and measuring change in large systems, a grand-design action-research strategy. Until Likert, few managers thought of organizational systems, being more inclined to see the workplace as an aggregate of jobs, following Taylor's lead.

Likert changed their viewpoint by quantifying "soft' processes like control, influence, decision making, and goal setting. He fed this data back to natural work groups. Asked to compare "what is" with "what's desired," people usually opted toward System 4. Problem-solving skill training helped them move that way. Periodic surveys provided progress measurements.

Likert had done a considerable feat. He codified the critical forces in the field and organized them into a questionnaire that could involve hundreds, even thousands, of people in the process of unfreezing, moving, and refreezing. Keying on leadership, he made McGregor's Theory Y assumptions into a comprehensive organization development and information system.

When I started my consulting in 1969, I visited Likert in Michigan and wrote several articles about his work. I understood his ideas intuitively from relating them to the business I had managed for years. In the 1970s I did several surveys using Likert's ideas and methods, though rarely his exact instruments. I report on two of these in the next chapter. The survey is one of those tools that doesn't care how you use it. Surveys can be built on a specific problem like turnover (see Chapter Eleven), treated as a thermometer in a systemic "health checkup," or aimed at company-wide tangles like high costs.

My colleague Eileen Curtin used her own variation on survey feedback more than twenty times to improve office productivity in divisions of General Foods and other companies. She had two major goals: better jobs and lower costs. She would form a participative study team. They would modify a standard survey of common office practices: phone calls, typing, photocopying, dictating. Every person from president to janitor took the survey. The study group fed back its findings one department at a time, seeking consensus on changes to be made.

Curtin's objective was neither to measure change nor to quantify systems behavior. It was to mobilize energy for problem solving by having everybody validate systemic conditions to be changed. Her survey goal was *to build a mandate for change at all levels*, in Lewinian lingo "influencing the gatekeepers" — supervisors and workers — to become involved. The study team validated key issues across departments and recommended actions to top management. The most frequent next steps were task forces across functions, or work-redesign teams in selected departments. These groups consistently improved jobs and cut costs 15 to 40 percent.

Task Forces

The most widely used action research vehicle (though it is probably not thought of that way) is the ad hoc task force. These task
forces became essential to functionally organized companies,
especially in high-tech industries, because functional structures
don't cope very well with fast-changing markets or technologies.
"Participation" was often the reason given for task forces, on the
vague theory that including people was a good thing. Many of us
struggling in the early 1970s with participative management were
unhappy with this simple-minded translation of Lewin's work. We
wanted business-centered participation, and legitimate tasks for
each participant. We insisted that people bring something else,
such as information or skill, in addition to their warm bodies. We
believed that Theory Y assumptions were useless in companies
where every policy, procedure, and system screamed out in contradiction. People needed to work on important tasks, not simply to
give input.

Mary Parker Follett, a person light-years ahead of her contemporaries, had recognized this phenomenon years ago. "It is not the
face-to-face suggestion that we want," she wrote, "so much as the
joint study of the problem, and such joint study can be made best
by the employee and his immediate superior or employee and special expert on that question" (Metcalf and Urwick, 1940, p. 60).
The ad hoc task force made possible such joint study, for it allowed
people to bypass formal structures while they figured out changes in
policies, procedures, and systems. With any luck — Lewin again —
this could be done in such a way that people would learn how to
learn, would absorb the general principles for using task forces on
their own. In Chapter Eleven I recount cases showing the growing
dilemma of enacting these methods while holding fast to values of
productivity, participation, and learning.

Chapter Eleven

Methods of Diagnosis and Action: Taking Snapshots and Making Movies

> According to Lewin, bringing about lasting change means initially unlocking or unfreezing the present social system. This might require some kind of confrontation or a process of reeducation. Next, behavioral movement must occur in the direction of desired change, such as a reorganization. Finally, deliberate steps must be taken to ensure that the new state of behavior remains relatively permanent. These three steps are simple to start but not simple to implement.
>
> —— *W. Warner Burke*, Organization Development: Principles and Practices, *1982, p. 48*

During the 1970s I explored every method I could find for helping organizations change using Lewin's generic road map. I did surveys, interviews, participant observation, research, and so many varieties of groups they all blur together. I used a dozen organization models to plan the questions and structure the diagnostic snapshot. My assumptions were based on the only change model I knew. The consultant was a change agent, whose objective was to help systems unfreeze, move, and refreeze. The diagnosis — from surveys, interviews, or whatever — was intended to confront the gap between what people did and what they said. I never questioned that this step was essential for unfreezing.

Lewin's model assumed the natural resistance of systems to change. It also assumed (a Taylor-like belief right from the old paradigm) that social science could do something proactive about that. Participation (a social process) and force field analysis (a rational problem-solving tool), or some variants thereof, could make enough heat to melt any iceberg.

Lewin had described — magnificent paradox — the "creation of permanent change" (1951, p. 224). Who would not wish to do that? I fell in love with the concept of diagnosis, with its rich overtones of prediction and control. I also discovered systems thinking. I became aware that my group dynamics training led to defining problems in social-psychological terms, mainly related to personal styles, interpersonal relationships, and group norms (unwritten rules). "Social researchers," wrote William F. Whyte of this adaptation of Lewin, "tended to concentrate almost exclusively on human relations. We gave lip service to the importance of technology but tended to treat it as a constant instead of as a variable, which could be changed along with changes in human relations" (1984, p. 168).

In my six-box model (Weisbord, 1978b) I sought to remedy this by introducing purposes, structure, rewards, and helpful mechanisms connected to relationships and leadership. I still used medical terminology, a paradigm in transition. Working in medical schools, though, I realized that the best doctors used their own model sparingly. "There are three things I can do for a patient," my friend Dave Wagner, a surgeon and a founder of emergency medicine, told me one day. "I can cut them, I can drug them, or I can counsel them. Increasingly I find myself counseling them."

No sooner had I written a book on diagnosis but I grew uneasy with the medical concept — and said so in the book (Weisbord, 1978b, p. 67). I began using the terms *snapshots* and *movies* in place of *diagnosis* and *action* as a way of reducing my own subtle reinforcement of processes I found self-limiting. The snapshot was a picture of the action frozen at one point in time long enough to identify conditions to be changed. A good movie, I believed, required that a large cast join in taking the snapshot, owning up to the dilemmas, taking corrective actions. Two of the cases that follow employ a generic survey method that can be used with any diagnostic theory to fit many organizational problems. One survey used Likert's diagnostic model (1967), another a model devised by Paul Lawrence and Jay Lorsch (1967). All cases employed a feedback meeting. They assumed that systems required consultant-induced unfreezing before they could move.

These cases exemplify the consulting practice Peter Block, Tony Petrella, and I sought to develop when we teamed up in the early 1970s. We wanted to develop a consultancy built on consequential business goals, rather than vague concepts like team development, participation, or organizational effectiveness. We also wished, paradoxically, to bring process learning more into the foreground, to encourage people to think of management as an interplay between task and process. Sometimes we used no specific, formal theories of organization to take the snapshot. Often we derived actionable theories from the client's own experience, what Max Elden (1983b), working with similar ideas in Norway, called "local theory." Above all we were committed to the power of intangibles like dignity, meaning, community, support, openness, responsibility, and collaboration. What we learned is that these come alive only when people are involved in doing important tasks.

Of course we had our failures, especially in training workshops based on somebody else's diagnosis and prescription. In retrospect, I think we were successful more often than not because our business focus led us to high-risk, high-payoff situations. The motivation for change, I now believe, came from the compulsion of people in authority to scratch a persistent itch. This factor, as I suggest in Chapter Sixteen, was more important than the "unfreezing" power of our methods. But that is getting ahead of my story.

These cases were largely problem-focused and consultant-centered. However, there was an evolution taking place, visible with 20/20 hindsight. Our methods and models were changing, propelling us toward new forms for snapshots and movies and greater unity of the two concepts. In the 1970s my colleagues and I became increasingly aware of how external forces — the marketplace, suppliers, regulators — influenced solutions as much as interpersonal and group skills. Our telephoto lenses gave way to wide angles. In parallel we grew increasingly uneasy about doing so much of the diagnostic work for clients. We wanted them more firmly in charge of the camera and the writing of the script. The first case illustrates classic Lewinian action research, problem-focused, showing the best that participative experts could do back then.

Case 1. Classical Action Research: The Food Services Turnover Problem (1970–1971)

> Heck, we have data from India, Pakistan, Sweden too. Beer salesmen in Sweden. The more the supervisors use System 4, the more beer the salesmen sell. But if you don't think it applies to you, collect the data. Find out what the differences are between your own high- and low-producing departments.
>
> —— *Rensis Likert, in Weisbord,*
> Conference Board Record, 1970, p. 16

The president of Food Services, operators of cafeterias in factories, colleges, and hospitals, wanted to bring social science thinking into his fast-growing firm, which then had no management training. A voluntary seminar was convened of operating managers, dieticians, and financial and personnel staff to consider new theories, methods, and experiences in other firms. (Some company names in these case histories have been fictionalized.)

Rensis Likert's "human resource accounting" ideas immediately attracted the group. Likert (1967) had said that treating hiring, training, and people development as investments rather than costs could change the way a company is managed. Our seminar soon found a high potential opportunity to test that idea: food service unit turnover, a social problem with serious economic consequences.

The Costs of Turnover. A typical cafeteria had from ten to sixty employees: manager, cashier, chef, cooks, food preparers, servers, dishwashers. People worked long hours for low wages under adverse conditions. Human resource accounting revealed that it cost an average of more than $300 to recruit, orient, train, and set up files for each new-hire. The previous year this company of 35,000 people issued paychecks to more than twice that number — more than 100 percent turnover. Even by conservative figures (double-checked by the financial staff), unit turnover was costing more than $10 million a year, an amount equal to total profits!

The company had accepted high turnover for decades as an unalterable business cost. Yet a curious thing was going on here. Turnover varied from 6 to 800 percent across units within the same company. Why the differences?

Scanning turnover figures from more than 100 units, we defined "high" as 120 percent a year or more, and "low" as less than 60 percent. We soon noticed that *all* categories — utility, supervisory, and food preparation — turned over two and a half times as often in the high-turnover units as in the low. This pattern suggested major unit differences that had more to do with the work system than with job categories.

Mark Frohman, then a graduate student at Michigan, and I devised a comparative study of high- and low-turnover units, using a home-built variation on Likert's survey. We interviewed managers and collected their turnover theories, which were associated with type of union contract, geographic location, percentage of women, employees' ages, type of service contract, number of shifts. We added other theories based on work at the Institute for Social Research, such as manager support for new-hires, tools and equipment, and on-the-job training. We tested a thirty-nine item survey, then selected ten units for the formal study, four with low turnover (40 to 60 percent), two medium, and four high (120 percent or more).

Both high- and low-turnover units showed similar patterns in employee ages, length of service, job categories, types of union and

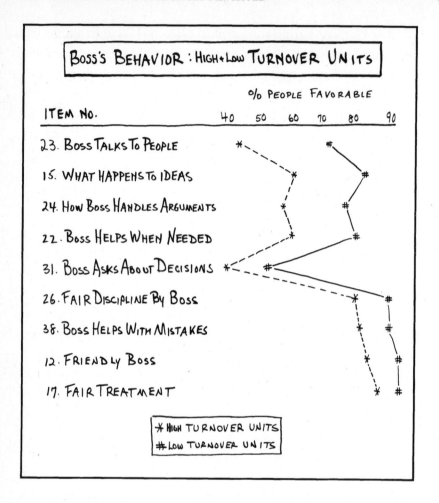

service contracts, number of shifts, and labor and food budget deviations. None of these accounted for turnover. The survey data strongly confirmed differences in manager behavior. Low-turnover unit people responded more favorably than high to thirty-one of thirty-nine questions. Most striking was that employees in low-turnover units believed they had better orientation and training, more helpful and friendly unit managers, and more chances to advance than those in high-turnover units. They also showed greater satisfaction with their jobs and pay (even though all were paid the same in each job).

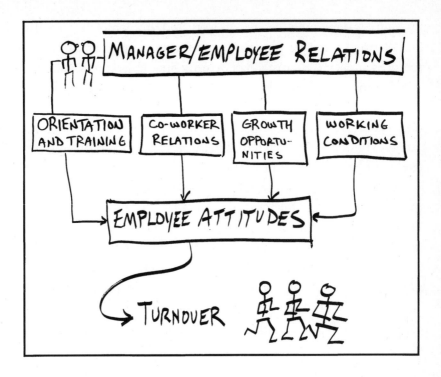

A set of graphs made the point dramatically. "Boss's Behavior" shows the response pattern on one cluster of nine related items. (Note this corporate version of the democratic behavior used by Lippitt and White in their pioneer studies of boys' club leadership described in Chapter Four.)

To help managers interpret the graphs, we drew a map of the turnover problem, based on Likert's theory of management behavior (see "Manager/Employee Relations" chart). Turnover resulted from employee attitudes shaped by management actions in four specific areas, which of course might differ in other companies.

Reducing Turnover. With one region's managers we worked out an experimental program to change turnover-related conditions. Unit managers were offered training based on survey and turnover data collected from their own units, which they could compare with the company-wide study. In four workshops they reviewed their own survey data, practiced supervisory and problem-solving skills, and planned turnover-prevention activities. Action research was repeated at each step. Instead of hearing how-to lectures, managers listed things they thought new employees wanted to know and things they needed them to know. Then they role played orientation meetings and critiqued their own ability to get across important points. They also met with senior managers to discuss problems that could not be solved at unit level.

We compared turnover in units whose managers took the training with those whose managers did not. Of twenty-seven participating units, twenty-four reduced turnover. One twenty-nine-person unit, which had thirty-seven turnovers the year before, had none the year after the experiment. The experimental region cut its overall turnover rate by 50 percent in a year when the company-wide figure climbed to 143 percent — a dramatic confirmation of participative action research for solving previously unsolvable management problems.

Change took many other forms. New policies and procedures were established; training was extended to other regions by internal company staff (who learned with us). District managers, one level above units, also asked for training. This led to a series of week-long district manager workshops, the start of a management development curriculum. Within three years the use of experience-based training methods went from nonexistent to an integral part of the company management — the president's objective in sponsoring the original seminar.

Limits of Likert Theory. Mann and Likert developed their organizational survey forms and methods with business firms. Likert's industrial research showed that System 4 organizations were likely to outperform System 1 organizations over time. Food Services is one of many business firms where I have repeated his findings. The methodology also has been adapted to schools, nonprofit agencies, and government departments. I have found applications in human service agencies and colleges much more problematical than in factories. Likert-type surveys illuminate systems where goals are concrete, formal authority is easily recognized, people must work together to get results, and output is easily measured. Remove any of these conditions and you see that the systematic effects of a particular management style begin to blur like an out-of-focus photograph. Physicians and scientists, for example, expect to maintain control of their own work, no matter who their boss is. They have little understanding of task interdependence, organizational goals, and output measures.

The Likert lens can't "see" what is going on in nonlinear systems because it is designed to look for patterns more firmly anchored in high interdependence, repetitive work patterns, and measured output. Likert himself recognized this. Years ago I showed him a medical school survey, using his instruments. Maintenance, housekeeping, and food service units varied the way they should, influenced by supervisor behavior. But academic departments were all over the map; they showed no consistent response patterns within or between. Likert examined the profiles, smiled, and said, "What you have here is System Zero." How do you induce change in such systems? Not with surveys, not by focusing on the boss's behavior. In Chapter Thirteen, I show in Case 5, based on a project in the same medical school, that "System Zero" needs new structures to influence cooperative action.

Turnover Update at Food Services

Food Services metamorphosed several times after I left in the mid-1970s. Founded as Automatic Retailers of America (ARA) in 1959, the company grew rapidly. In the late 1960s it got into magazine and book distribution, and later added uniform, environmental, healthcare, and child care services. As a public company, it became a candidate for hostile takeovers. The management organized a buyout, acquiring 70 percent of the company. By 1994, still growing, it changed its name to ARAMARK. By 2000 it had numerous divisions in business and campus food and many other services, and it became a public company again in 2001.

Although my old contacts were gone, in January 2003 I spoke with the human resource vice president for the Business Services

Division, David Kahn, and sent him a copy of the earlier case study. "It's remarkable how little things have changed," he said, "You were certainly ahead of the curve with turnover thirty years ago." "Manager quality is surely the key to cutting turnover," he continued. "People don't quit companies, they quit managers." He did a rundown of the extensive manager curriculum that had evolved at ARAMARK. In offsite workshops new managers learned the importance of imparting clear goals and expectations, offering feedback, and providing chances for employee development.

Manager trainees also were assigned to selected units where experienced managers, trained as coaches, helped them learn the ropes. Kahn also pointed out the importance of a stable hourly force, used to being supervised by a string of trainees and willing to assist in manager training too. Also it was company policy to provide more full-time jobs with secure pay and benefits, a key to developing a mature workforce. In consequence, turnover, Kahn said, was now averaging about 62 to 65 percent at ARAMARK, and considerably less among managers. "If you treat people poorly they're not going to stay," he added. "If you make it a great place to work, people respond, and do a much better job of serving customers."

Industry Norms in 2003

Back online, I checked out the current state of employment in the food services industry. Sure enough, turnover, like death and taxes, remained a certainty. Rates of 100 percent or more were still common. With better manager and employee training and orientation, many firms were able to keep a lid on this expensive headache (Ebbin, 1999).

Some had won industry awards for turnover reduction. Buffets, Inc., for example, with restaurants in thirty-seven states, cut manager turnover from 38 percent to 24 percent over the five years starting in 1997 by focusing on training and rewards. A comparative study showed that hourly employee turnover rates were 20 percent lower in restaurants participating in one of its employee-focused programs.

Another chain, Ground Round Grill & Bar, won an "Employer of Choice" award for reducing general manager turnover, considered key to successful attraction, hiring, education, training, retention, and inspiration of other employees. Through coaching, workshops, rewards, newsletters, and surveys, the company cut manager turnover from 70 percent in 1997 to 29 percent in 2002. More importantly, the managers, in a validation of Likert's model of leadership behavior, decreased unit employee turnover from 150 percent in 1997 to 90 percent in 2002 (Source: National Restaurant Association Educational Foundation website).

In summary, the 1970 objectives and programs at Food Services were by the end of the century an industry norm. Given the nature of front-line food service work, only a few firms had figured out how to keep hourly employee turnover below 100 per cent. ARAMARK among the largest, with a workforce approaching 250,000, was still on the frontier.

Case 2. Enlarging the Playing Field: Chem Corp's Client-Centered Survey Feedback (1978–1979)

> From this vantage point we can see why conflict must be accepted as a continuing result of living in a complex civilization. Resolution is not then put up as some final Utopian answer, but simply as a sensible solution to today's issue — with awareness that basic and legitimate differences will generate new conflicts to be resolved tomorrow. From this baseline managers can move more directly toward designing procedures and devices that are adequate for processing the flow of conflicted issues that will surely arise.
>
> —— *Paul R. Lawrence and Jay W. Lorsch,* Organization and Environment, *1967, p. 224*

This case describes a problem-focused survey of a different order from Food Services. First, the angle of vision is wider, taking in relationships among all departments in the company. The snapshot is taken with a homemade survey tool derived from a different research tradition than Likert's — based on studying how functional departments adapt to their environments.

Second, I learned here that, for surveys to work, it is not essential that consultants collect and feed back data. It may not even be desirable. In this case the clients helped develop the survey, collect data, and interpret results, becoming more central in their own movie. And the feedback was handled by those with the biggest stake in making improvements — the managers themselves. Here's how it happened.

Every department in Chem Corp — engineering, manufacturing, sales, and finance — criticized R&D. Maybe it had to do with the new glass-and-steel building from which only a trickle of new products emerged. Maybe it had to do with perceived slow responses to emergency service calls. Whatever the reasons, the scientists were under pressure. I learned of this situation in a team meeting of the president's staff.

The vice-president in charge of R&D, an outspoken company veteran, was viewed by his peers with affectionate mistrust. R&D, as in many other companies, played a dual role. It was responsible both for developing new products and for trouble-shooting process glitches. The vice-president argued that his department spent much of its budget on crises in many small plants scattered around the country. He did not have the resources to make a first priority of both long- and short-range goals.

The vice-president readily agreed to a meeting of *his* team to talk over what they might do. Nobody liked the situation. Everybody had a favorite "bad guy" in another department. An action-research plan soon emerged. We would design a customer survey (considering other departments as "customers" of R&D) to pin down dissatisfactions and air the resource-allocation dilemma throughout the company. It would be given only if the vice-president's peers agreed to participate. That meant encouraging their people to respond and to review results afterward with their R&D contacts.

A Company Priority. Top managers quickly sanctioned the project. Cooperation with R&D became a new priority. The R&D managers brainstormed everything-they-always-wanted-to-know-about-their-relationships-with-other-departments-but-were-afraid-to-ask. I drafted a simple R&D effectiveness survey testing each item: response time, quality, service availability, new product development, cooperation. Space was allowed for open-ended responses.

To get at the process side, I added conflict management questions from Paul R. Lawrence and Jay W. Lorsch (1967), whose contingency theory I had found useful with scientists in medical schools (Weisbord, Lawrence, and Charns, 1978). This theory says that when organizations set up departments with the right goals, time horizons, and boundaries for their *own* environment, this inevitably means conflict with departments needing other structures. Managing conflict constructively, not getting rid of it,

---

Sample Question.

22. Have you in the last 12 months experienced strong disagreement or conflict with anyone in R&D?
    _____ No   _____ Mild Disagreement   _____ Yes

If "yes" please compare the way conflict was handled by R&D and by yourself using the definitions below. Check two modes most often used by self and two by R&D.

Self R&D

Self	R&D		
___	___	Forcing:	People use "power plays."
___	___	Smoothing:	People discuss differences as if no substantive issues exist.
___	___	Avoiding:	People avoid raising sticky issues.
___	___	Bargaining:	People split differences trying to maximize their own interests.
___	___	Confronting:	Despite tension, people openly discuss differences seeking mutually acceptable solutions.

```
┌─────────────────────────────────────────────────┐
│   ┌──────────────────────────────────────────┐  │
│   │ CHANGING PERCEPTIONS OF R+D              │  │
│   └──────────────────────────────────────────┘  │
│                                                  │
│   "CUSTOMER" UNIT            % CHANGE 1978-79    │
│                                                  │
│   SUBSIDIARY A                  +  0.9           │
│   CORPORATE PLANNING            +  5.6           │
│   ENGINEERING                   + 13.5           │
│   STAFF OPERATIONS              + 14.8           │
│   FINANCE                       + 16.2           │
│   PLANT OPERATIONS              + 21.7           │
│                                                  │
│   OVERALL AVERAGE               + 10.9           │
│                                                  │
└─────────────────────────────────────────────────┘
```

becomes a criterion for success in high-performing companies. The engineers and scientists liked the more practical and honest assumption that conflict was a two-way street with traffic going both ways. See "Sample Question."

More than 100 forms came back. The R&D managers and I spent a day analyzing the data and organizing a feedback plan. One interesting finding was the tendency of other functions to see R&D forcing, smoothing, and avoiding more often, and themselves bargaining and confronting more — just the opposite of R&D's view. Another was that the more different a department's orientations from R&D's, the more likely the two would be in conflict, which was predicted by Lawrence and Lorsch's previous research. The most significant result, however, was not in the data. It was a new spirit among research managers, who shucked the "poor us" posture and set out to confront the resources question.

Discussion Meetings. Each R&D manager scheduled feedback meetings with other functions. They conducted these themselves, reviewing the data with their "customers" and planning joint action steps. Informally I asked people in other departments how

COMPARATIVE R+D PERFORMANCE

	APRIL 1978	JUNE 1979	% CHANGE
TIMELINESS	3.59	2.65	+26.2%
TECHNICAL QUALITY	2.77	2.38	+14.1
UNDERSTANDING AND SUPPORT	3.20	2.37	+25.9

1 = MOST, 5 = LEAST FAVORABLE

things were going; their responses ranged from "It's about time" to "I still don't trust them but at least we're talking." Many action steps came from these meetings, including closer cooperation, more frequent exchanges of information, and budget reallocations.

A resurvey the next year showed dramatic improvements in several key indicators. One way results were dramatized was to average responses across seven items: timeliness, technical quality, business mission, sensitivity to department needs, understanding/ support, competence, and performance. Averages were compared for each department with the previous year's figures. See "Changing Perceptions of R&D" and "Comparative R&D Performance" — two of several charts used in feedback discussions.

Again the R&D managers fanned out to address problems highlighted by the survey. The R&D vice-president remained on the job and the function became more respected and important. From 1978 to 1986 R&D produced more than 150 new product ideas.

It is hard to say how "frozen" Chem Corp was before the survey. The ready agreement of top managers to join in the effort was certainly a function of the need for new products to complement the flat sales of the company's major commodity. However, the survey, framed on ideas from Lawrence and Lorsch, was intended as a survey feedback exercise to change intergroup dynamics. It was based on comparing mutual perceptions and stimulating energy to problem solve issues raised across each boundary. I see its value now as demonstrating (contrary to conventional survey feedback practice) that clients could facilitate their own changes. They did not need a consultant present in each joint discussion to make sure the correct diagnosis was reached and action steps written down.

Chem Corp Twenty Years Later

In the spring of 2000 I phoned an old friend at Chem Corp. He had been a key player in the R&D work more than twenty years earlier and remained in senior management. We exchanged pleasantries and caught up on each other's families. What, I asked, at last, had happened with R&D?

There were, he told me, a spate of new products in the eight years following the project. During that time the feisty head of R&D retired. The survey was forgotten. Chem Corp R&D still occupied the same laboratory building, although the corporate headquarters had since moved. The number of staff employees fluctuated with market conditions.

Despite the new ideas from the 1980s, despite the greater acceptance of R&D by other units, few new products were coming off the laboratory benches. To improve customer relations, the company had given the business managers a dotted line responsibility for technical staff related to their businesses. Engineering, for example, a particularly sticky wicket, was now housed under plant operations.

The company again had trouble scaling up new products from pilot plant to production. The vast cultural divide between the people of science and the people of action widened once more. "The business managers," said my friend, "want a project that needs a year and $15 million, to be done for $8 million in six months." As a result, they had frustrating delays, missed deadlines, and longer lead times to market. In short, our survey feedback project of twenty years earlier had great short-term impact. Like Solcorp (Case 4, to follow), no form of consultation could make up for inherent dilemmas of managing a technological swirl in a volatile marketplace.

When I spoke to the former president in 2003, he agreed that departmental relations with R&D backslid in the 90's. That was not the whole story. The company also did well with a new product technbology on which it had the inside track. From 1970 to 2000, he pointed out, the cumulative increase in shareholder return on equity was 7 1/2 times that of the Standard and Poor's 500 corporation benchmark. "We moved from a paternalistic, high control company to high involvement starting with the work you did back in the 1970's," he said, referring to team building and leadership workshops that were done in parallel with the work with R&D. "We felt the long term impact of that work throughout the company for years after."

Inventing "Local Theory." Next, I will revisit two cases built on another action-research spin-off, the invention of "local theory" from the pooled perceptions of those closest to the problem. This is still consultant-centered work, at least initially. However, the effort to enlarge the snapshot beyond relationships and motivation — to show connections among relationships, structure, and purpose in local terms appropriate to each client — reflects a further evolution of practice. In this case we are moving toward making two forces — open systems thinking and the empowerment of clients to act for themselves — increasingly practical.

One case involves an effort to improve productivity in a factory where management had made unfounded assumptions about employee capability, the second a race to save a new solar energy company from strategic ruin. In each, top managers had concluded that the problem called for changing people's behavior. In practice we make outside forces more central in the snapshots. The consultants still do a lot of the work, but we are enlarging the context of the discussion to include history, the changing marketplace, and changing technology in addition to the behavior of key players.

Case 3. Wrong Problem, Right Solution: Packaging Plant Meets a Mess in the Marketplace (1979)

> They're good people. They're just not used to
> cranking out large quantities. I want them more
> involved in running the business.
> —— *Vice-President for Operations, Packaging Plant*

For years Packaging Plant's lackluster products made a comfortable living for its family owners. When it was sold to an international giant, the new management — professional marketers to the core — began a Madison Avenue blitz to wipe out emerging competition. Suddenly sales went up like a rocket. The plant could not meet consumer demand. The operations vice-president attributed this setback to the fact that workers had never been asked before to produce so much so fast — a kind of work ethic crisis. He agreed to an experiment.

We assembled twenty-eight people who might know something about how the products were packaged — lead operators, schedulers, a production planner, mechanics, quality control inspectors, managers, supervisors. Two consultants (William Smith and I) offered to interview people individually about the situation and conduct a meeting to talk over what we learned.

People were skeptical, wary, unsure what management was really after. In interviews, however, they readily described what was going on. Two weeks later the consultants papered the conference room with newsprint charts about the current problems, the company's history, and its dramatic changes — in technology, government regulation, the marketplace, and relations with the parent firm. We included a map of four conditions that must be met for a packaging operation to function:

1. Quality control must release good product from manufacturing.
2. Bottles, labels, boxes, brochures, and cartons must arrive from inventory.

3. A mechanic must spend four to eight hours setting up the line for a new run.

4. Operators must start up and test the line.

Unless all items arrive before the mechanic does, the line cannot run. See "Coordination Means . . ."

At this company, production planning (a Taylor invention) controlled schedules using a master called the green sheet. It actually was blue, and it was often wrong. It showed labels in inventory that were on the unloading dock, supposedly released product that was still in manufacturing, bottles available but not the right size. Things were changing so fast the green sheet could not keep up. When mechanics showed up to do a line change, they often found a necessary component missing. Market swings reverberated through the system to show up as missing items at setup time. The problem was coordination, not worker competence. See "Market Conditions."

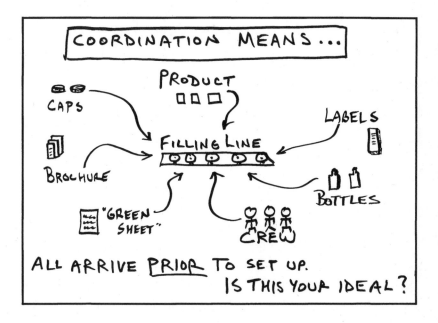

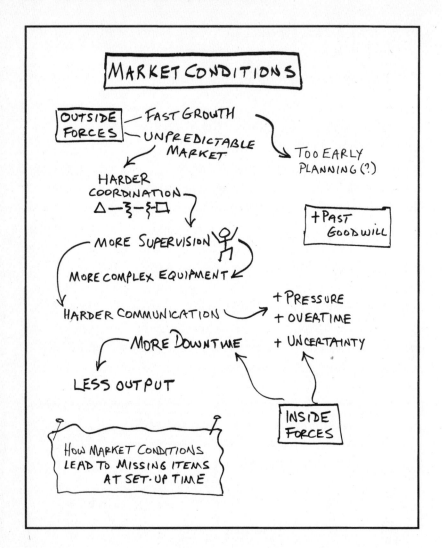

The workers, middle managers, and staff people had a richer, more complex systems view of what was happening than the boss did — a phenomenon I had experienced as a manager in the 1960s, and one confirmed by Elden's "local theory" experiments in Norway (1983b). Managers everywhere had begun to experience this phenomenon more and more often from the 1960s onward. It was no longer functional to go right into problem solving. We needed what Geoffrey Vickers (1965) had called an "appreciation" of the whole system before the right problem could be solved.

Spurred by the broader interpretation of their own data, the group acknowledged that hourly workers had no control over what was happening. This confirmed the intuition of a systems analyst assigned to improve the green-sheet system. Until then he could not get a hearing for his ideas. A multifunction task force was organized. They mapped the system together in detail, identifying exactly where things went wrong. Within a few weeks they ironed out many problems that had plagued the factory ever since sales increased. Production went up dramatically. The green sheet, however, stayed blue.

Packaging Plant Revisited

About ten years after the events just described I received a call from a Packaging Plant staff person. The company was enjoying boom years, sales going up, with new products in the pipeline. The pressure was on for production, quality, and cost-cutting. There had been many plant managers since I was last there. Now an energetic newcomer had taken over. I sent the new manager the work design chapter from this book. We set up a lunch. He embraced with great enthusiasm the idea of an employee-based plant redesign. He thought people ought to own their jobs, take pride in their work, and feel responsible for results. He couldn't wait to start.

Jill Janov and I undertook interviews to test the feasibility of a work design project. When asked what they thought of getting everyone involved, many managers said, in effect, "Not much." As one recalled years after, "We had no model for trusting one another. The risk was pretty big. We were conditioned to operate independently, making ourselves look good and being rewarded for it. The workforce was used to an endless parade of managers coming in, declaring productivity, safety, or whatever to be the most important thing, getting some improvements, and moving on." Suffice to say there was a long ramp-up for this project — months of meetings and many conversations centering on "readiness." (We still were doing a form of time-intensive diagnosis to gain commitment. I doubt people would sit still for this ramp-up today.)

As the dialogue spread among the workforce of 260 people, some enthusiasts began to emerge. One by one several second-tier managers fell into line, agreeing to support a redesign effort. For some it reflected a wish to please the boss. For others, the idea of workforce involvement had a powerful appeal. The plant manager's boss, the director of manufacturing, agreed to go along on one condition: in two years or less the plant had to show significant gains. If at any point he felt they were not moving that way, he would pull the plug.

Eventually we followed the guidelines in Chapter Sixteen, devising an early version of what Dick Axelrod (2000) would call *The Conference Model*®. Four volunteer teams representing every function in the plant came together to redesign four different processes. Each team included operators, supervisors, engineers, quality inspectors, and managers. The teams decided they wanted everything in plain sight. So they had a soundproof room built in the middle of a cavernous, noisy factory floor. Into this space some sixty employees, a fourth of the workforce, came each week to document the existing system and design a better one.

The teams engaged in a series of two- to three-day workshops, each looking at a different aspect of the factory. The first workshop created an umbrella of values, mission, and goals and was done in the "future search" mode described in Chapter Twenty. The second had people analyzing the technical system, the third the social system, the fourth focused on systems redesign, the fifth on implementation. Between workshops the design teams briefed the rest of the plant on what they were learning and tested new ideas.

Not everyone wanted change. Many employees, hourly and staff, not just managers, were happier with the devil they knew than the one they didn't. "I remember one meeting in the auditorium," a former supervisor told me years later, "where an employee asked the plant manager, 'When is this change going to start?' And he said, 'It already has!' The person didn't know it was happening. We needed strong leadership because so many people didn't want to do it."

Employee-Designed Work Teams

The work came together in dramatic presentations — looking back from the future — of how the various redesigned areas — compounding, filling, processing, packaging, mechanical support services, and others — were "now" operating. People attended from all functions. Many staff from the main corporation, who had offices at the same site, sat in. They were awed and baffled at what the employees had been able to accomplish. The company had never seen anything like this.

The teams redid supervisory functions into a team leadership model. They streamlined paperwork, set up troubleshooting task forces in all areas to root out longstanding problems. They shortened and sped up the product pipeline, rationalized inventory control, making numerous changes to systems and procedures that would surely have bemused Frederick Taylor. Each quarter the plant managers sat down with the manufacturing hierarchy to review the numbers. They were positive and improving.

The transition was hardest on former supervisors. A decade later one recalled how the redesign effort "was scary, different than anything we ever did before." As a team leader, she lost many supervisory responsibilities that now went to the hourly workers. Despite extreme skepticism about the increasing role of hourly people in running the factory, the manufacturing vice-president kept his word and continued to sanction the project. The plant manager was overjoyed. In mid-1989, employees began implementing their plans, setting up a radical new way of managing the plant. Weekly open meetings were held to talk over novel and unprecedented problems. And the numbers kept getting better.

Aye, there's the rub, to steal a line from the leadership secrets of William Shakespeare. A manager who got results like these in a corporation of any size could not expect, and would not want, to remain in the same job too long. Career path planning dictated that you move every few years or see your career stagnate. Inevitably, as the project reached a crescendo and people began to learn how to manage this new culture for the long pull, the plant manager received a job offer he could not refuse. In line with corporate policy, he had no say about his successor, who was brought in from another business to run the plant.

Remembering Changes Past (2002)

When I called the former plant manager twelve years later, I found him in a pre-retirement holding pattern at corporate headquarters. He anticipated the day, not far off, when he could take up a new career of service to his church and community. "The project was not popular with the new management that came in," he recalled. "It was seen as very quirky by the manufacturing establishment. I was an outsider. I only survived because we made the numbers. They put in an engineer to follow me who had grown up in manufacturing. His attitude was, 'We have to put it back to the way it was.'

"After I left," the former plant manager went on, "my new office was still in the building. People would come up to me in the hall to say, 'They're changing things.' Rumors held that there was too much power in the hands of the people, and the new manager was not buying into it." He felt pangs of remorse as people told him how their enthusiasm and commitment were draining away. There was guilt, too, for having raised expectations so high only to have them dashed by his successor. As he saw it, coordination and control were being shifted back to managers and supervisors. Many people were demotivated. Key staff people and managers left the company to take other jobs.

A former team leader remembered the exercise somewhat differently. "Whether you like it or not depends on what happens to your own job," she said. "You can always find people who were enthusiastic and others who simply had to leave." She herself had moved on to a series of staff jobs. In 2002 she was among a very few leaders left who had survived the initial redesign.

Was It Worth the Effort?

When I asked her if she would do it again, she did not hesitate. "Absolutely!" she said. "We went through a huge cultural change, something none of us ever had gone through before." She recalled that the new manager within a few years conducted his own reorganization, in which the employees were also involved. "We could not have done it without the first one," she said. And she added, "I think we should do this sort of thing every two years. The technology and customer needs change so fast that none of these systems lasts very long."

I asked the production manager who had raised the question of trust whether he thought it was worth the effort. "How can you say a system that delivers such positive results is not worth the effort?" he replied. "Isn't management's primary responsibility to optimize shareholder value and work toward the overall health and profitability of a company? Doing it with a fully engaged workforce is what we all should be striving for."

"The most satisfying part for me still," said the former plant manager, "is talking with the people who lived through that first redesign and seeing the impact it had on their lives." He mentioned Donna, an engineer now with a consulting firm, and Mike, a product line production manager now running a non-profit children's agency. "What struck me too," he added, "was how people who were not trained engineers could make such significant changes in the factory. One guy, an hourly line worker, said the most moving thing to me. 'In the old days,' he told me, 'I could check my brain at the door. Now I go home and I worry about the business. I can't help thinking about it. It's part of my life now.'

"The ones who suffered most in this situation," he continued, "were the rank and file workers who struggled to make the turn, had all this excitement and enthusiasm and commitment to the business, and then were told to go back to their machines and stop thinking. Suddenly people had no influence over what was going on. No question, the impact of their work was obvious. The numbers were there. We validated the business model in a very short time frame."

I asked him if he would do it again after what happened. "Oh, certainly!" he replied. "But I would want more control than I had then. I'd need agreement at the highest levels that succession planning would be included, that this was a long-term cultural change, not just an experiment. I would have to be free to hire people who would be open to doing things a new way instead of doing whatever they wanted to make their own mark. I'd need assurances that whoever followed me would carry on in the same spirit.

"When you put so much of yourself in it's revitalizing and exciting to get so much accomplishment. When I look back on my career, that project is what I am most proud of. And I have such high regard for the leadership team that came so far with me in that project. Many of them found new paths for themselves."

He felt no rancor. "The new guy who came in and turned things around again had to make his numbers too. He must have done it or he would have been gone. I guess there is more than one way to do this work."

Learning from "the Environment"

Packaging Plant, like many corporate divisions, had little control of systems that determine the longevity of projects. They were part of its "environment," controlled by remote executives overseeing a global empire. There was a direct link between workplace innovation and corporate career planning. A typical career path policy — move every two years or stagnate — was just the tip of a policy iceberg holding innovative ideas hostage. Had the plant manager stayed, he soon would have come up against corporate cost accounting, compensation schemes, personnel policies, quality initiatives, reporting systems — all sorts of centralized practices that did not reflect a high-performing system's real value.

In a big company it is difficult to make "systemic" changes when you cannot control key parts of the system. Since nothing stands still, systems redesign is a never-ending task. Those who aspire to this work would do well to get over the idea that there are powerful change technologies, even "large group interventions," to bypass all this. It's easy to say "flatter organization" and "get the supervisors out" than to figure out how to help redundant people find new jobs or how to put in measurements that account for the economic value of motivated workers.

That does not make systems improvement less important. We do better, though, when we shelve notions that we can create a new, unified, systemically integrated, holistic, organic, good-to-the-last-drop, for-now-and-forever, workplace culture in a sea of contradictory agendas. No one should expect to improve a corporate culture and have it stay that way. We cannot "build in" policies, procedures, and norms that will outlive all those who come after. Each new crop of managers will want to do things their own way. The best any of us can do is to give every project our best right now. Realistically speaking, we ought to act as if there will be no next time. For most managers in large corporations, that is a fact of life.

Case 4. The Old Paradigm Breaks Down: Strategic Trauma at Solcorp (1981)

> I think our goals are unrealistic — I mean having a
> production line when there's not enough product
> knowledge in this system to have anything other
> than an R&D facility.
>
> —— *Engineer, Solcorp*

We come at last to the end of the road for experts on the one hand and problem solving, even the participative kind, on the other. Solcorp was founded in the early 1970s to develop an innovative process for making electricity from sunlight. Its creator sold out to a large company eager to commercialize the process. In no time the division had 250 engineers and scientists and a building full of high-tech equipment and a factory actually making solar energy cells. The trouble was, they cost too much.

After a few years (way too few, it turned out) the parent company increased pressure on its new venture to cut manufacturing costs and get cracking in the marketplace. Production targets were missed for four years running. To stem the cash drain, a fourth of the work force was laid off, leaving the survivors in a quandary. Skilled technical people were bailing out as fast as they could get their résumés typed. Tensions among marketing, manufacturing, and development ran high. The parent recommended consulting help.

The president, a scientist, had no formal management training. He was convinced that procedures were needed to set goals and hold people accountable; that a lack of system, subordinated to development, was the heart of the problem. He had nagging feelings the company was off track, and wondered whether they could meet the current objective of a viable product this year and worldwide sales within four years more.

Cotton Cleveland and I agreed to use his concern as a hypothesis, an unproven theory to be tested by a joint diagnosis of the whole system. Like many managers, he was backed into a participative process by events he could not control. He identified twenty-five staff members from every function who knew the problems and whose commitment was needed for solutions. He laid out the dilemma. A joint diagnosis was planned. The consultants took more than 100 pages of interview notes. Many comments confirmed the president's observation about goals:

"I don't really know what the goals are."

"There are no goals. None."

"Our goals have been wrong. With 20/20 hindsight it's easy to say that."

Still, people had a strong sense of mission and were excited about the work. It appealed to their social values — finding a pollution-free, benevolent energy source. It appealed to their professional aspirations — pioneering a frontier technology.

"I'm engrossed in the high technology. The end result is visible, and it gives me a warm-all-over feeling."

"The public desperately wants an alternative to oil. The sun is too attractive to be ignored. It has to be pursued. We are pioneers, no doubt about it."

"This company is strong in its technical capability. People simply believe in what the company is trying to accomplish. It's something potentially beneficial."

In spite of perception about lack of goals, the company had in fact had a clear mission for five years — to make and sell a cheap product based on their new technology. The oft-noted lack of clarity was attributed to the fact that neither production nor sales goals had been met. People believed, deep down, that these were the wrong goals. The comments revealed a deeper strategic dilemma: the plight of a firm seeking to market a product not yet fully developed.

"We lack process knowledge. The basic work hasn't been done. We go by empiricism rather than knowledge — there's a lot of witchcraft and black magic here."

"There's a frustrating shift in quality and nobody knows why. We change direction to make the problem seem to go away."

"We can't produce and then repeat a stable product."

"We should never have gotten into manufacturing as early as we did."

As a result, the company was not a secure place to work. The president had been single-mindedly tuned in to the high-potential technology. His optimism (unfounded, as it turned out) brought economic pressures from a corporation happy to believe that profits were just around the corner. The social consequences had become too grave to ignore. Nobody had hope — a classic example of the way technical, economic, and social problems interact. Top managers took to public blaming, a symptom of anxiety and fear.

"I've seen people ripped to shreds in group meetings."

"I don't want to be humiliated in front of my peers."

"Upper management always takes comments as personal attacks."

The twenty-five people, including the president, reviewed these and a hundred other comments in a day-long meeting. They readily owned up to five conclusions based on their own (heretofore never shared) observations:

1. The product was not ready for market without more basic research.

2. Nobody could say how long this would take.

3. The sales force was promising potential customers more than the factory could deliver.

4. The factory was in a constant state of crisis, trying in real time to iron out the bugs of a technology not fully developed.

5. Each function went its separate way, with little interchange, coordination, or joint problem solving.

In short, it was a research lab trying to act like a business. Each year new shortcomings were revealed. People were continually fighting fires. The president desperately wanted to believe that the solution was just one experiment away. He knew research findings could not be scheduled, that some breakthroughs take minutes, others years, others forever. Manufacturing goals — which *could* be scheduled — proved unrealistic because of quality breakdowns. If the theory of the new cells was right, how come so much unexplainable variance occurred? To succeed they had to make the same product the same way with the same costs nearly every time. See "Cat Chasing Its Tail," a local theory for this situation, and "Ideal Solcorp" for the gap between reality and aspiration.

It was probably too late to salvage the dream. Involving employees more fully might minimize the damage. Two alternatives emerged from the joint discussions. Solcorp could stabilize a minimally acceptable product, maximize sales, and decouple production from R&D. This would mean a very narrow market in the short run, hardly enough to stem the losses. Or it could eliminate

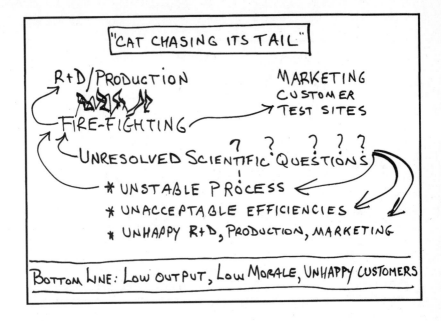

marketing entirely, reduce manufacturing to a pilot plant, and free up the researchers to move as quickly as possible — to become again an R&D facility.

In follow-up meetings, the top-management team decided on the second course of action. The consultants, not cognizant then of participative options for downsizing, terminated their work. Within a year, the parent had agreed to further cutbacks; half the work force was laid off, and the facility focused on R&D.

From the standpoint of this book's theme, several interview comments also reveal the depth of the need to be involved in the problem solving and decision making from the start, to have influence on the future:

"This meeting is the last chance. It can't go on. Management has to change or people will leave."

"If we change direction, everybody should share in that and the sooner the better. But I need commitment behind me."

"My people and myself want to help and don't know how."

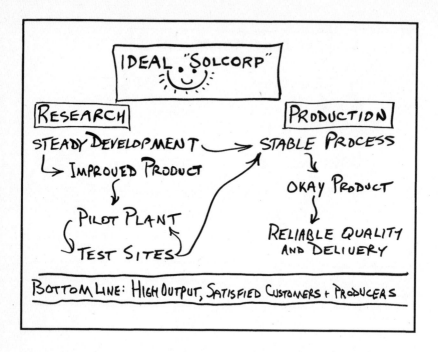

"For representing such a large number of people, I don't feel part of the team. That makes it extremely difficult to plan."

"We have great difficulty working in concert and it's clear we can't work independently and be successful. When I go home at night I think about the source of the problem and I can't find it."

"We changed course, but I don't hear about it. Perhaps I could make a contribution. I sit pretty high in management, but so what? I have lots of ideas. But do I really become part of the management team where we set the course for the company?"

Searching for Solcorp. Solcorp, real name Solar Energy Systems (SES), fell off the radar screen in the 1980s, not long after the events just described. I learned of its demise while seeking to contact someone who had been there. I called a company with a vaguely similar name located in the area where SES had been. Wrong company. One veteran executive recalled SES and even remembered the president's name. He had no idea where to find him. He could not recall the year they closed up shop.

In the 1980s SES was a Shell Oil subsidiary, so I checked the company website. Like most oil companies, Shell again had an active solar entity. Headquartered in Europe, the new division had no connection to the old. The online history made no mention of SES. I called Shell and exchanged emails with people in Texas, California, and the Netherlands. I could find no one with specific information on what had become of SES. An industry historian thought it had folded in the 1970s.

On the web I found that the cost of solar cells had fallen by 50 percent since 1990. "Photovoltaics," said an executive vice president of Shell Solar, "is one of the fastest-growing of all the renewable energy technologies. We have the people, the reach, and the resources to build a sustainable, commercially successful solar energy business around the world."

When I visited the website a few months later I found that the company was closing two European factories and laying off 170 people. "These have been difficult decisions for us and job losses are deeply regrettable" said the same VP. "The PV market faces a glut in supply and . . . we believe the way to maintain a competitive edge is to focus on our leading position in technology development and our sales and marketing operations" (de Renzy-Martin, 2002). I was encouraged to note that the company planned to help all those laid off to find new jobs. The technical problems of the early 1980s had been solved. The industry remained volatile and uncertain. Anyone who sought to do "change" projects in such companies could expect a bumpy ride.

The story illustrates, under the worst conditions, the hunger for productive workplaces. It also shows how technical values tend to drive out social values in the workplace, and the power of collaborative action research for untangling the mess. Without the involvement of all his managers, the president could not gain perspective on his own sinking feeling that he had been wrong to hold on so long.

Without focusing on the whole system, he could not confront the parent with its unrealistic expectations. This sort of dilemma has become increasingly frustrating to managers in every field caught in an avalanche of new technologies and markets at the end of the 20th Century. The movie was merging with the snapshot. That called for a wholly new way of building on Lewin's road map.

Chapter Twelve

Rethinking Organizational Improvement: New Perspectives on Consultation

> If you want to understand what a science is, you
> should look in the first instance not at its theories
> or its findings, and certainly not at what its
> apologists say about it; you should look at what the
> practitioners of it do.
> —— *Clifford Geertz*, The Interpretation of Cultures,
> *1973, p. 5*

Peter Drucker (1976) once pointed out that the trouble with Taylorism wasn't Taylor; it was that the engineers who followed him stopped where he did. Lewin's descendants face the same dilemma. We can get caught in the labyrinth of technologies, lose sight of core values, break off chunks of social-psychological reality, and end up prescribing activities nobody really wants. To the extent we do that, we mock Lewin's contributions. To mistake his methods for his insights and values is to apply a model of diagnosis and action that no longer fits the world we live in. In this chapter I will critique the cases just presented to show the direction required for a new practice theory of managing and consulting.

To appreciate why I want to refocus the playing field, I would like you to join me on a trip through the thickets of organizational-change theory. Case studies in organization development for decades have reflected two different theories of improvement, coexisting uneasily. One was a theory of process diagnosis based on the expert's data-collecting abilities — what I call snap-shooting. Another was Lewin's brilliant theory of participative change-oriented action —

what I call moviemaking, which is quite different from Hollywood's. Most practitioners know that the two theories are really one. How we take the snapshot determines the quality of the movie. Yet all of us have one foot in what Eric Trist, the originator of sociotechnical thinking, called the old paradigm — Taylor's cause-effect reasoning.

There are two critical decisions associated with snap-shooting and moviemaking: (1) What should be pictured? (2) Who takes the snapshot? The only Lewinian requirements were that (1) people and situation be looked at together, and (2) consultants and clients work as a team. Any problem, large or small, could make a movie, so long as its dynamic aspects were considered, meaning people's feelings, perceptions, and behavior. Action research, despite our whole-systems rhetoric, has often been problem-focused. That's no surprise when you consider the concept's origin.

Social science early on imitated medical science. "Diagnosis" is medical jargon for specifying the gap between sickness and health. As biology exploded in the 19th Century, the human body, like the workplace, was divided into manageable components. The medical profession evolved in parallel with Taylorism, both clinically and conceptually. Specialist physicians became the industrial engineers of the human physique. Their claim to expertise was based on their ability to factor in every variable and thus heal the sick. It is no surprise that early psychologists thought the same way about mental processes. Indeed, until the biologist Ludwig von Bertalanffy proposed a general systems theory (see Chapter Eight), people educated in Western societies could hardly think any other way.

Process Thinking

Lewin enlarged the medical model. He highlighted processes unseen in the 19th Century because nobody had a conceptual lens that could see them. Lewin's force fields made possible "process" snapshots — the feelings, motives, intentions, and other intangibles related to results. Lewin portrayed diagnostic gaps in more dynamic terms: as an interaction of relevant social forces — personal, group, company-wide, societal. Who are the gatekeepers, he asked, whose behavior must change to assure constructive action? What forces prevent or encourage their involvement? In that way, he showed more precisely under what conditions action taking led to change. Still the old medical vocabulary endured. From Lewin I inherited two change concepts that made possible my transition from manager to consultant. One, the task-process relationship, is a snap-shooting concept. The other, changing a system by unfreezing, moving, and refreezing it, is a concept of the movie's purpose.

Task-Process Snap-Shooting. The task-process relationship describes a subtle chicken-egg interplay between ends and means, methods and goals, motivation and output. A task is concrete, observable, and thing-oriented. You can convert it into criteria, measurements, targets, and deadlines — just the way Taylor did. Tasks pop up in every relationship, even between parents and children.

Devise a plan for reducing turnover 10 percent in Region A by January 1. That's a task. Survey the relationship between R&D and other departments and hold discussion meetings with them all in the third quarter. That's a task. Find out what's wrong with the packaging lines, and get production up. That's vaguer, but it's still a task. Plan one outing a month with the kids, and one with just the two of us. That's a task. *Task* refers to what is to be done.

Process describes the "how." It reflects perceptions, attitudes, feelings, reasoning. When you think process you ask, "Why aren't we making progress?" Or, "Do people really feel involved and committed to this?" Not when, where, and how many. Rather why, how, and whether. Process thinking stimulates questions about who needs to be involved and how much influence they will have. It leads to another kind of question. Do the kids help plan their own outing, or do we do it for them? Do we start with a blank sheet of paper and brainstorm places to go? Or do we pick three places and give them a choice? Those are process questions. There are no right answers — until you know which principles you wish to enact. What do you want the kids to learn from this outing besides local history?

Reprinted from *Gestalt Therapy: Excitement and Growth in the Human Personality* by Frederick Perls, M.D., Ph.D., Ralph E Hefferline, Ph.D., and Paul Goodman, Ph.D. Copyright ©1951 by Frederick Perls, M.D., Ph.D., Ralph E Hefferline, Ph.D., and Paul Goodman, Ph.D. Used by Permission of The Julian Press, Inc.

   A Dual Image Paradox. Task-process thinking can be likened to the famous visual paradox of the Old Woman/Young Woman, reproduced here. Do you see a young beauty facing away or a wizened crone in profile?

   You can't see both at once. By some mental gyration you can learn to shift between them. Does one picture cause the other? Cause-effect thinking that gave rise both to Taylorism and the medical model led, in Western societies, to a relentless propensity to see one form of task only as *the* task. The language of the workplace described only one picture, as if defining a goal causes its achievement. Western industrial managers developed an exquisite left-brain approach: linear, rational, A causes B, three steps, nine phases, finish by Tuesday, let's be precise, don't waste my time, gimme the bottom line. Diagnosis, even of processes, is a task requiring structure and precision. Whether your categories are "hard" or "soft," listing and prioritizing puts your left brain into high gear.

Action, on the other hand, reflects pure process. We guide it largely on automatic pilot, fueled by little explosions of energy in the right brain — explosions of creativity, energy, synthesis — especially when choosing among uncertainties (Mintzberg, 1976). Lewin ingeniously expanded left-brain thinking. He shifted the diagnoser's viewpoint to focus attention on the other picture — on *processes*, always present and invisible only because nobody was looking for them.

From his work came my simple practice theory: *process issues will always block work on tasks*. Through trained observation you can find ingenious linkages. If the work isn't getting done, look for what is *not* being talked about, rather than what is. This quickly becomes a hall of mirrors. The concept, like the picture of the women, is an artifact of how our brains work. Your train of thought can be derailed by either picture — too much or too little task orientation. And you can fasten on any issue or combination.

You will find tasks and processes every place you look. But neither is by itself an adequate description of reality. They exist only in relationship to each other. And Lewin does not tell you how broad or narrow your gaze should be, only that you should look at the person and situation both. If Food Services has too high turnover, what is there about its people and the company that makes folks leave? What is the link connecting cost, motivation, output, and manager behavior? If your framework is narrowly economic, you might say (with Taylor), engineer the jobs for speed and pay more. You might even get a group to participate in that. From a social systems perspective, you might conclude (with Likert) that manager behavior and conditions of work must change. And you might then proceed to change them without involving anybody.

Task-Process and Systems Focus. Many of us started early on to take more of a systems view of reality, to see the task-process linkage in terms not only of interpersonal relations but in terms of an organization's relationship with its environment. My six-box diagnostic model (Weisbord, 1978b) reflected this effort to move toward a more complete view of reality than group dynamics alone would permit. (It included purposes, structure, relationships, rewards, leadership, and helpful mechanisms — all in a context of outside forces or environmental demands.)

Two realities make task-process applications problematical. One, social engineers can abstract process issues out of their economic and technical contexts for problem-solving the same way industrial engineers break down machine operations. That's because all economic and technical problems have a process side related entirely to people's behavior — the unwritten rules (norms) informally evolved to cope with work. However, just because norms are diagnosable does not make them treatable, even when people participate in the diagnosis and write action prescriptions. Suppose the process issues lie with the structure of the work itself? The sort of organization development I was practicing in the 1970s did not permit the raising of that question. Moreover, my clients, still not shaken enough by world events, would not have found the question actionable.

Second, even with a systems model it is possible (even probable) that you will become problem-focused too soon. Managers hate to sit still, looking at something from all angles; they like to get on with it. In our left-brained industrial world, with computers tracking output, Wall Street watching quarterly results, and the Dow Jones stock index changing daily, you can hardly avoid it. It is tempting to zero in, once you learn task-process thinking, on a process issue in one box and start fixing it instantly. You say, "Let's get a new reward system in here," and in no time a compensation expert is working out the details, independent of the impact on purposes, relationships, or anything else. You say, "I want effective communications around here," and in no time everybody is in workshops (communicating to each other how unhappy they are to be there).

A manager's aspiration, of course, should be to go back and forth between task and process, structure and behavior, the way a pilot scans the instruments — from gas gauge to altimeter, to air speed indicator, to artificial horizon — continually keeping all of them in sync. As soon as one dimension checks out okay, you shift your gaze to another. If you see a serious deviation, say you've let yourself drift 1,000 feet too low, it would be disastrous to keep focused on the compass heading. You'd better correct your altitude or you're going to run into that big jet inbound at the same height.

You Can't Fly on the Compass Alone. Unfortunately, left-brain diagnostic thinking, perfected by scientists for more than 100 years, leads us to pay attention to the compass and to consider the altimeter a luxury or a frill. The assumption is that the diagnoser stands outside, impartial, objective, and aloof from what is observed. If you add to this our propensity to defer to authority — parents, bosses, experts, all the negative Theory X voices in our heads — you have a setup for disappointment. If ever a whole civilization was built on left-brain behavior, it is the world of work in industrial societies. None of us is immune.

Group dynamics' great contribution to management — whether from the Bion or Lewin traditions (see Chapters Seven and Eight) — was its relentless gaze at the process picture inseparable from the accomplishment of the task, the diagnoser inseparable from the diagnosis, a leader's skill inseparable from follower contributions. One big *ah-ha* for me in unstructured learning groups was that my anxiety and frustration were self-induced, cumulative, and self-reinforcing. My efforts to do things perfectly, and to make sure everybody else did likewise, had less to do with the trainer and more with my inability to see the other picture, to realize that my own negative voices declared unfounded assumptions about who was allowed to do what. That process issue affected the output of the whole group.

The big *ah-ha* for a task force making no progress in setting or achieving goals is the need to resolve process issues. Chem Corp's

R&D department could not achieve credibility through team building at the top. A great many managers at many levels had to become committed to working on the blockages. Until these were cleared out — either by spontaneous remission or deliberate diagnosis and action — things could only get worse.

There is no unique, perfect, by-the-book process issues list, by the way. One clue that things are off track is in your own reaction to what's happening. If you hear the same information recycled without being acted upon, that's a process issue. If you want to contribute something and hold yourself back, that's a process issue. If people run away or fight, abandoning the task either way, that's a process issue. All can be seen as the "hows" that block the "whats."

Unfreezing, Moving, Refreezing

My second important practice theory I call "Lewin's Law." Lewin saw human systems as almost but not quite static and resistant to change. A consultant's goal was to accelerate both the rate and direction of change, and to stabilize new behavior. These processes were initiated, in Lewin's mind, in response to a social problem or conflict. What was to be unfrozen were the *processes* of action, the unconscious behaviors that worked against productivity. In the four previous cases my diagnostic snapshots were intended to make people want to act, to melt the ice of indifference or ignorance or uncertainty and unfreeze the system. Once melted, it would follow more natural channels, flowing downhill, so to speak, until cooled enough to refreeze in more functional and congruent patterns.

At Chem Corp, Food Service, and Packaging Plant, I think the need to unfreeze was a defensible hypothesis in the 1970s. While all three firms experienced "turbulent environments" (Emery and Trist, 1963), most employees did not know it. In Packaging Plant, for example, nobody but top management sees anything amiss with the filling lines until the consultants assemble a cast of twenty-eight people and hold up a mirror to the dilemma. At Chem Corp, although the top team and R&D managers want to do something,

other departments are relatively indifferent until the survey creates awareness throughout the company of the need to act. At Food Services we see turnover as an assumed business cost, not a horrendous symptom of systemic dysfunction. The carrot of cost reduction attracts some top managers to study what had been, until the consultant raised it in a seminar, a non-problem. Hence the elaborate comparative survey used to entice people to take a second look. The diagnosis was of significant help to the clients. Though a traditional unfreezing diagnosis was attempted at Solcorp, I believe it was largely for the consultants' benefit. If I were doing it again I would not diagnose the system's failures; I would seek to mobilize energy for change. In that case I probably still would be too late.

Change Theory

Now, let us visit the linkage between the task-process cycle and the process of unfreezing, moving, and refreezing, Lewin's formula for systems change. This linkage made possible the profession of organization development (OD). Unresolved process issues accumulate in organizations like junk in an attic. People freeze in dysfunctional patterns; nobody listens, appreciates, celebrates, communicates. Output and quality suffer. Reacting to crises drives out future thinking — clearly the case in Solcorp. This self-perpetuating ice storm over corporate headquarters was what Lewin sought to unfreeze with action research.

If the stored-up stuff could be got out in the open, if people could express their resistances and skepticism, if undiscussable topics could be talked about, energy would be released. People would become aware of their own contributions to their problems. The blockages would be removed (a formulation, incidentally, also central to psychoanalysis) and new behavior would emerge — a possibility that might be accelerated through skill training. Unfrozen, people would redo strategy, policy, procedure, relationships, and norms more to their liking. Implementing new action plans would move the system, and reinforcing mechanisms — periodic review meetings, for example — would refreeze the system into more functional patterns.

Could you measure the results? The best answer was to check people's attitudes and actions before and after, and compare their answers with the task outputs: service levels, product quality, quantity, cost, profit. That's what Likert did with his systems surveys. At Food Services and Chem Corp we measured the outcome of an intervention that indicated new behaviors had taken root with excellent results. At Packaging Plant we changed the production system, and the old fallacy disappeared.

How long would the refreezing last? A long time, we hoped. But not a moment longer than the perception that unfreezing was needed again. That became the rub. How does a system become self-regulating? What does it take to spot and free up process blockages as you go along, instead of building up to a crisis before doing anything? The key was believed to be learning — not just learning how to solve the problem in cause-effect terms (if I do A, then I get B) but also learning how to flip back and forth between task and process, and to realize that both "pictures" are there all the time.

Learning to shift your gaze between task and process could become a way of life rather than a project. Results were feedback loops, a built-in monitor for self-regulation. In the cases in Chapter Ten we intended that managers not only solve their problems, but that they evolve a new way of doing business. In this new way, people would approach future dilemmas with a more open-ended data collection and more thoughtful diagnosis. They would take responsibility rather than play helpless or blame others. They would stop jumping to conclusions and become more aware that involving others would lead to faster, better, and more committed action. They would, in effect, learn how to learn, to generalize new behavior into better future responses. Those were the OD assumptions of change. They beautifully capture the spirit inherent in Emery and Trist's new paradigm behavior in contrast to a more mechanistic, manipulative Taylorism.

All OD cases fit this framework of diagnosis and action. At the heart of the diagnostic act was a confrontation: the clients had to accept the incongruity between what they want or need and what they have — the normative demon to be exorcised before healing could begin. Lewin's model does not necessarily assume sickness. However, sickness is easy to infer for those of us socialized to life as a medical model with diagnosis its most sacred expert act. Lewin believed action research should be a joint venture of experts and stakeholders — the people with the problem. While action was the client's bailiwick, unfreezing the system was clearly the consultant's. As long as OD consultants considered unfreezing their special province, they could not avoid the role of expert, despite models and rhetoric to the contrary.

In the 1950s people began working out a new form of third-party behavior — consulting skills — to facilitate these assumptions. It was based on Lewin's insights that people are more likely to act on solutions they have helped develop. It included a minor fiction: that questions, methods of inquiry, data presentation, analysis, and action steps would be jointly planned. I say "fiction" because the methods inevitably belonged to the consultants, and so did the theories of task and process, unfreezing, and the rest. The feedback meeting was the pivot point of social change, the payoff for action research. There the data were accepted, the system melted, and movement initiated.

Four Cases Revisited

The four cases in Chapter Eleven represent stages in both my own development and that of OD practice in the 1970s. They reflect travel along two paths toward better snapshots and better movies. Better movies require progress toward greater stakeholder involvement in every aspect of change. We can make them to the extent we can follow Lewin's 1923 signpost, his insight that improved farm tools await a collaboration of farmers and researchers (see Chapter Four). The path toward better snapshots leads from analyzing discrete problems toward understanding whole systems — the subtle interplay of economics, technology, and people.

The logic of Lewinian thinking requires a convergence of the two paths. Indeed, they are like Route 1 and City Avenue northwest of Philadelphia near where I live: both designations for the same highway. What keeps us from converging the paths is the proliferation of managerial and consulting techniques — narrow expertise, if you will — for unfreezing systems, sorting problems, and solving problems, all products of our formidable left brains.

In Chapter Sixteen I suggest some guidelines for developing a practice more congruent with our aspirations, a merger of snapshots and movies that makes simple and more radical managerial and consulting projects feasible. To appreciate them we must acknowledge the shortfalls of older methods: focusing groups on too narrow a problem or having too few people in on the diagnosis. Worst case, we do both — the agony of the expert problem solver.

From Problem Toward System Focus. Problem focus means worrying over one piece of the puzzle unconnected to all the others — economics alone, or technology alone, or people alone.

System focus means treating the whole system as one piece of a larger puzzle, for example, one that includes world markets *and* employees hungry for dignity, meaning, and community in work.

If we look at the four cases along the snapshot continuum from problem focus to systems focus, we see this picture:

Problem focus	Transitional	Systems focus
Food Services (turnover)	Chem Corp (inter-departmental relations; innovation)	Packaging Plant Solcorp (economics, technology, people)

At Food Services we worked on manager behavior and orientation, not the organization of a food service unit. At Chem Corp, we did not look at how the company was organized for innovation. We sought to improve relations between R&D and everybody else — a classic OD intervention, but with a do-it-yourself "new paradigm" survey twist. At Packaging Plant we started with a problem focus — getting more product out — and found the solution not in people's motivation but in the way the whole system functioned, clear back to the marketplace. At Solcorp, which was already swamped by change, our action-research orientation moved us quickly from teamwork in setting goals toward the heart of the issue: the connections among strategy, technology, markets, structure, and behavior. In short, we used (appropriately) a wide-angle lens, even when the president wanted a telephoto.

There is no necessary connection, however, between the wideness of the lens used for snap-shooting and the degree of stakeholder involvement. To make good our participative aspiration, people have to be deeply involved from the start in methods, concept development, data collection, and diagnosis. To make good our whole open-system aspiration, we need to put the system *and* all its problems at the center of the action, and not any one problem alone. If we would fully experience the snapshot and movie as one process, nothing less will do.

My cases reflect a mix of old and new paradigms in action. When all the stakeholders were involved — top team, R&D, other departments — and the clients generated hypotheses and led feedback meetings, the movie tended toward the new (Chem Corp). When consultants made problem maps for the client (Packaging Plant, Solcorp), the movie looked more like the old, even though the maps themselves, being of the whole system, were state of the art.

In short, a quality movie requires systemic participation in the snapshot. People need to describe their own gaps, make their own maps, find their own variances, instead of having consultants do it for them. The more technically competent consultants are, the greater the challenge to transfer their knowledge.

From Expert Toward Stakeholder Involvement. If we now put the cases on a movie continuum — from expert involvement to stakeholder involvement in the *whole* process — we see this:

High expert involvement	Mixed involvement	High stakeholder involvement
Food Services Solcorp	Packaging Plant	Chem Corp

In my four cases my colleagues and I still did most of the front-end diagnosis. In our zeal to be effective we became another kind of expert, striving to understand the client system, to draw maps of how it works, to explain it to those who work there, to build surveys and provide concepts, seeking to transfer "ownership" of the problem by negotiating questions to be asked, timetables, and objectives. In short we did whatever it took to unfreeze them. But *we* did it.

The four cases reveal varying degrees of whole-system focus and high stakeholder involvement. The best systems analysis was at Solcorp, where the clients had the *least* involvement in the diagnosis. The best client involvement was in Chem Corp. The cases reveal assumptions and aspirations for both snapshot and movie beyond the scope of my techniques. Nonetheless, I easily persuaded myself that unfreezing by third parties, movement by principals and third parties together, and refreezing by the principals constituted a strategy for cultural change.

Science could be mobilized to beat back authoritarianism and bureaucracy. If the norms of data collection, communication, relationships, and problem solving were changed, all else would follow. What made this different from Taylorism were its behavioral components and participative techniques — learning to do things with, not to or for, others. Whatever its shortcomings, this brand of action research, like scientific management in 1900, was a great advance over what people did before. Now we must go further still.

Rethinking Lewin

I now find my old practice theory unsatisfying from two perspectives. First, global markets, technologies, and worker expectations change so fast that a frozen workplace is a temporary phenomenon. Today change goes more like a bullet train than a melting iceberg. The rate has accelerated since Kurt Lewin died in 1947, too fast for experts to pin down, even the process experts. Conventional diagnoses may serve many useful functions, but unfreezing systems is not one of them. We change our behavior when we are ready to do it, not because of a force field analysis, or any other kind of analysis. Nobody is skilled enough to push the river. That is supported by consulting experiences clear back to Frederick Taylor. The best a consultant can do is create opportunities for people to do what they are ready to do anyway. If we apply a linear bag of tricks, only the content differs from Taylor's. The process comes out uncomfortably the same.

Second, despite my use of systems models, I cannot know enough about the ins and outs of any system to isolate, analyze, and synthesize its many moving parts. My systems perspective is the most useful thing I have. However, the perspective, or way of thinking, matters more than the factors, dimensions, or boxes in my model. Systems models are best thought of as tools for coalescing people to do something together, helping them to undertake a systems-improvement task.

If you accept that proposition, you will see why I worry more about responding to needs for dignity, meaning, and community in work, which means improving your own system, than in supplying "right" answers. There is considerable anxiety and confusion everywhere. I think it is wrong to assume our mutual dilemmas mean sickness, as if only the diagnostician were whole and in control. Nothing holds still long enough to be diagnosed and changed anyway. So consultant-centered diagnostic activities intended to unfreeze systems, even when welcomed by clients willing to defer to authority, even when holistic in concept, may inadvertently distract people from taking charge of their own lives.

To honor Lewin now requires reconfirming his values and insights. It also requires that we go beyond him in devising methods closer to our aspirations for wholeness, involvement, and self-control. We need new processes for managing and consulting that I do not fully understand. I'm conscious of profound paradoxes. I have at my fingertips diagnostic techniques for every issue in the cosmos. On my bookshelf I find more models for fixing things than there are stars in the galaxy. Yet, I am strangely undernourished by this intellectual cornucopia. My objective, I keep reminding myself as I pant to keep up with change in a new era, is not to diagnose and heal sickness, but to help people find dignity, meaning, and community in work.

The consultants' dilemma is that we always arrive in the middle of somebody else's movie and leave before the end. The script has many subplots and informal directors. The consultant negotiates a role — sometimes major, sometimes minor, but always limited by the willingness of others to play along. My view of the consultant's role has turned upside down from what I once thought it was. I imagine it now as helping people discover a more whole view of what they are doing than any one discipline or perspective can provide, including mine.

I find that proposition fraught with uncertainty. Is it doable? To the extent I can help people integrate their values and tasks, I make an important contribution. Yet that means being at some level an expert and accepting people's projections of authority, even when I don't act the authoritarian. None of us knows, exactly, how to be both an expert and also just one of the gang — when we value collaboration and mutual learning more than being right. I know that people can learn how to learn. But that any of us can *teach* others explicitly how to do that is in my opinion an old paradigm theory full of iffiness.

Toward Assessing Possibilities. We come at last to the heart of it: it is not always practical or desirable to negotiate a consulting role that, at its simplest, is helping people do what they are going to do anyway. The consultant's task in the movie is to see confusion and anxiety through to energy for constructive action, and to learn along with everybody else. That has an odd ring to somebody like me, who grew up at the tail end of the Industrial Revolution. I now believe that assessing the conditions (and they are narrow) under which such an unusual partnership is feasible should be the first task of consultation. Not how to help, but whether to even make the offer. That means a different kind of snapshot from the unfreezing variety.

Diagnosis, the gap between sickness and health, is not the right word for what I mean. Postindustrial change is not a sickness, although some consequences can be. Anxiety is not a sickness; it is a sign of learning and potential energy. We need another term. Maybe *assessment* will do. Managers today need simple ways to assess the potential for action, focus attention, and help people learn together about the whole contraption. That is quite different from having a consultant build a problem list and prioritize it. I am not against expertise, only the assumption that the specialist (or boss, or consultant) knows *everything* required to resolve the situation defined by the specialist's expertise or authority, without personally having to do anything new or risky. This is especially true in complex work like reorganizing. That's a developmental task, governed largely by the right brain, and not amenable except in discrete details to ordinary problem solving.

Moreover, we should not mistake human resource management for new-paradigm practices. A major limitation on action is the belief that a human resource department on the eighth floor, just like the strategic planning department on the fourteenth, somehow makes us immune from reductionistic, linear, rigid solutions. Staff-centered activity is not necessarily conducive to productive workplaces, whether named "participative management" or "dynamic synergistic holistic transformation." It doesn't matter what you call it. If people don't join in planning their own work, it's old Fred Taylor all over again, with social-psychological window dressing instead of time and motion study.

Whose Movie Is It? It is important to grasp this point if you wish to enact productive workplaces infused with dignity, meaning, and community. An effective snapshot, seen as a dual image — task and process — portrays the whole system in relation to a valued purpose. It can do that accurately only when the whole system, to the extent possible, takes the snapshot, appears in it, and looks it over together. When the whole system is in perpetual motion, every relationship changing, no one person can take a coherent picture. As soon as people start making a collective self-portrait, it is not a snapshot. Suddenly it's part of the ongoing movie, a form of cinema vérité, as messy as life itself.

Only those most involved can make such a movie. The best role a consultant can hope for is stage manager. Kurt Lewin showed that during World War II, when he discovered participative management by having Iowa housewives decide whether to change their food habits (see Chapter Three). Nobody has improved on the principle — that the wisest decisions, given as much information as we can get, are the ones we make for ourselves. This discovery has never been more relevant. People benefit most, I'm convinced, from talking with one another and deciding what to do. Increasingly, this dialogue does not require elaborate consultant-centered unfreezing exercises. Most systems are destabilized long before a consultant comes in.

To influence committed action today we need a practice theory that (1) respects the past, (2) enhances productive workplaces, and (3) is responsive to the tide of change. Such a theory requires imagining under what conditions people will work on improving whole systems together, which is the manager's dilemma, and under what conditions a consultant can help. In the next chapter I report on two more cases from my own practice that have bemused me for several years. I find in them the seeds for a new consulting practice and a new way of managing that many people are seeking now to evolve.

Chapter Thirteen

Improving Whole Systems: Alternatives to the Report-in-the-Drawer Phenomenon

> We are witnessing the most rapid, complex and thoroughgoing corporate restructuring in modern history.
>
> —— *Alvin Toffler*, The Adaptive Corporation,
> *1984, p. 4*

At last I will revisit two cases markedly different from the earlier ones. They contain the seeds for new managing and consulting practices that many people now seek to evolve. These cases provide the missing pieces to an altogether different jigsaw puzzle of whole systems thinking, and whole systems involvement, based on methods that have the potential to match our values and aspirations.

Case 5. A Whole System Looks at Itself: Participative Planning at Medical School (1969–1971)

The president and dean of Medical School, faced with dramatic changes in medical education in the late 1960s, charged a faculty/administration task force to come up with a "plan for planning." Members included the planning and development vice-president, physicians, a hospital administrator, heads of nursing, microbiology, radiology, social work. Another member, an associate medical dean, having heard that I had done something like this for a large foundation, contacted me. I visited with the chief executive. He described the pressing problems of medical administration, which could no longer be handled by a few top administrators. His own dual role had become an anachronism (he didn't put it that way). A few years earlier medical deans performed surgery before breakfast, taught a class in midmorning, saw patients in the afternoon, and ran a faculty meeting over dinner. To be both president and dean now meant more fund raising, less everything else.

That was no picnic. Research dollars were growing scarcer, escalating resource allocation conflicts between older and newer specialties. His medical college and teaching hospital were at odds over their respective missions. Cost-containment pressures and a shortage of primary-care professionals triggered a clash between advocates of broad-based care and those eager to advance medical technology into finer specialties.

In my first task force meeting I saw that faculty and administrators could hardly discuss the weather without arguing. How to proceed? As a former journalist I knew how to interview people. As a former manager I knew something about business.

In my only previous consulting assignment I had interviewed people. I proposed interviews with department heads and other key people on behalf of the task force, seeking clues to the relevant planning issues and the form their problem solving might take.

People Talked About the Process. Interviews revealed the mistrust and skepticism of many faculty toward the planning effort and the dean who initiated it. There was a deep rift between faculty and administration, and between medical school and teaching hospital located at opposite ends of the same building. Indeed these issues came up much more often than the problems of medical education. Years later I would learn formal concepts about how external changes upset relationships and lead to personal conflicts and internal strife. Now I was hearing it without fully comprehending.

I thought consultants should make recommendations. So I made one. Why didn't the dean and hospital administrator move next door to one another instead of having to schedule meetings two days in advance and walk a quarter-mile each time there was a crisis? There were a lot of reasons why not, sounding vaguely like a philosophy of the separation of church and state. (Years later their successors actually did relocate.)

Next to conflicts with the dean and administration, the department heads mentioned three major problem areas requiring planning: mission; organizational structure; programs and budgets. I reported to the task force the widespread skepticism, the perceived needs, and the obvious conflicts. What to do now? I had little experience to draw on. Medical schools, like the printing business, could not spend more money than they took in. That much I knew. Medical schools too had customers and employees. But the managers (called "administrators") had nothing like the respect accorded their counterparts in industry. That was reserved for professors, researchers, and clinicians, with one exception. The dean was considered a super-being, on whose shoulders all problems of medical education were (appropriately) placed. If doctors were God, medical deans were the whole Trinity.

When deans fell short (as inevitably they did in the late 1960s), the earth shook and planets threatened to leave orbit. Ordinary administrators charged with integrating medical systems had the least standing to do it. The supreme commander who had the standing could not get enough information or help. I followed all this in a myopic sort of way the way I follow Spanish in Mexico, understanding some of the words but missing a great deal for not having lived in the culture. Managing medical education, except in the most global way, was not the same as managing a printing business. More, it was not, to hear doctors tell it, the same as it used to be.

There comes a time, in Mexico or medicine, when you have to speak up, even when you're not sure of the syntax. I had recently come across Rensis Likert's ideas (1961) for managing information and problems across departmental boundaries in business firms. I suggested to the task force that we apply knowledge developed at the Institute for Social Research about large-systems change and participative processes — something that had worked in industry. It was a gamble, certainly, but it seemed like the sort of gamble the tense situation called for. We would treat the planning process as an experiment in changing the school. It was pure action research, and the research flavor appealed especially to the basic scientists.

Using Link Pins. So we adapted Likert's link-pin concept to the planning problem. There would be three participative planning councils, linked to one another and to top managers. Each would include doctors (both full-time and voluntary), nurses, basic scientists, students, trustees, and administrators. Each would have two members in common and two members who served on a coordinating body with the president and vice-presidents. (One link pin, task force members insisted, was not enough. People missed meetings too often, or ran out in the middle. Backups were needed. So two links were named to each group; see "Link Pin Planning Structure.") This process would address the three major areas of need (the content) *and* the demoralizing skepticism of those who felt they had no influence (the process).

Volunteer council members, some forty of them, attended a two-day startup session. They reviewed research on the importance of coordinated planning in hospitals (Georgopoulos and Mann, 1962), discussed how link pins would operate, wrote their own "prescriptions" for leadership, and chose heads for each council. They received brief training in cooperative problem solving from a moonlighting friend of mine who worked in a corporate training department. We rewrote a famous conflict management exercise, "The Prisoner's Dilemma," in terms of allocating space among medical departments. It was so realistic nobody thought of it as training.

Over several months the councils met weekly and studied their institution in depth, recommending changes in mission, structure, priority setting, and budgeting. As each council prepared its report, it scheduled meetings with every constituency — medical staff, nursing staff, trustees, students — to review early drafts before finalizing its proposals. The process gave influence to people previously left out and angry. It provided a practical means for building commitment to engage pressing dilemmas in mission and budgeting. The meetings,

tense and mistrustful at first, turned to problem solving as council members, armed with the information they had collected, talked with their peers. The problems were being solved by a great many people weaving an interconnected web.

Changes. There were many repercussions. The mission planning group revisited the famous three-legged stool of academic medicine — equal commitment to research, teaching, and patient care — and proposed local variations appropriate to the school's history and community. The organization planning council worked out a new concept of relationships between administration and faculty, medical school and hospital. Its work extended far beyond one school. It led to organization studies (another form of action research) with nine academic centers and twenty-five hospitals, carried out under the auspices of the National Institutes of Health and the Association of American Medical Colleges (Weisbord, Lawrence, and Charns, 1978). These studies influenced other medical change projects (Weisbord, 1974), none so successful as the case here.

Still, Medical School was never a bed of roses. The concept of having all the stakeholders represented was not hard to understand. Nor was having them work on core issues like structure and budgets. Doing it, though, required great commitment and persistence from people already loaded down with the exigencies of medical practice and education. Many people at Medical School worked extremely hard, fighting anxiety and frustration for several months to establish a new way of operating. Some people left. The president and dean eventually moved on and the two jobs were separated. A candidate accepted the president's job, met with the planning task forces, announced his acceptance, and then backed out. Those who stayed reorganized their medical school. The program and budgeting planning council's successor group still functioned as a key mechanism for setting priorities fifteen years later. One of its more active physician members was eventually named president of the school.

Medical School Revisited (2003)

Thirty years went by in an eye-blink. The need for confidentiality was gone, along with most of the players. What had been Women's Medical College in 1969 became Medical College of Pennsylvania (MCP) in 1970. And MCP survived egregious mismanagement more than two decades later. Allegheny Health Systems, a Pittsburgh-based for-profit health care company, purchased the school and hospital in the late 1980s. The institution was merged in 1994 with Hahnemann Medical College into a corporate medical megalith, the MCP Hahnemann School of Medicine of Allegheny University of the Health Sciences.

Allegheny, presaging the executive scandals of 2002, went bankrupt in 1998. Several Allegheny executives were indicted for fraud. To cite one example, they used earmarked research grants for private purposes, including foreign junkets. Some departments lost their entire research budgets (Stark, 1999). At this point the California-based Tenet Healthcare Corporation took on Allegheny University's facilities as part of an acquisition of Philadelphia-area hospitals. Soon after, the assets of Medical School were transferred to a newly created nonprofit entity that became in 2002 the Drexel University College of Medicine.

Recalling the Planning Councils What I could not write in 1985 is central to understanding what the planning councils actually did. Perhaps the most significant change was that the only all-women's medical school in the United States decided to admit six men (10 percent) into the class of 1971. The decision resulted from heated debates in the Mission Planning Council. For many graduates and board members this breaking of the gender barrier was an act of betrayal to a mission dating from 1850. For decades few women could receive a medical education in largely male schools. (In 1969, only 6 per cent of U.S. medical students were women and 50 per cent of all U.S. trained woman physicians were graduates of Women's Medical College! By 2003 the national male-female medical student ratio was roughly 50–50.)

From the smallest private medical school in the United States, the merged entity, which became Drexel University College of Medicine in 2002, was now the largest. Dave Wagner, the surgeon who had sparked the planning project in 1969, was now chair of emergency medicine, the only remaining department head to have lived through decades of non-stop change. In the intervening years he had become a founder and past president of the American Board of Emergency Medicine. With his help, thirty years after,

I convened a meeting with planning council members from a bygone era. These included two faculty, Phyllis Marciano, a pediatrician and 1960 graduate of WMC, and June Klinghoffer, an internist who had graduated in 1945.

Bernard Sigel, now retired, a respected surgical researcher who had became dean and president at the height of the crisis (and later dean of the University of Illinois School of Medicine), attended. So did Donald Cooper, chair of surgery in 1970, later vice provost, also retired. We met in the emergency medicine conference room.

The project remained vivid for all of them. The issues in 1969, said Dr. Marciano, were two: whether to admit men to an all-women's school and where to find money. The two issues were inextricably linked. They were losing good students to co-ed schools after two years, and, as a women-only school, were denied access to much government funding in the early days of the gender revolution.

The talk turned to outcomes. "There was no tangible outcome from the planning councils that I can recall," said Dr. Cooper. "I have thought a lot about it. I later came to believe it didn't work for two reasons. One, you need good will and we lacked it then. And, two, you need time to achieve consensus and we were out of time. Two-thirds of our budget came from outside sources, government, and state. The financial VP and hospital head kept a tight rein even though the dean/president was the nominal head. The issue was how to manage without authority." He was referring to a structural artifact from the days when a medical dean had a part-time job, the hospital and college were managed as one entity, and a full-time financial officer made budget decisions affecting educational priorities.

What, then, were the benefits? Why did people stay with it? "We talked like we had never talked before," said Dr. Klinghoffer, "across all lines. We were all in it together." Added Dr. Marciano. "We ventilated, we expressed our views, and it was helpful in that regard. What came out of it," she went on, "was a much better understanding of each other's problems."

"Given what you know now, would you do it again?" I asked at last.

"Absolutely," said Dr. Sigel. Several heads nodded in agreement.

"Why?" I asked. "The planning process kept us from flying apart at a critical time," said Dr. Sigel. "Had we not been involved, I don't know whether we would have survived."

"It was a good way to go," added Dr. Cooper. "Under the circumstances, I surely would do it again."

Finally, Dr. Wagner reiterated a point he had made fifteen years earlier that was still operative. "In my opinion, faculty involvement in planning and budgeting to this day is traceable to the work we did in 1970. That was a key turning point for all of us."

Implications for Practice What lessons did I derive from this story three decades later? One, we can never know going into a project what will come out of it. All we know is what we hope for. "Deliverables" represent a form of wishful thinking. Two, creating dialogue across all boundaries is a healthy response in open societies, no matter what happens after. Three, what we call "managing change" may be more an exercise in endurance rather than management. And that, in my opinion, is not necessarily a bad thing.

Of all my cases, oddly enough, this was the best example of organizational learning, although not in the usual sense. Remember that there were three planning councils, not one. Nothing was implemented from the Organization Planning Council (chaired by Dr. Cooper) that had worked so hard rethinking the relationship between the school and hospital. What people remembered decades later were the passion and the dialogue. The admission of men to an all-women's school resulted from the work of the Mission Planning Council. And faculty involvement in planning and budgeting over the next thirty years was traceable to the Program and Resources Council set up in the tumultuous transition of 1970. Moreover, the critical learning, based on the Organizational Planning Council's work, eventually became the basis for an extension of differentiation-integration research that influenced medical school management everywhere (Weisbord, Lawrence, and Charns, 1978). Chapter Fourteen tells more of that story.

Learning (the Wrong Lesson) from Experience. Some years and many medical schools later — now an "expert" — I wrote a controversial article, "Why Organization Development Hasn't Worked (So Far) in Medical Centers" (Weisbord, 1976). I chose not to report the preceding Medical School case because I did not understand that it represented (and still does) one of the few cases on record where physicians had worked with many other stakeholders, many of them nonphysicians, to improve an institution. Instead, I referred to the more formal action research that Paul R. Lawrence, Martin P. Charns, and I had done (1978), showing how significant differences in physician training and orientation led them to disdain collaborative projects across levels, functions, and hierarchy. I know now that Medical School is an excellent example of the practice theory I want to see applied everywhere — it is based on real business dilemmas, future-oriented, requiring action on the whole system by those with the biggest stake in it.

The Phantom Report. Working with the planning councils in 1969, I often heard members mention a health care firm's consulting report. It was said to contain much data and many ideas subsequently used. It had been created three or four years earlier, and nobody knew where it was. It rattled like a skeleton whenever someone opened an organizational closet. "Oh, yeah," somebody would say, "that consulting report recommended we should _____." (Fill in the blank with whatever discovery your planning council had just made.) Now I think I know where that report is. But that is getting ahead of my story.

Case 6. Do-It-Yourself Reorganizing: Getting Printing Inc.'s Report Out of the Drawer (1981)

I began actively studying the report-in-the-drawer phenomenon in 1981, a decade after Medical School. I had developed an interest in organizational structures and change processes in both medicine and industry. One day I got a call from the general manager of Printing Inc., a small division of an international corporation. His boss at world headquarters had told him he needed team building, and the corporate consultant recommended me.

Their market, the general manager told me, had been flat for a long time. Some products were holding, some dying, a few growing, some high-tech, some no-tech, but all made and sold in roughly the same way by the same people. The rising star, an electronic marvel, was buried deep in development. The old functional organization wasn't functioning like it used to. Everybody specialized, nobody cooperated.

My potential client was an ex-bomber pilot, meticulous and careful, a planner, not a spontaneous risk-taker like the fighter jocks who used to fly cover for him. When I asked him what *he* wanted, never mind his boss, he reached down into his bottom left desk drawer and, using both hands, pulled out a manuscript with more pages than *Gone with the Wind*. He opened it to two organization charts, which I have simplified here as "Now and Proposed." Two years earlier, unable to grow, he had called on a firm famous for its organization studies. Several consultants spent months talking to employees, doing library research, holding meetings. This was the result. They had recommended a decentralized product line organization that would be more flexible in the marketplace.

Why had he not implemented it? He hemmed and hawed for five minutes. The long and short of it was that the report was controversial. It would change every manager's job. My god, old Charlie had run manufacturing for twenty-three years. This general manager, like many top executives, considered himself a sensitive "one-on-one" manager. He had talked the report over with each person privately. No sale. Everybody had a different opinion about what to do, but on one thing everyone agreed: none wanted their jobs changed. They never had discussed it "as a team" since the day the consultants presented it and said good-bye.

That afternoon the general manager convened his team (his non-team). We began to talk about the report like a black-sheep

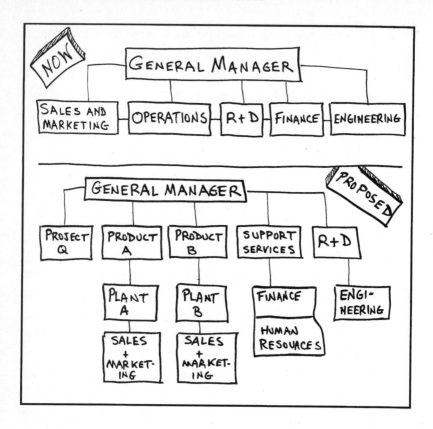

relative who had skipped the country. Finally, not knowing what else to do, I asked whether they would be interested in comparing what was in the report on the table (furtive glances would it explode?) with other structural ideas they had raised in the meeting.

Guided Self-Reorganizing. There are, broadly speaking, three ways to organize a business: by function, by product lines, or some combination, called matrix. Variations are possible on each form, depending on local realities, technology, number of products, geography, how fast things are changing. An organization study tends to recommend whatever you don't have now. That is based on the theory — faultless, when you think about it — that if what you have now isn't working well, you need something else.

Functional and product-line organizations both reach their limits after a while.

Functions tend to build in-depth expertise — and high walls. They make it hard to bring in new products. Product-line organizations maintain flexibility; the cost may be in losing touch with state-of-the-art marketing, engineering, manufacturing, and human resource concepts. Big central staffs reassure top managers they still have control — an illusion bought with high overheads. Small central staffs mean lower overhead and more local control — and more uncertainty at the top. (Nothing comes free.)

Companies reorganize because *any* structure's weaknesses eventually sap its strengths (Weisbord, 1978b). I knew that from my years of medical school research with Lawrence and Charns, and from consultation in many companies reorganizing from this to that, or vice versa. The need to reorganize, I had learned, does not mean that things are screwed up. It's a sign of growth, evolution, the earth turning on its axis just the way it should.

At Printing Inc. we discussed the options for an hour. Then the managers divided into three voluntary groups. One championed the old report; the others devised alternative structures. Each listed the pros and cons of their proposal (another way of saying "force field analysis"). We agreed that the first task was to come up with a structure they truly believed they could operate well. Suppose you were the sole owner? How would you organize this business? Once that was agreed upon, the job would not be finished until we had found appropriate slots for each manager.

The meeting was equal parts excitement and anxiety over the impact on everyone's jobs. Within twenty-four hours the managers had added some wrinkles to the expert consulting report and closed on a new structure. After two and a half years of aggravation, the report was implemented in a few months. A new job was found for each staff member. Old Charlie, after two stressful years worrying about being put out to pasture, took over a plant in another city.

A New Structure, or just a Report? I have reflected on that experience for years. What bemuses me are two questions:

1. Why do reports — especially excellent ones — end up in bottom desk drawers?
2. Under what conditions can they be implemented?

I have two answers to question number 1. The first is that some managers want reports, but they do not necessarily want them implemented. It has taken me a while to accept that, a triumphant integration (for me) of right-brain intuition with relentless rationality. Expertise has many uses besides solving the ostensible problem. Creating documents chock full of correct solutions is only one of them. Why would you want a report you do not intend to implement? Lots of reasons. One might be political — to satisfy a boss that you're on the case, yessir, or to placate a boss by using a highly recommended resource, let's say the parent company's favored consultant. (That, after all, is how the general manager started out to use me.)

A second reason might be unconscious — to act by turning the problem over to an expert. Most of us have ambivalence about tough dilemmas. Wilfred R. Bion, the psychoanalyst whose work I told about in Chapter Eight, could explain that one. The wish both to struggle through and to run away from the labyrinth is played out as dependency on the consultant. If the consultant acts out the assigned part — expert authority — and accepts the task of coming up with the perfect solution, the client is off the hook. The analysis and recommendations may seem too idealistic or too complicated, and so need not be implemented. Not doing anything becomes a prudent decision.

It is easy to put the rap on the consultant. Indeed, the more comprehensive the expert's work, the harder it is for anyone else to get a piece of the action — the perfect "successful failure." Two University of Pennsylvania social systems consultants have described this pattern as unconscious forces that can trap unwary consultants. The better the consulting job, the more helpless the consultant becomes (Gilmore and Krantz, 1985).

As for the second question — how to get reports out — just as some people only want reports, others (like the general manager in this case) want implementable solutions. They shelve the report, either because they don't see how to implement it, or because it violates a deeply held value. Those reports — and only those — are easy to get out of drawers. However, getting the report out calls for a different form of diagnosis from what the document contains. It calls for a process assessment — whether to try, how to do it, and who should be involved. Printing Inc.'s general manager got a diagnosis of the marketplace, the technology, and the limits of the existing organization structure. It was state-of-the-art content thinking. It assumed that given the "right" technical and economic solutions, reasonable people would do the right thing. That was precisely what Frederick Taylor assumed in 1893, an assumption smashed to smithereens by the machinists' union in the Watertown Arsenal strike of 1911 (see Chapter Three).

Rethinking Diagnosis. It is much easier to see now that implementing technically correct solutions calls for a different form of diagnosis. At Printing Inc., economics and technology got their due, but not the social side of the equation. The displacement of every manager (an identity crisis in every sense) was a problem worthy of the same attention as organizational structure. In fact, it was the organizational structure problem! That is a process diagnosis. The managers knew they needed a new structure. The consulting report made it plainer and said flat out what the structure should be. That's what gave everybody fits. Until those affected got into it, the general manager was sitting on a report he could not implement. Here was his paradox: he could not see how to invite participation when the outcome was so threatening.

"Ah," say you hard-nosed realists, "the solution is obvious. Forget participation. Tell people to take the new job or go see a headhunter." The general manager knew he had the power to do that. But here is the kicker: He would not *because it violated his values*. His integrity and self-esteem were at stake. He would not force people to act against what they saw as their own best interests. More, he believed forcing them would hurt the business.

Sure, the experts had presented a good plan. They were on the right track — but for one thing. In music stores you can buy jazz CDs of standard tunes entitled "Music Minus One," a full band except for piano or bass, drums or saxophone. Supply the missing line and the room swings. Without it, it doesn't sound right. The consulting report was a music-minus-one exercise, containing all the right changes on technology and economics. Until the general manager learned how to play the people part, the band could not swing. It did not meet the needs of a productive ensemble. That, above all — though neither he nor I could express it that way — was what both of us wished to create.

The action needed to create it is so simple that people often cannot, will not, believe it works. It requires that those with the biggest stake in the change sit down together and figure out, from all angles, the right thing to do. Their emotional stake in the outcome is not a reason for avoiding the issue. It is exactly the reason they should be included. At Printing Inc. that course of action supported the manager's values. He had been a prisoner of old assumptions, feeling that he alone had to meet everybody's needs, just the way the dean did at Medical School. He could not imagine how to do that constructively, given the radical change that was called for. And he was right.

The Missing Health Care Report. Working with Printing Inc.'s general manager, I experienced *déjà vu*. A few days after the offsite meeting, I was walking the factory aisles, watching a blur of labels stream between the printing heads. Suddenly I was back in the marble halls of Medical School. I knew what had become of the health care consulting report! It had gone into an administrator's file drawer. Probably it was still there. It could not have been implemented. It required a level of cooperation among clinical and basic science departments, hospital services, and administration unattainable in the 1960s.

Unprecedented changes called for unprecedented actions, such as the link-pin planning process. I had recommended that step out of ignorance of the rigidity and traditions of medical education. The planners accepted it as a desperate last-ditch stand. This process made possible a series of content changes heretofore inconceivable. Had I known more at the start, I am certain I would have assumed it would not work. Indeed, when some years later I *did* know more, I wrote an article analyzing why physicians resisted direct involvement in management, without drawing on my earlier experience to the contrary. The more interesting question to me now is why certain physicians became so deeply involved and committed. My personal doctor, the leader of the mission planning council, still talked twenty years later about the ways it influenced the management of his own office.

Printing Inc. Revisited (2002)

After reorganizing at the top, Printing Inc. undertook a series of successful work redesigns. People joined planning teams from all levels in customer service, art and graphics, and planning and scheduling. Each group devised its own multi-skilled, self-directed model. With each implementation, lead times from order placement to delivery were reduced, along with errors and costs. At last even the press room reorganized. By the early 1980s, the employees, from a sense of ownership bred of designing their own work, turned an ink-spattered slap-dash area into an industrial space clean and neat enough to be a cafeteria.

In 2002 I called the plant and was told that it soon would be no more. I arranged a visit and a few days later drove the seventeen miles that would take me back twenty years. I drove slowly, my car a time capsule, remembering the turns that would take me from the freeway through a shopping district to a middle class residential street. Some blocks later I found the plant on my left, a one-story stone-faced building sitting all alone on a large tract across from a row of 1950s perma-stone duplex houses.

This February day there were patches of snow in the street. A sign at one corner of the building announced, "Available 117,000 square feet, 11.8 acres." The reception area was as I remembered it. The last time I was there the woman who greeted me from a glass booth to the left of the door would have been a team member rotating from other work. Now she was a dedicated receptionist.

The controller in a sports shirt and casual shoes greeted me, a squarish man with a brush cut and a nice manner. He quickly informed me that his main job was closing down the plant. The customer service and printing operations were moving south. Only the machinery business would remain either as tenant or in a new facility. He took me on a tour of spaces I had not seen in twenty years.

We entered a light, bright, open office, once the customer service and art and graphics areas. The old partitions were gone. I noted big modern desks to the left and right, half of them vacant. The place was informal, subdued, more casual and friendly than I remembered, and still businesslike. I recognized Don, a former plant manager, immediately. Having outlasted seven general managers in as many years, he now ran order processing and customer service. Don was the same, smiling, garrulous guy except twenty years older, in a sweatshirt, still slender and with most of his hair. He talked to me with one foot up on the desk.

He informed me that of the forty-four people in his area only eleven remained. There was no tension, but a pall of sadness hung over the room, for this was a good place to work. Now the remaining dozens of people would lose their jobs. I met a woman who had participated in the work redesign years earlier. She was now a team of one. She sat at a computer terminal, headset around her ears, doing the whole job much like the folks at my old company were doing in the new century.

"We had ninety middle managers at one time", said Don. Now operations had four supervisors, but needed only two "They are called team leaders," he added, "but they do little leading. They provide support and problem solving if needed. They have their own accounts and their own jobs. We found that the multi-skilling worked so well that teams became unnecessary. People know what to do, have all the tools to do it, and work on their own." Most had their own customers, and they could also back up anybody else because the computers gave everyone access to every account.

The work that began two decades earlier had continued, despite several reorganizations, clear up to the year 2000. "Actually," Don went on, reflecting on the past, "the multi-skilling and teams were in conflict. You don't need teams when everyone has their own customers and knows what to do. The focus now is on how good your system is. And hopefully you develop the system with the people who do the work. That's what we do now, and have done ever since you left."

In the factory the machines remained as the design teams had rearranged them years before, in clusters of different sizes related to certain markets. However, the workers were back in functional teams based on the size and type of press. So jobs were grouped not by customer but by the presses on which they would run. "We tried organizing around the customer with three different machines," said Don, "but that turned out to be flawed thinking." Now, the organization was okay but the old layout worked against them.

"Efficiency is high," the controller said, "the quality good, and the customers like us. We just can't afford to keep two plants. Our overseas business is growing, but domestic sales are dropping 10 percent a year as more apparel manufacturers move offshore." This day, he pointed out, only three of ten machines were running, on a mid-week, mid-morning shift. Compared to the early 1980s the place was relatively quiet, and few people were to be seen.

The manufacturing was going south, even though some functions had been brought back from Mexico for a big customer that required American-made tags and labels. But it all would be consolidated in North Carolina. Local employees had been given nine months' notice, and many would receive up to a year's severance.

The company had set up counseling and job search services for all who wanted them.

Some months later, Don, now retired, sent me an email. "I wish there was a way to capture the real story. The endless parade of 'Professional Managers,'" he wrote, "and the decisions ranging from questionable to really bad, the individuals who refused to listen because they 'knew' that theirs was the only way and the focus that moved off of what was good for the customer and onto making the 'numbers' look good." In short, Printing, Inc., like many small acquisitions of global giants, had become, despite the best intentions of its workforce and middle managers, a dysfunctional stepchild.

Implications for Practice. This story repeats experiences clear back to Frederick Taylor. In a market-driven business, no matter how good the work system, no matter how involved and happy the people, a workplace lasts only so long as its economics satisfy the backroom strategists. At Printing Inc. key decisions came to be made by itinerant managers with no stake in the hard-won designs of those doing the work. In such cases there is nothing we can "build in" to assure continuity. This lesson is especially poignant in publicly traded global corporations. Employee and customer satisfaction may be highlights of the mission statement. In the new millennium, distant market and stock price strategies determined the work lives of countless people around the world.

The Case for Process-Focused Assessment

The four cases in Chapter Eleven have the consultants doing most of the initial analytical work. They act as unfreezing and diagnostic experts. At Printing Inc. and Medical School we see another, simpler way to help under conditions of rapid change. In neither case was unfreezing needed. In fact, the consultant was called in because the systems were not frozen; they were caught in the bumpy turbulence Emery and Trist had described as a growing phenomenon in 1963. Profit-making business and nonprofit college alike were responding to dramatic changes in their markets and employees. Medical School already had a planning task force struggling to figure out how to proceed. Printing Inc. had a good content diagnosis and recommendations in a consulting report. It prescribed a structure to close gaps in an organization no longer responsive to its markets and new technologies. To get things moving, a process diagnosis was required. It took only a half-dozen brief interviews and a two-hour meeting to help the managers own up to their dilemma: (1) They needed to reorganize. (2) They were stuck procedurally, not in conflict about whether to do something. With attention focused on both realities, it became possible to make a movie that was not implicit in the proposed reorganization scheme.

At both Medical School and Printing Inc. you notice that further content diagnoses were done directly by the clients, as they got together and began scoping out action plans. In the first case that happened because I hardly knew what to do about medical education. At Printing Inc., however, I had a good grasp of the content. I was, after all, an ex-printer. I had a good grasp of costs and markets, production and sales, capital and labor from having managed for a decade and consulted for another. I knew the pros and cons of this structure versus that one, or this reward system, or that marketing strategy. I could have told my clients which policies or procedures would solve their organizational problems.

There are two things wrong with this approach in a world spinning faster, driven by microchips, knowledge work, rising expectations, and a crisis of values, both personal and general. One, I could be wrong. I could be wrong for the same reasons that any extrapolators of past data for future purposes are wrong. I could be wrong for the same reason the engineers were wrong when they told Jimmie Lee Jones, the Jet Press operator, that he did not know how to improve their contraption (see Chapter One), I could be wrong for the same reason the aerospace experts were wrong when they excluded the astronauts from the capsule design. Experts rarely have enough data.

Two, most people would not take my advice unless it squared with what they wanted to do anyway. They might pretend. That's always a good way to hedge a relationship with authority figures.

They would not follow through. It might be against their own best interests.

Yet management, besieged on all sides with problems and opportunities, asks consultants for help in ever more ambitious undertakings. Changing a corporate culture — a breathtaking idea to somebody like me who has trouble cleaning up his desk — has become a commonplace aspiration. Strategy zigzags, mergers, reorganizations, downsizing, decentralizing, centralizing, retraining, redesigning work — that's all very complicated, high-level stuff. If managers don't know how to do it, and consultants can't give them answers, how can we possibly get at it? That answer is that there *are* answers, just not the sort we have come to expect.

The snapshots needed now are of a qualitatively different kind from either the Taylor model *or* the Lewin model. Diagnosis no longer means unfreezing. Its function now is finding the leadership and focus likely to turn people's anxiety from the impulse to fight or flee into the constructive energy and mutual support needed to transform the system. Accept that problems are everywhere, like flowers in the woods. But not everybody is ready to be helped, nor every culture amenable to remodeling. There is a season for this work.

You can't separate structure from behavior any more than you can economics and technology from people. Engineers can't do it; psychologists can't do it; physicians can't do it. Neither can you or I. However, that is not the only point behind the need for a new practice theory. I also believe that the task-process linkage is a whole-system concept, not a discrete technique. For that reason I think that solving the big problems of corporate life — costs, markets, quality, customer satisfaction, money-making, fulfilling work — lie in systems improvement, not in problem solving.

Systems can be improved only to the extent that everyone who works in them understands how they work. Dignity and meaning come from deep engagement. Helping people rethink the whole system is the best way a systems consultant can reinforce dignity, meaning, and community. That requires a qualitatively different activity from simply soliciting input.

One of the earliest and most ambitious examples was British Airways' efforts in the 1980s to anticipate increased competition by "putting people first" — customers and employees both. They repeatedly brought thirty to forty thousand employees to London for day-long events geared to learning more about one another's jobs, airline economics, customer preferences, teamwork on behalf of internal and external customers, competitors' advertising and service (even eating other carriers' in-flight meals). Volunteer employee teams continued the effort worldwide. It was an ongoing systems improvement strategy British hoped would make it the "best airline in the world" (British Airways "Customer First Newsletter," spring 1986, issue No. 5). With the proliferation of "large-group interventions" since 1990, dozens of similar examples now exist (Bunker and Alban, 1996).

You can buy all sorts of useful advice. I will give you some for nothing. If you want a plan implemented, a company reorganized, work redesigned, or many problems solved all at once, get as many key stakeholders as possible in one room and ask them to work on the task together. Use a wide-angle lens. Reaffirm dignity. Help people find meaning in their work. Move toward *your* vision of community in the workplace.

It's not quite as easy or simple as that. It's certainly not the "one best way," to borrow a phrase from Taylor. It is quite simply the only way, if what Lewin called "life value" matters as much to you as technology or money.

Chapter Fourteen

Management Training in Academic Medicine: Whose Resistance Is This Anyway?

Historically, health professionals have tended to learn management skills in their own groups, physicians with physicians, nurses with nurses, and so on, thus replicating the model in which professional training was provided. However, effective management practices require integrative behavior and nowhere is this more obvious than in the relatively new and rapidly expanding area of primary care.

—— *Rachel Z. Booth, Associate Dean,*
University of Maryland School of Nursing,
December 4, 1979

Diagnosis means specifying gaps between the way things are and the way they should be. Both "are" and "should" are loaded words, for the first law of diagnosis can be summarized as follows: "Seek and ye shall find." In workplaces, if you look for resistance you will find it everywhere. When I went into organizational consulting in 1969, the systems reputed to be most resistant to change were those where expert professionals worked — medical schools, hospitals, laboratories, law firms, and universities. Professional experts demanded answers and advice from consultants. Answers they treated skeptically. Advice they were reluctant to take. Few systems were less receptive to organization development than those of physicians in the 1970s.

During a decade of consulting and research in ten medical schools and twenty-five teaching hospitals, I learned a great deal about resistance to OD. I reported on this work (much of it in collaboration with Paul Lawrence and Martin Charns) in a series of articles, notably one on why OD had not worked (so far) in medical centers (Weisbord, 1976). While writing this new edition, I decided to revisit this work too to see what I could learn. My last academic medical project was with the University of Maryland's primary care program between 1978 and 1980. In helping to develop an interdisciplinary training seminar, I was able to apply everything I had learned about medical systems. That learning, and how I came to revise some of my cherished ideas, is the subject of this chapter. Like any good mystery story, there are a few twists. These I will save for the end.

The DIAGNOSIS: Great Differentiation, Little Integration

OD, as we have seen, grew up a hybrid of many streams of inquiry dating back decades. Some of its origins were odd indeed. The leadership style industry is traceable to the studies by Ron Lippitt and Ralph White of preadolescent boys' clubs under Kurt Lewin's supervision at the University of Iowa in 1939 (Chapter Four). The self-managing team concept came from efforts by Wilfred Bion and Eric Trist to select field officers for the British Army early in World War II (Chapter Eight). Participative management stems from Lewin's studies with Margaret Mead during that war to change the food habits of Iowa housewives, steering them toward "variety meats" (for example, Spam), so as to save prime rib for the armed forces (Chapter Four). T-groups and later team building came from the founding of NTL Institute following workshops with the Connecticut Interracial Commission, also a Lewin-directed project, to improve leadership skills in tense communities (Chapter Five).

Output- Versus Input-Focused Organizations

Despite their diverse, non-commercial origins, OD techniques found their most enthusiastic reception in business and industry. If you looked at academic medical centers in the 1970s, the reasons for resistance to planned change were not far to seek. *Academic medical centers were upside down from business firms*. Exactly those systemic factors that made businesses amenable to OD were missing. On four critical organizational features, business firms and academic medical centers were mirror images. Business leaders managed *output-focused* organizations, emphasizing quantity and quality of goods and services produced.

Output-focused systems typically had

1. Clear-cut formal authority;
2. Concrete goals;
3. High interdependence; and
4. Agreed-on performance measures.

Customers evaluated businesses on the "output" end, based on satisfaction with goods and services. Academic medical centers were *input-focused*, evaluated by the staff's professional credentials and state-of-the-art technology. Such systems tended to have

1. Diffuse authority;
2. Abstract and often conflicting goals;
3. Low interdependence; and
4. Few or no widely accepted performance measures.

Professionals, of course, had personal standards for quality care, based in part on individual patient needs. So variable were (and are) these standards that it was (and is) hard for third parties to impose standard diagnoses and treatments to control costs. Indeed,

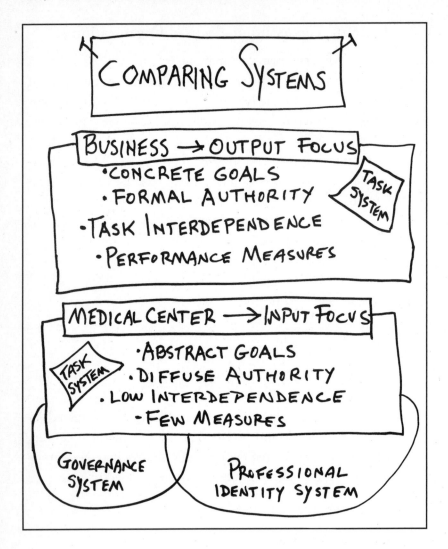

until hospitals began competing aggressively in the late 1980s, there was little organized effort to satisfy the patients. Today, in an age of free market medical care, I see TV testimonials from patients for medical centers and more emphasis on outcomes. None of this was evident in the 1970s. (See "Comparing Systems.")

There was another key difference, peculiar to academia and greatly amplified in academic medicine. In industry, people tended to wear only one hat at a time: production; sales; R&D; engineering; or other aspects. Coordination meant getting everybody to collaborate

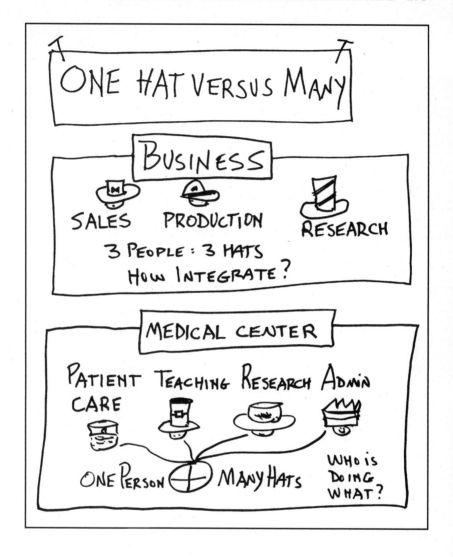

for a shared bottom line. Industry honored general managers who could integrate specialized functions (Weisbord, 1978). In medical schools, each faculty member wore as many as four hats at once: administration; patient care; teaching; and research. Each had two, three, or four individual bottom lines. (See "One Hat Versus Many.")

Administrators could hardly keep track of who wore which hats on what days. Faculty could pick research, patient care, or educational goals, depending on the month, the day, or the hour. They could switch in an eye blink, a phenomenon I came to call "the hat dance."

Indeed, individuals had no trouble sorting out their own work. Often one program's budget was used to subsidize another's. Those in charge, however, could hardly keep track of, let alone prioritize, so much differentiated activity. This was made more mind-numbing by nearly two dozen board-certified specialties (medicine, pediatrics, obstetrics, surgery, and so forth) and numerous subspecialties. No wonder medical faculty shunned administrators. Their attempts to integrate threatened everybody's freedom.

During many years of action research in academic medical centers, my colleagues and I interviewed scores of faculty (Weisbord, Lawrence, and Charns, 1978). When we asked about leadership, we often heard stereotypical personal characteristics named as problems, particularly for associate and assistant deans. This one was too young, only recently out of residency. ("Prejudice toward youth?" I wrote in my notebook.) That one was a woman, and women had a hard time gaining acceptance from male faculty. ("Women too?") Another was black, at a time of few black faculty members. "No prejudice," an interviewee assured me, "but . . . you know." (What I knew was that I could find racism anywhere. "Prejudice toward nonwhites, too?" I mused.)

Then there was the veteran faculty member, semi-retired, who was "over the hill." ("I think they don't like seniors, either," I wrote.) But the interviewee who confounded me was the one who said of a distinguished, prize-winning clinician, "I don't know what happened to him. He used to be a pretty good doc, but ever since he got on the dean's staff, he seems out of touch with everybody." ("They don't even like each other!" I observed.)

One day at my desk I took out my notebook and began contemplating this grim litany of isms. Except for a storm of negative projections, what, I asked myself, could these diverse medical professionals have in common? And then lightning struck me too. They were all *administrators*! Their goal was to inject order, predictability, and modest controls into systems where personal preference and free choice defined the work. Each was seeking to integrate a system whose members thrived on differentiation. Standard procedures and paper-work were unwanted bureaucratic intrusions.

People in diffuse structures with few organizational constraints tended to personalize everything. Anyone who sought to integrate the many hats of medical faculty on behalf of the whole was seen as acting in ways inimical to good research, teaching, and patient care. No wonder I found so few takers in professional systems during those years for methods advancing self-awareness, teamwork, and commitment to shared goals. (This was not true then of nursing, for nurses were trained to deliver coordinated care.)

In business firms, rewards and prestige went to generalists who could manage on behalf of the whole. In medical care, rewards went to awe-inspiring specialists. Consulting to business firms and medical schools, I lived in contradictory worlds. I became aware that most management technologies were adopted first by industry. All were designed to affect what I called the "task system," the core process of delivering products or services. Task systems thrived on clear authority, goals, interdependence, and measures. Business was relentlessly bottom line: higher profits, lower costs, increased share-holder value. Self-awareness, personal growth, and collaboration — core OD values — were touted as paths to more productive work-places, not just better human beings.

Medical centers in the 1970s, by contrast, represented a force field of three interlocking systems. There was a task system, to be sure, producing education, research, and patient care. And administrators ran the task system, with its diffuse goals, dispersed authority, unrecognized interdependence, and few measures, as best they could, seeking to impose structure, policy, and procedure amid piles of paperwork. Indeed, as Just Stoelwinder, an Australian physician and medical administrator, pointed out, physicians controlled up to 90 percent of hospital costs in the 1970s. Doctors decided who was hospitalized, what treatment and medicines patients received, and how long they stayed in. Administrators were left with supporting these decisions as efficiently as possible. (Weisbord and Stoelwinder, 1979).

The professional medical staffs, however, danced to more subtle melodies than the relentless drumbeat of bureaucracy. The two most powerful of these I dubbed the "identity system" and the "governance system." Professional identity in medicine was based on academic training and certified by outside agencies and licensing boards. Credentials were the name of that tune. If you asked the general physician with the little black bag who visited your grandparents' house in the 1930s what he did for a living he would say, "I'm a doctor." If you asked your personal physician forty years later, she replied, "I'm an internist" or "I'm a family practitioner." They were board certified, their identities validated, updated, and policed by diverse civil and professional agencies — the governance system — where the rules for professional conduct and competence were made.

It is no wonder so many medical professionals, socialized by training and licensure to autonomy in thought and deed, resisted methods intended to make them collaborative. Why should psychiatrists care whether surgeons showed up for work in the morning? Few specialists saw the value of behavioral science based training for managing work. Many considered administration a necessary evil, inimical to good patient care, research, and teaching.

The PRESCRIPTION: Training as Action Research

It was from this perspective that I began working with William S. Spicer, Jr., a feisty physician heading up the Office of Coordination of Primary Care Programs (OCPCP) at the University of Maryland in Baltimore in the late 1970s. Spicer's goal was a joint training program in medical management for primary care doctors, nurses, and pharmacists. He wanted all to become competent service coordinators, and he hoped to train a generation of professionals capable of integrating multiple disciplines. The vehicle would be an annual three-day workshop for interns, residents, and practitioners of medicine, nursing, and pharmacy.

Spicer, who had attended the Management Advancement Program of the Association of American Medical Colleges, recruited a physician and hospital administrator with a master's degree in management from MIT and a noted nurse-educator to plan the program. I was invited to join the staff by virtue of my consulting and research in medical systems.

The plan was to develop content similar to what the physicians had learned at MIT, then pilot the course with primary care faculty. We would start with a five-day workshop for faculty members in the three disciplines. They would be expected to support and in some cases staff three-day training events with graduate students. Modules included large systems change theory, management practices, group dynamics, interpersonal skills, and personal leadership.

I would coordinate the workshop design, and "stage manage" the faculty workshop. Something troubled me about the plan. My many years of research and consulting in medical schools had taught me that the managerial bag of tricks was much more highly valued by administrators than by medical professionals. The theory and practice of OD taught in business schools derived largely from industry. I was reluctant to prescribe this medicine for doctors, nurses, and pharmacists without more systematic clinical trials.

Kurt Lewin, the pioneer social scientist behind field theory and the primary ancestor of "change managers" today, held that reducing forces resisting change was easier than increasing driving forces. Pushing content that some professionals considered antithetical to good medical practice might increase negative forces in this system. For years I had heard colleagues in medical systems tell me that doctors insisted that you be an expert too, a projection I resisted, although with much anxiety and self-doubt. How could I force collaboration on people and unilaterally insist on more democratic practices? I considered my medical school consulting a form of Lewinian action research. None of us could say for sure what would work in upside-down organizational settings. We needed to enter into joint inquiry with the professionals.

In this sense I consciously emulated Lewin's model of shared agreement between clients and consultants on goals, procedures, and outcomes. That medical systems might require an exception to this core practice always troubled me. I wasn't ready to advocate techniques that medical professionals might not appreciate the same way I did. In fact, as our research had shown, much integration in medical schools actually took place *inside individuals* — who did some mix of patient care, education, and research — rather than by administrators. Even Spicer's title reflected this. He was the "coordinator" of primary care programs. He couldn't order anybody to do anything.

Building on Individual Autonomy

With these thoughts rattling in my head, I proposed another format for the faculty workshop. Instead of treating the OD repertoire as essential knowledge for medical professionals, why not invite the faculty to do action research with us? We would present the proposed training modules for their evaluation. These would include personal style instruments, interpersonal, group, and meeting skills, role analysis, and problem solving, and large systems change strategies. The faculty/participants' task would be to (1) try each activity as potential content for graduate training, and (2) decide what should be dropped, modified, or presented to graduate students. We would work out with them the relevant connections to medical management.

Nobody was expected to change his or her personal behavior, work systems, or organizational norms. Participants needn't like everything. We needn't defend anything. The deal was accepted and we conducted this experiment with twenty faculty members in January 1978. Despite much anxiety, the event was successful. We refined the program's content, emphasizing aspects of the training repertoire faculty considered most useful for medical professionals in building program manager skills.

No Right Answers

A key feature of the Maryland program centered on cases written by faculty members based on their actual experiences. Students, as part of their training, would use the cases to "diagnose" organizational problems and work out new solutions. One typical case had a person coming into the primary care clinic with severe dizziness. She says she is taking "pressure pills" four times a day. Except for unusually low blood pressure, the nurse practitioner finds nothing wrong. A medical resident confirms her findings. "Just get her to take her pills right," says the resident. "You've got to educate these people if you give them this sort of medicine." The nurse points out that the patient took her medicine for months and was fine until now. The nurse also notices, though, that the records show a different dosage than the patient's bottle. "The pharmacy messed up again!" she says. "I'm calling them."

"Don't bother," says the resident. "They don't listen anyway. Give her a new prescription." The nurse practitioner writes and the resident signs a new Rx. A few days later the woman is back in the emergency room after a fainting spell. This time she brings two bottles of the same medicine, one generic, one brand name. She is taking both, thinking she has two medicines. A resident on duty calls the pharmacist, who finds two prescriptions written two weeks apart.

"You should have caught this!" says the resident to the pharmacist. "Don't you talk to your clients?" To which the pharmacist replies, "This is what happens when doctors just countersign Rx's and don't really evaluate the case!" Whereupon the screening resident calls the clinic resident and both agree it was the nurse's fault for not taking the first bottle away from the patient. The nurse practitioner says, "This is what happens when you have physicians sitting around in offices reading journals instead of helping us out!"

Finding an Organizational Solution

To work on the case, we formed groups differentiated by specialty: nurse practitioners; pharmacists; and physicians. We asked each group to "diagnose" the situation. How did the patient get into trouble? After each group presented a diagnosis emphasizing its blameless behavior, people were reorganized into cross-disciplinary groups. The integrated groups were introduced to the technique of "responsibility charting." (See page 363.)

The diverse professionals were asked to make a responsibility chart ensuring that this troubling case would not occur again. Each of several groups came up with creative solutions. However, there was a big surprise. No two solutions were exactly alike. What happened next made a tableau etched in my memory. One of the physicians jumped up from his chair, clapped a hand to his head and said, "Omigod, there's no right answer to this!" He had found the outer limit of expertise. Putting the system at the center of the action, he realized that the right answer could only be collaboration. The best answer had to be the one everybody agreed on.

The workshop, with similar cases, was repeated for several years thereafter. It had considerable faculty support and a big impact on the primary care program. Which brings me, at last, to what I learned from all this.

Learning from Experience

Two noteworthy things happened in Maryland, challenging ideas that I had considered OD gospel. First, we expected the primary care faculty to put systems theory and matrix management high on the relevance list for graduate training. After all, these were the keys to understanding the system's many ins and outs at the theoretical level. We expected personal, group, and interpersonal skills training to rate relatively low. This was the "soft" stuff that people needing to be in control found so threatening. In fact, the faculty rated all the content as relevant, hard and soft alike. However, for graduate students, the faculty proposed, much to our surprise, that the large system concepts and theories be sacrificed in favor of personal, interpersonal, and group methods of interaction. Personal skills, they said, would be instantly useable on the job!

Huh? This was the very content that for years medical professionals in other contexts had dismissed as "touchy-feely." Given first-hand experience, no pressure, and no expectations, the faculty wrote their own prescriptions. Despite the temptation to play the medical game and prescribe desirable techniques, our training staff got more openness to new ideas by treating the techniques as hypotheses for action research. Had we not done that, the faculty would surely have confirmed our built-in prejudice about their built-in resistance.

Whence Cometh New Behavior?

My second "ah-ha" had to do with "transfer of training," the conditions under which people apply at work what they have learned in seminars. Earlier research had shown that newly learned skills and attitudes faded quickly once a workshop ended. To overcome this, people in training seminars were invited to make action plans. Up to 20 percent of my workshops in those days was reserved for "back home" applications. People would write and even rehearse action plans. Despite this, they often had a hard time affecting their systems. This was especially so when people came alone and went back to find that existing organizational norms, policies, practices, and/or leaders did not support new behavior.

In the faculty workshop, participants were not expected to use what they had learned. There were no "back home" exercises. All we asked was help in refining the curriculum. What we did not anticipate is that the faculty — researchers, clinicians, and teachers all — began applying what they had learned anyway! In followup interviews, many reported using responsibility charting, conflict management techniques, and meeting skills back on the job. OD wisdom had it that "just training" was an inferior way of inducing organizational change. Here we saw the stirrings of significant changes in the way primary care professionals worked with each other. Our faculty was not constrained by the corporate sanctions reported by business people. This was not "organizational change" in the strict sense. Yet many people were acting in new ways.

How could this be happening? I concluded that the same features that led Cohen and March (1974) to call universities "organized anarchies" also made possible effective action by individual faculty. In systems with diffuse authority, abstract goals, low interdependence, and few performance measures, all were queens and kings of their own domains.

"If the fans won't come," baseball's legendary phrase-maker Yogi Berra is reputed to have said, "nobody can stop them!" In academic medicine, if faculty wished to act in constructive ways, then nobody could stop them! Professional autonomy could work for, as well as against, better organizational practices. After Maryland, I stopped stereotyping experts and dropped "resistance to change" as a category of problem to be solved.

Chapter Fifteen

Productivity After Taylor: Systems Learning Replaces Expert Analysis

"... the process of becoming increasingly competent amounts to an increasing understanding of a subject in what can be called systems terms. What [successful learners] become good at is not fragmented for them, not isolated from its environment, not isolated in time or in space. They know the relevant elements and their interrelations intimately. These learners have a feeling for the meaning of the subject beyond its technical details and its formal structure. They have operative knowledge about this system, which is to say they know how to get this complex something to work in the way they intend . . ."

—— *Peter Vaill*, Learning as a Way
of Being, *1996, p. 111*

I started my history of productive workplaces with Frederick Taylor, "father of scientific management." For more than twenty years I have lived with a keen awareness of the secret niche that Taylorism fills in the human psyche, shaping workplaces to this day. You need not look far to find "electronic sweatshops" that use employees' computers rather than stop watches to dehumanize work (Garson, 1989). Yet, paradoxically, many old economy giants by the 20th Century's end had shucked the yoke of Taylorism. One notable example was Bethlehem Steel Corporation, the place where scientific management came to flower a century ago.

I cannot overstate the priceless lesson in systems thinking that I got at Bethlehem in the early 1980s. What I valued most about that experience I could not put into words until years later. Now I can say it in a sentence: *Systems "thinking" is useful in workplaces only to the extent it can be made experiential rather than conceptual, using structures that enable people to act on the whole*. My rethinking of systems thinking began in a steel mill, and that is the theme of this chapter.

Getting Ready for Labor-Management Cooperation

Frederick Taylor had exited Bethlehem Steel in 1901, forced out by managers whose power he usurped during three tumultuous years on the bumpy road to higher productivity. Some eighty years later Bethlehem invited my consulting firm to help it shake off the residue of a troubled labor-management history. The late Ben Scribner, an erstwhile operations researcher whom I had met in an organizational diagnosis seminar in the 1970s, recruited us. Ben, an idealistic, persistent, and doggedly effective engineer, was determined to help Bethlehem throw off the yoke of Taylorism. In mid-career he had taken up process consulting and earned a doctorate in psychology. He told me he was driven to integrate the "hard" and "soft" sides of managing and would one day invite Block Petrella Weisbord (BPW), my consulting firm, to help. This I considered a foolish pipe dream, given that even the executives in his company until recently had punched time clocks. So I was surprised to receive a phone call one spring day in 1981. "The time is now," said Ben.

Frederick Taylor had left Bethlehem with a modern cost accounting system, doubled stamping mill production, materials handling costs cut by half, and hourly wages 60 percent higher than when he arrived. By 1981, though, Taylor's ingenious 19th Century solutions had regressed to mindless time-and-motion studies and a tangled mess of 20th Century labor problems. The company had eleven steel plants, fourteen levels of management, 3,400 wage incentive plans, and 400 industrial engineers timing jobs and setting rates. Steelworkers were among the highest-paid blue-collar employees anywhere. Bethlehem's workforce averaged 130 percent of base pay. Yet, the company was losing $80 million a month. One estimate pegged the cost of poor quality alone at $1 billion a year, almost exactly the losses. And labor-management antagonism, a chronic problem in Taylor's day, had now reached mythic proportions.

A consulting study had pinpointed labor-management cooperation as a key to Bethlehem's future. After decades of labor strife, however, management was not ready to cooperate with the union. Our task was to devise a "readiness" program. We visited the plants, met the top managers, and proposed a plan for involving people at many levels in preparing for more cooperative union-management relations. The strategy included teaming with line managers in each plant dedicated to a concerted effort to change management assumptions and practices.

Although top executives supported this idea, we, like Taylor in 1898, found skepticism everywhere. Mid-level managers believed the hierarchy impregnable. United Steelworkers of America leadership rebuffed a bid to include union members. This hot potato, they said, was management's alone. Unable to involve the union on management's behalf, we determined to ready management to reach out for itself. Working with designated line managers, we started programs shaped by local needs in plants across the country.

Sparrows Point Plate Mill, 1981

Thus began my practical education in translating whole systems from a theoretical construct into action plans involving everyone. Sparrows Point, Maryland, was a company city, a sprawling complex of blast furnaces and finishing mills, company housing, schools, and stores. It was one of half a dozen major plants where Tony Petrella and I came looking for openings that would enable "readiness." We soon learned that the giant Plate Mill would shut down early in 1982 for maintenance. Workers would be furloughed for two weeks with pay while technical crews tore down, refurbished, and reassembled the mill.

That meant that some eighty non-union managers and staff (five levels!) could be available for readiness training. Here was a chance to go through work with the whole system and all its leadership. John Dupre, then a young BPW associate, and I met with the mill managers and the internal consulting and training staffs. Several had just returned from Japan. They described their shock at seeing the integration of new technologies with employee participation into work systems that defined the term "world class." We discussed what it would mean to involve everybody in improving the Plate Mill. Could people imagine a world class Sparrows Point?

What I recall most about that seminal meeting was the anxiety. It was palpable, bouncing off the conference room walls, a vortex of fear, fueled by the possibility that we might, just might . . . do . . . something . . . new! The norm for training was twenty people or fewer for a few days at a time. The human resource staff was understandably nervous at having eighty managers in one room all working at once, not for just a few days but two full weeks. What would we do for all that time? Would hands-on managers used to grime, grit, and the tangible satisfactions of piling up steel plate in the yard put up with a long talk fest? Even if the talk was tied to making plate steel?

Scribner talked in favor. The consultants talked risks and benefits. The grizzled old mill superintendent at last threw up his hands. If top management wanted it, that's what we would do. The issue was settled. We would find out soon enough the results of involving everybody in the whole mess, the way they did in Japan. In the words of Kris Kristofferson (1970), "Freedom's just another word for nothing left to lose." In the Plate Mill in the dark days before Christmas 1981, people had nothing to lose. The shutdown would take place early in the new year. For the first time the staff, instead of taking a vacation, would study the whole system together. We consultants had an opportunity unprecedented since Taylor's time, carte blanche to use our entire experience-based consulting and training repertoire — individual, group, and organizational activities — in one place at one time with all the key actors. Nobody could say, as we had often heard, "The wrong people are in the room!" Or "What's all this stuff have to do with making product?" We had all the right people and ample time to connect learning with doing.

A Two-Week Systems Workshop

The two-week workshop plan was as follows. All eighty Plate Mill managers — superintendent and assistants, foremen and their assistants, and service staff — would study the whole together. "The system" was defined as relationships within and among five centers of action:

1. Individual ways of thinking and acting;
2. Interpersonal relations with co-workers;
3. Team work;
4. Mill-wide organizational problems; and
5. Customers and suppliers, the mill's "environment."

People would work alone and in four groups: pairs; natural work teams; cross-functional problem-solving teams; and customer and supplier study teams. (See "Whole Systems Learning.") My knowledge of systems theory was then largely conceptual. I had done "open systems planning" exercises, usually with natural work groups or task forces. I could diagram environmental demands and constraints on a flip chart. I had never tried to facilitate learning on every level with so much of a system in the room. In short, I could imagine doing what I am about to describe. I did not imagine what would happen. It has taken me many versions of that experience to appreciate what power people can exert on their systems when they have access to ideas, authority, resources, customers, suppliers, and each other all at once.

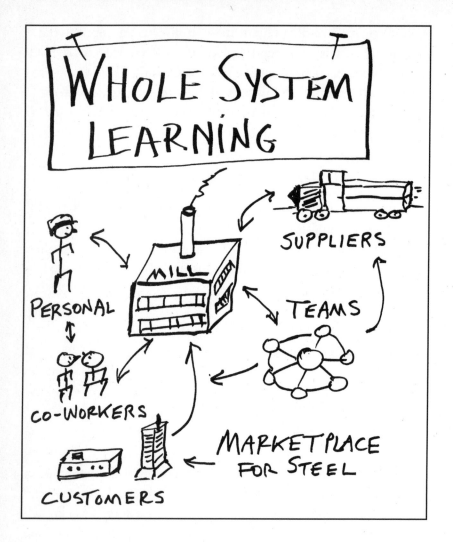

Experiencing the Whole System

In advance of the two-week seminar, managers and staff met to talk about what was keeping them from doing their best work. We introduced group problem-solving techniques. During the first week cross-functional teams began devising solutions they could implement. We then integrated group problem solving with each person's studying his or her preferred ways of doing things. Staffers filled out a "personal style" survey on their own attitudes and behavior and found out how their ways of thinking and doing affected their working together to do the job. On other days, people met with their supervisors. They talked about the changing role of supervision, from goals imposed by management, for example, to shared goals set jointly.

Teams studied their own "process issues" such as communications, control, trust, decision making, motivation, and the use of each other's capabilities. This content was integrated with personal styles and problem solving. At each step people were asked to make notes alone, to share them with others in their groups, and then to report out and discuss what they were learning. A typical question might be, "What do personal styles have to do with the mill problems we worked on this morning?"

At the start of week two, sales and marketing staff, who might as well have been Martians, came with overheads and spreadsheets. Everyone filed into the auditorium and saw the big picture on a large screen — the marketplace for steel plate and what was known about customer uses. In late morning, groups of five or six got into their cars and went to visit customers within driving distance of the plant.

The next day they reported to each other what they had learned. The room crackled with excitement as each group told its story. One veteran foreman told a story that raised the hairs on my neck. "This customer bought a crane," he said, "Spent $25,000 on it, just to turn our plates over. They said we were shipping 'em 'upside down.' Hell, we don't care which side is up. We told 'em we'd ship 'em right side up from now on. They didn't need that crane anymore!" That day we heard many similar stories, of changes easily made to the work system as a direct result of meeting customers face-to-face and seeing how the product was used.

Later that week the groups visited their raw steel suppliers, Sparrows Point's blast furnace and steel-making department. Many had never been there, although it was less than a quarter of a mile away. Again, reports, and again, revelations. "I've worked here thirty years," one man said, "and I've never seen those guys make steel. We do a lot of complaining about what they send us. Well, I can tell you they have the same problems we do, and they are busting their butts the same way we do. We have to work with them if we're going to keep our quality up."

Systems Thinking as Systems Doing

At Sparrows Point I first became aware of what ought to be a core principle of workplace education: *"Systems thinking" becomes useable in workplaces when people experience the whole for themselves.* Drawing "environmental scans" on flip charts is no substitute for interacting with those who *are* your environment. During those two weeks I gave up a fantasy that had haunted my consultant identity, that if only I could master systems concepts, tossing off words like "equifinality" and "negative entropy," I would, at last, become a transformer of workplaces. Such ideas could not be acted on unless people identified systems improving with everyday experience. They simply had to gain control of their own work. At Sparrows Point, without any big words, we expanded systems thinking into everyday experience, linking minds, hearts, and hands with making steel plate.

In the months that followed, the internal consulting staff got the "whole system in the room" repeatedly as each mill shut down for maintenance or closed temporarily for lack of work. Eventually they involved 2,000 people in studying the whole and improving their own work systems. Soon, customer-supplier teams sprouted up throughout the plant. One group, for example, took on the problem of moving raw steel from primary to finishing mills while still warm, eliminating a costly reheating process. Soon, these teams became standard procedure for all cross-functional problems. Eventually, union leaders in each mill, wanting to be part of the action, officially unable to back the effort, began attending readiness sessions anyway.

The internal staff sought training in socio-technical work design and began involving workers in the redesign of their own systems.

Management and the United Steelworkers of America signed a local memo of agreement assuring cooperation on new technology. For the first time, a joint labor-management team installed a new continuous caster that became one of the best performers anywhere. At Sparrows Point "readiness" metamorphosed into effective action as managers and steelworkers implemented new forms of cooperation. BPW also developed a team training program to enable the use of Joseph Juran's statistical process control methods. We taught it to thirty Bethlehem managers who implemented it with teams in all the plants. Sparrows Point also sought help from Eli Goldratt, the Israeli engineer who had written a novel called *The Goal* that elucidated a "Theory of Constraints" for systems improvement (Goldratt and Cox, 1985). They changed everything after that — new markets, new products, the works. By the end of the 1980s, Sparrows Point became what seemed an impossible dream a decade earlier. They were a world-class operation.

Sparrows Point Fifteen Years Later

In 2000 I called up John ("Rocky") Rockstroh, lead internal consultant for the Sparrows Point work. Retired now, facing cuts in health and retirement benefits because of steel industry instability, still he was glad to reminisce. "From '81 to '83 the culture changed," said Rocky. "We realized the way to manage the business was to get everyone involved. We put a stake in the heart of Taylorism. We changed the role of the industrial engineer." By the year 2000 the IE's, instead of just timing jobs and setting rates, also had become process and methods improvement experts, doing postmortems on outages and other problems.

"The place was never the same after the Plate Mill project," said Rocky. "It became natural to ask, 'Who else do we need in the room to solve this problem.'" Rocky recalled how one manager, after seeing what the finishing mills had done, insisted on systemwide readiness training for the "hot" side, even though it included furnaces that could never be shut down. "I was

Systems Improving 101: If You Can't Get the "Whole System" Use the "Three-by-Three Rule."

From Sparrows Point I derived my Three-by-Three Rule, a practical way to start people improving the whole. This is not quite a recipe. You will have to choose your own ingredients, preparation time, and serving size.

Pick your bureaucracy. The key thing is that you have a legitimate reason for calling a meeting. Be clear about where you sit, what your responsibility is, and which others you need to get action. Whether you are staff or line, high or low, doesn't matter, only that you have the standing to invite others.

Pick an issue that affects people at more than one level. Make it something in which people have a big stake, where the solution would be a blessing, not a threat, to almost everyone. (I say "almost" because I never found an issue so benign that it didn't threaten somebody. Be good to yourself and accept reality. You will never please all the people all the time.)

Make it an issue where you have to act. It helps if you are not sure what you ought to do, but even if you know what you should do, this is the fastest road to surfacing potential roadblocks and to getting help. You are inviting people to advise you on what to do. You are not giving up your responsibility to decide.

Here is the key step. Do not compromise. Get a minimum of three levels in the room from the unit where action is required (vice president, director, supervisors, or directors, supervisors, workers) and a minimum of three interested functions (manufacturing, sales, research; finance, human resources, engineering) depending on the issue.

Have everyone hear from everyone else about his or her stake in the issue before proposing anything. In groups of thirty or fewer you can keep everyone together; ask each person to make a statement in a minute or less. In larger groups, have each group talk together for fifteen minutes about its stake and report to the whole. This is called "differentiating," which is the key to integrating anything.

Organize cross-functional groups — if necessary — to plan action steps.

Have everything happen in public. Don't end the meeting until all say what *they* will do next.

fresh from a consulting skills workshop," Rocky recalled, "so I used words I had never said in my life. I told him that for me to help him there were certain things I wanted him to do too." He would have to get together managers from all the operations to help solve the problem of training everyone while keeping the furnaces hot. Eventually they came up with a plan to get one-fourth of the managers together in each of four workshops that would include a cross section of people from operations, electrical and mechanical departments, and staff. What had he gained personally from this, I asked Rocky. "Always look downstream and upstream to learn the whole system," he said without hesitation.

Today, the Sparrows Point training program seems overloaded to me. It was state-of-the-art circa 1982. We threw in everything we knew. The critical learning, however, was what the steel makers went out and got for themselves. Today there are many large-group processes for involving everybody and many elegant experiential learning methods (Holman and Devane, 2001). Some processes (future search is one) do not require new skills or self-awareness training at all before people improve their systems. Nonetheless, the general idea remains durable. Getting the whole system in the room and giving all a chance to learn from one another is surely a no-fail productivity enhancement strategy, no matter what procedures you use.

Bethlehem Steel in the 21st Century

On the Internet I also did a little review of the new millennium steel industry in the United States. While steelworkers became ever more productive, globalization had altered the face of steel production. Modern mills in Europe, Asia, and South America were making good steel with lower labor costs and shipping it around the world. Consolidations were taking place everywhere.

Interested parties debated endlessly whether governments ought to subsidize critical industries like steel making.

In the 1980s and 1990s Bethlehem Steel closed or merged one facility after another, going from eleven plants to four. Having lost $1.5 billion in 1982, the company started making money again. But not for long. In 1995, the erectors of the Golden Gate Bridge and the Empire State Building ceased making structural steel altogether.

In December 1997 the corporation announced the closing of the coke works in Bethlehem, Pennsylvania, its hometown, ending 140 years of steel making there. The last unit of the plant where Frederick Taylor had created the world's most efficient machine shop, invented high-speed steel, and studied the "law of heavy laboring," was no more. Henceforth, the Sparrows Point blast furnace would import its coke from China and Japan. About the same time Bethlehem bought Lukens Steel, a company with two plate mills. The Sparrows Point plate mill, world class at last, was shut down again, not for maintenance but for good.

In September 2001 the corporation hired a noted turnaround specialist, Robert Miller, Jr., as chairman and CEO. He had his work cut out for him. The firm now supported six retirees for every active employee, a $5 billion liability. A month later *The New York Times* reported that Bethlehem Steel had filed for Chapter 11 bankruptcy protection. They would go on with a reduced workforce and radically changed product lines. New talks began with the United Steelworkers aimed at an unprecedented realignment of workplace restrictions built into earlier contracts that would mark the complete demise of Taylorism at Bethlehem Steel. "We need a comprehensive restructuring," said Miller, "so that our employees can be part of a globally competitive steel industry in the future" (Miller, 2002).

In 2003, I received a note from Connie Fuller, who had worked with Ben Scribner years before at Bethlehem and was now a human resource manager in another company. "I think a case could be made," wrote Fuller, "that the change initiatives enabled the company as a whole, and Sparrows Point in particular, to remain viable for much longer than it would have otherwise. I know that the work done at Bethlehem Steel changed the culture forever."

A few days later I read that the company had cut off health and insurance benefits to retirees and arranged to sell its assets to International Steel Group of Cleveland, a firm noted for innovative work systems. The major remaining facilities at Burns Harbor, Michigan, and Sparrows Point, Maryland, would be renamed ISG/Bethlehem. On April 30, 2003, roughly 100 years after Frederick Taylor invented scientific management and twenty years after I had learned to increase productivity by getting the whole system in the room, the Bethlehem Steel Corporation was no more (Caruso, 2003).

Part Three

LEARNING AND APPLYING NEW PRACTICE THEORIES

Perhaps life is not a race whose only goal is being foremost. Perhaps true felicity does not lie in continually outgoing the next before. Perhaps the truth lies in what most of the world outside the modern West has always believed, namely that there are practices of life, good in themselves, that are inherently fulfilling. Perhaps work that is intrinsically rewarding is better for human beings than work that is only extrinsically rewarded.

—— *Bellah and others*, Habits of the Heart,
1985, p. 295

In Part Two I reviewed several projects concerned with developing better workplaces. I suggested that in "permanent whitewater" new methods are needed to realize our values and keep businesses viable. Just as throwing money at problems sometimes makes them worse, so does throwing technology, even of the human relations sort. I can sum up the story so far on one flip chart: "A Century of Learning."

Our society has learned a great deal about what works — practically, politically, and morally — these last 100 years. Now we must come to see learning, not training, as a way of life. Training is something we make time for. Learning happens routinely every day as we go about our business. Workshops are wonderful milestones in personal skill building, but unless we keep learning every day, no amount of training will help us stay up with new technology and markets. That means structuring work so that we can keep on learning.

Question to myself: what must we learn?

Answer: how to get everybody improving whole systems.

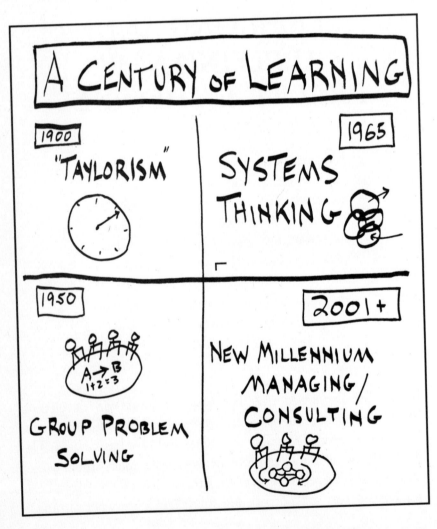

Merging Two Traditions

Part Three begins (Chapter Sixteen) with a new practice theory for managers and consultants, my road map toward getting everybody improving whole systems. It includes (Chapter Twenty) a case employing this map in the rescue of an economically troubled company. The case brings together learning from many places I have visited in this book. It illustrates an effort to integrate two new forms of action seeded in the 1950s — organization development (OD) and sociotechnical systems (STS) design — both stimulated by Kurt Lewin's fertile mind, both intended as correctives to bureaucracy, fragmented work, and authoritarianism. Both traditions focused on learning first. Sharing Lewin's practice-theory road map and values, they specialized in different pieces of the same jigsaw puzzle.

OD, a spin-off of NTL Institute's human relations laboratories, evolved as a strategy for reorienting management behavior. It was invented by people frustrated at transferring T-group learning into the workplace. The task-process lens, attached to an action-research camera, revealed new dimensions of work life not considered important before. More, this tool became useful to unfreeze, move, and refreeze systems. OD practitioners worked primarily on perceptions, feelings, relationships, attitudes, group norms, and communications skills among people at the top and middle of organizations. They advocated self-awareness to improve relationships in teams, among functions, and throughout systems. Their assumption was that openness and responsibility for self are existentially good conditions on which better work systems depend (Neilsen, 1984). OD practitioners, influenced by Bennis's passionate vision (1966) of an integration of science and democracy, aimed for flatter organizations and more egalitarian relationships. Yet the techniques and methods were rarely applied to such mundane matters as factory and office work or used with union members and hourly workers.

OD and STS — The Same Coin

When I became a consultant in 1969, I expected to do what I had done as a manager — help people install autonomous work teams. However, I came in through the NTL door, went to T-groups, and learned team building. In short order I found myself working in country clubs and boardrooms with chief executives and top managements. Imbued with Beckhard's concept (1969) of a large-systems change as a top-down strategy for reorienting management culture, I had faith that, layer by layer, every corporate onion could be peeled. Eventually I would help the hands-on operators take charge of their work, too. After some years I realized that my OD projects always stalled somewhere between the top and bottom or between the staff and line. I might survey workers at the bottom but rarely consulted with them. I might train supervisors, but I only saw the people being supervised during a quick walkthrough. What I hoped to do (I did not know it then) belonged to sociotechnical systems (STS), a tradition practiced in different circles from the ones I was going around in during the early 1970s.

STS designers sought to reduce the need for management and supervision by increasing skills and responsibility lower down. Where ODers sought new behavior and relationships, STSers designed new organizational structures. Inevitably — an open-systems discovery — each method found need for the other. ODers pushed up against the limits of assumptions about supervision, spans of control, and staff-line relations. STSers, some at least, realized that novel structures required perceptual, communications, and leadership skills that could be learned through group dynamics training.

STS design metamorphosed in the 1970s into a worldwide movement labeled "quality of working life" (QWL). It became especially attractive as a tool for uniting management and organized labor in making work more secure. It emphasized high-quality products, services, and relationships across functions and levels and between customers and producers. OD meanwhile moved toward "organizational transformation" (OT): discontinuous, rapid culture change helped by novel questions about myths, heroes, rituals, unwritten rules, values, and so on. Each movement inevitably adopted methods, techniques, and perspectives from the other. Structure and behavior constitute two sides of the same coin. Productive workplaces, I think, require continuous work both on ourselves and on our structures.

Emerging New Millenium Practices

Chapters Seventeen through Twenty-One illustrate a growing synthesis of methods for what I call "21st-Century management and consultation." It is based on open-systems thinking that includes economic realities, technological change, and democratic values — the dignity of each person and the responsibility of each for the common good. It is first and always a broad learning strategy, one that includes self-awareness, interpersonal, group, and technical skills, economic knowledge, and social responsibility.

I describe preferences, not certainties. These surely are not the only methods that embody my beliefs. They are simply the ones I know best. They come from Lewin and laboratory learning, from McGregor and Lippitt, Emery and Trist, and many others — all infused with my biases, my managerial and consulting experiences. Snap-shooting, as we shall see in Chapter Sixteen, has a dynamic purpose inseparable from moviemaking: to turn anxiety into creative energy and to mobilize support for constructive action taking. To bring the two processes closer together in a way that our changing reality says they should be, that constitutes a methodology for productive workplaces. The growing literature on the use of the "whole brain," the importance of intuition in decision making, and a host of nonrational processes suggest that, as knowledge proliferates, the medical model proves less and less satisfying for workplace improvement. Something novel and unquantifiable happens when the whole system joins in an important task. The new arena for action is networks of people learning and deciding together what to do next, based on open-systems maps, freely available information, and the evidence of their senses.

At the dawn of the 21st Century, we are groping toward a wholly new way of envisioning these processes: as purposeful, idealistic, tradition-conserving, radical, discontinuous, and innovative all at once. There is arrogance in believing one or a few people hold special unfreezing techniques. If we wish to find community and identity in democratic societies, harmony between personal and general interests, we must work together on economics and technology. The abstract forces that pull us apart also provide the crucial cement that binds us together — in finding more humane and sensible solutions. If I could ask one thing of a crystal ball in every new situation it would not be "What's wrong and what will fix it?" It would be "What's possible here and who cares?"

Three Leverage Points

There are three powerful levers in every workplace to turn anxiety into energy: purposes, relationships, and structure. Each is linked in an endless chain with the others. Purpose or mission — what business we are in — embodies future visions on which security and meaning depend. Relationships — connections with co-workers that let us feel whole — require cooperation across lines of hierarchy, function, class, race, and gender. Structure — who gets to do what — affects self-esteem, dignity, and learning. In my 100-year journey through the work world, as manager, consultant, historian, I find myself attracted to three processes, each starting with one of these levers.

For *purposes*, I like the "future search," a powerful exercise for any organization at a strategic turning point (Chapters Twenty and Twenty-One). If you only have time for one meeting, this is the one to have. Future search enables people to articulate key values, create attractive futures, and build commitment for action very quickly. Paradoxically, people often improve their relationships too as they do tasks of mutual concern. Future search may lead to structural changes too, for the meeting enables new forms of action beyond the capability of the existing system — until now.

Since the first edition of this book, I have seen future search extended in ways not imagined twenty years ago. It has been used to create new visions, to gain commitment to existing visions, to create strategic plans, and to implement plans already made and stalled for lack of buy-in. In 2003 I had a future search experience undreamed of until recently: redesigning a global distribution system, together with an implementation plan, and commitment from the top down in eighteen hours (rather than the usual six months) as a result of having people from all functions and parts of the world in the room (Chapter Twenty).

For *relationships,* I like guided team development for learning to maintain innovation in a sea of change. The sort I advocate (Chapter Seventeen) depends on developing awareness, skills, and cooperation within a natural work group against a social and business backdrop. This mode is most useful in support of other development strategies. Its strength — encouraging *this* team to accept responsibility for its work — is its severest limitation. For a team succeeds only when it can also work up, down, and sideways. Still, the face-to-face work group remains the building block for every organization.

For *structure,* customer-focused work design (Chapter Eighteen) is the best method I know to create better jobs, higher output and quality at lower cost, greater system flexibility, increased self-control. This mode involves people from many functions and levels in rethinking how they operate in light of changing customer needs and technologies, and in making their own implementation plans.

The three modes are not substitutes for one another. They are mutually reinforcing. The use of any one heightens the need for the others. Each could be a step in a strategy for ongoing development. Indeed, elements of each always surface in any one. It couldn't be otherwise in an open system. Any combination — you have to make up your own — makes a powerful large-systems change strategy. I describe one example in Chapter Nineteen. Finally in Chapter Twenty-One I sum up what I learned from revisiting my cases.

While I'm glad to share my experience, I doubt that it is repeatable. If you want *the* strategy, you have to find a promising opportunity and plunge ahead. Chapter Sixteen, coming next, provides a new practice-theory road map to stimulate your imagination.

Chapter Sixteen

Managing and Consulting in the 21st Century

The results of this generalized speedup of the corporate metabolism are multiple: shorter product life cycles, more leasing and renting, more frequent buying and selling, more ephemeral consumption patterns, more fads, more training time for workers (who must continually adjust to new procedures), more frequent changes in contracts, more negotiations and legal work, more pricing changes, more job turnover, more dependence on data, more ad *hoc* organization. . . . Under these escalating pressures it is easy to see why so many businessmen, bankers, and corporate executives wonder what exactly they are doing and why. Brought up with Second Wave certainties, they see the world they knew tearing apart under the impact of an accelerating wave of change.

—— *Alvin Toffler,* The Third Wave, *1980, p. 230*

Any reader of the daily newspaper knows that a sea tide of change has been surging through the work world for two decades, different from anything before. Futurist Alvin Toffler (1980) called it "the third wave" to differentiate it from the agricultural and industrial revolutions of bygone eras. Now firmly into the new century, we are changing ever more rapidly from physical to knowledge work, mechanical to process technologies, manufacturing to service economies, and central to local control. Here, I use the term "21st

Century" to describe the ever-changing conditions we face and the new practices we are evolving to better meet them.

In this chapter I will sketch the broad outlines of an integrated practice theory for recovering dignity, meaning, and community in a stormy sea of change. A practice theory, in Peter Vaill's (1979) words, is one which resembles a formal theory but is in no sense identical. It is based on experience, not systematic research. It constitutes a mental map of what's important and what to do about it. I have no doubt that research studies can be devised to substantiate what I will say. However, I base my theory on mental maps drawn up while rethinking the cases in Part Two in light of the history in Part One.

My new practice-theory road map is summed up as "Learning Curve." In 1900 Taylor had experts solve problems for people — scientific management. In 1950 Lewin's descendants started everybody solving their own problems — participative management. About 1965 experts discovered systems thinking and began improving whole systems *for* other people. Now we are learning how to get everybody improving whole systems. The purpose of this chapter is to accelerate that trend.

I will suggest practices for those who want to go beyond problem solving and participation to the heart of the matter: giving people direct influence over the economics and technology of their work. I believe that by keeping this objective in mind we can think our way out of narrow methods that make things worse, techniques that don't work, and panaceas that only disappoint. By centering on these purposes, we might undertake projects — flying like birds — previously considered impossible. The guidelines that follow reflect my vision of what managers and consultants can do to make the new paradigm live in the workplace. Some people apply them now without knowing it. Others mix these practices with more traditional ones. They do not constitute a formula for day-to-day managing, or a cookbook of planned change. I have sought to describe emerging practices consistent with history, current knowledge, the great dilemmas we face, and wide aspirations: for dignity, meaning, and community. They are practices to help us move along the learning curve, toward the point where everybody is involved in improving whole systems.

Though I write as a consultant now, most comments apply to managers too. "Ninety percent of living," comedian Woody Allen once said, "is just showing up." Hidden in the joke is a grain of wisdom. Getting the right people together is probably 90 percent of 21st Century managing. The other 10 percent is helping them commit to valued purposes and tasks. That means having their own experience.

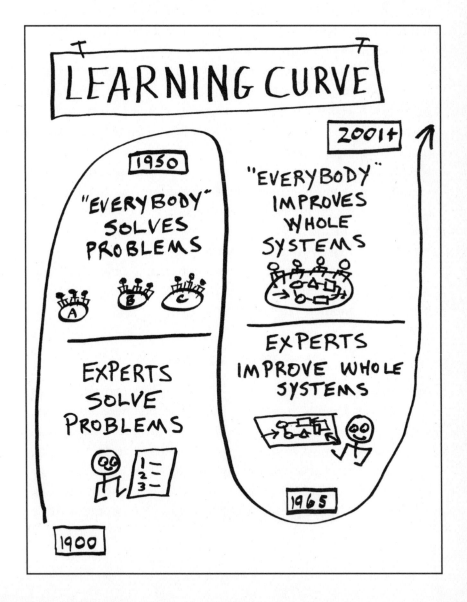

No person, not even an expert, unfreezes another. We move in our own way at our own pace, regardless of techniques used. We change as we have face-to-face contact with others and get new information. We change when we listen and respond in new ways, listening to our own inner voices, hearing ourselves say things we never said before. We change when we can think out loud *together with others whose actions affect us*. Applying social science techniques (or any techniques) piecemeal to problems, big or little, probably makes things worse. Looking together with an eye on the future at how the whole system works is the shortest route to solving handfuls of problems at once.

This calls for another way of talking, different from medical lingo about diagnosis and treatment. As a consultant, I am learning to assess whether I can make a contribution, in other words, to find out if the season is right for action rather than sell a new technique. I also have moved away from flagging discrepancies between words and deeds — an act of narrow verbal abstraction that, in my view, has little motivating power — toward testing people's willingness to take on important tasks together. If I were managing today, I would ask myself every morning which principles I intended to live by that day. I am not saying these are the only valid perspectives on managing and consulting, only that I find them compatible with my belief in the centrality of dignity, meaning, and community. They help me say "yes" or "no."

Four Useful Guidelines

In reviewing my projects since 1969 I find recurring patterns related to leadership, energizing situations, and energized people; under these patterns I work better with others. The leaders I have learned most from seem to me to have certain knacks. *They focus attention* on valued aspirations. They *mobilize* energy by involving others. They face *the unknown* without answers. All the cases in the previous chapters vividly document these knacks.

My leadership observation underlies the first of four practical guidelines that make up my 21st-Century practice theory for moving everybody toward improving whole systems. The other three depend on what comes of the first. I consider these guidelines plausible (though far from trouble-free) alternatives to traditional analytical procedures and action steps for improving organizations. They focus on enacting dignity, meaning, and community by involving people in the kind of learning required to navigate through "permanent whitewater." Notice that I say "enacting," not talking about them. I do not see lectures, models, or videos, or CDs as a *change strategy*, though all might help to heighten awareness. I am advocating more direct involvement of people in restructuring their organizations and their work.

The practices I will describe are well known among current practitioners, though not well articulated. Many of us — we can hardly avoid it — continue to mix them indiscriminately with less effective procedures. I believe that as we use these guidelines more confidently, we will enable many more reorganizations and work redesigns in the spirit of dignity, meaning, and community.

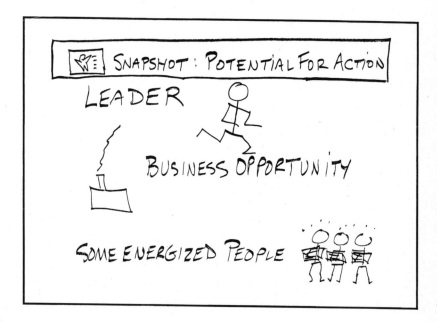

SNAPSHOT: POTENTIAL FOR ACTION

LEADER

BUSINESS OPPORTUNITY

SOME ENERGIZED PEOPLE

Four Practical Guidelines

1. Assess the potential for action.

2. Get the whole system in the room.

3. Focus on the future.

4. Structure tasks that people can do for themselves.

Guideline 1: Assess the Potential for Action

This guideline has three parts, as shown by the flip chart "Snapshot: Potential for Action."

As a consultant I have moved away from diagnosing gaps between the way things are and the way they should be; that's the client's job, not mine. Instead, I find myself asking under what conditions I could make a contribution. That leads me away from problem lists toward an assessment of three dimensions in the organization: leadership, business opportunities, and sources of energy.

Committed Leadership. Do the people authorized to hire me have itches they want to scratch badly enough to put their own rear ends on the line? Consultants make better contributions when a person in authority says, "I think this is so important I'm willing to take a risk too." I'm wary of requests to fix somebody else or to supply unilateral "expert" answers. I like leaders who stand up and say to co-workers, "We're in this together."

Good Business Opportunities. Good business opportunities come in packages labeled "economics" and "technology." These can be the rich source of dignity, meaning, and community — or the death of them. So I listen sympathetically to the "people problem" list, but I don't focus on it. Rather, I focus on the opportunities for cooperative action, chances to innovate products or services, and ways of making or delivering them. These occur most dependably in mergers, acquisitions, reorganizations, declining markets, overhead crises, nonfunctioning structures, new technologies, and changes producing the need to save jobs. The potential benefit has to be worth the cost. There should be no economic reasons for not using these guidelines.

Example: The Medical Products Division of Atomic Energy of Canada, Ltd., in 1985 rescued itself from economic disaster and mass layoffs by assuring jobs for a year and employing much of its work force in market studies, work redesign, and new employment opportunities. The payoff was a viable business with revenues of $30 million a year, managed participatively by its employees. That's a good business opportunity. I tell this story in Chapter Nineteen to illustrate these guidelines in action.

These two conditions — a leader and a promising opportunity — can't be behavioral-scienced in, or engineered, for that matter. Frederick Taylor understood their importance in 1900. He did not know as much as we do, though, about commitment and support. Taylor assumed that only the expert's diagnosis and prescription counted. Thanks to action research, we know a great deal more about commitment and support than our grandparents did. We have many choices about how we focus attention and mobilize energy. We know that every task needs a viable process, that every process exists only in relation to a valued task. We also know that task and process cannot be integrated *for* people. The underlying theory (pure Lewin) is that involving those most affected leads to better solutions and quicker actions. Yet participative techniques, or economic ones, for that matter, are useless in the absence of leadership and purposeful goals.

Energized People. The third dimension is a little trickier. We all drag our feet some days and burst with energy on others. What is the significance of this simple observation for changing large systems? Claes Janssen, a Swedish social psychologist, has devised a simple tool for visualizing where the potential energy is. Each person, group, department, company, says Janssen, lives in a "four-room apartment" (1982, see sketch). Note how the rooms correspond to the positive and negative sides of Theories X and Y as described in Chapter Seven (see chart on p. 140).

We move from room to room, depending on perceptions, feelings, or aspirations triggered by external events. The rooms represent cyclical phases, not unlike the process of death and dying. Indeed, change represents a "little death," a letting go of the past to actualize a desired future. We change rooms as we grow. However, it's not an ever-upward spiral where things only get better. It's a circle game. Our feelings and behavior go up and down as outside pressures impinge on our own life space. How much energy we have for support and commitment depends upon which room we're in.

In Contentment, we like the status quo. We are seen as — and feel — satisfied, calm, and realistic. Any change — a merger, reorganization, new leader, new system, market crisis, job threat — can move us into Denial, where we are perceived as unaware, afraid of change, insensitive, though we do not (consciously) feel that way. We stay there until we own up to fear or anxiety. That moves us through the door into Confusion. Here we are seen as — and feel — different, out of touch, scattered, unsure. Mucking about in Confusion, sorting out bits and pieces of our lives, we eventually open the door to Renewal. Now we are perceived as — and feel — sincere, open, willing to risk.

Anxiety (in Gestalt terminology, "blocked excitement") is the emotional decor of the Confusion room. Far from a state to be avoided, it signifies readiness to learn (Perls, Hefferline, and Goodman, 1951). Anxiety is the place we store energy while deciding whether to invest it. Every new project, course correction, major change requires optimal anxiety. If there's too much, we are paralyzed; too little, unmotivated. In every Confusion room there are people already taking constructive action. It is they who will carry the movie forward — if they can be brought together to learn how their initiatives integrate with the whole. So I seek to assess which room people live in right now, and how they are

acting there. That helps me decide how I can act constructively in the situation.

People in Contentment or Denial are not frozen. Events will move them soon enough. Little can be done to hasten the day, although rational problem solving can certainly delay it. We can make our presence felt and accepted by acting appropriately with people in those rooms, supporting their right to stay there as long as they wish. To mobilize energy, we need to be with people in Confusion or Renewal. I believe if someone were to revisit OD cases from this perspective they would see that "failure" correlates closely with "excellent" action-research methods foisted onto people living in Contentment or Denial. The flaw in Lewin's Law is that there is no cause-effect connection between these techniques and transforming systems, or even developing them. The seeds of success are sown in Confusion and sprout in Renewal. Those are the rooms where people welcome flip charts, models, and OD techniques.

Lewin showed that the attitudes and feelings of those being diagnosed are critical to the change process. He also showed that situations matter as much as personality. What you do is a result of both and changes both at any moment in time. If you want a diagnosis to lead to action, said Lewin, you *must* include those who will have to act. That changes the diagnostic objective from "being right" to "helping others learn" — focusing attention. It modifies the action objective from "making decisions" to "building support" — mobilizing energy. Lewin altered irrevocably our views of what ought to be diagnosed, who should do the diagnosing, and how a diagnosis might be used.

I think Lewin missed one particular that is better understood today. Focused on obvious problems, he was not aware of the dilemmas associated with Contentment and Denial. He knew that to get past resistance, people have to express it out loud. He did not know that letting go the past is a precondition for moving on the future, and that letting go happens in its own time. The forces working against a given change can be charted in a force field analysis. They are not always subject to rational problem solving, even of the group variety.

The urge to hold on — to old habits, familiar patterns, relationships, and structures (whether they satisfy or not) — is as old as human history. Donald Schön called it "dynamic conservatism," defined as "a tendency to fight to remain the same" (1971, p. 32). Robert Tannenbaum and Robert Hanna, developers of a powerful learning laboratory for "holding on and letting go," explain this tendency as the profound losses that change represents for each of us — loss of identity, of certainty, of meaning itself. Under these conditions no unfreezing techniques are likely to help. "Realistic patience and a sense of an appropriate time scale must underlie and guide the change process itself," counsel Tannenbaum and Hanna (1985, p. 114). We can help by giving people a chance to come together, to experience their mutual dilemmas more fully, to make their own choices about when and how to move.

Oddly enough, the T-group, a closed-system application of action research, was initially taken up by Lewin's successors as *the* way to induce change in the workplace. It could not succeed because by design it eliminated past and future, created an isolated cultural island for learning, and removed everyday tasks so that people's here-and-now behavior would come sharply into focus. What the T-group did do was heighten our understanding of the task-process relationship. It taught us firsthand that feelings and perceptions can block task accomplishment as surely as lack of money, time, or tools.

Any task, at some point, may shake people into Denial when the going gets rough. When that happens I don't know what to do except to keep talking and wait it out. The movement toward Renewal is always in doubt. We are all subject to anxiety and craziness under stressful change. People need support to stay where they are a while longer under those conditions, not admonitions to hurry up and change faster. "Managers," write Tannenbaum and Hanna, "must be deeply concerned about sanctioning processes within organizations that might release unpredictable and often powerful feelings" (p. 119). And yet — paradox — real transformation awaits the constructive expression, conscious or unconscious, of such feelings.

Pockets of Innovation. There is something else to look for, too. Some people seem to have the knack for constructive action, even when all hell is breaking loose. They need to be found and got together with those who don't know what to do. Often the two groups ignore or mistrust each other. Creative seeds tend to sprout independent of each other. See "What to Do in Each Room."

A notable example was the simultaneous discovery, each unknown to the other, by an amateur chemist in a Paris suburb and another in an Ohio college town of the electrochemical process for extracting aluminum, the seeds of a new industry. This sort of simultaneous innovation — in methods, procedures,

WHAT TO DO IN EACH ROOM

CONTENTMENT:
"I LIKE IT JUST AS IT IS."

LEAVE PEOPLE ALONE
(UNLESS THE BUILDING'S
ON FIRE).

RENEWAL

"WE HAVE TOO MANY GOOD
IDEAS."

OFFER HELP
FOR IMPLEMENTATION.

DENIAL
"WHAT, ME WORRY?!"

ASK QUESTIONS. GIVE
SUPPORT. RAISE AWARENESS.
No ADVICE.

CONFUSION
"WHAT A MESS! HELLLPP!!"

FOCUS ON FUTURE.
STRUCTURE TASKS.
GET PEOPLE TOGETHER.

improvements — goes on constantly in organizations, in pockets isolated from one another. They are likely to be overlooked exactly when they are most needed — when every department is in chaos, everybody is working overtime, and nobody knows what's happening except in their own bailiwick.

Consultants only add to the resistance when they merely collect the data and present back what others have already figured out. We have more power than that — we have the standing to bring people together and make new things happen. In the reorganization of

McCormack & Dodge, for example, a task force had worked out a comprehensive product development life cycle critical to the company's future. Yet relatively few people knew about it, and even fewer knew how to implement it — until fifty top managers began working it out in redesign meetings.

Hooking together many disconnected activities requires only a little linear planning. If we provide the right container, people will fill it with the right elixir. This happens spontaneously as the other guidelines — getting the system in the room, focusing on the future, constructing doable tasks — are applied. Important tasks, mutually defined, building on existing initiatives, greatly enhance both survival and self-control.

The "Should We/Shouldn't We" Dialogue. The activities I like best, because they involve whole systems, are joint planning of business strategy (external focus), work redesign (internal focus), and reorganizations, which embody both strategy and structure. In each mode the people most affected help devise and test various structural models, using consulting help. I don't mean to make this sound easy as pie. I usually find myself in long "should we/ shouldn't we" dialogues, hours or days of hashing out the pros and cons of whether the action should be opened to many others, whether there's time to do it all, whether short-term results will suffer, what good alternatives exist. Above all, each of us uses the dialogue to decide whether to become personally involved.

So I look for a leader, a business opportunity, and a "should we/shouldn't we" discussion. If we decide to team up, I help people plan how to raise a crowd, structure a task, and provide some methods for getting started. And they should be left-brain methods. As right brains are activated, they take care of what can't be planned in advance — as long as the present task against a future focus is maintained.

Now I take up the three others, what we might call the "Movie Guidelines."

Guideline 2: Get the Whole System in the Room

There are many ways to get a whole system together. A system can be there, for example, in your head — a conceptual rather than logistical feat that most people can master. For example, try the "All-Purpose Viewfinder" and see how fast you can become a systems thinker.

ALL-PURPOSE VIEWFINDER	INSIDE PICTURE	OUTSIDE PICTURE
ECONOMIC$	COSTS + OR - ?	REVENUE + OR - ?
TECHNOLOGY	DO SYSTEMS WORK AS INTENDED?	ARE PRODUCTS + SERVICES BEING IMPROVED?
PEOPLE	HOW DO PEOPLE FEEL ABOUT WORKING HERE?	HOW DO CUSTOMERS FEEL ABOUT BUYING HERE?

However, knowing what's going on is not the same as enacting dignity, meaning, and community. People need shared perceptions to make their contributions. That means getting together to *live* the open system. How many functions, levels, managers, operators, staff, line can be mustered to work on their own organization all at once? Could customers and suppliers be involved?

My own inclination is to push for more and let others say what's realistic. I don't know how to involve a cast of thousands all at once. Yet keeping that benchmark helps me remember what I set out to do. It's a systems problem. We solve it for rock concerts and football games. If the Wright brothers figured out how to fly like birds, somebody else will figure out how to get the whole XYZ Corporation into one place to enact its future and reorganize its work. Maybe it will be done through computer networks, but it will be done. That's as obvious to me as sunshine on a clear day.

Meanwhile, we settle for what's do-able. My former partner Tony Petrella, for example, has these guidelines for a reorganization team: that its members (a) represent key functions, (b) be highly credible,

(c) have lots of experience, (d) be reasonably open-minded, and (e) work full time on an analysis of how the whole system actually works.

Companies get better when employees cooperate on joint tasks. When people meet across levels and lines of status, function, gender, race, and hierarchy, when problems are seen as systemic rather than discrete, wonderful (and unpredictable) things happen. Long-standing lockups, assumed to be intractable, are resolved. Relationships improve, walls come down, problems are solved, norms change — without any directed exercises. These results can't be planned except in the sense of making them more probable. Such happenings lead to more creative and committed actions, more secure and engaging work. During the months that a design team works on a plan, its members use what they are learning on the job every day, making small improvements that help the system function better. They experience their power and influence early in the game, although they often are reluctant to believe it really is happening.

Examples:

• In the merger that created Sovran Bank, at the time the largest financial services institution in Virginia, the operations departments used an interlocking chain of team development conferences, starting with three top executives from each bank, cascading to the next two levels, culminating in a mass meeting of several hundred people. People planned their own roles and divided up work — an exercise many believed was impossible.

• Bethlehem Steel's Sparrows Point Plate Mill, the focus of Chapter Fifteen, reorganized during a two-week training marathon attended by eighty people — all managers, supervisors, and staff-who specified in advance which problems they wished to manage better. Together they studied every aspect of the mill: its internal dynamics, its marketplace, corporate connections, and relationships across levels and functions. They visited the co-workers who turned out raw steel and the plate customers in distant cities. As workshop inputs linked up to their own experience, they quickly changed mill practices to serve customers better. They could do this because of an unusual business opportunity: the annual maintenance shutdown.

The key new management behavior: paying people to come in and learn instead of taking a two-week vacation.

• A fast-growing software development company, McCormack & Dodge, lacked the structure to implement a new strategic plan. Top management convened four conferences for fifty people representing all levels and functions. Design teams organized by product line analyzed the system and created new organization designs. The design specs included a 1990 strategy, their own values about employees and customers, and their analysis of how to close information gaps, improve career paths, and develop more accountability and self-control. This was the unpredictable part: twenty-four hours into the first meeting they began making changes to existing practices as information gaps were discovered. Long before a design was finalized, people already were acting in ways neither planned for nor diagnosed in advance. As a design emerged, the fifty talked over implementation issues with 1,000 others, extending to all the influence over next steps.

There is a further benefit to having a whole system present. New patterns of action achieved in the room often are carried outside it *because* all the relevant parties enacted them together. There is less sell needed when three or four levels come to the same conclusion at the same time. See "Notes on Getting Whole Systems in a Room" for some specifics.

News Note 2003

Perhaps it will come as no surprise to you that the organizations in all three examples above no longer exist. I don't know what happened to Sovran Bank except that it disappeared in a tidal wave of bank mergers. The Sparrows Point Plate Mill, after becoming "world class," was shut down in 1997, as described in Chapter Fifteen.

As for McCormack & Dodge, there was a bit more to the story. Dun & Bradstreet acquired the company in 1983, about two years prior to the events just described. Under Frank Dodge, a founder and CEO, the company grew profitably from $38 million to $180 million in annual sales, reaping the fruits of its employee-managed reorganization. At the end of 1989 D&B, without consulting Dodge, acquired a leading competitor and put the two companies into a D&B Software division, headed by the rival CEO, whereupon Dodge left.

In a few years, the company went through several "cultural" changes, none driven by values of inclusion. After the merger, it lost money for three years, laid off much of its work force, and was sold to a Canadian firm, having gone through, according to industry analysts, about half-a-billion dollars. When I spoke to Frank Dodge in 2002, he had a new career as "executive in residence" at Babson College in Boston. "This could be a case study," he said, "of how large holding companies fail when they try to acquire entrepreneurial firms."

Guideline 3: Focus on the Future

This guideline derives from work by Ronald Lippitt (1983), coiner, with Kurt Lewin, of the term *group dynamics*. In 1949 Lippitt began tape-recording planning meetings. The tapes revealed that people's voices grew softer, more stressed, depressed, as problems were listed and prioritized. You could hear the energy drain away as the lists grew longer.

In the 1950s Lippitt started using what he called "images of potential," rather than gripes, as springboards for change. In the 1970s he created new workshops merging group dynamics with future thinking. He had people visualize *preferred futures* in rich detail, how they wish things to be two, three, five years out.

This simple concept has enormous power. If untangling present problems depresses, planning future scenarios energizes common values. Taking a stand for a desired future provides purposeful guidance for goal setting, planning, and skill building. Successful entrepreneurs, notes Charles Garfield (1986), are uniquely skilled at projecting alternative futures. They get "feed-forward" from their imaginings, a qualitatively different experience from feedback on past behavior.

Notes on Getting Whole Systems in a Room.

1. I don't like one-shot events. Town councils meet repeatedly. A one-shot business conference is not adequate to the needs of dignity, meaning, and community in a workplace.

2. I seek to *reduce* dynamic tensions. A decision to work with groups of twelve is a decision to train group leaders or facilitators — a step away from self-management. Subteams of four to eight work well for many tasks; in this mode 100 or more people can work in one room on their own. I suggest that people make time for small groups to participate in whole-system reviews, so everybody finds out what the others are up to.

3. I contract to manage time boundaries and task structures. In self-managed conferences, I suggest that people monitor their own processes and be responsible for output.

4. I like organizing the inquiry as much as the data. I don't withhold my observations or perspectives or knowledge. But I don't want to make them the center of the action either. I like to see task structures — worksheets, lists, hints, glossaries, exercises, bibliographies, handouts, overheads — devised with client help. Some people need lots of printed material. They should have it — in addition to, not instead of.

5. I aspire to give people formal information when they can use it or when they call for it, not all at once in long lectures. This does not square with what some people want from consultants. I am unable to help people who are convinced there's a lot more.

6. I like having the task front and center, directed toward output, shifting to process only to get the task back on track. I am not against struggle, anxiety, bewilderment, or frustration. We have to go through Confusion to get to Renewal. I tend to become more involved when asked or when I see people running away from the task or fighting with each other. I do not always know what to do. Fortunately, someone else usually does.

7. I want to help set norms for productive learning. I reduce my involvement as people get past initial anxiety and take over the work. I heed Merrelyn Emery's advice (1982) to avoid attaching to a particular subgroup and becoming its informal leader for managing larger events.

8. I like rooms with windows and plenty of light. Hotel dungeon rooms depress groups and make productive anything very difficult.

9. None of these practices is "the" answer to anything — except how one consultant and ex-manager seeks meaning in work.

A word of warning. This concept — "visioning" is one name for it — is so attractive most people want to go out and run a group through it. This technique *will not work* in the absence of committed leadership, a business opportunity, and some energized people. It won't work with people in Contentment or Denial, either.

Guideline 4: Structure Tasks That People Can Do for Themselves

What structures make it possible for people to do learning, futuring, and action planning for themselves (assuming leadership, opportunity, and energy exist)? A conference series designed by clients and consultants together is one way to make dignity, meaning, and community come alive instantly. I'm talking about task-focused, working conferences, to reorganize work or refocus effort — not add-ons or data dumps. I am not suggesting a laissez-faire attitude: "let 'em struggle and they'll work it out." Rather I believe all people in the room have a unique contribution to make to rethinking the work, the strategy, the future scenario. To make it, they need structured tasks, with time frames and expected output clearly spelled out. In Chapters Seventeen through Twenty I give some examples.

For a consultant to manage such events requires, first of all, sanction from credible parties. If that exists, then any plausible bag of tricks will do. It is here, at the very last, we get to techniques — OD or any other. If the other signals say "go," then we need a few of what Hackman and Oldham (1980) call "task performance strategies." One example (of hundreds) is responsibility charting, a simple way of symbolizing whether people are expected to be active in a decision or passive (Galbraith, 1977). Others include simple worksheets (derived from sociotechnical analysis) to help people analyze and redesign their own work.

Merrelyn Emery, a leading advocate of this perspective, points out that the purpose of consulting technique is to create a learning climate, not solutions. This is a subtle and important distinction.

It is essential that we do nothing that would reinforce the idea — both undemocratic and unscientific — "that people cannot make sense of their own experience." Creating a learning climate, points out Emery, results in "an almost immediate increase in energy, common sense, and goodwill" (1983, p. 4).

New Way of Consulting

Working in these ways, I find myself doing things that don't come naturally. I have had to shift my focus — a real mental wrench — away from content diagnoses and problem lists, even from process issues. I still need to understand what a company is up against in the marketplace, what it takes to create committed customers. But I add the most when I can assess the potential for action rather than the solution required. So I look for a leader, a business opportunity, some energized others — the conditions no consultant should leave home without. When they exist, I have faith that I can make a contribution to the most complicated reorganizations. I have learned to accept my own anxiety that I will always do too little or too much.

I have stopped fantasizing that one or two experts — even the process kind — are smart enough to figure out alone the right learning structures. That's 1950s thinking. Anybody who offers to sell you an exemption from the clarifying experience of muddling through to Renewal is a charlatan. The more we experts know about our own specialty, the less likely we are to see our favorite solution's impact on a system. When the whole system gets into one room, when people have a valued systems task to accomplish, when the focus is future potential rather than past mistakes, I believe the right diagnoses and action steps occur in real time. Designing somebody else's work is not in any way, shape, or form an expert task.

Nor do I imagine that I can take away by any known magical mystery trick, technique, system, jargon, book, speaker, or dog-and-pony show, the travail, confusion, chaos, and anxiety that are as natural to our species as breathing. These conditions fertilize growth, excitement, creativity, joy, energy, and commitment. As a consultant I often am invested with the power to grant people exemptions from Denial and Confusion. Alas, like the Wizard of Oz, who knew he was a fraud, pretending that his technologies worked (Baum, 1900), I can't do it. I don't believe you can either.

Instead, I seek to reduce anxiety (my own and others') through simple procedures that allow people to sort and use their own experience. I help those who wish to design their own futures. I hate to hear anxious people labeled "change resisters," as if the natural cycle of human experience is an evil legion to be defeated by superior methodological firepower on the force fields of organizational strife. Resistance is as natural as eating. I am learning to accept my own resistance too, especially to client expectations I cannot meet. The people I work with are moving, too, in some or all of these ways:

Away from	Toward
"Solve the problem."	"Create the future."
"Give it to an expert."	"Help each other learn."
"Get a task force."	"Involve everybody."
"Find the technique."	"Find a valued purpose."
"Do it all now."	"Do what's doable — in season."

In sum, I believe that elaborate consultant-centered (or manager-centered) diagnoses are unnecessary to reorganize workplaces flooded by sea tides of change. That may surprise some fans of my widely used six-box model (Weisbord, 1978b). Yet that model, as many have discovered, has all sorts of uses besides diagnosing problems. It can advance organizational learning, for example. It encourages thinking about how the whole contraption fits together. That is its strength. If I used it today, I'd steer away from zeroing in on problems *within* boxes. Rather, I'd seek connections among whole sets of problems to the values, beliefs, and assumptions that support them. That describes any model's "expert" function — to make better open-systems analysts of each of us.

However, a model's "everybody" function need not be diagnostic at all. Its best "everybody" function (for those who can accept it) is as a future planning tool. What sort of system do we want to see three, five, ten years from now? In terms of purposes, structures, relationships, rewards, and helpful mechanisms? (Or any categories that highlight networks of connections inside and out?) Does our work design or reorganization plan account for each category in a way that's consistent with our values?

A model may reduce anxiety and frustration, but it can't take them away. I have learned to greet them as familiar traveling companions in every whitewater voyage. I try to rejoin them each time with good humor and to forgive myself when I can't. I recall Rudyard Kipling's poem about keeping your head "when all about you are losing theirs and blaming it on you" (Sisan and Sisan, 1973, p. 69). Dignity, meaning, and community in the workplace are for me the anchor points for economic success in democratic societies. We need to preserve, enhance, and enact these values for reasons at once pragmatic, moral, humanistic, economic, technical, and social — take your pick.

Quality of working life — which is far from cultural change — can be seen as a serious effort to conserve our culture's deepest values against erosion by narrow economic and technocratic thinking. That for me is the song and dance of restructuring workplaces. I am interested in preserving economic stability beyond quarterly dividends because I believe that democratic societies depend on creating employment. More, I would like to use these guidelines to discover new ways to help people manage economic and technical innovation, to stimulate new economic activity, so that all of us find dignity, meaning, and community in work.

Chapter Seventeen

Transforming Teamwork: Work Relationships in a Fast-Changing World

Conventional organizational theory has focused almost exclusively on the individual as the main building block of the organization and has tended to ignore the problems of groups or teams and their development. Changes that have affected organizational life over the past twenty-five years have forced students and practitioners alike to reexamine their trends. Certainly, a strong strain of individualism is alive in all of us nurtured in the spirit of democracy. However, the complexity of the environment and the goal structure of the enterprise create a situation in which it is no longer possible to comprehend or conduct the operation of the enterprise without some form of teamwork and team building.

—— *Douglas McGregor,*
The Professional Manager, *1967, p. 181*

Teamwork has been a contradiction in American society clear back to Alexis de Tocqueville, that astute French observer who coined the phrase "habits of the heart" to describe our folkways. "Each man is forever thrown back on himself alone," wrote de Tocqueville in the 1830s, "and there is danger that he may be shut up in the solitude of his own heart." He called this tendency — lest you wonder where we got that word — "individualism" (de Tocqueville, in

Bellah and others, 1985, p. 37). It is our great strength, the bedrock of the entrepreneurial spirit and innovation. Overused, it becomes our strongest weakness.

Productive workplaces need both individual effort and team-work. And teams get much lip service. We call every work group a team even if they rarely see each other. "Team" rivals "quality" as a business cliché. "I have to see my team about that," says a company president. "Individually, of course," she adds. "I don't want to open a can of worms."

Sometimes people develop teamwork spontaneously, like schoolyard kids in a basketball game. That's what my self-managing teams did in the 1960s. Serving customers, rather than a boss, drove them to cooperate. Sometimes teams need help. In 21st-Century managing I think this help must include two perspectives: (1), unlearning deeply ingrained, self-limiting assumptions about individualism, authority, and responsibility that defeat coopera-tion and, paradoxically, individual success; (2), looking outward toward the wider social and business networks that shape their mutual effort. People need both perspectives — relationships *and* environment — to make sense of the workplace. Integrating both to move from competition and individualism toward cooperation and wholeness is what I mean by transforming teamwork. There is no more important task for 21st-Century managers.

Teams and Team Building

Teamwork can be transformed using a particular learning structure a few times a year. It derives from the most widely used and pre-dictably helpful tool in the OD kit: team building. The methods have been greatly refined since McGregor's still-pertinent 1967 observations. There is no standard procedure. Team building evolved in the early 1960s as a solution to the transfer-of-training dilemma — how to use workshop learning in real life. A T-group was (and is) an education in self-awareness. For willing members it offers learning that simply can't be got any other way. The exchange of perceptions of self and others unites groups in powerful ways.

People learn to accept themselves, to trust one another, and to resolve their differences.

Two insights emerged, however, from efforts to repeat these results in companies in the 1960s. One, people who attended learning laboratories with strangers had powerful *ah-ha's* that they could not describe to co-workers, or translate into new organizational policies or procedures. Two, when they sought to remedy this defect by running T-groups *within* organizations, they found people dredging up emotional issues too remote from the tasks at hand to be properly dealt with in that setting.

Developing self-awareness remains an essential but not sufficient activity for changing companies. A T-group changes by observing its own behavior as a temporary system. To use this knowledge, we don't transfer T-groups to the workplace, but only the learning principle. Teams benefit from observing together their own behavior *in the organization they wish to change,* in all its richness of environment, economics, and technology. Group norms and interpersonal feelings are pieces of a large jigsaw puzzle.

Businesspeople, aware that process skills could help them put the puzzle together faster, sought a format that would make these skills learnable in the workplace. Organizational realities had to be worked with — formal leadership, for example. That meant validating mutual goals, both personal and organizational. It meant opening the agenda to past, present, and future, instead of keeping it only "here and now." It meant giving the decision to proceed over to the whole team. And it required task structures different from, but not alien to, real life. The T-group was a closed system by design, so that each person could focus inward. To transform team building requires inquiry into the team's open system — personal, company-wide, global, past, present, and future. It takes in every agenda.

Not everyone defines it that way. Team building has come to mean everything from interpersonal encounter among co-workers (a format I do not recommend), to joint work on tasks of mutual importance for the future (a format I strongly support). The earliest modes used an exchange of interpersonal feedback as the key building block. In my practice now I am more committed to helping each team member take a public stand on critical issues the team faces, the ones most likely to shape the future. The most powerful team building occurs in the mutual revisiting of an organization's future, its central tasks, the design of its jobs, policies, and systems — and how people move toward or away from these tasks.

Many Methods. Modern methods are available from many sources — everything from self-guided workbooks and cassette tapes to facilitators and consultants. Team building remains durable, flexible, and broadly useful in a wide range of situations: starting new teams and task forces, reorganizing, untangling conflicts between departments, setting goals, strategy planning, cultural change — any activity people cannot do alone. In such team meetings, well-motivated groups routinely learn how to manage with less frustration and higher output. They usually report more openness, more mutual respect, higher trust, and more cooperation over time.

I stress well-motivated because that is the building block for all constructive change. You can't play winning football if half the team doesn't give a hoot. The same is true for producing, selling, or managing. That's not to say it takes no work. Even the best-intentioned groups find they must flounder for a while the first time they endeavor to have this sort of meeting. You can't get to Renewal (see Chapter Sixteen) without crossing into Confusion. After that, maintenance requires perhaps two meetings a year, during which team processes are part of the agenda. This becomes more important if, as is common, the team gets new members.

Conditions for Success. Team building succeeds under four conditions:

1. Interdependence. The team is working on important problems in which each person has a stake. In other words, teamwork is central to future success, not an expression of ideology or some misplaced "ought-to."

2. Leadership. The boss wants so strongly to improve group performance that he or she will take risks.

3. Joint decision. All members agree to participate.

4. Equal opportunity for input. Each person has a chance to influence the agenda.

In one typical scenario, the boss calls a meeting, states some personal goals, and asks for discussion. When (as is common) a consultant has been asked to help, the parties need a get-acquainted meeting. (I will describe the meeting from both consultant's and manager's perspectives. I think you will find them often interchangeable.) Often the consultant interviews team members to discover their concerns and wishes. Questions might include each person's objectives, tasks, problems, and the extent of help needed from others. Responses always encompass costs, markets, innovation, and other business-related issues.

Clients (some consultants too) often treat interviews as if their main purpose is for the consultant (doctor) to learn enough to prescribe the right cure. An experienced team-building consultant, however, knows that the prescription is voluntary dialogue. Interviews have two other purposes more important than the consultant's education. One, they help team members collect their thoughts and feelings, zero in on what they really want to say. Two, they reduce the fantasy about the consultant's motives and working methods. The consultant will learn about the organization in any case. What the consultant wants most to know is how much each team member will take responsibility for the meeting's success.

Deciding to Proceed. The consultant presents a summary of interview themes to the team, inviting discussion of the pros and cons of continuing. If the team decides to proceed, it schedules a two- or three-day offsite event. This meeting has a dual focus that makes it different from typical staff meetings. The team works directly on an important task identified by members: strategy formation, reorganizing, dealing with technologies, costs, or markets, quality or customer problems. Here a future scenario — "X Corporation Five Years Hence" — can be a powerful lightning rod for attracting constructive dialogue. Team members also specify what it is about their own processes they wish to improve. This makes it possible for them to periodically step back and observe what they are doing that helps or hinders progress. This discussion can be helped by process-analysis forms like that in "Rating Teamwork (page 358)," a grandchild of early group dynamics.

Such forms are easily constructed. You can spend days in the library tracking down the issues that decades of research have shown go hand in hand with output and satisfaction. Or you can ask the team members, and get roughly the same list in ten minutes. Nine times out of ten one item on the list will be "trust" — a validation of Jack Gibb's contention (1978) that without it nothing else of consequence is likely to happen.

Making such a list is a focusing device, a learning tool. It is useful when used once or twice to help people internalize key processes. Done by rote, it becomes a meaningless ritual, the social analogy to turning out reams of numbers in a quarterly rollout nobody pays attention to.

A more powerful way to help people experience their own processes is with videotape. Reviewing ten minutes of a meeting and asking people to recall what they were thinking or feeling is probably the simplest way to facilitate team learning (the same way sports teams, tennis players, skiers learn by watching themselves on tape).

The dual focus on task *and* process is the team-building meeting's unique contribution to productive workplaces. I have three success criteria:

1. The team resolves important dilemmas, often ones on which little progress was made before.

2. People emerge more confident of their ability to influence the future.

3. Members learn the extent to which output is linked to their own candor, responsibility for themselves, and willingness to cooperate with others.

Practical Theory

I want to describe the underlying theory in business terms, borrowing from an extraordinary consultant, the late Mike Blansfield, who pioneered the method years ago with TRW and other companies. He called his concept "Team Effectiveness Theory," outlined on the chart on page 359. Blansfield's method, which I will not describe, was based largely on interpersonal feedback. Yet he had a strong practical grasp of business issues that is reflected in his theory. I think it is a major contribution to the transformation of teamwork, fitting in with any agenda you can name. The key to team building, I believe, is its *dual* focus on task and process under conditions of rapid external change, not a narrowly interpersonal focus.

Blansfield's concept highlights universal processes that work teams rarely connect to results. The chart makes the linkages by bringing together a managerial vocabulary for output with a vocabulary for teamwork. Most managers define positive results as higher productivity, better quality, more profits, and lower costs, listed at the bottom of the chart.

When something on that bottom list goes wrong, people often feel out of control and (secretly) incompetent. They initiate a search for mistakes in techniques, policies, systems, plans (the middle list), or they seek to finger a villain. In extreme cases, if they have the power, they may fire somebody. Few consider the impact of their own behavior on the *key processes* affected by the situation. These are the three factors on the top list.

From Taylor to Lewin to McGregor to Emery and Trist, observers have identified management's own behavior as *the* starting place for improving anything — systems, labor-management relations, output, work satisfaction, culture, whatever. Blansfield's model highlights the differences between managing a problem one on one and managing a group in which people depend on one another. To do the latter requires an appreciation of task and process applied to teamwork in an unpredictable world.

RATING TEAMWORK

1. PURPOSES
AMBIGUOUS   1   2   3   4   5   CLEAR

2. IN/OUT
I'M IN   1   2   3   4   5   I'M OUT

3. ELBOW ROOM
I'M CROWDED   1   2   3   4   5   I'M EASY

4. DISCUSSION
GUARDED   1   2   3   4   5   FREE

5. USE OF SKILLS
POOR   1   2   3   4   5   FULL

6. CONFLICT
AVOIDED   1   2   3   4   5   WORKED ON

7. SUPPORT
SELF ONLY   1   2   3   4   5   EACH TO ALL

I quickly learned to appreciate this model because of my management experiences years ago. About 1960, in the days of the eighty-column punch card and key verifier (remember when, senior citizens?), I installed a computerized order processing system in the business described in Chapter One. Outside systems analysts told us what we needed. Programmers instructed the computer. The rest of us waited expectantly for results. I never considered that this new technology would change everybody's job, including

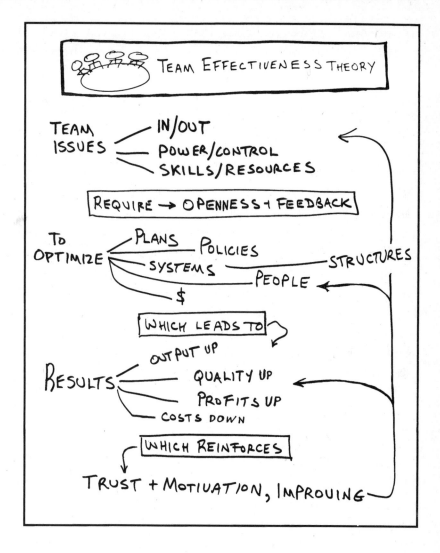

mine, reduce our control over customer policy, and force us to rethink many non-routine problems. I had never seen a computer before. Hardly anybody had. In the days before user friendliness, it was an aggravating initiation.

Little did I appreciate what strong feelings this innovation would stir, or how feelings, attitudes, and actions would combine to frustrate my intended result. It never occurred to me to get together the people affected and plan the implementation. I simply instructed all to carry out their assigned tasks, never imagining that people so instructed have an unerring tendency to thwart one another unless they plan together.

I vividly recall the disruption, missed deadlines, angry customers, tearful order processing clerks, bewildered systems analyst, and general turmoil that cost two resignations and several lost customers. Who knows what our collective blood pressures were, how many got ulcers, how many smokers and drinkers stepped up their intake? I fell prey to a common tendency of task-driven managers. When things started to go wrong, I did what I knew best harder and faster. I pressured people to work overtime. I chided the office force for not cooperating. I reiterated my goals for rapid implementation. I fiddled with the system, rerouting Form A from Desk B and Desk C, with a carbon copy to Person D. I checked up and made sure that a copy went to Accounting. In short, I belabored the daylights out of the effectiveness factors, as if feelings and motivation had nothing to do with it. Managing one on one like a whirling dervish, I drove everybody nuts, including myself.

Adding Teamwork to Effectiveness

My motor had a missing cylinder. I thought I was managing computer system technology and acted as if each person were a cog in the machine. I triggered a set of social dynamics about which I knew nothing — the factors listed at the top of Blansfield's model. Each person in a work group continually struggles with three questions that are never answered "once and for all." They are in jeopardy at every turning point, and must be resolved over and over again.

1. Am I in or out?
2. Do I have any power and control?
3. Can I use, develop, and be appreciated for my skills and resources?

In or Out. Most of us want to belong, to be valued, to have tasks that matter, and to be recognized as insiders by others. The more "in" we feel, the better we cooperate. The more we feel "out," the more we withdraw, work alone, daydream, defeat ourselves and other people. When I sought single-handedly to patch up the computer system, I drove everybody else out.

Power and Control. Power and control need little explaining after Taylor, McGregor, and the astronauts. We all want power. Faced with changes we can't influence, we feel impotent and, in turn, lose self-esteem. It doesn't matter how smart we are, how skilled, or how far up the ladder of success we have climbed. Faced with something we can't influence, we may work harder and do worse, losing self-esteem until we gain control again. That happened to me in the 1960s, and I made it worse for everybody else.

Skills and Resources. Tremendous skills, experience, and common sense exist in every workplace. What keep us from tapping them are outdated assumptions about who can and should do what. Often, jobs are defined so narrowly people can't use the brains they were born with, or even the training they have received. During my computer installation, I thought that people's years of experience with the old system were irrelevant. I pressured folks to turn on a dime and learn something nobody had any experience with. Lacking a team concept, I saw no way to help people support one another over the learning hump. In short, I was not only managing a computer installation, I was managing the destruction of a social system of trust, motivation, and commitment built up over many years.

Here is the simple truth: there was no way, in the face of the interdependent changes we were making, to manage this changeover successfully one on one. The three team process issues can be resolved only when the tasks are seen as team tasks, not the boss's problem to be solved. That is not to say they automatically *will* be resolved. They won't — unless two things occur. We need to learn how to be open about what's on our minds, and responsive to others. We need to give and get feedback.

Candor and Feedback. These two processes, openness and feedback, link team issues with results. We need a place where we can talk over what each person needs to do and our anxiety about doing it. We need a chance to own up to uncertainty and express differences of opinion constructively. We need to discover that others are in the same boat. We need one thing more. I've been in dozens of these meetings. Sooner or later somebody always brings up the importance of trust. Commitment is built on a foundation of mutual trust, and everybody knows it. Trusting one another is the most secure way to manage through tough times. The team-building meeting is one way people learn how to develop trust.

Feelings about membership, control, and skills influence our motivation, which in turn determines the quality of our work. If we talk *only* about results, tasks, and plans, without observing our ability to listen and hear, to discuss differences, to solve problems and decide in a way that builds commitment, we ultimately defeat the results we claim to value. It's all one system. Pull on any thread and you untangle the whole net — the task of a dual-focus meeting.

Structure. Such a meeting is helped along by structure. Usually a team-building meeting starts with a discussion of goals and agenda. Often there is considerable discussion just to get a meeting of the minds about the major agenda: why, how, what, who. Sometimes there are prearranged "stop-action" points when people fill out a process observation form or review the videotape. Sometimes a consultant will call time out if people are fighting or running away from the task. Usually a short process discussion is enough to get things tracking again. Sometimes it takes several hours of dialogue. Each team's own process requirements should be kept front and center.

If people identify interpersonal conflicts or difficulty in communicating as sources of frustration, some device on personal style (maybe a self-report paper-and-pencil survey) may trigger half a day's discussion. In such exercises people learn to value their differences, to accept their strengths, and to express themselves more clearly.

Sometimes teams engage in role negotiation, a procedure devised by consultant Roger Harrison (1972). Each team member writes down what he or she wants each of the others to do less or more of, and what to keep doing the same. These requests are posted and negotiated. For example, "I'll give you at least a week's notice of schedule changes, if you'll refer customer complaints directly to me." There's no deal unless both parties agree.

Another useful format, responsibility charting, is indicated if the team's self-diagnosis is that important tasks are falling between the cracks. An "R" chart (see flip chart) lists who makes which decisions, who must be informed, who must support, and who has the power to veto (Galbraith, 1977). All these activities increase communication, provide feedback, take account of each person's needs, more equitably distribute influence, and promote orderly procedures for managing interdependence.

"R" CHART

R = RESPONSIBLE   A = APPROVE
C = CONSULT   I = INFORM

DECISIONS \ ACTORS	GENERAL MANAGER	PROJECT MANAGER	FINANCE DIRECTOR	MARKETING MANAGER	HUMAN RESOURCES
CHANGE BUDGET					
ASSIGN PEOPLE					
CHANGE SCHEDULE					
CALL RE-VIEWS					

Leadership and Consensus. Nearly every team gets around to how the boss makes decisions — the authority-dependency issue highlighted by Bion (see Chapter Eight).

The boss laments, "They act like children, bucking everything to me." The team members echo, "He treats us like children and does too much himself." The commonest discovery on both sides is how each acts to reinforce the other's perceptions, unconsciously accepting (even relishing) their roles in this age-old parent/child drama. Inevitably this triggers talk about the meaning of individual versus group decisions, when each is appropriate, what the practical limits of formal power really are, what the risks and payoffs can be when acting without consulting others, and whether consensus means "doing what the group wants."

I find consensus decision making the least understood and most useful dimension of teamwork. Consensus means support derived when each person feels heard and understood. Unanimous decision is a desirable goal. With or without it, a boss has the responsibility to decide. This task is made easier if each team member feels free to speak openly on important matters. Indeed, the simplest team-building technique is the "go-around," where all participants have a chance to say how they see it and what they would do. Bosses can facilitate this task by openly sharing their own dilemmas and willingness to hear people out. To maintain team cohesiveness, all should be satisfied that they had a chance to influence the decision and declare their willingness to support it. When any team member can't do that, the team has a serious problem.

The Future of Team Building

A team-building meeting can become a procedural nightmare of consultant-orchestrated exercises. It also can be run simply, directly, and to the point. Tony Petrella (1974), for example, has evolved many procedures to put responsibility firmly in members' hands. In one variation the consultant interviews each person in front of the others, asking questions all have agreed to in advance.

Everybody takes notes. People review their notes in subgroups and diagnose their team's needs and priorities. The diagnoses are discussed, an agenda built, and the remaining time spent solving problems, working out new relationships, or improving policies and procedures. In another variation Petrella and Mike DiLorenzo interviewed managers and wrote down everything they heard — the traditional approach. In a follow-up meeting, before unveiling their notes, they simply asked people to repeat for one another what was already said, a request carried out with enthusiasm.

The objective of these simpler procedures is to reduce passivity and put people more firmly in charge of their own lives. The consultant's role is to help people talk constructively about their work, to learn, and to act. I share Petrella's conviction that most folks can discuss, learn, and act as readily with a little structure as with a lot. If you consider the "right" answer the best one that is implementable, this less-is-more approach will be welcome in many situations where participation and commitment are important to success.

Teamwork is essential to large system success. Team building is useful at some point in any change program. Most team members come away feeling more "in," more influential, more competent, more supported, and more committed to their common enterprise. They may also have solved some problems, devised a new strategy, moved toward a new structure, consolidated a future vision. They are still stuck with the dilemma of implementing action among those who were not there. That's where the future search (Chapters Twenty and Twenty-One) and work design (Chapter Eighteen) come in, offering complementary activities for transforming teamwork by involving people up, down, and sideways.

Chapter Eighteen

Designing Work: Structure and Process for Learning and Self-Control

> The company doesn't see QWL as democratization
> of the workplace. I do, and if I have a mission,
> that's what it is. People in our plant are responsible
> for millions of dollars in equipment. . . . If we can
> make decisions at work, surely we can make
> decisions about work. . . . If we are talking about
> job redesign to make our jobs more interesting, we
> have to be concerned about company effectiveness.
> That's not just a management concern. It's part of
> our increased responsibility for ourselves. Our
> livelihood is too important to leave to managers.
> ——*Judy McKibbon, chief union steward,*
> *Shell Sarnia,* QWL Focus, *1984, p. 15*

Designing New Structures

The quickest way to increase dignity, meaning, and community in a workplace is to involve people in redesigning their own work. That is also the shortest route — in the long run — to lower costs, higher quality, and more satisfied customers. I learned that lesson first in my own business in the 1960s. Having repeated that experience in factories and offices, large and small, union and nonunion, in chemical, pharmaceutical, steel, printing, banking, and many other businesses, I'm more dedicated than ever to this mode of workplace improvement. The simplest way to get started is to have workers, technical experts, and managers sit down together and look at how the whole system works. If they listen to each other and hang in long enough, they can create satisfying and effective workplaces beyond Taylor's most extravagant dreams.

Work-Design Protocols. Work-design methodology is relatively simple. The values behind it, however, challenge more than a century of reductionist practice. A protocol of strategy, structure, and procedure has emerged. Relevant stakeholders form a steering group. It includes at minimum top management and union leaders. It formulates or reiterates the values and philosophy — the new-paradigm thinking — that have led them to a design effort. It makes people aware of the *meaning* of the effort. It also chooses one or more design teams to analyze work systems and recommend options. Regular progress reviews are set up. See "Work Design Structure."

Design team membership cuts across levels and functions. Teams differ from traditional task forces in major ways. First, line workers and engineers, top executives and staff supervisors serve together. Second, they look at the whole business together, seeking Emery's "joint optimization" of technical and social systems. This form of social learning, unavailable in traditional systems, *changes management and worker perceptions of the problem and the nature of the solutions*.

The perceptual shift can't be overemphasized. *All* parties see aspects of their business they have never seen before. To do it, they must get past strange feelings born of invisible walls between jobs and levels. Nobody quite knows how to work together in this odd mixture of status, role, level, gender, knowledge, skill, and authority sitting around the same table. It can be very uncomfortable at first.

Orientation seminars help. Going through a joint simulation exercise, reading cases, and visiting other companies are good team-building tasks for new work-design teams. Low-key group and interpersonal process work can help. A few hours with a simple personal-style instrument (for example, the Work-Style Preference

Inventory [McFletcher, 1983]) may accelerate mutual acceptance and support. Brainstorming lists of appropriate behavior for group members and leader can set useful norms. Teams are best focused at this stage on tasks — learning about their own system and how to redesign it. If they get into fights, run away from the task, or insist that the consultant "give us the plan," they may need more explicit discussions of norms, processes, and styles to get back on track.

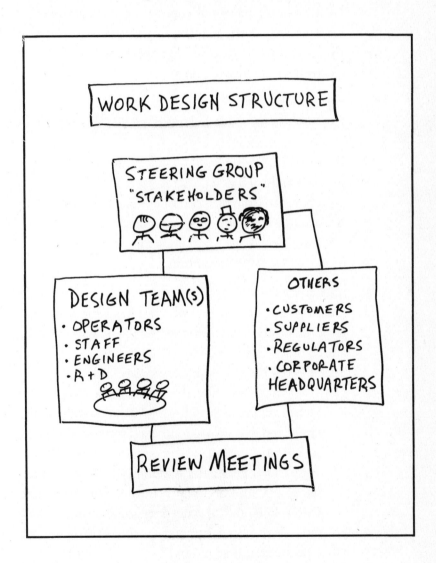

The Generic Menu. Here is a generic menu of typical tasks work designers do. I have derived it from managing or consulting in organizations seeking to translate into action the principles first articulated by Emery and Trist.

- A person who has formal authority *usually:*
    1. Identifies the window of opportunity, the compelling business need, and invites outside or internal help.
    2. Encourages others to visit innovative sites, attend workshops, read up on what's happening.
    3. Convenes a steering group.

- The steering group *usually:*
    1. Restates the organization's purposes and the objectives of the design effort.
    2. Begins articulating values and philosophies a new design should embody.
    3. Selects design team members or criteria for self-selection.
    4. Reviews design team progress regularly.
    5. Validates new designs and implementation plans.
    6. Manages the implementation.

- A design team *usually:*
    1. Examines outside forces to which the organization must respond: customers, regulators, suppliers, government, and so on.
    2. Specifies the most desirable responses.
    3. Does two analyses of how the system works now:
        a. Technical: linear layout, what "steady state" means, where and why errors or upsets ("variances") occur.
        b. Social: what constitutes "good jobs," what skills are required to operate the system in steady state, handle upsets, and do administrative work, who has which skills, and who needs training.
    4. Educates itself about innovative solutions (visits to other sites, reading, seminars).
    5. Drafts one or more new scenarios.

6. Presents emerging scenarios to the steering group and (in redesigns) to other departments to let people know the changes being contemplated, and to get feedback on feasibility.
7. Prepares a design plan and implementation proposal.
8. Discusses the plan and proposal with all affected parties *before* its approval by the steering committee.

The design team nearly always includes one or more members of the steering group, a very practical application of Likert's "link pin" in action. A useful detailed guide for getting started is William O. Lytle's (1997).

Implementation follows a learning curve. It doesn't happen all at once. Consider a graphic illustration of the ups and downs of order processing in a redesigned customer service department, which once needed nineteen days to process new orders; see "Customer Service Weekly Progress." A design team estimated the job could be done in three days. The chart shows how a multiskilled customer team achieved this standard as jobs were learned. In seven months the teams had reached a new level dramatically better than the old.

Design Contingencies. The best-known innovative workplaces have been startups ("greenfields") like the Gaines Foods pet food plant in Topeka, Kansas (Walton, 1982), and the Shell Sarnia oil refinery in Ontario, Canada (Davis and Sullivan, 1980). However, a great many organizations are now undertaking redesigns, reorganizing work in ongoing operations.

Based on physical work in mines, mills, and factories, work-design principles for both startups and redesigns have been found applicable to offices, research laboratories, government agencies, and service businesses. Their spread into new settings mirrors that of scientific management in the early 1900s from machine shops to government offices. This new revolution, however, differs significantly from that earlier one. Work-design techniques now have been put directly into the hands of those who do the work. They have been used with equal success (and failure) in union and nonunion settings, with young and old, men and women, blacks, whites, and many other ethnic groups. Multiethnic workplaces present special problems of language and culture. Yet the principles hold for those able to see work design as an action-research process rather than implementing a predetermined structure.

"Work Design Contingencies" (page 378) shows factors designers usually consider. A unionized office doing accounts receivable and billing calls for different procedures from one for a nonunion research facility or a batch processing factory.

Applications vary tremendously with geography, local community, work force composition, even between sites with the same products or services. The "right answer" is best worked out by local teams from all levels, functions, degrees of expertise. This is called learning. Although a lot of folks tried and a lot of folks died, nobody has found economic or technical substitutes for people learning together what to do and how to do it.

HIGH PERFORMING
STARTUPS

	PRINTING	MAGNESIUM
CAPITAL	$60 MM	$90 MM
PEOPLE	300	400
AGE OF PLANT (1985)	3 YEARS	10 YEARS
LINE MGRS TO PEOPLE	1:17	1:50
STAFF MGRS TO PEOPLE	1:32	1:30
MONTHS TO CAPACITY PLANNED	9	18
ACTUAL	3	1
TURNOVER RATE	2.5%	3.0%
ABSENTEEISM	.2%	1.7%

——— COMPARED WITH "SIBLINGS" ☺ ———

	PRINTING	MAGNESIUM
PEOPLE NEEDED	−15%	−14%
PRODUCTION COSTS	−5%	−10%
QUALITY	EQUALS	EXCEEDS
OUTPUT	+5%	+110%

*THANKS TO JACK OLLETT

Three Analytic Tasks. Design teams do three analyses. One is a map of "environmental demands" — what the customers, regulators, suppliers, and the community want from the organization and how it responds now. Another is the technical analysis, a flow chart of how the system functions, and where and how often errors occur. This is done against a growing understanding of raw materials, conversion steps, and what customers consider to be high quality. The group analysis of key variances always excites and stimulates people. A third is a social analysis, looking at how satisfying each job is now and how to build a system where every job is a good one.

There are many wrinkles at each step. The classic procedures originally formulated by Emery (1980) can be found in many places. Consultants have invented endless variations. Appliers as quickly modify them, a sign of "ownership" heartening to those of us who like to see their ideas implemented. The classic procedure is to scan the environment before doing anything else. My preference is to start with technology and flow charts, because the product or service itself is often the only thing the diverse people around the table have in common, besides membership in the human race. Each analysis is needed to fully understand the others, a chicken-egg paradox that leads to iteration — going around the same mulberry bush several times. Inevitably people discover deeper meanings in what they do, and modify the work accordingly.

The exercise starts slowly. This unprecedented task baffles groups at first. If you start a design team, expect some frustrating "why are we here?" meetings. Some managers see this as a defect in the process, a waste of time, which efficient techniques should cure. Why doesn't the consultant just give them the "right" structure and get on with it? In fact, everything we have learned about group development since Lewin supports the view that floundering around is an essential precondition to learning and high output. No championship football team ever became a winning combination on the first day of practice. Neither do steering committees or design teams. They have to discover their own potential by playing the game.

Laying Out a New Work System. Eventually every design team arrives at a new analysis of how things work now. Now they try out some alternative designs. They seek to create systems that (1) eliminate errors and (2) have no crummy jobs. The boundaries among functions, departments, and tasks are redrawn. Jobs become larger. Departments take on more responsibility. Supervisory and staff functions are redefined.

Every important traditional factor must be accounted for in a new system: hiring, firing, training, controlling, planning, scheduling, compensating, repairing, filing, reporting, and so on. In unionized places, task force members try to distinguish between problem-solving issues and collective bargaining issues. That is not possible in work design. The contract specifies work rules, division of labor, and compensation — exactly the issues a redesign brings into focus more sharply, the same way that scientific management did over eighty years ago. To maintain union-management cooperation in such an effort requires considerable behind-the-scenes negotiating and political skill of team members. Visible outcomes tend to be embodied in new contracts guaranteeing secure jobs, for example, in return for task flexibility.

Designers eventually devise a new supervisory pattern. Sometimes that means fewer supervisors, and nearly always the title changes to "coordinator" or "team leader" or some other nontraditional name. In every case — a new design cannot succeed otherwise — the supervisory role changes. Control shifts to workers when skills and knowledge are enlarged. Leaders manage resources, training, and relations with other departments. Since few of us know how to do that, we need to learn how, something teams must constantly be reminded about.

However, the job does not stop there. In new sites, we must draw up hiring and training plans. In redesigns, we need a plan to secure employment and use the skills and experience of every person, regardless of the staffing called for by the ideal design. We must offer choices to workers who are not needed, interim methods (and incentives) devised for the transfer of people's skill and knowledge, new coordinating procedures worked out, and new supervisory activities learned.

None of this is quick or easy. Taylor estimated two to four years to install scientific management. That estimate held good for sociotechnical redesigns too until the late 20th Century. In the 1980s design teams might work from three months to a year to come up with plans they had confidence in. By the turn of the century, though, the rate of change outran the ability of design teams to keep up. This called for quicker ways to do the job. It also made obvious that the solution was not a one-time fix but a work system in which people continually updated what they were doing. The process is analogous to the annual software update every computer user accepts as a cost of higher productivity. You'd better do it even if you'd rather not. Many ideas have emerged for accelerating work systems design (Lytle, 2002). See also the IKEA example in Chapter Twenty for an experiment in which six months of (old style) design team work was compressed into under three days using future search principles. In new designs people worry continually about whether "it" will work, whether they can get competent people in, whether they will start on time. As "High Performing Startups" shows, when a team takes its time and does things right, startups can be accelerated dramatically. Note also that the original results from the coal mines — higher output, lower cost, better social systems (as evidenced by turnover and absenteeism) — are achieved repeatedly by those who stay faithful to the original principles. Note the two ratios in particular: staff experts to workers, and managers to workers. These indicate how broadly skills and responsibilities have moved directly to operators.

Special Problems of Redesigns. Redesigns involve more ambiguity and anxiety than startups. The biggest worry among designers and steerers alike is "What happens to me?" This is a legitimate concern. Evidence from many projects confirms that a design done right alters every job, from janitor to president. Functions are combined, eliminated, farmed out. Supervisory functions don't disappear; they are managed differently by different people. This often reduces the number of formal leader positions and changes the nature of those left. It is very common for *all* members of a self-managing team, for example, to acquire more skill, knowledge, and responsibility than their former supervisors used to have. That is what makes teams so flexible, cost-effective, and challenging. It also reinforces the threat to middle managers and supervisors.

This reality requires additional principles in redesigns:

1.   It is wrong and impractical to ask people to design themselves out of work. A way must be found to assure employment for people, even as their jobs change. This means gains cannot be taken through unilateral layoffs. They accumulate instead through attrition (not replacing dropouts), doing more work with the same work force, offering early retirements, transfers, retraining, career counseling, help in starting their own businesses for those displaced by redesign. There are creative options — new technology and market teams, special projects, ad hoc training groups — that add value not accessible before. As new technologies arise, a great many more people will be displaced. We cannot apply sociotechnical redesign without also imagining new forms of economic activity, a reality I explore at length in Chapter Nineteen.

Displacement also is a two-way street. Many people who could and would be employed in a new design find, like some of my supervisors in the 1960s, that they don't want to work this way. That leads to the second principle.

2.   Choices should be offered. In many redesign situations jobs are rebid, leadership roles opened up to all who think they meet the criteria. Those who are not selected to their first choice retain their former pay and benefits until equitable arrangements can be made.

3.   Displaced people need influence over their own futures. Displacement is a joint problem, caused by economics and technology. If it is to be solved in socially viable ways, management should not assume unilateral responsibility for redeploying people. That means enacting a policy decision that problem solving should include those most affected, who will be treated as adults.

These principles alter the old authority-dependency games between labor and management. One practical observer has gone further and suggested that management and labor reverse their traditional roles: management should take responsibility for job security, labor for productivity (Hickey, 1986). Later, these principles were built into several innovative labor-management contracts, notably one between the United Steel Workers and National Steel Corporation cited in Chapter Two.

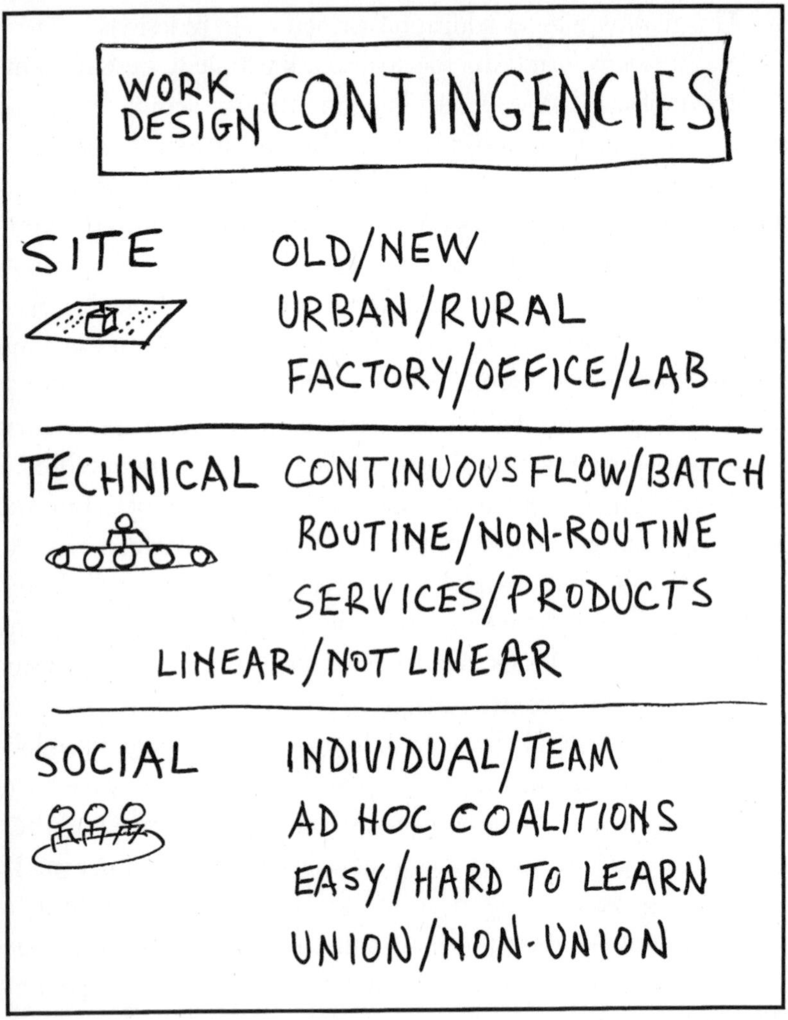

WORK DESIGN CONTINGENCIES

SITE
OLD/NEW
URBAN/RURAL
FACTORY/OFFICE/LAB

TECHNICAL
CONTINUOUS FLOW/BATCH
ROUTINE/NON-ROUTINE
SERVICES/PRODUCTS
LINEAR/NOT LINEAR

SOCIAL
INDIVIDUAL/TEAM
AD HOC COALITIONS
EASY/HARD TO LEARN
UNION/NON-UNION

Supervisory and Staff Roles. The last things to be designed are leadership roles. These are best considered after all other aspects of the work have been figured out. Unless this practice is observed, people tend to reinvent traditional supervision, defeating their own new design. One sign that learning is taking place is when a supervisor on the design team says, usually with ambivalence, "Well, I do that now. But with what we're talking about, you don't need a special person." A "Responsibility Chart" developed by a design team in General Motors' Packard Electric division shows what might happen to staff and supervisor roles in a redesign. I have found this chart useful for helping people visualize the changeover problem. You can see that the tasks listed include most staff and *supervisory jobs*. *All* are potential team tasks. However, teams start with only a critical minimum number, because newly formed teams (1) do not have all the skills and knowledge and (2) cannot know what coordinating problems they will have with other departments.

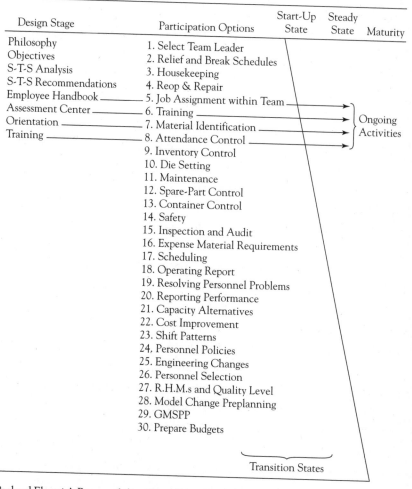

Packard Electric's Responsibility Chart (from Zager and Rosow, 1982, p. 133. Used by permission.)

So the tasks are phased in over time, teams taking on new responsibilities gradually. Former staff people and experts help with training and implementation. The transition also gives them time to find new ways to contribute or to relocate.

Special Problems of Professional and Managerial Work. In a routine technical analysis, the system is flow-charted and errors pinpointed. In a routine social analysis, tasks are merged and blended to create, "whole" jobs that better match the technology. Anyone who tries to clone this procedure for project management, product development, or planning quickly discovers that knowledge work happens differently from repetitive production work (a continuing source of irritation between scientists and cost accountants). The flow chart spills in all directions. People already have multiskilled-jobs, with considerable decision latitude. What they lack is a map of the informal processes — apparently random — most likely to produce optimal results.

One sociotechnical design scheme to account for this reality uses a map of a nonlinear system's tasks in terms of the discussions that *must* take place on the road to a solution, invention, discovery, decision, or plan (Pava, 1983). Pava calls these "deliberations," a word that covers everything from new-product development to sales and service policy. The places where deliberations happen Pava calls "*forums.*" These might involve anything from doodling on the backs of envelopes over coffee to long offsite meetings.

A map of required deliberations compared to actual reveals the kinds of teamwork needed among individual contributors, already multiskilled, for whom the classic work team would be inappropriate. To enhance the social side, Pava specifies the shifting cast of characters who come in and out of the deliberations as they progress. These he calls "coalitions," formal or informal allies thrown together by mutual need to carry out individual and common tasks.

A non-routine design team's technical analysis, then, consists of mapping necessary versus actual deliberations and coalitions, then designing a realignment of forums which people predict will produce more satisfying outcomes. Sociotechnical principles remain intact. The methodology changes with the nature of the problem: equifinality in action again. John Dupre and I modified Pava's procedures and applied them during 1986 to the reorganization of McCormack & Dodge, a 1,200-person software development firm, in the case cited briefly in Chapter Thirteen. One innovation that emerged was each staff vice-president taking on a product or customer service responsibility in addition to support functions like human resources, finance, or information systems. The top team also devised a dozen corporate-policy forums in each function. Each included specialists from business units and field offices, so that those most affected directly influenced what happens. They rejected the alternatives — building large corporate staffs or having a full-scale matrix organization — as (a) too expensive and (b) contrary to people's aspirations for broader career paths.

Implementing New Work Designs

Events to Ponder Department: Thomas Edison, the inventor, spent ten years on the nickel-iron-alkaline battery. After 8,000 experiments, an assistant suggested giving up, seeing as there were no results. "Results?" said Edison. "We have lots of results. We know 8,000 things that don't work!"

——*Popular story*

When a design team draws up a new plan, you can bet your last nickel that the designers have concluded that many old practices will not work. You can be equally sure that they do not know which of the new ones will. Uncertainty abounds. Nobody has gone down this road before. In the interim between design and new reality, ad hoc structures are required to help with learning. People who have been doing one task for years don't suddenly become multiskilled. Supervisors used to handling daily problems themselves don't suddenly become "boundary managers." It can take months or years to build new capabilities. Work must go on in the meantime.

So companies need transition structures. In one case, for example, newly created multiskilled work teams were complemented for nine months by a temporary technical team, which included former supervisors and staff experts. It had two tasks: (1) transfer its skills and knowledge to the other teams and (2) explore and develop new roles for its own members.

There are some useful guiding principles. An obvious one is "Try it out." One steering committee was skeptical of a design team's plan to put orders into the shop in three days instead of two weeks. They gave five design-group volunteers a room of their own and began feeding them orders. In a week the team got the cycle down to three days. They also learned new wrinkles that were incorporated into the emerging plan.

Minimum Critical Specs. Another basic is minimum critical specification, a breakthrough concept devised by David (P. G.) Herbst (1974) during the redesign of Norwegian merchant ships. It is a central principle of work design, wholly contradicting the old-paradigm notion of several contingency plans worked out in advance. Minimum critical specification means not making decisions for another group that its members ought to be making for themselves. By this principle, a steering group passes along "boundary conditions" — values, philosophy, and limits of space and money. The design team recommends basic structure, quality, output, and safety requirements, legal and ethical considerations, a process for member and leader selection, a training plan, and such personnel policies as the steering committee may require. Many problems people actually encounter, as the Three Mile Island disaster showed, often cannot be foreseen.

So details like housekeeping, job rotation, relief schedules, and monitoring safety are best left to those closest to the work. Specialists or supervisors may need to remain in ad hoc support roles, gradually transferring what they know to the work teams. Creative companies offer staff and line people promotions if they serve well in this role for a time.

Teams and management evolve an ongoing negotiation over skill acquisition, tasks, and responsibilities. Much experimenting takes place. Which skills and tasks will be acquired by people on the line? That is a design question, to be solved through ad hoc teams, teachers, or other arrangements. One company invited retirees back part-time to teach its new plant teams special technical skills, a creative arrangement that met everybody's needs without adding to permanent payroll. Certain kinds of outside expertise will always be needed, especially for new product and technology development. In new-design sites, however, engineers, scientists, and marketing specialists tend to interact with line operators regularly, a practice unheard of in traditional places.

Many how-to-do-it treatises exist on sociotechnical systems design. Case studies abound. Find them in the library or by keying "sociotechnical systems" into any business publications data base through your computer. A common thread of these cases is that each site writes its own textbook, a thick binder of philosophy, mission, values, assumptions, and specific solutions for its problems. Each organization reinvents the process and adds its own twists. Sometimes it invents new analytic tools. There are so many ways to skin this cat nobody can imagine all of them. The only constant is a repeated question: "Which principles do we want to preserve?"

Perhaps 500 factories had been designed in North America by new-paradigm principles from 1975 to 1985, and hundreds more since. Nearly all have features similar to what my customer service teams worked out in the 1960s (see Chapter One). They integrate work and learning, pay skill-based salaries, organize around natural production segments, include maintenance, safety, and clerical tasks in work teams, have workers train one another and rotate jobs to acquire skills, have joint team-manager evaluations for pay raises, and coordinate through a committee or task force system. The most successful ones treat their own culture as a unique feature requiring constant attention. Many install a process review board to keep their norms and principles intact (Hirschhorn, 1984).

Implementation: Possible Pitfalls. People can mess up new-design implementations too. The reasons, broadly put, are too much structure or too little. In some cases management panics when production curves drop during early stages. In one innovative plant the management initiated ad hoc "assistant coordinators" to shore up slow-learning teams, angering team members who were not consulted. Although the decision was necessary, the process was seen as contrary to espoused principles of participation (Hirschhorn, 1984). Anxious managers are prone to recreate features of traditional supervision at the slightest hint of variance. This works against learning. It becomes a self-fulfilling prophecy.

Managers may also abdicate responsibility, leaving people too much on their own, without clear goals or enough skill to proceed. Some avoid direct statements for fear of being labeled authoritarian. They defer to participation, imagining a collective magic born of good intentions that absolves them from making tough choices. Laissez-faire management, as Lippitt and White showed years ago in Iowa (Chapter Four), creates as many problems as capricious authoritarianism. Too little structure is as bad as too much.

Managers everywhere discover, as Lewin pointed out years ago, that while authoritarianism is everybody's old friend, democratic methods can be alien indeed. Effective managers learn to provide goal focus and instruction, and not to overload people with too many tasks in the early stages of a new design. Effective participation requires leaders to take a stand without becoming authoritarian. They learn to give over responsibility gradually to teams, a trick mastered only by doing it.

Relearning to Manage. This calls for a form of leadership training still not well defined. All of us, no matter how good our intentions, grew up with one foot planted in the old paradigm. How do you learn and lead at the same time? How do you walk the tightrope between taking over and leaving people alone in emergencies? How do you speak for your own goals and visions without preempting other people's? How do you lead and simultaneously develop other leaders? How will you reassure people when you don't have answers? How do you maintain the short-run economic integrity of an enterprise so that people can learn to keep it viable for the long haul? These are challenges the new paradigm poses. There are no textbook answers. Each company writes its own treatise.

Experiments founder on two other kinds of shoals. One is a change in leadership. The new leader does not know how to leave a self-managing system alone and inadvertently, or deliberately, recreates traditional supervision to reduce his or her anxiety. My own 1960s experiment lasted about three months longer than I did, because the managers who followed me had not been involved in the design and could not understand results based on self-control. They settled for less output and more turnover as the price of lower anxiety.

A more common situation is the boundary that can't be bridged. This happens especially to experiments contained within one department or division of a large company. The other departments continue business as usual. Eventually the maverick is swallowed and digested. One large corporation fostered sixty self-managing team experiments, only one of which survived into the late 1970s. The others sunk without a trace, leading researchers to observe that the umbrella of values and commitment must be particularly strong from top to bottom for these innovations to survive (Trist and Dwyer, 1982).

What about workers who refuse responsibility? A few years ago the United Auto Workers sent a delegation to Volvo in Sweden to study alternatives to the assembly line. These factory hands concluded they would rather have high wages and machine-paced work than assume the responsibility the Swedish system entailed. They could not imagine a system where control was turned inside out.

Eric Trist observed that management commitment and learning over time are likely to convert resisters (an observation also made by Taylor about scientific management a century ago). The design of such auto factories as the joint Toyota-GM venture in California and the General Motors Saturn factory in Tennessee suggest that this is happening even in the highly traditional auto industry. Management is learning how to offer job security, unions to offer greater flexibility and focus on output. These unprecedented arrangements lead both parties down a path fraught with unknown pitfalls — and exciting possibilities. (At General Motors, the United Auto Workers' Irving Bluestone injected QWL into contract negotiations as early as 1973.)

The only safe work-design strategy, in this fast-changing world, is to build up workers' ability to learn how the "black box" works so they can detect errors no one has seen before. We are in a tug-of-war as never before between output and learning, what Larry Hirschhorn calls "developmental tension." People fail if there is too much to learn too quickly. Managers who rush into the gap with more structure may cut out future learning essential to success. External controls are self-perpetuating; the more you have the more you need.

People also fail if management does nothing to support them over the hump. People become demoralized when they lose faith in their ability to learn. People can also fail where there are too few product, market, and technology changes to sustain worker interest over time. Boredom and alienation can overtake a new design plant, too. Novelty is needed at intervals.

Another dilemma is the multi-skill system itself, by means of which everybody can eventually reach the top rate. Designers are learning to plan job progression so that people don't move too fast, compromising safety, quality, and learning. The emphasis must be on knowledge and skill, not rapid advancement. Even so, teams could experience malaise when everything becomes routine and everybody has mastered all skills. Introducing new products or equipment and systems is one way to keep work teams fresh. Another solution is continually providing new learning opportunities, inside or outside the system. Some companies pay for job-related college courses for workers. Others encourage community service or transfers.

The problem is a relatively new one in the world. It is likely to get worse. The more successful a new design, the quicker the demand for novelty, stimulation, and new challenges. (Managers and staff specialists, bored out of their socks when work becomes routine, register surprise when hourly workers mirror their aspirations. Taylorist assumptions die hard.) In my own 1960s experiment, people began prowling the office like restless cats after the day's order processing crunch was over, looking for excitement. I know of another case where one work team stole another team's work just to keep busy! Compared to boredom and alienation, those are good problems to have. However, it takes constant attention to devise novel solutions.

Finally, people resist peer salary reviews. It takes a mature, experienced work team to make peer review work without any input from management or the human resource department. In practice, skill-based evaluation responsibility seems to work best when shared between teams and management.

Changing Consultant Roles. If workers, managers, and supervisors move toward new learning, can consultants do less? It is one thing to advocate new paradigms from the sidelines and skewer those who fall short (the old paradigm in spades). It is quite another to get into the ballgame, which means joining in the vulnerability, risk, and egg-on-the-face messiness that attends jumping off the edge into the unknown. Can consultants keep up their old ways and expect to succeed? An early answer from Norway, where they had been thinking about these matters for a quarter of a century, was "No way." Max Elden (1978), at the Institute for Industrial Social Research in Trondheim, wrote about third-generation work democracy as a synthesis of sociotechnical thinking and participative change.

Elden's first generation (the 1960s — he skips the coal miners' 1950s innovations described in Chapter Eight) aimed to prove that industrial self-managing teams, of the sort discovered spontaneously in the mines, were feasible elsewhere. Sociotechnical experts did the diagnosing, designing, and implementing. In this period the process side of sociotechnical redesign eroded, the mechanics of work analysis overriding change skills derived from Lewinian thinking. Experts sought to get the "right" merger of technology and social psychology.

In the second generation (late 1960s, early 1970s) the goal broadened — to change the pay scheme, to alter middle-management and supervisory roles, to apply new concepts to service and educational organizations. The expert became a consultant, contracting for a limited number of days to help organizations redesign their work. In this evolution, the influence of the NTL Institute, group dynamics, and the consulting practice that flowed from them, became more important.

While consultants involved clients more in diagnosing and prescribing, they still directed and often performed the search. They also devised an ever-growing repertoire of models for new techniques like environmental scanning, variance analysis, role analysis, demand systems, and core transformation processes. It became hard for people to "own" their daily lives reinterpreted through so many unfamiliar frameworks.

What coal miners had invented spontaneously now became a grueling process. Groups started and could not finish. Just as Taylor built scientific management from pieces tried out in different places, consultants imagined comprehensive change strategies manufactured the same way, incorporating all of social science "knowledge," but leaving out common sense — like the fact that people can remember only a few things at once, that short-term problems drive out long-range thinking, that people in Contentment or Denial are not ready to change, that dogged leadership is required to finish anything.

In the third generation — there are more than fifty examples of employee-managed redesigns in Norway (and a growing number in the United States) — we are moving even further away, paradoxically from outside experts. I say "paradoxically" because more knowledge exists, thanks to Lewin, Emery and Trist, and their followers, than ever before. Hundreds, perhaps thousands, of managers have now had the sort of firsthand experience I did in the 1960s. Many now understand how to find novel, workable solutions to unprecedented problems by turning them over to players once considered ineligible for the game.

Fred Emery, in particular, devised some simple methods for transferring sociotechnical knowledge (Emery, 1982). He invented the participative design conference working with the Royal Australian Airforce in 1971, simplifying the methods to reduce dependency and extend his own efforts. He introduced the procedure into Norway in 1973. It requires that natural work groups, given a few simple inputs, then assist each other in doing redesigns, a procedure I find less workable as technologies grow more complex and a wider range of skills is called for. My firm has used variations in the United States in printing, textiles, contact lens manufacturing, and in steel mills. We have found ways to make useful contributions throughout the design phase and into implementation without doing the work for people. By economic and technical standards, results have been dramatic. See "Printing Inc. Redesign" for one example achieved without layoffs.

"PRINTING INC." REDESIGN

	1983	1984
PEOPLE	227	195
SHIPMENTS	$15.9 MM	$18.1 MM
DIRECT COSTS	45.2%	43.1%
VARIANCES	$557 MM	$337 MM
INDIRECT COSTS	23.7%	20.5%
OVERTIME WEEK-ENDS/MONTH	4	1
GROSS PROFIT	26.8%	33.6%

BOTTOM LINE: +25% NET

Two Important Lessons. Sociotechnical experts have learned two profound lessons from all this work.

First, given some minimal guidance, most work groups produce designs 85 to 90 percent congruent with what the best outside pros can do — with vastly more commitment to implement. Nobody can implement commitment for you.

Second, a work design is not an all-at-once activity to be finalized, the way plans for a house might be. Rather than try to do it all, managers and designers must learn to do as *little* as possible *for* others who will be involved. Herbst's "minimum critical specification" is a key new-paradigm design principle. It means, bluntly, don't try to figure out every contingency in advance. The best engineers can't do it, as Hirschhorn's (1984) studies of Three Mile Island show, and neither can you or I. Even if we could, doing it would cut down others' chances for learning, self-control, and ownership. Paradoxically, in the work-design business, slow is fast, less is more.

Under suitable conditions, people often invent the self-managing work team as I did in the 1960s. This happens enough that some folks believe work design means, by definition, work teams. That is an understandable mistake. The defining factors of work design, in my opinion, are (1) participation in the analysis and problem solving by all relevant players and (2) changing the supervisory role to managing boundaries instead of the work itself so people can learn self-control.

For routine and repetitive work, multiskilled teams are an excellent solution, socially, technically, and economically. It should be obvious, though, that such work teams do not fit all work, especially the individual contributor kind like computer programming. In one study of 134 projects, multiskilled teams showed up in 53 percent of the cases (Pasmore and others, 1982). People who do non-routine work tend to invent different kinds of solutions. They are most likely to be helped by the form of analysis recommended by Cal Pava (1983). You also can find excellent guidance in William O. Lytle's (1998) comprehensive work design textbook and in the team-based organization book by Mohrman, Cohen, and Mohrman (1995).

Back to Group Dynamics. In our effort to understand what it takes to do complex work under conditions of continual change, we come at last, in an age of cybernetics, robotics, and sophisticated process controls, back to group dynamics, Lewin, Lippitt, and the Iowa studies in authority/democracy and participation (Chapter Five). How important is group skills training? What kind? When?

I am attracted to a classic piece of action research showing that a balanced use of leadership and authority is the key to effective self-managing work teams. Videotapes by Beth Atkinson reveal people using information, expertise, connections, communications skills, and charisma to exercise influence in positive and negative ways (Hirschhorn, 1984). People willing to risk disclosure of feelings and ideas and to confront differences created a better power balance and more effective teams.

Atkinson changed the climate of self-managing groups by teaching people to use, not abuse, power, and to recognize abuses by literally raising little red flags in meetings. Not surprisingly, she also found that pep talks and exhortation, such as "win one for the Gipper," had little value in motivating quality or output. "People who use charisma as a base," notes Atkinson, "produce the most stifling group climate" (Hirschhorn, 1984, p. 146). They abuse others, and powerless people (as Lippitt and White showed long ago) cease to act.

This confirms for me that the T-group, which put these issues in stark relief, is an important *learning* structure. It became problematical when enthusiasts tried to transfer its learning as pure process, leaving out an organization's extended social field. The self-managing team, focused on customers and externally driven tasks, can, paradoxically, improve its performance enormously through a deeper appreciation of its own process, as I have suggested in Chapter Seventeen. But only when its members accept their common task.

We have discovered, as the British coal miners did in the 1940s, that higher levels of technology offer a chance for more humane work relationships. Technology, however, doesn't care what we do with it. So we can easily fall into the trap of creating "electronic sweatshops" too (Garson, 1989). To gain the full benefits of new technologies, we should consider new structural arrangements, involving those who do the work in its design, coordination, and control. In summary, feelings, trust, and openness need structures neither too tight nor too loose; and new structures are likely to bog down if people cannot achieve the necessary group and interpersonal skills.

I conclude that cross-functional teams from three or more levels can invent innovative systems with minimal direction. To operate them over time, however, they need help to learn. In team settings, people need to build up their power bases, to talk to one another on an equal footing. Most of us cannot do this without greater skills in supporting and confronting others, and in taking and yielding leadership in groups (Weisbord and Maselko, 1981). For practical guidelines in developing personal power in large corporations, I recommend Peter Block's book (2004) on constructive politics.

It is worth noting here that the Emerys, working in a highly unionized country, Australia, believed that gaining the legal right to control and coordinate your work renders group, interpersonal, and communications techniques unnecessary. In the United States, given our enormous diversity and political pressures, I find that attractive hypothesis hard to test. I take it seriously because of my 1960s experience with self-managing teams. If I could go back to the 1960s again, I would certainly figure out how to transfer whatever knowledge and skill in managing the task-process relationship I now have. The dilemma, I think, is not whether but rather when and how to do it so that we do not deprive people of choice and control.

We have come full circle — from early group and leadership experiments to T-groups to coal mines to textile mills to nuclear power plants to a merger of technical and group processes drawn from all these settings. Such is the convergence of OD and STS, two social learning traditions, one dug out of the British coalfields, the other stumbled upon in a Connecticut race relations conference, each concerned with the subtle interplay of work and feelings, the one highlighting structure, the other relationships, one developed by Tavistock Institute, the other by NTL Institute, both influenced by that "funny little man with the German accent."

Chapter Nineteen

Managing and Consulting Beyond the Design Limits: Changing Everything at Once

> Transition begins with an ending. Human beings cannot move into new roles with a clear sense of purpose and energy unless they let go of the way things were and the self-image that fit the situation.
>
> ——*William Bridges, "How to Manage Organizational Transition," 1985, p. 28*

The case that follows describes a permanent whitewater rafting trip down an uncharted river — a hair-raising adventure more and more companies are finding they cannot avoid. Numerous industries are caught in this dilemma — having to rethink both costs and markets in real time in a period of relentless discontinuity. There are no shortcuts to transformation here. It is not simply a little vision linked to some future scenarios. It is a profound letting go — of past assumptions, habits, familiar niches. A future vision *costs* emotionally — in anxiety, stress, expectation, anger, resignation, and hope. The leap into new spaces is never made in comfort.

No textbooks exist on this management frontier. Each company writes its own. This case documents one company's experiences in pushing beyond severe economic and technological limits by removing the limits on employee involvement. It embodies the guidelines discussed in Chapter Sixteen.

A Division in Trouble:
Technology Meets Economic Limits

Atomic Energy of Canada Limited (AECL) is a Crown corporation (government owned) dedicated to peaceful uses of nuclear energy. It operates world-class research facilities and businesses competing in global markets. One business, the Radiochemical Company (RCC), had for years profitably made and sold radioisotopes and related equipment for diagnosing and treating cancer, and had developed methods for medical, industrial, and food irradiation.

In recent years RCC's various operations had their own customers, production, and technical support. The Medical Division — subject of this case — manufactured and sold cancer treatment and treatment planning equipment. In the 1950s Medical, backed by AECL's sophisticated research reactors, built the first commercial cancer treatment device using cobalt 60, a highly useful radioactive element, and became the world's leading supplier of cobalt machines.

In the 1960s a new technology, the linear accelerator, began replacing cobalt. By 1972 RCC knew that it had to be in accelerators to continue as a radiotherapy leader. It began investing profits from its other divisions in an advanced linear accelerator — the Therac 25 (T-25) — to replace cobalt 60. An innovative research breakthrough promised a new high-energy machine smaller and less expensive than the competition's. Ironing out the complexities proved harder than anticipated. At $1 million a copy, the new machine had a limited market. AECL faced serious doubts about the T-25's commercial prospects.

In 1982 Bill Hatton, a chemical engineer reputed to be a stern taskmaster, was transferred to RCC after upping productivity in a heavy-water plant. A story is told about Hatton that reveals his stubborn side. Ken Round, the last of many project engineers managing the accelerator, years earlier had been technical manager in Hatton's heavy-water plant. During a drought the lake was dangerously depleted. Round told Hatton they would shut down in a week for lack of process cooling capability. "That's totally unacceptable," said Hatton. "You *must* make it rain. I *know* it's technically feasible." Round hired Indian rainmakers and aerial cloud seeders. What happened? "It rained," said the teller of the tale. "In that part of the country it always rains if you wait long enough."

This time, however, Round could not make rain. The T-25 was a technological marvel and an economic nightmare. Even if its bugs were ironed out, the market was too small to recoup the investment. Hatton and his team soon proposed two drastic steps to AECL: one, withdraw from accelerators; two, slash costs. Neither move would be easy, particularly as more T-25 development work was needed to support units already in the pipeline. Still, if costs could be cut, the product might break even and be a technological success. Late in 1983 Hatton reluctantly sought approval to downsize by 20 percent — 220 people through voluntary retirement and layoffs — RCC's largest reduction ever. Cuts were made across all product lines. People in profitable segments were demoralized and worried. With no new T-25 orders in prospect, more layoffs there were inevitable.

Hatton asked his human resource staff to suggest remedies. Their report pulled no punches. Most people were job security oriented, knew little about customers, and had never met top management. Planning was secretive; functions were rationalized that probably shouldn't have been done at all. From the report:

> Structure appears to be inflexible and resistant to
> change. ., resistance to intergroup cooperation. . .
> assigning blame for problems to other groups. . .
> limited job structures. . . considerable duplication of
> responsibility. . . buck passing. . . decisions pile up at
> the top . . . exclusion of almost all employees from
> decisions. . . complicated and unclear policies . . .
> low morale.

The report also noted that other companies had turned bad situations around by reducing layers, increasing teamwork, and devising more flexible systems. They recommended outside consulting help to explore a cooperative approach between labor and management.

In July 1984 Maurice Dubras, a mechanical engineer and a twenty-year AECL veteran who was now the company's internal consultant, introduced me to Hatton. "I've got a $3 million problem and no way to solve it," Hatton said. "The only way management knows is to lay everybody off. We have 100 surplus people right now. I'm not sure exactly what to do. I know that what we went through before is *not right*. I want to redirect that effort."

Dubras, I, and Dominick Volini, an experienced member of our firm and a Windsor University graduate who had lived in Canada, met with RCC's management team. AECL's motivation was not just cost cutting. It was also to avoid further layoffs — a source of guilt, anger, and despair among senior managers. We agreed to assess the feasibility of a participative rescue effort. Managers would discuss our findings throughout the company. Only then would we decide whether to go forward together.

In July 1984 Dubras and Volini were joined by Eileen Curtin and Jack Ollett of our firm. All had facilitated reorganizations in many offices and factories. Curtin and Volini had recently helped a small Philadelphia manufacturer reorganize, cutting costs $1 million a year without layoffs. Dubras hoped the approach could be applied in RCC and the learning transferred to other parts of AECL.

The team interviewed fifty-eight people across levels, functions, and labor/management lines, using the technique of following the flow of paperwork in the office and raw materials to finished goods in the factory. These interviews showed that the local union presidents — Ed Devaul of the Energy and Chemical Workers (ECWU) and Frank Amyot of the Public Service Alliance of Canada (PSAC) — were open, helpful, and worried. So was Reg Waterfall, the local head of the Commercial Products Professional Employees Association (CPPEA), an engineers' group active in the company. Managers and supervisors were discouraged. All knew that the lack of T-25 sales was a cloud of doom for the existing work force, even though other product lines had exciting futures. Many wanted to help if a way could be found to involve them. Yet they had little confidence in management's leadership.

Could Medical's issues be resolved before they compromised the profitable divisions? Three tangled dilemmas threatened the company's future. One, while many products had future potential, none could be realized because the T-25 tied up major resources. RCC had to let go the T-25. Two, tangled systems, inefficiencies, and traditional work rules kept everybody busy. Three, while stopping work on the T-25 and redesigning work would mean more layoffs still, these steps would not save the company. Solutions also required sales, and the market did not look promising.

Time had run out on incremental change. Further layoffs were imminent, making a cooperative salvage effort improbable. Survivors would be overworked and demoralized. And managers were split on the future. A few remained stubbornly committed to accelerators. Others argued to expand manufacturing, still others for marketing agreements with Japanese or European firms.

In our feasibility summary we wrote, "In terms of our model for required starting conditions — e.g., committed leadership, a significant business problem, and a high degree of awareness and energy to solve the problem — RCC qualifies on all three counts." But initiatives were needed on two fronts at once: costs and markets. I could hear in the situation uncomfortable overtones of Frederick Taylor's magnificent failure at Simonds Ball Bearing (Chapter Two). By focusing on production, he had cut costs, raised wages, reduced working hours — only to see the firm fail when the price of bearings went through the floor in a volatile market. Unless we addressed markets and strategy along with production, we faced a similar prospect.

Hatton was attracted by the example of Lincoln Electric Co., an innovative "guaranteed employment" company that had weathered a recession by giving redundant workers a crash course in selling. Could that notion work in a government-owned company with no entrepreneurial tradition? Canadian law required sixteen weeks' notice of impending layoffs. Suppose RCC put 150 redundant people to work exploring options instead of out on the street?

Suppose labor and management cooperated to search for new markets, better technology, more efficient methods, or alternative employment? The responses of RCC's top team ranged from skeptical to incredulous. Opening the company to influence from so many directions would release forces that management could not control.

Yet Hatton also had tentative support. Ken Round, responsible for T-25 development, desperately wanted to iron out the bugs, set up customer support, and cut the product loose. The former manufacturing head, Frank Warland, an expatriate British engineer and AECL veteran known for his exuberance, had grown discouraged at his own inability to influence change. Bob Wolff, in charge of the human resources department, had good relations with union leaders and liked the idea of increased people involvement. Yet he saw many pitfalls because of traditional practices and animosities on the shop floor.

Hatton's group discussed a radical proposition. Guarantee employment for a period longer than normal if people would participate in the rescue operation. The options for employee involvement included everything from work redesign to the phase-out of the T-25, an internal job search agency, entrepreneurial training, sale of existing business to employees or outsiders, new services based on existing technology, product line extensions, joint ventures. The list mocked rational management. How can you redesign work when you don't know where your market is? Or search for new products and markets when your internal systems need overhauling? It was a chicken-egg tangle of interlocking dilemmas. Managing so many diverse explorations in parallel represented an enormous leap into the unknown.

In the film *Starman*, an alien sent to study the planet Earth is pressed to explain his culture's motives for wanting to know more about human beings. "You are one of the most interesting species in the universe," he replies. "You are at your best when things are worst." That's as good an explanation as any for the events that followed.

Building a Company-Wide Mandate

While RCC was considering how to implement the consulting proposals, AECL's corporate management independently had decided on a bold move to contain accelerator losses. "We had made classic mistakes — merging winners and losers into one company," said President James Donnelly, a pragmatic Scotsman with high standards. "It didn't work." To give viable products a fighting chance, he proposed to reorganize yet again.

A new division, AECL Medical Products, would be set up to contain the losing accelerator lines, cobalt therapy, simulators, treatment planning, and manufacturing. RCC, a viable radioisotopes business, would stand alone and become a major customer for Medical. AECL would withdraw from accelerators, while supporting existing customers. The new division would lay off 150 of 480 people and the rest would take their chances. Those in the downsized RCC would have relatively secure jobs.

Still many aspects troubled Donnelly. "It was more than just going out of the accelerator business," he said later. "It meant going out of the cobalt therapy business, and that was a much harder problem." Customer anxiety about the company's future could jeopardize successful products. Donnelly also wanted to tell employees that this was the last layoff — the same message as a year earlier.

At this juncture Hatton brought Donnelly the proposal that he and his team had worked out with the consultants. He wanted a fighting chance to turn around the existing RCC. Donnelly offered him an unattractive option — heading up Medical, the weaker division split off from RCC, and managing its further downsizing and withdrawal from accelerators. Harry Hughes, AECL's corporate human resources vice-president, urgently believed participative activities were needed in AECL. Hughes and Donnelly asked the consultants what could be done to help Hatton *after* downsizing. Now we had a dilemma. We did not wish to be identified with a unilateral layoff, both for moral and practical reasons. I called my friend Eric Trist. "Tell them exactly how you see it," he advised.

"This could be a damaging situation, socially and politically, and 500 people could lose their jobs."

Next day we met with Donnelly and Hughes. We said we couldn't help if they undertook a unilateral layoff first. The survivors would not want to participate in saving a business that had laid off 40 percent of its work force — many of their friends and relatives — without increasing its market prospects. Moreover, it would be a mistake to tell people layoffs were over. No seeds for a turnaround existed. AECL's credibility would take a nose dive before the year was out. The only way we could imagine saving the business was to put the redundant people to work searching for innovative solutions.

Donnelly pondered the pros and cons. "If we guarantee jobs, and search for ways to save the business," he reflected at last, "we can tell people the truth! We are dropping accelerators, protecting our customers, and looking for options to carry on. We could satisfy ourselves that we had explored every choice."

All at once the meeting turned to problem solving. The cost to guarantee 500 jobs for a year when only 350 people were needed would be $5 million in wages and salaries. But dropping accelerators and laying off 150 people would cost $3 million in any case. What was it worth to save the medical business? Quite a lot — socially, economically, technically, and politically. Even if Medical floundered, involving people in searching for new businesses might set a learning precedent for the company. With a hiatus in peaceful uses of nuclear power, layoffs were in prospect throughout AECL. Demonstrations were badly needed that the trend could be reversed.

Now the ball bounced back to Hatton. Would he take the Medical assignment if it included a layoff moratorium and search? By now Hatton was invested in the idea of all-out participation as the only solution to so much uncertainty. He also abhorred the "hatchet man" label he had acquired in previous posts. He concluded he had no choice but to go for it.

Hatton's team was understandably ambivalent. The proposition made more sense to them before the decision to split the business, when they still had the hedge of profitable product lines.

Had they been tapped for self-liquidation? Round characterized it as "an appallingly difficult problem, caught in conflicting objectives between employees, customers, and shareholders." Wolff, the human resources manager, could not imagine how the various union jurisdictional problems could be solved. The two locals would each be split. How could they bargain jointly now that one company was surviving, the other in jeopardy? Top team members and consultants met for days on end, bouncing back and forth between how to do it and whether anybody really wanted to. Many questions were simply unanswerable. No one knew whose input was needed to figure them out. Which people would run the existing business; which would search for new options? By what means could they be selected? How could the process be kept voluntary? If some people were tagged "redundant," would that not amount to a layoff with twelve months' notice? Who should manage the transition, besides management and union leaders? Suppose the unions balked?

It was now late December. The announcement of the company split was set for January 15. That day new Medical Products Division employees would be told of the proposal to put a one-year moratorium on layoffs in return for a cooperative effort to save the company. Meanwhile, word of the impending split had to be kept secret. Yet two unions and the professional employees, society would have to be involved and agree to cosponsor any plan before it could be set in motion.

A Tangled Web. In tense meetings between Christmas and New Year's 1985, Hatton and his team worked out the complicated details — announcements, reassuring customers, offers to the unions, employee briefings, starting up the search for new products and markets. Several times they reached dead ends. Did they really want to go through with this? Each time they iterated options, they all looked unattractive — a tangled web of uncertainty.

Warland, problem-focused again, somehow found in the ambiguous challenge extraordinary reserves of energy and enthusiasm. Each night he recharged his batteries by writing out notes and plans on his personal computer, coming in next day with printed "to do" lists, ideas, questions, schedules. His energy fed the rest of us. Inevitably we decided there were no ideal alternatives, no expert solutions, no obvious way out. The financial manager, skeptical of this approach, opted for transfer. His place was taken by Rod Arnot, who called himself a "bean counter" but who proved to be a great deal more. With enormous anxiety and misgivings, the group decided to plunge ahead.

A formal proposal went to the AECL board: defer layoffs for a year while the division engaged in a participative program to explore new uses for existing assets, create jobs for all within AECL or outside, fulfill customer obligations, supply basic products to RCC, and enhance AECL's reputation as a responsible employer.

If the unions agreed, up to 150 people would be engaged in exploring every option they could devise, including the redesign of work systems. Others would maintain the existing business. A third track, still ambiguous in structure and timing, would explore out-placement. Medical Products in transition would have two major departments, Operations under Warland to carry on the existing business, and Search, guided by Round. The latter would include new markets and products, work redesign, and outplacement. A transition team, representing all employees, would manage the effort. Somebody noted that, even if employees agreed, they really didn't have a year. The law required sixteen weeks' notice for lay-offs. That reduced the practical window to eight months. It seemed a near impossibility.

The wish to preserve employment, more than any other value, united the actors. It represents to me the foundation of productive workplaces, a corporate analogy to the barn raising. The barn rais-ing was a ritual of mutual survival. It enabled each farmer to remain independent in the face of adversity, maintaining all as contribut-ing community members. It symbolized both independence and collective security, assuring all that help would arrive should they need it. Of all the acts managers perform, none is more hateful than deliberately burning the barn — involuntarily depriving others of livelihood. The practice of involuntary layoffs grows from deep-seated, unexamined Theory X assumptions — that people are spare parts, that neither workers nor managers can influence impersonal economic forces, that management is unilaterally responsible for figuring out what to do in good times or bad.

In a layoff everybody loses. The victims lose self-esteem. The survivors suffer guilt and demoralization. The community endures economic and social hardship. The unemployed and their families may be severely depressed, especially if caught unaware and given no chance to find options. Usually a last resort, layoffs compromise a firm's ability to rebound. The assumption that layoff is a necessary management tool is what makes layoffs necessary. That assumption can be altered, McGregor would have said, only by testing it anew in each situation.

Achieving a Mandate. There began an emotional roller coaster of euphoric highs and depressing lows, an all-out effort to salvage a business many of its employees, managers, and directors had written off. Between Christmas and mid-January a "buy-in" of all parties — AECL board, union leaders, middle management, professionals, unorganized employees — was sought in tense meetings. Hughes called a meeting of top management, consultants, and national and local officers of the Energy and Chemical Workers Union (ECWU) and the Public Service Alliance of Canada (PSAC) to discuss the proposal.

Henri Gauthier, ECWU's articulate national representative, posed tough questions. "Why are we always junior partners in good times and senior partners in bad?" was the first. Management replied that participation would be a way of life at AECL Medical if the company were saved. The company would open its records to union officials over the weekend. Gauthier also challenged what he called the consultants' "blueprint." He recalled another company where the union had been handed a plan and told it could not be changed.

This proposal, he learned, was open-ended. A transition team sanctioned by labor and management, representing all parties, would form two steering groups to organize search and work redesign (see "The Blueprint"). All further decisions would be theirs. A joint U.S.-Canadian consulting team would assist. To test each other the parties had to plunge ahead. Gauthier, in fact, had had more experience with labor-management cooperation in Canada than any of the parties. His union had been partners with Shell in the startup of the Sarnia, Ontario, chemical plant, a notable innovative work site. He knew the potential if the parties could learn to trust each other. He also understood the pitfalls in a traditional plant with a history of directive supervision. Union officials proposed other conditions. There would be no changes in job descriptions or the collective agreement without mutual decision, and either party could terminate if it wished to.

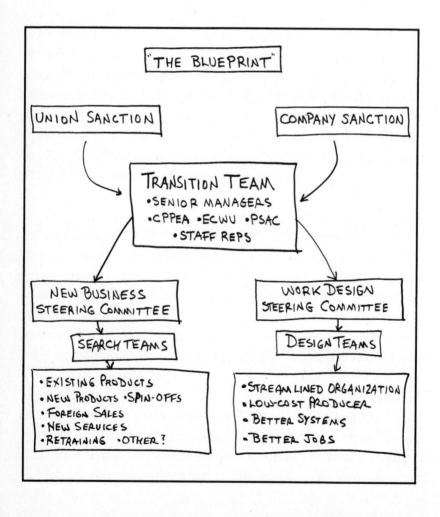

A major hurdle to overcome was union leaders' resistance to the idea that nonunion office workers be on transition and steering groups, though inclusion of all parties was a basic principle of participation. "They're unorganized. How can anybody represent them?" said one union official. In this uncharted water, past rules, norms, and labor-management practices offered little guidance. After some old-fashioned bargaining it was agreed that the transition team would include five top managers, one representative each from employees' association, middle management, and unorganized workers, and two from each union — the local president plus a national official — thus keeping significant union influence. The deal would be contingent on union votes after a public announcement.

Next day Hatton told his "old" RCC management of the plan. "We would like to see unions, managers, and all employees involved with us on teams," he said. "This will work if we practice openness, honesty, and participation." The next day Donnelly announced the new AECL Medical to an employee mass meeting. "While existing business conditions and work load would traditionally dictate a layoff," he said, "we will undertake an innovative participative management program for twelve months to involve and tap the creative energies of all employees. We feel it has a reasonable but by no means guaranteed chance of success."

Now began a frantic three days of communicating and asking for a buy-in among Medical Division employees. Managers, supervisors, and union officials were given special briefings, asked to assume leadership, communicate to their people, bring back questions. What will happen, asked a shop steward in a union leader meeting, if we go along and pull it off? Hatton: "I think we'll look a little smaller, walk a little taller, and make a little profit. I'm just giving you my personal feelings, because in this I'm one of 486 people."

Supervisors and middle managers now had to communicate and manage a risky transition wholly outside their experience. They received a list of anticipated questions and answers worked out by Warland: how people were sorted into divisions, under what conditions a layoff might occur, whether the company would sell assets to employees, what to tell customers. Volini reviewed tips for dealing with likely reactions to the change. (See "Guidelines for Helping People in a Major Change.") All managers agreed to circulate and collect additional questions that afternoon.

Next day the entire managerial group — sixty-five people — pooled the collected questions and concerns, and worked out answers to be distributed in French and English. They identified twenty high-priority themes to be addressed at a company mass meeting that afternoon. Confusion was evident. "It's worse than two years ago," said Hatton to his managers. "I take full responsibility for that. What we're discussing here is whether we will buy into a new way of trying to turn it around."

Voice from floor: "Will it be democratic or management veto or what on this transition team?"

Hatton: "It will be all things — tough, soft, mixed up. Until I get on the team, I don't know."

Facing Facts. At the mass meeting Hatton outlined the facts. The new company had few orders, was losing $1 million a month. To survive it had to turn around by 1986–1987. Although there was too little work, employment would be guaranteed for a year if employees joined in searching out new markets and redesigning work. The goals were two: employ everybody; become profitable. The transition team could meet only when all parties had agreed and picked representatives. People talked it over at their tables with union leaders, managers, and supervisors. That evening both unions voted separately to participate. Professional employees and supervisors voted yes the next day and unorganized workers a few days later. All recognized that the choices were few and unattractive.

Mobilizing a Productive Workplace

On January 23, 1985, less than a month after AECL's decision to embark on this risky form of employee involvement, the division suddenly had a transition team consisting of top management, leaders from two unions and a professional society, middle managers, and unorganized office workers — a diverse stakeholder group that had never worked together. They were starting cold turkey with a tight deadline. How would leadership be handled? Hatton said that he expected all major company decisions to be ratified in this forum. He would serve only as another group member. It was a startling (and unsettling) statement from an executive viewed as an autocrat. Uncharted water again. The consultants agreed to run the first few meetings until transition team members figured out an acceptable mode.

Guidelines for Helping People in a Major Change.

Mostly, it's common sense. Here are practices usually found helpful.

1. Give as much information as possible. Repeat as often as needed. You may not be heard or understood the first time.
2. Tell the truth. Nobody has all the answers. It's ok to say, "I don't know but I'll find out and get back to you."
3. Don't argue. If you feel misunderstood, ask people to repeat what they thought you said. It can save a lot of explaining.
4. Accept all feelings — good and bad — as real honest expressions of the other person. Don't tell people how they "should" feel. It's okay to be down. Your feelings change eventually, even if you don't do anything.
5. Guard against self-fulfilling prophecies, such as, "That won't work." We don't know yet what will work and what won't. We intend to explore every possible opportunity.
6. Let people see you write down things that need followup. It's reassuring.
7. Follow up all questions, rumors, or concerns. Don't let anything go by. Get the facts!
8. In short:
   • Give information.
   • Listen, accept feelings.
   • Make notes.
   • Follow up.

The transition team began by naming a Business Opportunities Steering Committee (BOSC) and a Work Design Steering Committee (WDSC). Urgency and anxiety led to improvisations and goofs. The transition team decided not to have its members "link pin" with steering committees. Instead, mindful of employee suspicions that management might spy on activities and discussions in this more open climate, they offered each group maximum latitude. Management had backed way off to avoid being seen as manipulative. Ken Round, as search manager, would be link enough. But what was Round's real charter? Did the teams work for him? Or was he an ex officio member? His was a very ambiguous role.

Management also assumed that its U.S. sales force, handicapped by geography, could not participate directly. A few days later in Dallas, sales managers confronted Hatton: this was stepchild treatment from the home office. A conference call was put through to the transition team, suggesting a U.S. member be added. Union reps interpreted this as a management power play. "How can we exclude our U.S. operation?" asked Hatton. "They represent most of our sales." The dispute was resolved a few days later. Management agreed that only four of the five top managers would attend transition team meetings, to create a slot for a U.S. manager. The unions then accepted U.S. members on all steering groups.

The transition team began writing a charter (see "Transition Team Charter"). Someone suggested the team should have skill training. A union leader pointed to the long agenda and proposed training be deferred. Others concurred. There was too much else to do. With anxiety, touchiness, uncertainty, and vague mistrust, the joint rescue operation was launched.

Focusing on the Future. The Business Opportunities Steering group (BOSC) immediately organized a two-and-a-half-day search conference of 100 people from all levels and functions. Together they looked at the past, present, and future of AECL Medical. The conference featured a "skills fair." Every function touted its capabilities in booths improvised on the spot. BOSC also had collected more than 500 business ideas — novel, practical, farfetched — from

Transition Team Charter.

The transition team is a joint, representative, decision-making body. Our aim is to ensure employment for all employees of AECL Medical by making it a viable, participatively managed business with a strong customer focus. This will be accomplished by promoting the voluntary participation of all employees who will provide ideas for business opportunities and redesign of the work performed. We will assume an ongoing leadership role by managing the change process, by motivating and encouraging the free flow of ideas, and by ensuring that all necessary information is communicated promptly to all employees. With employee cooperation, we will make every effort to provide employment beyond the one-year guaranty within Medical, elsewhere in AECL, or outside the company.

those who stayed home to run the business. These were sorted by four tough criteria imposed by the TT. To merit further exploration, an idea had to (1) create jobs, (2) use existing skills, (3) require little or no capital, and (4) likely provide profits by 1986–1987.

A dozen ideas emerged. Nearly all involved expanding, refining, upgrading, or cutting costs on existing products. Union shop members overwhelmingly supported subcontracting, for example, selling excess plant capacity. High priority went to a low-cost cobalt therapy machine, a product line extension that could open new markets.

Managements biggest fear had been that people would opt entirely for "blue sky" pursuits. In actuality, most clung to their belief in existing products "if only" this or that happened. BOSC, alarmed that there would be *no* innovation, insisted on a second-round poll. It yielded endorsement of ideas such as a novel home decoration called an electron tree and X-ray machines to survey hidden structural damage in buildings and bridges. As traditional projects were completed or proved unfeasible, new teams would investigate ideas from the innovative list.

At last twelve volunteer search teams were organized. In a blur of anxiety, enthusiasm, and bewilderment, they wrote out criteria for team leader and member roles, reviewed purposes, picked meeting dates. What were they allowed to do? Whatever they believed was necessary. Who could they talk with? Anybody they thought could help. How much time could they spend? That had to be negotiated with supervisors. Suppose supervisors balked? BOSC or the transition team would deal with it — another unprecedented problem to be worked out. Claudia Chowaniec of our firm and Larry Schruder of AECL joined Dubras and Volini in consulting to the search teams.

Each team would meet monthly with BOSC and the transition team to report progress, review needs, decide next steps. The clock was ticking. Only seven months remained before a layoff decision had to be made. The monthly review was the only integrating mechanism available. It was based on the premise that if people sharing vital goals can be brought together to organize common tasks and exchange information, they will make the most of it — a productive workplace in action.

Search Crisis. Within a few days of startup, management made a high-risk decision: to place under BOSC two sensitive merger discussions already in the works. This meant opening up formerly secret negotiations to hourly employees, an unprecedented display of trust. The initiatives, mutually exclusive, would make work for different functions. Opening the issue to influence in advance, said management, was the only sure path to implementation should either venture pan out. Confidentiality agreements were signed — and respected. To stop the perception that this pet project would be railroaded over all opposition, Hatton and Warland now refused to take any further actions until BOSC decided who should join them on the team and gave them a mandate to proceed.

Hatton was taking an extraordinary stand: the transition team should become the company's management committee. He deliberately held back in meetings, insisting that the team confront all business dilemmas together. This discomfited both his own top managers and union leaders. The managers were frustrated that he was not more forcefully directing; the union leaders wondered whether they could, in light of their own politics, share management decision making and still bargain for their members' best interests. With heads of finance, search, human resources, and operations involved on the transition team, it became difficult to separate day-to-day operations from future-oriented search. More, the transition team became a forum for airing every ongoing division problem. The "Medical Products Division" chart shows the operating structure.

Were managements and labor's interests incompatible, aligned, or some of both? Were their relations grounded in natural law — adversarial to the end — or different in each situation? It was an issue baffling to those most committed to its constructive resolution. One thing was obvious. Both management and union leadership had to change. They would move together or not at all.

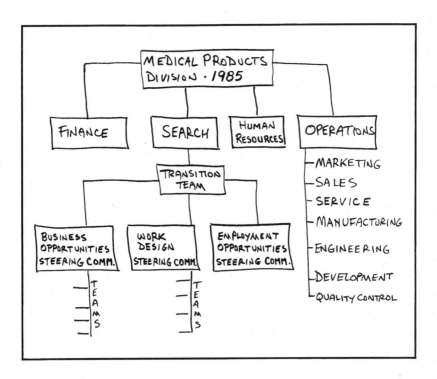

Nobody knew what was possible. Contrary to conventional wisdom, Hatton had created a leadership vacuum. His action stemmed from a complex set of motives — anxiety, faith in this process, uncertainty about what to do, acknowledgment that this management, exercising its prerogatives, had often made mistakes. He readily accepted that the buck stopped with him. Who would share the risk and join in thinking through the tough decisions? Would people fight, run away, or confront their mutual problems and solve them? The answer was not long in coming. Union members of BOSC insisted that hourly people be added to management's merger negotiating teams. High-level managers argued that BOSC itself included members of these teams already. Two union officers walked out of BOSC, saying that this was one more example of how management puts down hourly workers.

The issue dredged up long-buried resentments. The consultants, determined not to let people fight or run away, joined the fray. After tense discussions in the transition team and BOSC, relative harmony was restored. The issues would recycle many times as anxiety mounted about which potential businesses would be pursued. Some managers, upset at top management's patient acceptance of union members' volatile behavior, felt bruised and abandoned and began updating their résumés.

Starting Work Redesign. Meanwhile the Work Design Steering Committee (WDSC) set up tables in the company cafeteria and solicited ideas from all employees. Nearly 500 suggestions came in. The committee identified three priorities: order processing; building new product prototypes; improving the MRP (Materials Resources Planning) system. A fourth project on cobalt adjuster rod manufacturing was deferred because people were not available. Volunteer task forces received an orientation to basic work-design principles, flow-charted the existing systems, set goals, established ground rules for leadership and membership, and scheduled meetings. They would rationalize systems and work flows for products, technologies, and markets that in fact might not survive the search process.

Review Meetings: Getting the Whole System in the Room.
The first review meeting opened a Pandora's box of tangled systems, accumulated inefficiencies, and strategic dilemmas. It was the first time that the whole system's intelligence had been assembled in one room: manufacturing, marketing, finance, engineering, management, labor, factory, office. Work-design teams reported bad due dates and inflated factory lead times. Orders passed through production planning four times. Prototype parts needing sixteen hours of machine time took forty-eight days in process. Simple parts orders passed five times between three buildings and took fourteen working days to ship. New procedures could save $200,000 to $300,000 a year and vastly improve customer service.

Search teams reported customer interviews, analyses of service failures, costs, market data. Joint-venture initiatives in Japan and the United States were being explored. Teams had found many attractive markets and extraordinary dilemmas in tapping them. Customers preferred the competition's cancer treatment simulators, for example, despite the excellence of Medicar's. "We have to clean up our act, improve service support to existing customers, reduce irritations," said the team. Subcontracts surfaced a puzzling dilemma: the factory had excess capacity, yet existing products were consistently late — a clue to the linkage of marketplace and workplace.

People were stressed by the scarcity of resources to carry on daily work and at the same time explore options. There were sore backs, stomach aches, weariness from long hours and high anxiety. Despite supposed redundancies at all levels, few managers could work full time on teams. Fear grew that participation was too little, too late. After the meeting a marketing executive confided that he believed the division would close its doors by year end. As if to punctuate his remarks, two experienced engineers left search teams to take jobs elsewhere.

There was worse to come. Pressure on union-management relations grew. By April work-redesign teams realized that many order processing jobs held by PSAC members could be eliminated. Without warning, the national union withdrew its members, citing joint management of layoffs as a dangerous precedent in government service. PSAC members had been among the most dedicated participants in the process. Their union's unilateral pullout left them vulnerable to early layoff should management choose. Yet many continued on search teams as individuals, and management did not exercise its option.

Middle management was in disarray. Many of its problem-solving prerogatives had been assumed by search teams. A "management initiatives group" was convened to encourage this group — the one most threatened by change — to take charge of their futures. Only thirty-five of sixty-eight middle managers and supervisors responded. Many could not face the dilemma that when hourly workers had direct access to management through participative teams, supervision must undertake a wholly new role. Union members heightened the tension by using the more open climate to publicly criticize unpopular bosses.

"I don't see this process yielding anything new," said one. "Why not sell three good accelerators? We have the parts." Arnot showed the group the latest business plan. If nothing changed, they would lose $18 million in 1986, including the cost of letting go 250 people, and $3 million more in 1987, "tantamount to closing our doors." All products but replacement sources were losing money. They had no orders for the next three months. What next? A half-dozen volunteers agreed to organize work-redesign orientations for middle managers not on teams. Pessimism ran high. One subgroup offered to start exploring alternative employment and termination compensation.

By June the need to revamp marketing, sales and services, production, and control systems was apparent to all. Externally, the assessment was gloomier still. Although good ideas abounded, few could be taken far enough in one year to employ everybody. After each review meeting Arnot updated his spreadsheets, feeding in new data and assumptions, looking for a mix of product lines, services, and costs that netted a survivable business.

The Phoenix. A few bright spots emerged. The feasibility of a simple, inexpensive, high-quality cobalt therapy unit (nicknamed Elsie [LC] for "low cost") was quickly established by a search team. It would be ideal for Third World and rural hospitals, likely to take 33 percent of the market by 1989. Given the many factory glitches, it would take a year to produce one — a demoralizing conclusion. After weeks of seemingly fruitless debate, Warland seized the initiative. He got together union machinists and a cadre of engineers. "Let's cut the red tape and get on the market," he said. "Can you build a prototype together, without detailed drawings?" A union inspector asked what the quality specs were. "If you're proud of the finished product, Jack," said Warland, "that's good enough for me." The team produced a prototype in eight weeks. They named it Phoenix, symbolizing a reviving company. Two team members flew to Miami to display the machine at an October trade show — a big lift at a critical moment.

Another team identified a chance to market a U.S. firm's low-cost simulator overseas. It made no jobs, but was "one of the few things likely to produce revenue this year," strengthening chances for survival. A deal was cut. Still a third team identified a market for a mid-cost couch, using manual controls. Meanwhile the subcontracting search team had sold a new contract. This good news was quickly tempered by the discovery that filling in while new medical business emerged would not work. A subcontract job shop required different systems from a medical manufacturing plant. Although many knew this, it took the team's initiative to force strategic thinking. They must be selective in accepting jobs lest they foul up regular production.

Now BOSC sought to initiate a second round of search teams focusing on innovative ideas. Only seven people signed up. "If we have 250 people on a potential layoff list," asked one steering team member, "why aren't they available to us?" The answer seemed to be that it took all the experienced people to patch the system's inefficiencies. BOSC sought financial help to assess old programs, get marketing input on potential sales of new products, and train members in compiling and analyzing business plans.

On the work-design front, production control and engineering were being revamped despite some managerial foot-dragging. Three more teams started — in packaging, cobalt adjuster rods, service contracts. Potential efficiencies were identified at every turn. Yet the gap widened between the quality of problem solving and people's feelings about the future. In general the mood was glum. "There are many obstacles to better manufacturing," said one steering group member. "Morale is low. It's certain now we won't have 480 jobs come January." On paper, one-third of the jobs in selected areas had been cut out in the first three projects. People worried about implementation. How to choose the right people and assure work for those whose jobs would disappear? Strong leadership was needed. Where would it come from in this ambiguous participative climate?

Can This Business Survive?

Would *any* strategic scenario save Medical? Perceptions of the situation began to change. The division was not avoiding a layoff of 150 people. It was discovering whether the business could survive at all. By now financial manager Arnot was putting every team's analysis of costs and markets into spreadsheets weekly, and discussing the resulting scenarios in every forum he could reach. Employees at all levels learned the economics and technology of the business — an unprecedented sharing of information, knowledge, and responsibility.

Despite the anxiety, great surges of energy also had been released. Nobody knew how to run this unprecedented system. Yet run it did. Control had shifted from top management, where it was illusory anyway. Self-control at many levels emerged. It could not be seen, touched, or put into job descriptions, and not everyone had it. But some people, in this situation, had chosen that path. Something vital was happening.

By the June progress review, the mood was quiet, somber, rational — and sharply focused. Both anxiety and excitement had gone. Time had come for concerted action. "Our shop is underutilized," said Hatton. "Our sales force can do four times the volume with little increase in cost. But is the business there? We're in crisis now." A few days later, Arnot's spreadsheets for the first time revealed dim outlines of viable business strategies — with and without manufacturing, with and without marketing competitors' products, with and without divesting certain product lines. Each implied radically different futures. The alternatives were built around either high-tech fabrication or the medical marketplace. Hatton convened fifteen top managers to consider options. What would motivate them to want to build a future company? What sort of plan would get their support? The consensus: one that included a new management style, more influence from everybody, more ownership at all levels. And it had to have growth potential. They could build a survivable core business from the pieces surfaced by the search. It would take a lot of planning and managing to realize it.

The future rested on two major observations. One, cobalt therapy, the cash cow, was good for the foreseeable future, even without the T-25 accelerator line. It could provide secure revenue to underwrite new initiatives for some time — a real breather — if costs were cut and service improved. Two, Medical had to make a fair profit on sales to its sibling company, RCC, the customer whose orders provided a major source of stability.

Treatment planning was a potential star that might be marketed or sold to its managers. Equipment servicing could be extended to competitors' products, leveraging AECL's reputation and service network — if home office support could be improved. Selling other companies' lines instead of investing in development could also leverage a highly effective sales organization. Subcontracting might pay if focused on unique shop capabilities, not just selling time. A more efficient factory would keep open many new product options emerging from other AECL research facilities, as well as longer-range innovations surfaced by the search teams. "We must maintain a customer focus in the future," said Hatton. "Management must be much closer to the customers."

How many jobs could be secured? Perhaps 200. A layoff was still in prospect. Agonizingly, the transition team activated the Employment Opportunities Steering Committee (EOSC), under Bob Wolff's leadership, to consider alternatives to layoffs: career counseling, résumé writing, entrepreneurial training, early retirement, voluntary resignations. EOSC boldly proposed that union, nonunion, and management — people together create voluntary severance packages to meet as many needs as possible.

Meanwhile, pressure built at the top. At a private lunch, Hatton told Arnot, Round, Warland, and Wolff — the "direct reports" who had come this far with him — "I think my role is largely over. I realize people have had a hard time with my leadership. I'm ready to move on in AECL." The others had mixed feelings. Said Wolff, "I think Frank [Warland] is the man for the job. He has support in the plant, and can pull all the factions together." The timing probably should coincide with reorganization. That could be done when they had a process for reducing the work force and selecting a new management team.

By the end of June a consensus had emerged on a short-term strategic plan based on retaining manufacturing and keeping other options open (such as selling parts of the company or joint marketing arrangements). A few weeks later EOSC presented an employee-designed plan for early retirement and voluntary resignation. People would be given a month to decide if they wished to accept. Job-search and retirement-planning seminars were scheduled. Wolff saw enormous advantages in this plan over traditional labor-management practices. If people found it beneficial to relocate without following seniority guidelines, there would be no layoffs and no recall list. Yet self-selection meant that some skilled managers, engineers, machinists surely would go. Certain experienced people were offered inducements to stay through the reorganization. Round, for example, agreed to supervise the completion of the THERAC-25 engineering so that customer support services would exist for the discontinued product.

New Beginnings. In midsummer the transition team undertook a formal review of what they had done and learned. Big disappointments were lack of new products and difficulties in gaining middle-management support. Despite the lengthy decision process, diffuse leadership, and union-management dilemmas, none wished to scrap future participation. What parts did not work? Team members said they felt out of control most of the time, missed direct links to steering groups, lamented the loss of minority ideas, and (despite, or maybe because of, Hatton's laissez-faire approach) wished management had pushed harder.

What did work? Only one grievance was filed throughout this period. There was much better rapport between senior management and others, freedom to speak out at all levels, a great increase in employee understanding of the business. The value of having people who do the work redesign it was undisputed. However, the difficulty of achieving results when the outcome was loss of jobs was undeniable. Eliminating pyramids, identifying employee skills, more dependable feedback, and better decisions were all applauded. And one thing more was noted: the division had met its first-quarter financial objectives for the first time in living memory!

The future? The consensus was that a representative team could not perform ongoing management functions. Instead, they proposed a new employee advisory group, elected by each department rather than the constituencies previously identified. People at all levels should be consulted on policies and procedures. Employees in all departments would be directly involved in the design and planning of their own work.

By the end of August the future leadership was resolved. Hatton accepted a post with CANDU Operations, AECL's reactor business in Toronto. With little fanfare, his transfer and Warland's appointment as vice-president of AECL Medical were announced the first week in September, to coincide with the retirement and voluntary termination list. It had been little more than a year since the managers had first discussed salvaging the company. It was almost a certainty that the new organization would employ 260 people, many more than anyone dreamed possible eight weeks earlier. Most of the others, secured by generous severance, had found jobs elsewhere. No layoffs would be needed now or — as the survivors vowed — ever again. They would manage the business to assure employment security.

Management and labor, organized and not, had forged a community of interest out of the need to survive. These were the statistics:

Employees on January 1, 1985	486
Voluntary termination	118
Early retirements	47
AECL transfers	45
Other terminations	32
Total voluntary terminations by February 28, 1986	<u>242</u>
Net employment	244

In December Warland issued a notice in French and English headed "Participation." A few sentences are worth quoting:

"AECL Medical has made a firm commitment to Participative Management as the future style of the Division. We began with the formation of the Employee Council. . . . I am now pleased to announce a second step. The formal process of Work Design will be instituted throughout the Division. . . . I have appointed Bob Wolff to direct the Work Design Program and his first task will be to assemble a team of knowledgeable employees to formulate a master plan."

A Backward Glance. Rereading my notes at the time, I saw constant references to slow decisions, uncertainty, ambiguity, conflicting goals, short tempers, profound disagreements, misunderstandings. I found managers lamenting the lack of clear focus and concrete end points. I also found words like *energy, creativity,* and *innovation.* Now, more than a year later, I saw a division, unprofitable for years, that had in twenty weeks:

1. Evolved a new mission
2. Developed a new strategic plan
3. Reorganized its work force
4. Involved everybody who wished to be
5. Created a new level of labor-management cooperation
6. Turned around its sales and costs
7. Implemented a participative, no-layoff downsizing
8. Established a firm future base

Defying theory, AECL Medical had turned itself around, precisely as it had set out to do. It had retained employment for more than half its members and avoided further layoffs. By the end of 1985 its sales already were running ahead of projections. By early 1986 the shop was working overtime again. By early 1987 the company had shown a profit for six months in a row. (A renewed sales force had turned in so many orders the factory could not keep up, even working overtime. It became necessary to hire back people who had left. By April 1987, 309 people were employed.)

In April 1986 Medical surveyed those who opted out to determine, in Warland's words, "what your views are of what we did right and those things that could have been done differently." Most who responded agreed that participation was the right path. Many felt it came too late under too much time pressure. They were disappointed that more innovative marketing and work-redesign ideas had not been implemented before taking the decision to cut back. Several felt the termination options were implemented too hastily, that they had no way to judge whether they should go or stay. Some who left expressed regret now that the company was doing better. More than half said their economic situation was unchanged.

Supervisors, those people in the middle pulled apart in every change effort, remained generally negative about participation. Nearly everybody said they had learned "a great deal about how organizations operate and are managed." Two-thirds said they would participate again if given the chance.

Medical Products Fifteen Years Later

In the fall of 1999 I called Frank Warland, the retired former CEO, to learn how he viewed the AECL adventure now. "No one expected Medical Products to survive," he said. "That the company still exists is a tribute to the work we did together and a lot of resolve during some difficult times after that." The employees who had lived through the traumas of 1985 pulled together at critical moments in the years that followed. From early days, Warland recalled, they had faced the distressing deaths, due mainly to faulty software, of several cancer patients treated with the discontinued T-25 accelerator. The company undertook intensive remedial work. By 1988 they had fixed the software and upgraded the hardware too.

Thereafter, despite level sales AECL Medical made money into the early 1990s. Still, it was not in a good position to survive on its own. It had too little capital, too few products, and giant competitors. Its plant was too large a facility for the volume. The company cut costs by building offices inside the factory and moved from three buildings into one.

In the late 1980s the Canadian government sought to divest the two companies that had been split asunder years earlier. Medical Products became Theratronics International, and The Radiochemical Co. was renamed Nordion International, each with its own board of directors. Both were put up for sale under the umbrella of the Canada Investment Development Corporation. Nordion was sold to a global giant, MDS Health Group, and in 1991 became MDS Nordion.

Meanwhile, Theratronics' employees were given a chance to buy their company. They met with a financial consultant to explore the purchase option and decided their best chance for long-term health was a strategic sale to a going business. A Canadian-French partnership put in a suitable bid. Just as the deal was closing, the U.S. Food and Drug Administration, under pressure from legislators to crack down on imports, determined that Theratronics had fallen short in its Good Manufacturing Practices. It could not export to the United States until it had redone its policies and procedures. On its own now, sans government subsides, Theratronics put on hold a major new treatment machine and lost 40 percent of its product lines.

The firm went to 4 1/2-day work weeks, cutting income for management and workers alike. "If we hadn't gone through 1985," said Warland, "the place would have shut down long ago; we wouldn't have had the spirit to enable us to carry on during those tough times. I don't think there's any doubt that our union relationships were important. Both Hank Gautier (of the ECWU) and I spoke of the need to share the benefits and share the pain. And people responded with commitment again." A few years later Warland ran into a former employee who had lived through the organizational traumas and now had lung cancer. "I wouldn't be here," said the veteran, "if we hadn't pulled together back in '85. I now know what it means to be under one of our machines!"

After two years of struggle to upgrade quality, Theratronics became in 1993 one of the first Canadian medical device companies to qualify for ISO-9000 certification, a key condition for resuming U.S. exports. Now, however, the Canadian government would not approve its prospective merger partner. So the company began serious talks with David Evans, a senior MDS Nordion executive, who had been with the Radiochemical Company during the turmoil of the 1980s.

In December 1995, while talks were in progress, Frank Warland, CEO for ten years, retired. His successor, a popular marketing and sales executive, died of a heart attack some months later. Again the company was thrown into white water. Rather than recruit another president, the board set up a senior executive team headed by the chief financial officer. The government exerted pressure to get the company in shape to sell. Turmoil at the top reverberated through the workforce, affecting morale.

Everyone scrambled again. "Our middle and senior management," recalled an executive, "were by then a battle-hardened group. We had been through trials that few companies face, and we had an intense sense of accomplishment and pride in that." One tangible success was a computer-based treatment planning system that increased safety and effectiveness of cancer therapies.

Together Again!

Then, in the summer of 1998, this story, which began with an agonizing decision to separate two businesses, took a new twist. MDS Nordion acquired Theratronics. The two businesses that had been split off from each other thirteen years earlier were reunited! Unlike the original company, however, MDS Nordion had a long-term strategy. It had bought up several small companies, giving it a global presence with a wide range of related products. With access to capital, Theratronics introduced a new version of the old T-25, the Theratron Elite, with a state-of-the-art computer interface.

More, under MDS Nordion, a culture of employee participation and high involvement was enhanced and extended. In 2000, I spent a couple of hours with David Evans, who was then in charge of Theratronics. Evans had built a new management team. "We don't believe in autocratic styles," he said reflectively. "We believe in teamwork." Moreover, the company now had the resources to invest in training, team development, and regular meetings of the workforce. The company had survived another cycle of crisis management and market uncertainty to emerge stronger under a more secure corporate umbrella. "Still," one executive who had come through the bad times told me, "there is something about crisis and uncertainty that gives you an intensity of focus. There's a kind of high in that too."

In one of our conversations, I asked Frank Warland if, knowing what he knew now, he would go through the traumas of the 1985 employee-involvement effort again. "Yeah," he said, after a moment's reflection. "I'd do it again."

"Why?" I asked. "Because I was motivated to succeed and believed that we needed all the help we could get from employees to make a major cultural change. That was the only thing that would save us." He recalled how so many people pulled together to improve manufacturing processes, and what that meant to him as an engineer. "There were many who opposed the original search process at senior levels in AECL," he recalled. "Comments such as 'letting the inmates run the asylum' and 'having the animals running the zoo' were very hard for me personally.

"On reflection now, I was more concerned about the lack of respect for the knowledge and abilities of the employees. Even those who opposed us, such as the Public Service Employees Union, were important. While they couldn't support layoffs, many employees quietly helped us survive. When the labor disputes are over," he added reflectively, "you still have to work together. So we better learn to respect each other's views. Someday, I want my grandchildren to drive by that plant in Kanata and say, 'My grandpa used to work there!'"

Implications for Practitioners

What can we learn from this revisit? One, we have further evidence for a key point made in the first edition of *Productive Workplaces*: no amount of employee involvement and training can make up for lack of capital and market clout. That was true in Frederick Taylor's time. It's true now too. I'm certain that principle will endure until human beings find a way to create an economic paradise on earth. Nor can yesterday's innovations withstand new managers wishing to go elsewhere. As Ed Liddy, a Sears executive who helped shut down what was arguably the most famous mail order catalog in history, said,

"It's amazing how quickly you can dismantle a business that took a hundred years to build" (Cohen, 2003).

Two, with determined leadership, people are capable of incredible survival feats. That theme, too, is older than any of us, predating Taylor, predating modern organizations. The ancient Chinese, Greeks, Romans, Egyptians, and Polynesians knew that long before anybody conceptualized "development." The Theratronics case represents one modern example.

Finally, I reiterate something I did not have the words for, or the conviction, until I was deeply into the research for this edition. To get people together in the workplace, to involve people in the control of their own lives, work, and destinies, to "keep meeting like this," and to validate shared goals is existentially right, *no matter what the outcome*. I can think of no higher form of leadership. Acting in accord with economic values that also honor dignity, meaning, and community in the workplace is a widespread aspiration. That vision was the common ground for Frank Warland and many others I once worked with and revisited years later. Engineers, doctors, marketers, staff and line alike — all would do it again if they had the chance.

Chapter Twenty

Future Search: Evolving a Whole Systems Improvement Strategy

> On the way to the moon the Apollo astronauts
> made tiny "mid-course corrections" that enabled
> them to land at an exact predetermined spot. The
> corrections were small, but because the moon was
> far away they made a big difference. It is like that
> with us. Some of the changes we make in society,
> in our lives or in our organizations seem
> insignificant, but over the years they can have
> major impact.
>
> ——*Edward B. Lindaman and Ronald Lippitt*, Choosing
> the Future You Prefer, *1979, p. 4*

"In this chapter I will describe an extremely promising method for getting whole systems in one room and focusing on the future—the 'future search.' Like so many workplace innovations, its origins are traceable to creative extensions of Kurt Lewin's insight that you steer a ship by feedback from outside, not by how the rudder, engines, or crew are behaving. Innovators in many places began extending Lewin's work to larger systems years ago, responding to the psychological stresses of accelerating change."

Thus began in 1987 what was then Chapter Fourteen of this book. Future search, a derivation from Kurt Lewin and his followers, integrated into one short action planning meeting insights from the consulting cases and training workshops described in the previous section. I had found this method a practical way to "get everybody improving whole systems" without people having to do something else first. A few points from 1987 bear repeating.

From The First Edition.

Future search embodies three assumptions:

- Change is so rapid that we need more, not fewer, face-to-face meetings to make valid strategic plans.
- Problem solving old dilemmas will not work under fast-changing conditions. Each solution begets two new problems. Future focus is a better strategy.
- People will commit to plans they have helped to develop.

Future searches excite, engage, produce new insights, and build a sense of common values and purpose. They have been especially attractive to organizations faced with significant change: markets, mergers, reorganizations, new technologies, new leadership, the wish for a coherent culture and corporate philosophy.

The future search has proved to be a powerful tool of productive workplaces. Far from requiring conformity in thought and action, it provides a forum and norms that respect individual differences. Personal attitudes, thoughts, feelings, and styles are honored. People sometimes fear that past disagreements will intrude and prove disruptive. [Usually] this does not happen. A major strength of future search is its unifying effect on people even when they fear divisiveness.

A great deal happened on the future search front after 1987. Hundreds of people were able to repeat my experiences. Future search, much to my surprise, went around the world. People improved water quality through future search in Pakistan, introduced credit cards into Eastern Europe, demobilized child soldiers in the Southern Sudan, made business plans in Spain, improved school systems planning in the United States, cut factory costs in Brazil, shaped health care policy in Canada, developed women leaders in Siberia, got the bankrupt town of Stahnsdorf, Germany, out of debt, and formed coalitions to combat AIDS in South Africa, Senegal, Nigeria, and Ghana. These were just a few of many hundreds of examples.

Because it was a learning laboratory, not a definitive answer, many practitioners continued to contribute refinements. The meeting design was by 2003 widely available (www.futuresearch.net; Weisbord and Janoff, 2000). For those not familiar with future search, here is a brief summary. A typical event lasts sixteen to eighteen hours spread across three days. It involves sixty to eighty people, organized at various times in one of three ways: stakeholder groups (those with a similar relationship to the task); mixed groups of diverse stakeholders; and a meeting of the whole. The focus is always "the Future of X" in a given time frame, usually five to twenty years out, X being an organization, community, network of shared interests, or an issue needing cooperative action.

There are five segments—the past, present, future, common ground, and action. (See "Future Search Agenda.") At each step, people (1) build a database of their own experiences, (2) look at the whole together, and (3) interpret through dialogue what they are learning. At the end, those who wish make commitments for action. One difference between future search and some large group methods is that the entire group does the same tasks prior to action planning, giving everyone a view of the whole that none could get alone. The products are three: a "common ground" statement that every person present supports, action plans not imagined a few days earlier, and high commitment to follow through.

Principles Over Techniques

Many techniques are used, including time lines; mind maps; "prouds and sorries" lists; and future-oriented dramas. The techniques always are secondary to the principles. This point is worth repeating. *The principles are more important than the techniques* (see "Future Search Principles"). Indeed, hundreds of techniques could be found for these principles, although getting the integration right might take some doing. The principles are contextual. They assume (Chapter Sixteen) a leader with an itch to scratch, a "business opportunity," and support from people energized by the focal topic—whether company, community, network, or issue.

Let me say up front that people can misapply this method like any other. To the extent you ignore the context and principles, the more likely it is that you will fall short. I have not found methods to substitute for attractive goals, good leadership, and people who care. The success of future search is determined in the planning. The key is matching the task and participants so that people with authority, resources, expertise, information, and need are all in the room at once. Otherwise, it's just another meeting with novel procedures.

Future Search Principles.

Get the "whole system" in the room. The quotes imply that we never get everybody. It is possible, though, to have in the same room people with authority, resources, expertise, information, and need. Simply calling such a meeting is often a radical change, making possible many others.

Explore the whole before seeking to fix any part. Each person has a part of the whole. When all have put in what they know, every person has a picture none had coming in, and they can plan together in a shared context.

Put the future and common ground front and center. You can't chew gum and whistle. So problems and conflicts become information to be shared, not action items.

Invite self-management and personal responsibility for action. Groups are capable of doing a great deal more than they customarily are asked to do. Each time managers or consultants do something for a group, they deprive others of a chance to be responsible.

The Origins of Future Search Principles

The principles of future search emerged for me during many years of applying ideas from the "practical theorist," the social scientist Kurt Lewin and his followers. After the first edition of *Productive Workplaces* was published, I was surprised to hear from many people who said they had run meetings based on my brief account and were astonished at what had happened. People had an insatiable hunger for simple methods promising wholeness and new ways of cooperating. In the late 1980s I called these stories to the attention of Fred Emery and Eric Trist. Braced by their support, I began a systematic inquiry into the use of search processes. This led to the book *Discovering Common Ground* (Weisbord et al., 1992). While compiling that book I uncovered many experiments for involving people in improving whole systems. I found confirmation for the value of principles over techniques. Below I summarize how this inquiry into effective planning influenced Sandra Janoff and me as we began refining the practice of future search with members of Future Search Network in the early 1990s.

Learning from Eric Trist and Fred Emery

Emery and Trist invented what came to be called "the Search Conference" in a 1960 planning meeting in Great Britain. A merger had led to a serious market crisis in the Bristol/Siddeley aircraft engine company, one partner making piston engines, the other jets. Trist was asked to help, and he brought along his young associate Emery. The pair had recently begun work on the managerial dilemmas of "turbulent environments" (see Chapter Nine). To the firm's top managers they proposed a weeklong collaborative inquiry.

It would be a new kind of strategic planning meeting, one explicitly designed to bring alive "conditions for dialogue" that Emery had derived from the research of social psychologist Solomon Asch (Weisbord et al., 1992). When people experienced themselves living in the same world, subject to the same laws of nature, having the same psychic needs, and willing to accept each other's perceptions as shared resources, they would plan together effectively.

In the meeting, piston and jet engine proponents would compare notes on the state of the world and their industry before dealing with their differences. Talking about the same world changed the meeting dynamics in two ways. One, each person's perspective was validated and people stayed with the task without having to defend or attack any points of view. Two, having multiple perspectives before acting gave every manager a view of the whole that none had coming in. This wide-angle view enabled crucial strategic choices, including building a new jet engine, still in use forty years later, based on the capabilities of the merged companies.

In that historic conference, Trist and Emery (1960) had made two key discoveries. First, when people had a shared worldview, they were less likely to fight or flee than in a traditional problem-oriented session. Second, they discovered a contradiction in the consulting role. The consultants drew much hostility from the group when, having come in as experts, they refused the expert's prerogative of interpreting data and suggesting action. They concluded that *effective searching should not mix expert input with self-management*. Rather, people should be primed from the start to accept responsibility for their data, interpretations, and action steps (See the Barford Report, in Weisbord et al., 1992). The facilitator's job was managing time and tasks and staying out of the way when people were moving forward.

In future years Emery, collaborating with his wife Merrelyn, began a conceptual and practical expansion of the methodology (Emery, 1982). The Emerys' conference typically lasted two or three days. They began by mapping the networks of people and external pressures linked to the focal task, what they called the "extended social field." They ended with action planning. In between they drew on a flexible menu—history, desirable and undesirable features, constraints on change, values to be carried forward, desirable futures—based on data produced and analyzed by the participants.

Others made adaptations, from downsizing business firms (Hirschhorn and Associates, 1983) to refocusing social service agencies (Clarkson, 1981). Trist did a variety of conferences in this mode, noting in a memo to me the emergence of many search models, for example, Michel Chevalier's search position conferences in Canada for executives who couldn't be away more than one day a month and Russell Ackoff's idealized design sessions.

Design Dilemmas

Trist, Emery, and the Search Conference, then, inspired two of the four future search principles: (1) exploring the whole before seeking to fix any part and (2) having groups self-manage their work. The *techniques*, however, proved to be more of a challenge than I expected. While preparing *Discovering Common Ground* (Weisbord et al., 1992), I found that the Search Conference was closely held by a handful of practitioners trained by Fred and Merrelyn Emery, whose insistence on "the Asch conditions" for dialogue I considered a major addition to group dynamics theory.

In future search experiments, we had sought to activate dialogue by having each person record life experiences in parallel with global and local events, making people's personal histories part of the system. This quickly enabled the discovery of shared psychological needs, a key "Asch condition" for dialogue. I was surprised, then, to discover that the Emerys ruled out personal information in a task-centered conference.

The Search Conference design had other features that puzzled me. People were asked, for example, to list global trends of concern to them. Groups were asked to report what would happen if they "did nothing" about these trends and to contrast the inevitably gloomy predictions with their hopes and dreams for the future. Janoff and I tried this step and gave it up for two reasons. First, everybody was doing the best they could and we had never known a group decide to do nothing. Second, nobody could predict the future. Extrapolating a static present to arrive at a future based on a planning group's doing nothing contradicted people's experience. It seemed like an artificial wrinkle. People already experienced the present as far from ideal.

The Emerys also saw theoretical drawbacks to inviting customers, suppliers, family, or community members to, say, a company conference. "Outsiders" would dilute the use of the "second design principle" (Chapter Nine) intended to further democracy by flattening hierarchies, eliminating supervision, and placing control and coordination with those who did the work. From our point of view, redefining and enlarging a system's boundaries by inviting key stakeholders—"the environment"—was a way to put open systems into action, the essence of democracy.

That this step led to new forms of cooperation within and between organizations and communities had been confirmed around the world. Fred saw this as a dilution of his central goal rather than a parallel discovery. I considered this unfortunate, for the Emerys had made giant strides in workplace improvement practices, noted in many places in this book. Without them future search would not exist.

Parallel Universes

Ludwig von Bertalanffy (1968), author of general systems theory, once observed that the same ideas often spring up in parallel in diverse places. Many people in the 1960s and 1970s were seeking ways to bring diverse stakeholders into the room. Meetings cascading down from the top were a recipe for frustration in large bureaucracies in a speeded up world. New information came up in every meeting that was not available at the top.

Why go slowly nowhere in numerous meetings when one with all the right people could produce information and action both? Among the early practices I sought to emulate were the intergroup events pioneered by the late Richard Beckhard (1969) and the imaginative "collateral organization" design of Dale Zand that got people at all levels in a hierarchy looking at the same problems (Weisbord, Lamb, and Drexler, 1974; Zand, Miles, and Lytle, 1970).

By the end of the 1970s many of us became convinced that diverse "stakeholders" working together in real time was the key to rapid systems improvement. The person who opened my eyes to the use of very large groups was Ronald Lippitt, Lewin's student and colleague in the evolution of group dynamics. I was fortunate to spend many hours talking with Ron during several summers when we both were at NTL Institute in Bethel, Maine.

From the 1940s on, Lippitt, like Emery and Trist, had sought to extend group dynamics to large organizations, networks, and communities. Lippitt too had moved from small-group problem solving to future-oriented conferences with diverse participants. What started him down this road were tape recordings secured (with Douglas McGregor's help) of thirty strategic planning groups in action. Lippitt was appalled as he heard people build long problem lists, set priorities, generate solutions—a direct extension of his pioneer group dynamics work. He noted that voices grew more depressed as people attributed problems to causes beyond their control, using words like "hopeless" and "frustrating." Action steps tended to be short-term, designed to deal with symptoms and reduce anxiety. The motivation, noted Lippitt (1983), was to escape the pain induced in part by the method itself: the piecemeal listing of problems, the solution of any one of which might create still more problems.

Focusing on the Future

As early as the 1950s Ronald Fox, Lippitt, and Eva Schindler-Rainman (1973) began eliciting "images of potential"—envisioning what could be instead of lamenting what was. Lippitt also teamed with the late futurist Edward Lindaman, who had directed planning for the Apollo spacecraft that made the first moon landing. Lindaman believed that the future was created by our present ways of confronting "events, trends, and developments." The "preferred future"—an image of aspiration—could be a powerful guidance mechanism for making far-reaching course corrections. Lindaman and Lippitt (1979) found that when people presented future action plans as if they had already happened, they developed energy, enthusiasm, optimism, and high commitment.

In the 1970s, Lippitt and Schindler-Rainman, a dedicated community development consultant, pioneered large group future-oriented conferences for more than eighty cities, towns, and states, many organized by the Junior Leagues of America, Eva's long-time client. Diverse interest groups—community, business, labor, government, health care, education, social agencies, and so on—sometimes hundreds of people at a time—could jointly envision desirable futures. People were invited from all walks of life, ethnicities, and neighborhoods. Lippitt and Schindler-Rainman also devised a menu of activities geared to the past, present, and future:

a history, a list of events, trends and developments shaping the future, "prouds and sorries" about present operations, preferred futures, action planning.

Learning from Lippitt and Schindler-Rainman

Despite their success with communities, Schindler-Rainman and Lippitt's participative work (1980) with large groups had little influence in the business world of the 1970s. It remained for Kathie Dannemiller, of Dannemiller-Tyson Associates, to make the conceptual and practical leaps that would enable groups as large as 2,000 at one time in such companies as Ford and Boeing to do significant systems change based on the Lippitt/Schindler-Rainman foundation (Dannemiller-Tyson, 2000). Inspired by talks with Ron Lippitt, I too found myself lobbying clients to get more people into the room. I saw this step as the shortest and most practical path to valid information and committed action.

In the early 1980s, I made my first foray into community dynamics, using an NTL "organizational diagnosis" laboratory in Bethel, Maine. In years past we had sent teams out to visit single organizations. Now, eager to apply the large group knowledge then emerging, we decided to involve the community in a bit of action research. Teams would investigate the relationship between NTL's summer program and local sectors—stores, restaurants, churches, schools, medical facilities, hotels, and banks.

Each team would visit, interview, observe, prepare a report, and invite people to a large meeting of the whole. Coincidentally, Eva Schindler-Rainman, working that week in Bethel, also gave us the benefit of her years in community building. And she joined in the meeting that brought all the parties together. A major issue was the culture gap between lab participants and service people in stores and restaurants, leading to mistrust and mutual irritation.

One insight from the meeting was that townspeople for years had heard rumors that NTL planned to pull out, hurting the local economy. As a result, NTL took a public stand on remaining in

Bethel and invested in improving its conference facilities—a key ingredient in community building. Townspeople took over the writing of the summer participants' services guide. A joint committee of townspeople and NTL staff, facilitated by Eva, continued to build a productive community of interest. Only in a face-to-face discussion of the future by many stakeholders at the same time could this new spirit be infused into an old relationship. And I, for one, had my eyes opened to the feasibility of multiple stakeholders from many sectors planning joint actions when they shared an important goal.

What's Good for the Goose. . .

In 1983 the late Ronald Lippitt helped Block-Petrella-Weisbord organize a future search with client managers from AT&T. Bethlehem Steel, McNeil Consumer Products, Smith Kline & French, Soabar Corporation, Warner Cosmetics, and consulting colleagues from the United States and Sweden. Together we looked at the future of the work world, and the meaning for clients and consultants alike.

Our decision to open a private meeting to clients and friends was triggered by a startling statement in *Megatrends* (Naisbitt, 1982). Producers fear losing control if they invite consumers into strategy and policy discussions. "Too many corporations that should know better are terrified of this whole idea," Naisbitt wrote. "I do not think it an oversimplification to state that producers can only become more successful by learning how better to satisfy consumers" (1982, p. 178).

In our conference we compared notes on major trends reshaping business firms. All noted the need for constant retraining, the emergence of a world marketplace, a smaller gap between blue-collar and white-collar work, fewer jobs at the middle and top. The ways in which our company's future scenario must take account of these trends became plainer to us. My confidence in participative work design and reorganizations was greatly strengthened by manager comments in this conference.

Facilitator Dilemmas

Early in my journey I faced a contradiction between the principle of self-managing groups and the refined, technique-rich Lippitt/Schindler-Rainman meeting model. In 1969, when I took up group dynamics, I had learned to facilitate small groups using procedures (agenda setting, brainstorming, prioritizing) and process analysis (time out to look at decision making, control, communications, commitment, and so on).

Using this repertoire, to which they had been major contributors, Lippitt and Schindler-Rainman would train one lay facilitator for each group of ten, meaning twenty trainees for a 200-person conference. It was considered a good investment, for the facilitators were learning skills that would last a lifetime. While I liked the premise, I worried that the practice reinforced dependency and passivity in large groups when the intention was exactly the reverse. If a facilitator were assigned to lead a group, I as a participant had no need to concern myself if things went wrong. Instead, I sat back and watched what the leader would do.

Reducing Dependency

The facilitator's goal in those days was teaching people to observe their own progress and "learn how to learn." Such learning was considered as important as the content agenda, and would, many of us imagined, encourage people to monitor and self-correct whether facilitators were there or not. As some of us started working with future search, we became convinced by the Emery/Trist experience that people were capable of self-managing their work. If so, then a team of two could easily manage groups of sixty to seventy and more. This seemed both feasible and cost-effective.

Yet, as small groups grew to ten or more the need for facilitation increased. If large groups were organized into subgroups of eight, rather than ten, people's ability to self-manage was enhanced. A whole conference learning this do-it-yourself potential seemed to us to be valuable experience too. Why eight? You can find support in academic studies cited by Russell Ackoff (1974). While teaching future search in Singapore, Sandra Janoff and I also learned that eight was the luckiest number in Chinese culture and that eight groups of eight, our ideal structure, was lucky beyond imagining. Social science or Chinese numerology? Take your pick.

Despite my moving away from training small group facilitators, I considered as priceless the understanding of change strategy I got from Ron Lippitt and Eva Schindler-Rainman. They had discovered the incredible power of having a "whole system" in the room. They had proved the dynamic virtues of focusing on the future rather than the problem list. These tenets too I wrote into *Productive Workplaces*. Later Janoff and I adopted them formally as two of the four core principles of future search.

Honoring the Pioneers

The pioneers who inspired me all had made conceptual breakthroughs I considered unprecedented. The way that Ron Lippitt and Eva Schindler-Rainman defined a community to include everyone, high and low, rich and poor, all ethnicities and professions, and *actually got them there* was for me a triumph of moral imagination in action. More, their emphasis on the future was the precursor for visioning and futuring methods that would leap like a flash fire through corporate boardrooms a decade later. The way that Fred Emery and Eric Trist had built Solomon Asch's research into a task-centered meeting design to create conditions for dialogue I considered a model lesson in putting theory into practice. So too their discovery of the power of self-managing work groups.

Hence Janoff and I used "future search" as an apt name for the experimental methodology we were practicing. "Future" honored the community futures conferences of Ronald Lippitt and Eva Schindler-Rainman. "Search" acknowledged the seminal Search Conferences of Fred Emery and Eric Trist. We saw future search as a learning laboratory for theirs and many other ideas, where people could discover new ways of working together.

Notice that all of these trail blazers from whom I learned were mentored by Kurt Lewin, who pioneered action research and opened the door to collaborative consulting. Although I portray Lewin in this book as a long-dead giant in the history of applied social science, there are in fact only two degrees of separation between Lewin and you. I hope that many who read this will by inspired by this tale of origins to extend Lewin's reach further still down the generations.

Chapter Twenty-One

Improving Whole Systems Worldwide

> "The principle of surviving in a multi-cultural
> world is that one does not need to think, feel, and
> act in the same way in order to agree on practical
> issues and to cooperate."
> ——*Geert Hofstede* (Cultures and Organizatons, *p. 237)*

Future search by 2003 had been used equally well in corporations and communities on five continents. In nearly forty years I had not found a more cost-effective or time-efficient planning method. Nor one more responsive to values of dignity, meaning, and community. In this chapter I want to describe some of the ways future search has been used and disseminated. I also want to speculate on how and why so many diverse cultures have taken it up.

In this regard I must mention the central role of Sandra Janoff. When we met in 1987, Sandra had spent a decade teaching in an experimental school where city and suburban children formed a self-managed learning community. Her experiences paralleled mine in business firms. We had both come separately to the conclusion that structure was a shaper of behavior that people actually could control. Together we now began to fine-tune future search principles and practices. In particular, we sought to understand and apply structures that best enabled the dynamic journey people went on as they explored their systems and themselves.

I had been experimenting since the early 1970s with meeting designs aimed at involving the whole person and not just the "left brain." This meant offering ways for everyone to participate regardless of learning styles. Now Janoff and I began an elaboration of this idea. We set up tasks that would require people to move around, on the theory that if you want to move you start by moving. We gave everyone access to the walls and the markers to write or draw pictures from the very start. This showed that every person's experience counted and that the charts and markers belonged to all.

Adopting a Lippitt technique, we had people act from the future, describing their desired experiences as if they had already happened. This, we believed, engaged people physically and emotionally, making action more probable as they got the feeling of success in their very bones. Sandra also began to integrate into the facilitating work insights from her training in system-centered group dynamics. In particular she showed that so long as each person had at least one other who shared his or her thoughts and/or feelings, a group would stay whole and "on task." It was not necessary to process relationships, only to validate subgroups when issues became sticky (Janoff and Weisbord, 2003).

We refined these ideas with many types of organizations. One early effort was with Resources for Human Development, a nonprofit umbrella agency with 100+ human service programs, that later became home of Future Search Network (page 449). RHD was managing 25 percent a year growth in diverse and unrelated programs in housing, employment, mental health, child care, the arts, drug and alcohol abuse, among others, supported largely by (uncertain) government contracts. RHD sought to implement values of inclusion, diversity, dignity, responsibility, accountability, and cooperation while operating on 15 percent overhead or less. Many programs benefited, and five years later we ran a second conference to decentralize what was becoming a mini-bureaucracy with 3,000 employees.

Reaffirming Self-Management

A notable business example was a future search with a Quaker Oats pet food plant in Topeka, Kansas. Built originally by General Foods, it was then the longest-running employee-designed team-based factory in the United States. It had won wide notoriety for "the Topeka system," a low-overhead, high-productivity process driven from the bottom by the people who did the work. General

Foods, exemplary of Eric Trist's observation that such innovations rarely inspired imitation close to home, could not clone its system to other factories, even those making the same product. Eventually it sold Topeka to Anderson-Clayton, who sold it to Quaker Oats.

The future search celebrated Topeka's twentieth anniversary and was intended to set a direction for the Topeka system over the next twenty years. A subtext was the survival of that system in a corporation that neither invented nor understood it and was imposing corporate policies that speeded its erosion. Participants included workers, executives in the Quaker Oats manufacturing hierarchy, raw materials suppliers, and corporate human resources, finance, and information systems staff.

What I recall vividly years later was the passionate dialogue about the subtle shift away from self-management that happened under each new corporate owner. Workers looked increasingly for team leaders to solve their problems. Team leaders increasingly saw the workforce as inept and dependent. In the future search, both groups had a shock of recognition: each perpetuated a self-fulfilling prophecy, creeping Theory X driving out Theory Y assumptions.

The meeting ended with a resolve to restore autonomy and responsibility for results at all levels. For me the high point came when a senior Quaker Oats executive stood up and said in a voice quivering with conviction, "What I realize today is that when we acquired your company, we tried to 'Quakerize' you." A bolt of electricity shot through the room. "For that I apologize," he went on. "We did not appreciate what you were doing here." He then publicly charged his staff to collaborate with the plant in modifying corporate practices to support the local system.

One thing we learn from the past is that we never learn from the past. In 1996, Quaker Oats sold its pet foods division to H.J. Heinz, which moved quickly to "Heinz-ize" the operation. According to one account, "Management shut down half the plant, eliminated the team system, suspended all the costly ongoing training that made the team system viable, and cut 150 jobs." Six months later Heinz, faced with declining productivity in Topeka, did an about face. They restored training budgets and team meetings and revalidated pay-for-knowledge and self-management of job rotation. "The system in Topeka has evolved to a much higher level than any of our other plants," said a Heinz vice president. "We look at it as a model of where we'd like to go" (Kleiner, 1996).

Merging Future Search and Work Design

Perhaps my most eye-opening experience with future search came in 2003 when Janoff and I joined with Tomas Oxelman, an internal consultant with the furniture company IKEA, to do a feat of systems redesign I had thought impossible until now. The company had decided to overhaul its "pipeline," the flow of products from the drawing boards in Almhult, Sweden, to its far-flung factories, thence to assembly and distribution points, stores, and ultimately customers in thirty-six countries. With eleven major product lines, 186 stores, 1800 suppliers in fifty-five countries, and 70,000 employees, this would be a daunting task.

Oxelman and several executives had attended future search workshops. They persuaded us that extreme action was needed, and they observed that future search principles supported their corporate values, reason enough to work this way. They would guarantee the right people in the room for whatever time was needed. Together we adapted the future search method to a single product, the "Ektorp" sofa, to re-imagine its journey from design center to customer. This would be the prototype for all product lines. Catarina Bengtsson, the business group manager, set ambitious goals for Ektorp: double sales, improve quality, and cut the price 30 percent without cutting profit, make sofa shopping easier for customers, and cut delivery times.

In March 2003, fifty-two stakeholders, including suppliers from Poland, Mexico, and China, executives starting with the company president and top staff, and line people from Sweden, Canada, the United States, and other countries, and several Ektorp customers from Hamburg, Germany (site of the meeting), came together for three days. Many had never met before. Nonetheless, they described the existing system, documented required changes, proposed a variety of new systems, agreed on common specs for a new design, created an implementation plan, and obtained buy-in from all relevant levels and functions—design, production, distribution, information technology, retailing, and customers. In Chapter Eighteen, I described such processes as taking at least six months. Here the plan was made, validated at the top, and launched with multi-level task forces in eighteen hours of work.

The most astonishing outcome for me was the common ground specs for a new system. They included greatly flattening the hierarchy, involving customers and suppliers in design from the very start, providing direct contact with suppliers and stores, changing the roles of central staff, and modifying information systems to give everyone greater influence on the system's coordination and control. What made this remarkable is that people made this up on their own, with no prompting from consultants on how to think about systems design. They muddled their way from a traditional, centralized system, breaking down the silos, by taking seriously customer concerns and matching a variety of designs against the proposed goals. It was a vivid example of people following Mary Parker Follett's "law of the situation" (Metcalf and Urwick, 1940, p. 59). There was one more thing—leadership. Throughout, top executives joined the dialogue without saying what form a new system should take. Rather, the president continually reiterated the importance of the prototype to the company's future. Ektorp—that sofa sitting in a corner of the meeting room with a coffee table in front of it—was a means to a larger goal, not an end in itself.

Within a month, seven task forces were at work around the world, redoing every aspect of the system. The main coordination and control mechanism? A regular conference call buttressed by emails. Having all in touch with one another enabled a degree of self-organizing not previously seen. "I learned a lot and also got many insights into how we in IKEA cooperate amidst the complexity, and in how to run a workshop like this one," said

Catti Bengtsson, who has no formal line authority over most of the players. "We have complete documentation at our intranet site, which is updated continuously. The regular telephone conferences are helping us keep the focus and speed!"

Training Practitioners

By 1991, having done several future searches, Janoff and I seized on an opportunity presented by Gil Levin, director of Albert Einstein College of Medicine's summer Cape Cod Institute. We designed an experiment to see whether we could teach future search principles and methods in a seminar. There exists in such training a paradox. The success of a future search hinges on interdependent stakeholders. The dynamic tension comes as people find common ground across lines of class, culture, and status, leading to action plans none dreamed possible. We could describe this, show it on videotapes, and even role play it in simulation. What we couldn't do is provide the real thing. Workshop participants' only common concern is learning future search. Diverse and motivated they may be, but they cannot recreate fully the interactive dynamics. They simply have no ongoing business with each other.

So it was with skepticism that we approached Cape Cod. Nearly 100 people showed up, a group too large for our purposes. To make things worse, we selected the future of organization development as a simulation topic, thinking this would provide a common denominator. That turned out to be a little like choosing the future of metaphysical speculation, since OD encompassed a wide range of highly diverse practices, individual, group, and systemwide. More, OD consultants, like many professionals, usually work solo or with a partner. This would not be significant except for the fact that they earn their livings advocating collaborative teamwork for others.

So even were Cape Cod not a simulation, an actual future search to help solo professionals do collaborative action planning is largely a dead end. Future search is geared toward tangible actions with a visible impact, requiring groups that perceive their interdependence. (Even knowing this, Janoff and I later would run three future searches for professional groups with low interdependence. Lots of talk, little action. Eventually we would accept what we had learned at Cape Cod: ours was not the best meeting design for lone wolf practitioners.)

However, we learned a more important lesson. Many Cape Cod participants later ran successful future searches. Although they could not get the dynamics, they got the principles, tools, and techniques. Most also got a pleasant surprise. Faced with people who needed to cooperate, they had a *better* experience than during the training. So did their clients.

Launching a Future Search Network

In 1991 we also met with a social action group from the Philadelphia Region OD Network who wanted future search training. Together we designed an action research project to see whether consultant teams could run successful future searches after three days of training. To maximize chances for success, we invited clients and consultants to learn together. By "success" we meant enabling clients to do things after the future search that they could not do before. All of us would donate our services in the interest of creating new knowledge about change processes.

That project resulted in a dozen future searches in the Philadelphia area for organizations as diverse as an inner-city career agency, a statewide reading program, and a hospital for emotionally disturbed children. As clients reported planning breakthroughs, people in other cities requested training. Eventually the program was repeated sixteen times across North America, resulting in hundreds of future searches and many stories of effective action plans.

Thus began Future Search Network, founded in 1993, a nonprofit coalition of practitioners who began doing future searches across the United States and Canada as a form of public service. By 2003 the Network had 350 members in 25 countries on five continents. Members offered to put on future searches of public benefit anywhere, in any culture, any language, for whatever people could afford (see www.futuresearch.net).

To help fund the Network, we offered public workshops. By 2003, our colleagues and we had trained more than 3,000 people in Australia, Austria, Bangladesh, Canada, England, Germany, India, Indonesia, Kenya, Singapore, South Africa, Sweden, Thailand, and the United States. Hundreds, perhaps thousands, of future searches, in corporations, NGOs, non-profits, and communities, had been run and dozens of cases documented (Weisbord and Janoff, 2000). With minimal instruction many people, despite uncertainty and high anxiety, could run successful future searches the first time—if they let the participants do the work.

We decided also that the method, a product of so many hands and brains, ought to be freely available, unencumbered by certification and market concerns. As the Network grew, its members experimented with time frames, overall length, group size, task sequence, instructions, how to display data on walls, how to involve everybody in large groups, and with the degree to which people could and should do work formerly done for them by staff. All shared the learning. The method became simpler, instructions fewer, groups ever more diverse, and participants' involvement deeper and more passionate as we left more of the work up to them. All this we put into a detailed action guide (Weisbord and Janoff, 2000).

A Network in Action

In 2002, this work reached a high point in Southwestern Michigan. Future Search Network was invited into a model business/community partnership significantly redefining the boundaries of both systems. Led by Dave Whitwam, CEO of Whirlpool Corporation, a global giant based in Benton Harbor, the community had organized a remarkable development effort aimed at including all citizens in every aspect of local life.

Whirlpool's motivation was a history of racial and other tensions between Benton Harbor, a once-thriving, largely black town that had lost many businesses, and St. Josephs, its well-to-do, mainly white neighbor across the river. The growing gap between communities made it hard for Whirlpool to attract a diverse workforce at its headquarters. Whirlpool Foundation, the company's community action arm, retained Kaleel Jamison Consulting Group (KJCG), a diversity consulting firm led by Fred Miller, a colleague I had known for years.

KJCG mobilized hundreds of local citizens in workshops, seminars, and meetings. People met each other across economic and racial boundaries, discovering common stakes in working together. Future Search Network's task was to help channel this growing energy into joint community projects. Having the Network made possible the mobilizing in a few days of thirty-two highly motivated members from diverse racial and ethic backgrounds. Working in teams of four with community leaders and a KJCG team led by Marcus Robinson, they ran eight future searches in as many weeks.

Sandra Janoff and I conducted an initial future search for the executive steering group of The Council for World Class Communities. They confirmed their mission, defined "world class" and "interdependent," and created an action umbrella for seven more future searches—in business, communities of faith, community outreach, economic development, education and learning, government, and health care. More than 300 local citizens came together in cooperative action on dozens of plans. These included attracting new businesses, opening affordable housing, building children's playgrounds, cooperation among churches and schools, and inclusion of many citizens previously left out of local civic life.

Ripples in the Stream of Social Change

I cannot leave this future search review without commenting on two phenomena related to the rapid spread of this work. First was the discovery that diverse people could participate in future searches without needing to be trained in new skills and that many people could manage them without long apprenticeships. Second, the method bridged cultural boundaries none of us had set out to cross. In the 1970s I had learned how problematic it was to adapt business-based methods to colleges, universities, and medical schools, not to mention cultures not my own. Future Search Network members had involved participants from an encyclopedic list of the world's cultures in taking charge of their futures.

We had stumbled on a meeting methodology that people were using to validate their own traditions. Unity Church clergy, for example, adapted future search to congregational renewal, saying that the underlying principles embodied the core tenets of their faith. Many Episcopal and Methodist clergy came to the same conclusion. The Jewish Reconstructionist Federation undertook a future search, saying it represented "Reconstructionism in action." A director of the U.S. Army leadership center incorporated future search into officer training because the balance between structure and open-ended possibility seemed peculiarly suited to military officers. In Hawaii the planning committee for Ko'olau Loa, a community on the North Shore of Oahu, concluded that future search enabled a return to traditional Hawaiian values of the oneness of mind, body, and spirit. In Singapore, participants of Chinese descent said they experienced in future search a re-creation of traditional community values of mutual support and cooperation.

There were other clues that something out of the ordinary was happening. I was surprised at how many groups adopted their "mind maps" of trends affecting them as totems of a sort, putting them in reports, on the World Wide Web, and on the wall back at the office. I was equally surprised that the time lines had universal appeal and that dramatizing ideal futures gained wide acceptance, even in business firms. We often were astonished to see staid executives laugh, dance, and play act, displaying a talent for serious fun nobody knew they had. It was as if participants used future search to evoke archetypes that had great meaning now.

Why Was This Happening?

As I pondered this development, I thought of something my friend Bapu Deolalikar, an international development consultant, had told me years ago before future search had spanned the globe. "This method," Bapu noted, "is largely culture free. I think it could be done in India and many other places." At the time I recall mumbling my skepticism that such a thing could be possible. By the mid-90s, however, it became clear that Bapu was right. Future searches were tapping into something lodged deep in the human psyche. I'm confident this could not happen if people first had to acquire skills and attitudes they did not already have.

Far from adding new pressures into the field—theories, concepts, and strategies to be mastered, conflicts to be managed, problems to be solved—we were stripping away group dynamics technology a layer at a time. In Lewin's terms we had reduced the restraining forces enough so that the skills, experiences, and motivation people already had would sweep them toward the futures they really wanted. We had people doing real-time action research on themselves. We were actualizing Kurt Lewin's values while updating his concepts and techniques for a world of full-time change.

I would like to think this marked the beginning of the end of increasingly complex strategic management programs. Of course this wish could be pure fantasy too, as much so as the belief that mastering complexity calls for more of the same. I know that many of us by the year 2003 believed that in our drive toward faster, shorter, cheaper we had greatly increased the pressure on ourselves for techniques to keep up. We also were building up unconscious restraints in ourselves and others. What we called "resistance to change" could be renamed a healthy reaction of organisms pushed beyond their design limits. We didn't need better tools for handling resistance. There was a part of us yearning to transcend the tyranny of technology, the pressure for growth and achievement at any cost, and the relentless compression of time. Future search offered one forum for accepting ourselves and working with each other as is.

Future search—to be so widely embraced—had to be serving universal needs. That realization pointed me toward its mythic aspects. Looked at one way, future search was just another planning meeting. From another angle, it could be seen as a secular rite of passage, enabling people to make a perilous journey from one place to another, to do things this week that were unthinkable a week earlier. Its rituals were the time lines, mind maps, "prouds and sorries," and "common ground wall." Its myths were fanciful stories dressed up as "preferred future scenarios." Looked at this way, I could understand my friend Bapu's comment about crossing cultures. The human species has practiced living in community from the dawn of time.

For people from homogeneous cultures, the secular myths and rituals evoked familiar cultural processes that celebrated community milestones. In cross-cultural future searches, the processes provided a neutral bridge that diverse people could walk to find each other. Because the rituals belonged to no one culture, all could own them. It was as if people used the future search to re-create their own cultural contexts, projecting onto an empty screen labeled "past, present, and future" what they valued most. Far from being a "new paradigm," perhaps we had inadvertently tapped into our common heritage on earth, dating to when every tribe lived by myth, ritual, and the changing seasons.

Redefining Future Search

Then, in 1995, I was startled to discover parallels between future search and the ancient Taoist philosophy underlying traditional Chinese medicine. The catalyst was a seminar on "Redefining Health," a program of TAI-SOPHIA (formerly the Traditional Acupuncture Institute) in Columbia, Maryland. In the seminar we learned the seasons of five-element acupuncture, each matching an element in nature—fall (metal); winter (water); spring (wood); summer (fire); late summer (earth). We were asked to apply this metaphorical system to situations in our lives.

Each season has a condition associated with "effective actions for life." The model had us moving—in relation to the issue we had selected—around the seasons, from "honoring all concerned" in fall, to a place of inquiry and unknowing in winter, to a clear vision in spring, to partnership in summer, and to mutual agreement about what to do in late summer. (Acupuncturists who practice this way intend that people experience the five conditions during treatment. To be whole and energized is to know all five states.)

Observing this process in the workshop, I felt a tingle of excite-ment. This movement exactly paralleled the five phases of future search! We started with timelines honoring the experience of every person in the room. We made a mind map of global trends that was the basis for further inquiry into the complexity of our world. We moved to common ground and dramatic visions of a future people are willing to work for. Finally we sought voluntary partnerships, agreement, and action commitments. This cycle of experience had been known for thousands of years. Over a few decades we had replicated it experimentally. Its origins, I concluded, must lie in the collective unconscious (Weisbord, 2001). See "Ancient Wisdom/Future Search."

I cannot prove that future search does all this. However, I have little doubt that researchers will follow up my hypothesis. Someday we may see formal evidence that future search and similar methods succeeded not because they changed the paradigm so much as they helped people refocus on what had always been fundamental to our species—dignity, meaning, community, and productive work. In a tidal wave of change, most of it self-made and much of it self-defeating, many people were eager at the approach of the 21st Century to recover those parts of our shared experience that made working together one of life's joys.

ANCIENT WISDOM		FUTURE SEARCH	
Season	*Ongoing Conditions*	*Phase*	*Purpose*
FALL	Honoring all concerned; insight into who each of us is in this situation.	PAST	Validating every person's experience; developing a shared context.
WINTER	Knowledge; willingness to be in inquiry/unknowing.	PRESENT	Pooling all perceptions; inquiry; discovery.
SPRING	Seeing what your vision is with clarity about your intent	FUTURE	Living our dreams; Internalizing what we really want.
SUMMER	Opening the heart to create partnership.	COMMON GROUND	Confirming shared aspirations & values.
LATE SUMMER	Mutual agreement about what would be of service.	ACTION	Cooperating on next steps toward a future serving all.

Chapter Twenty-Two

How There and Then Looks from Here and Now: Ten Cases Revisited

"Can't help but wonder where I'm bound."
——*Tom Paxton, folk singer, 1963*

"This is not a one walk dog."
——*Dianne Connelly, practitioner of traditional Chinese medicine*

I based this new edition on following up ten cases from the earlier book. The six cases in Part Two were foundations for the "learning curve" on page 329. The curve showed an evolution from expert problem solving to involving everyone in improving whole systems. My insight was that this shift, driven by social, technological, and economic change, called for new ways of managing and consulting. Other cases told how I entered the workplace improving game (Chapter One) and illustrated my theory in action, notably the work at AECL Medical Products (now Chapter Nineteen). Revisiting these narratives fifteen to thirty years later, I wanted to know what happened after I left. More particularly, I wanted to see what I could learn about continuity in a world of unstable workplaces.

Ten cases is admittedly a small number. In retrospect I selected these because each involved one to three years of effort with committed clients, a good cross section of the 100 or so workplace projects I had done. It's possible, of course, that my experiences are so personal and idiosyncratic they cannot be generalized. Nonetheless, here are answers to some questions I found myself asking at this stage of my journey. See "Ten Projects Summarized."

Ten Projects Summarized

Cases	Dates	What Was Done	Situation 15 to 30 Years Later
Chapter One			
MW Family Business	1966-1968	Self-managing work teams started; increased productivity and morale, reduced turn-over, absenteeism	Company sold twice; part of successful conglomerate; "teams" of one did whole job
Part Two			
Six Key Cases			
Medical School	1969-1971	Planning process involving all stake-holders, with emphasis on alienated faculty; new mission	Changed owners twice, survived financial scandal; faculty remained involved in plan-ning and budgeting
Food Services	1970-1971	Turnover reduced through Likert survey and manager training	Turnover was still an issue for company and industry; manager training now key everywhere
Chem Corp	1979-1980	Survey feedback improves R&D/ relations with other functions and increases flow of new products	Old culture resurfaced; few new products
Packaging Plant	1978-1979	Packaging system greatly improved	
	1989-1990	Entire plant redesigned by 60 employees	Redesign of 1989-1990 did not outlast leadership changes
Solcorp	1981	Attempt to get R&D, marketing, and manu-facturing in synch	Company gone without a trace
Printing Inc.	1981-1983	Reorganization at top followed by redesign of work systems by employees	Facility closed; manufacturing moved

Ten Projects Summarized, Cont'd.

Cases	Dates	What Was Done	Situation 15 to 30 Years Later
Part Three			
Whole System Cases			
Bethlehem Steel Sparrows Point Plant	1981–1983	Whole system pilot projects to improve union/management relations and save company greatly improves quality	Plant closings; downsizings; climate of labor/ management cooperation sustained; company filed for Chapter 11 bankruptcy in 2002; assets sold in 2003
McCormack & Dodge	1985	Strategic reorganization by sixty employees in series of conferences	Company merged by new owner, lost money, sold abroad
AECL Medical Products	1985	Failed company saved through employment guarantees and total involvement becomes profitable	Company survived further crisis; sold in 1990s; remained viable as part of large, successful company

Q: *What Led People to Undertake These Projects?*

A: While statistics can be mustered — there are several in this book — to support involving everyone in improving the whole, I don't believe "the numbers" ever motivated skeptics to do it. Positive measures mainly reassure people who would do this work anyway. In my projects leaders were of two kinds. Some were under the gun to survive and were at the point where they would try anything plausible. Had things been going well, they would not have called consultants. Others believed that involving people was the right thing to do and the prospect of a return on investment made it easier to justify betting on consultants who shared their values.

Of the five motivated by survival, Solcorp's president was driven by an under-developed product and market pressures from his corporate parent. The Sparrows Point Plate Mill superintendent worried about the superiority of Japanese steel. Medical School's president faced financial pressures, an alienated faculty, and conflict between the school and its teaching hospital. The president of AECL Medical had come up against continuing layoffs and a possible shutdown. At Printing Inc. the CEO's own survival was at stake. The company was doing okay but he had fallen out of favor at corporate headquarters.

In five other cases, by contrast, leaders were blessed by rapid growth and increasing success. This complicates the hypothesis that change projects require a threatening crisis. There is such a thing as a crisis of success, when an organization outruns the experience of its leaders. This happens more as the work world spins faster, pushing people into novel situations. In such cases putting your values into action offers more certainty than recycling wornout methods. In the success/high growth cases, all the leaders were value driven, that is, believing that stakeholder engagement, influence, and commitment would improve economic viability.

My family business, for example, was growing 25 percent a year. I wanted a workplace founded on Theory Y assumptions because that touched a deep part of my identity. At Food Services the president gained valuable self-knowledge at a behavioral science seminar. He wanted the same for his managers. The turnover project evolved when a pilot group discovered at the initial manager seminar how much employee attrition cost. The regional president in whose area the research was done, however, had a deep belief in people and did several team-building sessions with me about the same time.

At Chem Corp, the HR manager and his boss, the president, had asked for team building to foster cooperation among functions. The R&D action research project was a spin-off from team members wanting better relations with an uncollaborative R&D chief. As a scientist, however, the R&D head liked the idea of quantifying relationships among departments. At Printing Inc. I came in after the president was pressured by corporate headquarters to shape up his leadership or else. The later work redesign projects were led by a vice president with an affinity for teamwork, openness, and a belief in having people control their work.

Packaging Plant enjoyed rapid growth and market leadership when I went there in 1979. The manufacturing VP who called me wanted greater responsibility for results shared by managers and workers alike. He believed in opening up the plant and finding new ways to cooperate. The plant manager had no choice but to go along. In the plant redesign ten years later, another plant manager valued employee participation and creativity and wanted everyone to have a chance to succeed. McCormack & Dodge was growing fast, too, and was a leader in mainframe financial systems software. The president had a balky and contentious staff, and he wanted departments to cooperate — an itch that led eventually to a total company reorganization by employees from all levels and functions.

Q: *How Did I Decide What Methods to Use?*

A: My choices had more to do with my enthusiasms than with existing OD methods. I started my consulting practice after a decade of business experience. I also knew how to interview from my years as a journalist. Putting together business and interviewing skills, I got through my initial consulting assignments. In year one I said, "Here's what I propose to do," drawing on what I knew. In year two, having added survey feedback to my tool kit, I could say, "Well, there are two ways to go at this." Attending workshops, I brought myself up to speed with process consulting, interpersonal skills, team building, group dynamics, and problem solving. By year five I had a menu that included the above plus intergroup workshops, management-by-objectives, ad hoc meetings, and leadership training, all within an action research framework.

I also had my eyes open for work redesign projects to repeat what I had done as a manager, though it took me 12 years of consulting to find the first one. In each case I proposed methods I was eager to try because they spoke to my sense of adventure. I was looking for the boundaries of social, technological and economic change. Indeed, until I committed in the early 1990s to future search as the embodiment of everything I believed in, I never did the same thing twice. Rather, I tailor-made each project from the whole cloth of my current passions linked to my clients' wishes.

In my family firm I had just read Douglas McGregor and was eager to start self-managing teams. At Medical School I first interviewed people because that was what I knew how to do. By the time we got to action steps, I had met Rensis Likert, internalized his "link pin" planning ideas and saw this as a reassuring structure for a school low on trust. At Food Services I built further on Likert's work, starting with his concept of human resource accounting wed to survey data feedback because I was eager to prove the bottom line value of social processes in a business not my own. At Chem Corp I saw a chance to develop a new use for the differentiation-integration theories I had absorbed while working with Paul Lawrence in medical schools. Packaging Plant in 1979 enabled an application of systems thinking, a concept I was attracted to intellectually and wanted to find a way of using with people who were systems operators, not thinkers. By the time I got to AECL Medical Products and McCormack and Dodge in the mideighties I had had 20 years of experience. By the second Packaging Plant effort in 1989, I was doing work redesign in a series of large group meetings, a significant scaling up of my earlier efforts. At each stage I was integrating everything I knew into every project, seeking the limits of workplace improvement.

In short, I liked the high wire. My safety net was the certain knowledge that doing projects nobody had done before in *this* workplace was the only sure path to new levels of both business results and learning. You can't "change" a workplace by repeating old dynamics. Nor can you do it by comparing an organization's needs with an inventory of all the possible ways for meeting them. I think Harrison Owen's (1997) principle for Open Space meetings applies to all OD strategies. Whatever you did is the only thing you could have done. Choosing a change strategy is like deciding what to wear each morning. You can only pick from what you have.

Q: *What Became of These Workplaces Years Later?*

A: Four organizations by 2003 were no more. Solcorp disappeared, having no market viability. Sparrows Point Plate Mill, world class at the end, was closed for strategic reasons when Bethlehem Steel acquired another plate mill, and Bethlehem itself was sold shortly after. Printing Inc., successful for a long time, had its manufacturing moved to points south for strategic reasons by a distant parent corporation. McCormack & Dodge, despite its success, was merged with a rival and lost its founding CEO. The parent company, having diluted its economic strength, got rid of a merged entity turned albatross.

Two organizations, Chem Corp R&D and Packaging Plant, enjoyed great short-term success from the OD projects and were ongoing successful businesses. Both were large corporations with several divisions, the only ones of my ten cases to have the same ownership two decades after I had worked with them. Both continued to bring consultants in every few years to revisit turf ploughed years before. Successive generations of managers need to walk their own dogs.

Three organizations — my family firm, Food Services, and AECL Medical Products (Theratronics) — were sold and thrived as part of larger companies. In my former family business, the work system I had installed in 1967 metamorphosed after the sale, obeying the laws of ever-more-powerful technologies. In Food Services manager training and turnover reduction became institutionalized, although not traceable to 1970. Medical Products was reunited with its sister company in a progressive, well-capitalized firm. All three companies had effective employee- and customer-friendly work systems under new management that knew nothing of earlier programs.

Finally, Medical School changed hands twice, survived scandal and economic mayhem, and went from the smallest to the largest of its peers in the United States. Thirty years later, faculty involvement in programs and budgets was a legacy of the 1970 project, although hardly anyone knew it.

Q: Do These Cases Represent "Culture Change"?

A: I have rarely used the term "culture change," thinking it a bit grandiose for workplaces. Still, many others do, so let me attempt a definition congruent with my beliefs. I'm aware from years of future searches that one tangible expression of culture is the circle, that ancient symbol of community. In workplaces, people in the circle are those with information, influence, control, power, and respect. Some sit in the inner circle, some the outer, and some hover on the fringe, hoping to be invited in. Here's my practice theory of culture change: *make the circle bigger and things get better; make the circle smaller and things get worse.*

As more people become involved with understanding and improving whole systems, the circles get bigger and the potential for making things better increases. For me the simplest example of "culture change" is when people accustomed to sitting in closed circles find themselves asking, "Who else ought to be in on this?" or "How can we get people with information, expertise, authority, resources, and need all in one conversation often enough to call it a way of life?" That is a formula for designing and maintaining productive workplaces, where dignity, meaning, and community are enacted daily as people go about creating wealth (business) or spending it for the public good (non-profit and public sector).

Q: Did the Circles Get Bigger in the Ten Case Examples?

A: In every case, the circle got bigger for some people. Indeed, as consulting projects expanded from expert problem solving toward involving everyone in improving the whole, more people got into the loop. Eventually they provided their own data, analysis, and action plans, using structures and processes managed by consultants. The four cases in Chapter Eleven, where consultants did the diagnosis and prescription — Food Services, Chem Corp, Packaging Plant, and Solcorp — had large numbers in the circle during the surveys and interviews and far fewer when it came to action. At

Printing Inc. and Medical School, a great many people participated at every step. These two projects had considerable impact, the first resulting in a total reorganizing of the work systems, the second in a strategic change of direction and inclusion of enough faculty to avoid splitting the system beyond repair.

The projects at Bethlehem Steel (Chapter Fifteen) and AECL Medical (Chapter Nineteen) involved the most inclusive circles and, perhaps no coincidence, had the most dramatic impact. Both led to significant changes in work processes, labor-management cooperation, using new technologies, and capability to weather quality and market crises. In both cases employee commitment and involvement staved off disaster — for a while.

In this regard I must also cite the future searches described in Chapters Twenty and Twenty-One. These, I think, encapsulate in one short event the dynamics required to get everyone on the same page and acting together. Paradoxically, many future searches have had greater long-term impact on a system than months or years of more narrowly focused activity — team building, for example, or leadership training, or surveys. I have many theories about why this could happen and no proof that would stand up in a court of science.

Oddly enough, the metaphors I use to explain to myself the impact of this work are more familiar to cultural anthropologists than to management consultants. "Rite of passage," "secular ritual," and "walk around the seasons" are a few that I use. These suggest for me the smallest containers big enough to hold what is easy to see and hard to believe: whole systems moving themselves in three days to new, more balanced ways of functioning. That has happened often enough in communities and organizations to be noted by thousands of people. Much remains to be learned about these phenomena. In 2003 Future Search Network had an ongoing "ripple" research project to document what people did after future searches that they couldn't do before. Maybe we'll discover we're doing culture change after all.

Q: How Can I Be so Sure That Making the Circle Bigger Has Both Economic and Social Benefits?

A: I enjoyed both benefits as a manager and for many years saw my consulting clients repeatedly get both, at least for a while. In my family business I saw a 40 percent increase in productivity within six months after starting self-managed teams and great esprit in the work force. Food Services saved millions of dollars reducing turnover by attending to employee needs, something the whole industry knew how to do by 2003. Chem Corp initially took some new products to market in a shorter time; Packaging Plant and Printing Inc. increased production capability; AECL Medical went from years of losses to years of profits; and Medical School did not go broke until it was taken over by a big for-profit corporation with loose ethics. Bethlehem Steel staved off disaster in the short run. It could not outrun the exigencies of a globalized steel industry. McCormack & Dodge did well economically while it had control of its destiny and was eaten alive after its parent company merged it with a despised rival. In every case motivated people produced good economic results. They were not achieved by consulting reports.

Q: What Comes After? Are There Natural Limits to This Work?

A: The "environment," that catchall concept from open systems theory, is what constrains us all. The environment got Taylor's ball-bearing company in the 19th Century and it got Bethlehem Steel and Printing Inc. and Solcorp in the 20th Century. That's the shadow side of participative planning. If you set your mind to it, you *can* get everybody improving whole systems. You know you can do it because thousands of others already have. But when Humpty-Dumpty, good egg to the core — organic, free range, and all that — falls off the wall, smashing to smithereens in the global marketplace, all the king's horses and all the king's men, even with the king's total commitment to openness and creativity, cannot put Humpty-Dumpty back together. That too is a tale reinforced by my cases, and confirmed dramatically when the dot.com bubble burst in 2001 and dozens of great places to work went under.

Chasing permanence in an impermanent world, then, is as self-defeating as a cat chasing its tail. We cannot stabilize cultural changes any more than we can get the planets to assume different orbits, the Nile to flow south or the Mississippi north. What's the alternative? Doing each day the best you can with what you know is right. "Shucks," say you, "I learned that in grade school!" Well, here at last is a practical application. Any time you include more people and help them to look at the whole before fixing the parts, any time you get people to focus on shared aspirations rather than problems, any time you set it up so people control and coordinate their work, that's a high order of systems change. Repeat this formula daily for as long as you can, and voila, you have "built in" continuity. You have it, that is, until the environment says "enough."

Getting everyone improving whole systems, I conclude, is an existentially right goal no matter what comes after.

Epilogue

Still Caught Between Paradigms: Where Do We Go from Here?

> I know of no safe depository of the ultimate powers
> of the society but the people themselves, and if we
> think them not enlightened enough to exercise
> their control with a wholesome discretion, the
> remedy is not to take it from them, but to inform
> their discretion.
> ——*Thomas Jefferson, September 28, 1820*

Suppose the whitewater isn't permanent? That's not so far-fetched if you believe that nobody has a crystal ball and the future is made up of a billion individual choices. Suppose we all got tired of change and settled down for a while? Peter Schwartz, former head of Royal Dutch Shell's Business Environment group, once foresaw a decade of unpredictable change followed by a long stretch of stability. "I think the world economy goes through these transitions, from periods of relative stability to relative turbulence to relative stability again," he told *Whole Earth Catalog* author Stewart Brand. "We're in one of these transitions. There's probably a relatively stable era of several decades ahead" (1986, p. 96).

I wrote the foregoing paragraph in 1987. In 2003, there was no stability in sight. In the United States the longest economic boom in decades ended with a collapse of many technology companies just after the turn of the century. This was followed by earthshaking corporate bankruptcies, notably Enron and WorldCom, driven by deceit, fraud, and mismanagement. Nobody controlled the global marketplace. Indeed, nobody, it seemed, controlled the global corporations. Insatiable for quarterly dividends, some firms were prone to substitute dubious accounting for accountability.

Global terrorism had become a fact of life, affecting the security and economy of every country in the world. People were adopting a raft of new technologies — in health care, recreation, warfare, communications, genetics, entertainment, biotechnology, and the media, to cite just a few — adding great complexity to daily life. You would not want to ask in most workplaces the facetious party question, "Are we having fun yet?"

Of course, the Peter Schwartz scenario above may still be correct. Few of us will be around to evaluate it. Regardless, the choices we make today have profound consequences for the future.

Consider the AECL Medical Division. Despite my satisfaction in having aided AECL's renewal, I feel uneasy too. The case raises many unanswered questions for each one of us: about the right relationships among economics, technology, and people in a political democracy; about the difference between authority, which we need for security, and authoritarianism, which threatens our survival; about what sort of meal really satisfies the hunger for community, dignity, and meaning in work; about the contributions managers, consultants, students, and teachers can make to our mutual survival; about the limits of fast-changing technologies; about our positive and negative voices, X and Y alike, tugging us this way and that between grit-your-teeth denial and purposeful involvement. In these closing pages I want to indicate some paths we can take, should take, will take if we care about the future of our workplaces and our planet.

People in the Middle

To start in the middle, there remains the peculiar plight of managers and supervisors caught in a time warp between the old paradigm and the new. It's one thing to recognize that new technologies and democratic values push toward greater competence at the bottom, less bureaucracy in the middle, and new forms of leadership across the board. It is quite another to revamp organizations that way. We must not be deterred by the difficulties. "The role of the foreman is so central to the traditional authoritarian system," writes Fred Emery, "that the first question to ask of any proposed scheme for democratization of work is, what does it do to the foreman's role? If it leaves that role intact then the scheme is fraudulent" (1980, p. 20). Traditional supervision may be the buggy whip of the 21st Century. It's time to move away from supervisory training toward developing team leaders and facilitators. Who needs better buggy whips?

Tough principles are involved, not just techniques. I list three that tie closely to dignity and meaning, and cast some (admittedly dim) light on the rocky path between what Tolstoy called "personal and general interests."

Principle 1: Secure employment is the bedrock of viable businesses and personal identity. Work redesign means fewer people have better jobs and produce more. We need to create new economic opportunities at the same time we streamline our work.

Principle 2: We cannot afford to preserve the special status, autocratic style, or expert turf of a handful of traditional managers at the cost of motivation, commitment, and growth for 90 percent of a work force. We should not be deterred from work redesign and participative future searches for new technologies and markets just because those in charge have not done it before. They should be encouraged to learn how.

Principle 3: Loyal people who did their best for years and suddenly find the game changed deserve options — to learn and lead, or to find new careers. While they have not earned the right to block changes that afford others dignity, meaning, and community, they *are* owed the means to get new roles and skills and the emotional support needed to take charge of their own futures.

It's important to recall, as I learned from Taylor, that resistance is a universal phenomenon. It is also temporary — unless hardened by constant pressure. *All* change, even when they desire it, threatens supervisors and managers. Worker participation is just one kind. New technologies, scheduling methods, ways of budgeting, executive computer terminals, appraisal systems — new anything — all threaten comfort, status, and identity. Yet somehow we find ways to move on. Managers and consultants continually face resistance, in themselves and in others, when pressured to learn new skills and alter familiar tasks. The journey from old to new paradigms is like that in "Star Trek," a five-year voyage into vast uncharted outer space where our species has not been. Few guidelines exist for getting us there, although we now have a long list of practices that won't.

We are in the midst of an unstoppable historic shift from global competition to cooperation. You can approach it as a war of the workplace to be fought by firing and laying off to cut costs (economics), imposing innovations unilaterally (technology), and manipulating decisions already made to "make people feel involved" (human relations). That's the old paradigm in action, making things worse every time we invoke it.

The new paradigm, I think, will one day be understood as a revolutionary turning point in human history — from expert problem solving circa 1900 to everybody improving whole systems in 2001 A.D. and beyond. We have been slow to recognize how quickly this model is replacing the old one in the workplace, just as automobiles once replaced horses and buggies in the streets. How people perceived autos in 1915 is, roughly speaking, the way we perceive work redesign, teamwork, and future search today. Many people have heard of them, few have actually seen one, not everybody wants one, and those who do are still focused on speed and cost more than a high-quality ride. As for those who own one, they find learning to operate it stimulating, irritating, threatening, miraculous, inspiring, frustrating, unpredictable, demanding, and hard to describe.

If you believe that dignity, meaning, and community — your own and others' — derive from taking charge of your own fate, then you face profound paradoxes. The way to help people move, for example, is to invite them to express their reservations. But skepticism gets you tagged. We ought not label people Theory X or

Theory Y or theory anything — when both X and Y capture the good and bad in each of us. To make it safe for people to express skepticism, we have to hear it without taking it personally. We have to be able to admit it in ourselves.

If you're leading anything, you have to take a stand *without a crystal ball*. There are no sure things, only sure values. I remember Don Thompson's statement to managers when he was operations vice-president in a company shifting toward employee-managed work teams. "This thing is a steamroller," he said. "It's a benevolent steamroller. It's only going three miles an hour. If you go five miles an hour you can stay ahead of it. If you go eight miles an hour you can even stop for a beer. But if you only go two, it's going to flatten you."

Helping People Caught in the Middle. The game has changed from telling people what to do or doing it yourself, to managing boundaries and helping others gain skill. Unless policies exist to learn how to do that — promotion, reward, support — there is no behavioral science alternative (or any other alternative) to rejecting previously loyal people. In Taylor's time, making it the engineers' problem did not work. In our time, making it the human resource manager's problem still doesn't work. It's everybody's problem. (See "Summary.") How can those of us who believe in dignity, meaning, and community learn to:

1. Treat each person as an adult capable of sharing risks and entitled to share rewards ?

2. Involve people in creating their own choices instead of assuming that a week's notice and an outplacement counselor in the next room are the outer limits of practicality?

3. Accept individual *and* corporate responsibility for inventing alternative paths, new economic activity, to reduce the anxiety released by the disappearance of old machinery, markets, and jobs?

If I were king in an ideal world, I would insist that those in the middle lead the change, and offer choices to those who opt out. After all, they have the most to lose, therefore the most to gain. But I'm never king, and the world is not ideal. My dilemma includes mountains of evidence that having groups represented helps only the representatives — and not as much as they would like. Ask any steering committee member. It has been known for some forty years — from Israel, Scandinavia, Yugoslavia, and West Germany — that putting workers on boards of directors and worker ownership does not reduce worker apathy or increase output where traditional supervision stays intact and people do narrow jobs (Bucklow, 1966).

Representation in planning enhances democracy. It is not sufficient for productive workplaces. Dignity, meaning, and community come from deep engagement in our work. Each person needs real tasks that make a contribution to the whole. That means a form of corporate democracy still being invented.

The ideal remains a tantalizing aspiration, just out of reach. It's the right brass ring to stretch for. If I were doing AECL again, I would make a strong pitch to the Work Design Steering Committee to treat the *whole* factory, not just critical subsystems, as the unit for redesign. I'm sure that would threaten many more folks in the middle. Maybe that's why we didn't do it. I'm also sure it's the shortest path to improving the whole. Redesigning the whole factory would have given those who remained the best shot at producing to their highest capability. Under time pressure, we gave in to participative problem solving in a tapestry so complex it could not be woven that way. We must get everybody redesigning whole systems; that's the basic principle. If you tell me my aspirations are impractical, I can only reply that so was flying before 1903.

Training — When and Where? In Chapter One I told how I installed self-managing teams in the 1960s with no training in group dynamics or problem solving. The teams had no choice. In 1966 I

Summary:
What Managers and Consultants Are Learning to Do.

Involve others in designing their work.

Advocate quality and customer service.

Get rid of *all* dumb jobs.

Help people make a contribution as well as a living.

Be involvers, facilitators, keepers of the learning environment.

Help others take stands on important economic and technology issues — even when they disagree.

Hold interactive stakeholder meetings, across levels and departments, and with customers and suppliers.

Walk the line between too much and too little structure.

Search for new economic opportunities and secure jobs.

Live with and accept their own inner dialogues, both positive and negative voices.

Help others build power bases, learn skills, talk to one another on equal footing across all cultural and ethnic boundaries.

Use the whole brain — intuition, values, experience, *and* rational problem solving.

Let go the need to know everything; help people write their own textbooks.

Accept the need for stability and the inevitability of change.

And a hundred others we forgot, or never knew, and have still to learn.

knew nothing about training. Forty years and hundreds of workshops later, I know a lot about training. I wish I could tell you — here, now, in this situation — how much training is the right amount, or when to do it, or even whether to. For years I have found myself too soon or too late with training. Not only that, the trainees — unless they include top management — always say the wrong people are in the room. I admire Eileen Curtin's ability (see Chapter Ten) to mix training, problem solving, and purposeful focus so skillfully in a work redesign that people learn just what they need exactly when they want it. It is an art I wish I could tie a ribbon around and give to each reader who sends in a postcard.

Instead, I leave you with a challenging paradox. We all need the best methods we can find for learning new skills. Unless our learning is self-motivated, we are unlikely to use it. Training needs to be voluntary, jointly entered into by people who work together, and safe in the sense that people will not be compromised by other's judgments of them. In short it is helped by joint planning between trainees and trainers — a difficult though not impossible move, as Curtin has shown. Putting everybody through this or that experience satisfies certain needs. Building productive workplaces is not one of them.

Economics, Technology, and People

Finally, there is the linkage among technology, markets, and economic success. My major *ah-ha* from writing this book was how concepts of improvement evolved over the last century, from experts solving problems piecemeal (Taylorism), to everybody solving problems piecemeal (participative management), to experts improving whole systems (systems thinking), and now everybody improving whole systems (21st-Century stuff). We chose that course at AECL Medical because all the others, given the enormity of need and the shortness of time, were unthinkable.

We encouraged entrepreneurship at AECL — a government-owned enterprise — through an extended search process. By conventional standards the time frame was too short even for bona fide entrepreneurs. Perhaps that objective was unrealistic. Yet a company once thought moribund turned around and sales went up dramatically. That result had never been obtained there through old-paradigm selling. More, the company survived and became part of a vibrant enterprise years later.

Despite imperfections in the AECL process, I, like most survey respondents, would do it again. Had we stayed cautious and realistic at AECL, I doubt that so many jobs would have been saved or a new strategy hashed out so quickly. Unless we reach beyond the boundaries of realism, we are unlikely ever to realize our full human possibilities.

Risks. Still, there are enormous risks in reaching far. Make no mistake about it, every stretch toward dignity, meaning, and community is shadowed by what my friend William Schmidt called "the fraughts." Fraught means "laden with . . . . burdened . . . . teeming," "weighted," "charged," "loaded." Every business is fraught with the temptation to exploit its work force on behalf of its stockholders, fraught with the risk of manipulating middle managers to preserve power at the top, fraught with the possibility that energy, commitment, and impulses toward productivity will be misconstrued by greedy directors with narrowly economic motives, technocrats driving people to exclude all else but the job from their lives, executives and union leaders alike climbing or holding on for dear life to a pyramid of status and power.

There is a fine line between exploits and exploitation. I cannot tell when or if we crossed it in AECL Medical. There were times when I thought that the process was inhumane, that the kindest thing management could do was give everybody sixteen weeks' notice and avoid a lot of stress. But is that the ethical course? I wish life were so simple. Who would get notice? How about those who stayed? Would they be more secure than before, with no new markets or technologies? I am troubled each time I see companies unilaterally go for layoffs ahead of using their human capital to search out alternatives. I believe 21st-Century managers must find methods that hand people back their own lives.

Union-Management Relations. One hopeful sign is the new willingness of firms to provide employment security and workers to accept responsibility for output, as embodied in the 1986 contract between National Steel and the United Steelworkers. The AECL case makes plain what a challenge it is to implement such wrenching changes to tradition. In an open system, you can't separate "the contract" from everyday problem solving. What is the role of union leadership when workers have direct influence in management? When a design team can rethink wage schemes? When a steering group makes personnel policies? By the mid–21st Century my children's children will know a lot more about those matters than I do. I find myself muddling through still, though more confident than twenty years ago that answers can be found.

Working on Ourselves. I think our limiting assumptions go beyond economics to the negative voices, X and Y, buried in each of us. Profit is far from the only driving force in professional managers or owners. Nor is job security the only drive in union leaders. The desire to control, to maintain hierarchy, is so strong that some executives reduce profits to keep their worst assumptions intact. Conversely, freedom may not be the only motive for those who "stay loose," resisting structure and commitment. Creating more ambiguity when there is already too much serves no social purpose. It's a subtle bid for control more insidious than authoritarianism. There is a lifetime of personal work for each of us in contacting the shadow side of our natures, integrating the voices that tug us away from creative and humane impulses. We' re never finished. My concern is that so many young managers from modern business schools never even start.

Political Democracy and New Technologies

Mediating between us and our personal tensions, we have a democratic political system 200 years old in the United States and a few centuries older in Great Britain. The importance to community of openness, trust, free expression, mutual influence, equity, rationality, acceptance of differences was not discovered in T-groups in the 1940s or invented by Douglas McGregor. These core values were imported into the New World centuries ago.

Thomas Jefferson asserted the worth and dignity of each person as "unalienable" (which means nobody can take them away). He affirmed universal rights to "life, liberty and the pursuit of happiness" in the Declaration of Independence — the bedrock symbol of U.S. culture. You can read the American Revolution as an action-research experiment (never finished) to find a better fit in human society between personal and community needs. What makes the experiment possible is freedom of expression, the guarantee of openness provided by the First Amendment to the U.S. Constitution. Has any society ever sought to reconcile through political equality so many differences across cultures, classes, races, genders, hierarchies, institutions, and vast geography?

What expectations were created! Does it startle you that workers have less commitment to plants where they have little to say about how the job should be done than those where they have a lot? Were those expectations built by social scientists and engineers studying motivation? Or were we socialized to them from kindergarten on, studying the exploits of the American Revolution? Is it surprising that the central issue of productivity has often been framed as the tension between authoritarian and participative leadership? That's how American revolutionaries defined their conflict with crazy King George III.

Why Not Open Workplaces Too? In the workplace, the latest experiment has hardly begun. The wedding of capitalism, bureaucracy, and scientific management created in the early 20th Century levels of output previously unknown in the world. It also made workplaces — especially in smokestack industries like steel and autos — that contradicted democratic values of society at large. The march of technology has made such factories and offices obsolete. To compete in world markets, they are struggling to become more productive workplaces. Many thoughtful companies are feeling their way to the linkage between democratic values, dignity, meaning, community, and economic well-being (see "Ethical Infrastructure").

The fact that free expression, mutual responsibility, self-control, employee involvement in work design are associated with higher output, lower stress, and more viable businesses is as much a tribute to democracy as to social science. Frederick Taylor saw the fruitlessness of dictatorial managers and supervisors. Taylor had himself be a peacemaker. He thought rational work systems would cut out abuses of authority common in 19th Century factories. For a while it actually worked — with non-English-speaking immigrants. That his system could not sustain its intentions is a comment on our baser impulses — the triumph of control, greed, mechanistic thinking, and technological fantasies over dignity, meaning, and community when more conscious choices were needed.

We need authority in business enterprises, people who accept responsibility for saying "yes" or "no." We cannot afford authoritarianism — the willful, uninformed exercise of power. Yet antiauthoritarianism is not the same as political democracy, nor is full participation the equivalent of representative government. In the workplace we need modes consistent with democratic values and more efficient than democratic governments. Indeed, as we have seen, political representation on task forces or in business firms has little to do with meaningful, productive work. Perhaps the United States' unique contribution to 21st-Century management is to do business in ways that preserve individual freedom, enhance community, support innovation in methods and markets, and provide each person engaging work. Other nations may inspire us, but the culture we have to work with is peculiarly our own. We have a lot to learn and a lot to offer.

For all these reasons, I have a hard time calling organization development, quality of working life, or business transformation "cultural change," except in the most local sense. The values I speak for — a voice in company policy, openness, trust, responsibility for controlling your own work — represent cultural conservation, holding on to what we value most. Company cultures have been compromised by abuses of technology, bureaucracy, and authority. Democratic values came on sailing ships a long time

Ethical Infrastructure.

"Our ethical infrastructure should recognize some facts of life in the world of work:

- People want to do a good job.
- Each person knows best how to do his or her job.
- Individuals must be able to participate in decisions that affect their jobs.
- They need information to make good decisions.

"A business ethic that recognizes these truths . . . should not seem new or strange to us. It is what the Declaration of Independence and the Constitution are all about. Our task today is to put these principles into industry as well as society. . . . Management's job is not to tell people how their work should be done, but to create a climate in which these principles can flourish and people can work most productively.

"I am talking about lofty principles of fairness and justice. They are both moral and right and should live for their own sake. They are also worth observing for the sake of American business and industry. Our human strategy and our business strategy depend on each other."

— J.J. Renier, Vice-Chairman,
Honeywell, Inc. (1986, p. 4)

before. We conserve our culture when we seek to extend these values in the workplace, to keep open a creative dialogue between individualism and the common good.

Democracy Needs Learning. Democracy is a tough way to live. With all its flaws, I think it beats the alternatives. I do not wish to have someone else, no matter how educated, well-intentioned, wealthy, or wise, decide unilaterally what is best for me. Unless we are deeply involved in our work, we cannot feel good about ourselves. Unless we work with others toward valued goals, we cannot infuse hope and aspiration into our lives. Unless we treat one another as equals, we cannot find dignity, meaning, and community in work. Unless we make our own mistakes, and learn to forgive ourselves, we cannot learn at all. Unless we cooperate, we cannot survive.

If we care about the future, we must learn to care *more* about economics and technology, to understand their social uses and abuses. Workplace improvement — viability in world markets — requires that each person learn to accept personal customer responsibility *and* interdependence with many others. Hundreds, maybe thousands, of business firms have publicly acknowledged that need, and are learning the behavior that goes with it.

The Time Is Short. That's the Good News. The bad news is we're running out of time. Observed Frederick Taylor long ago, "We can see our forests vanishing, our water-powers going to waste, our soil being carried by floods into the sea; and the end of our coal and our iron is in sight. But our larger wastes of human effort, which go on every day through such of our acts as are blundering, ill-directed, or inefficient . . . are but vaguely appreciated." And he went on, "Their appreciation calls for an act of memory, an effort of the imagination" (1915, p. 5).

Now appreciation calls for imagining the unimaginable — the interconnectedness of every last thing under the sun. In choosing to write about dignity, meaning, and community in the workplace, I am uncomfortably aware that we cannot sustain good work apart from our lives as members of an endangered species on an endangered planet. The whole world is becoming our community. We have become much more sophisticated about Taylor's issue: awareness of human resources. We have a long way to go to tie together forests, water, soil, coal, iron, and newer natural resources like oil, gas, and the sun, with the infinite capacity of the human brain wed to the computer. In nuclear energy, in chemical wastes, in acid rain we have set up our own end game. Only by playing it cooperatively can we hope to win. No boss, no leader, no expert, no person, no group, no company, no nation, no continent can go it alone.

We are all on an open highway toward wholeness, of perception and involvement both. To make a whole life we can live with, each of us has to become expert at integrating what we have to contribute with what the others have.

At the End of the Day . . .

Eric Trist observed decades ago that workplace innovations had lives of their own. They rarely spread within the companies that pioneered them. As word got around, though, the underlying ideas became public, and many distant workplaces benefited. There is a term for this phenomenon — "morphic resonance" — that, despite my distaste for jargon, I like very much. It was coined by Rupert Sheldrake (1989), the molecular biologist and maverick scientist, to describe how (perhaps) things change in nature without anyone's deliberately seeking to change them.

Take flying, for example. For thousands of years people aspired to soar like birds. Nobody could do it until the Wright brothers built the right machine and learned to use it. After that nearly anyone could fly. Until Roger Bannister ran a mile in under four minutes in 1954, that feat was thought beyond human limits. Now countless others have done it.

So it is with workplace innovations. Margaret Wheatley (1992), for example, was among the first to show the inherent potential and the beautiful order that exists amid apparent confusion. Before "chaos theory" became management lingo, most people were understandably skeptical of large crowds interacting, sharing information, planning, and committing to action — all without being coerced by zealots or exhorted by charismatic orators. As more people learn to do something, however, it becomes easier for others, even without prior exposure. The capability travels through space and time by processes not well understood, although the effects are observable. When we say a trend is "in the air" we are talking about morphic resonance. By the end of the 20th Century, many colleagues and I came to understand the transformative power of "the whole system in the room."

We recognized that a simple act — inviting the right people to an interactive meeting, something the average person could do without years of training — opened the door to constructive, time-efficient actions that no one could plan, program, or specify as "deliverables." The more we did it the easier it was for others. As a result, tens of thousands of people who once had the word "meeting" equate with "frustration" had attended highly productive forums. They had learned first-hand the action potential of what Wheatley had called a "self-organizing system." Paradoxically, in an age of shorter, faster, cheaper, the shortest, fastest, cheapest way to get everybody improving whole systems was to get the whole system in the room.

My favorite "Peanuts" cartoon has Good Ole Charlie Brown saying, "I wish I was four years old again knowing what I know now." Would I plunge again into the projects in this book, knowing that for most the half-life would be an eye blink in human history? Yes, I would do them all again knowing — as should anyone who takes on the awesome task of improving systems — that "outcomes" in a sea of non-stop change are as short-lived as butterflies in summer.

I would do this work again because I believe that:

- Dialogue and inquiry are good for us.
- Humane workplaces enjoy greater economic success.
- Helping people gain control of their work engenders hope, and we all need hope to get by.
- It is existentially right to encourage cooperation — social, technical, and economic — across lines of age, class, culture, education, ethnicity, gender, national borders, race, status, and occupation.

Finally, I would do this work again for the sake of future generations. Getting everyone improving the whole is a legacy from the ancestors honored in these pages. It is a legacy our grandchildren richly deserve from us. More to the point, in the workplaces of the future, it is the only one they are likely to find worth inheriting.

References

Ackoff, R. L. *Redesigning the Future: A Systems Approach to Societal Problems.* New York: Wiley, 1974.

Ackoff, R. L. "The Corporate Rain Dance." *The Wharton Magazine*, 1977, *1* (2), 36–41.

Aguren, S., and others. *Volvo Kalmar Revisited: Ten Years of Experience.* Stockholm: Efficiency and Participation Development Council, 1984.

Argyris, C. *Intervention Theory and Method.* Reading, Mass.: Addison-Wesley, 1970.

Argyris, C., and Schön, D. A. *Organizational Learning: A Theory of Action Perspective.* Reading, Mass." Addison-Wesley, 1978.

Axelrod, R. H. *Terms of Engagement: Changing the Way We Change Organizations.* San Francisco: Berrett-Koehler, 2000.

Bartlett, J. (ed.) *Familiar Quotations.* (E. M. Beck, ed.) Boston: Little, Brown, 1980.

Baum, L. F. *The Wizard of Oz.* New York: Grosset & Dunlap, 1900.

Beckhard, R. *Organizational Development: Strategies and Models.* Reading, Mass.: Addison-Wesley, 1969.

Beckhard, R., and Harris, R. T. *Organizational Transitions: Managing Complex Change.* Reading, Mass.: Addison-Wesley, 1977.

Bellah, R. N., and others. *Habits of the Heart: Individualism and Commitment in American Life.* Berkeley and Los Angeles: University of California Press, 1985.

Bendix, R. *Work and Authority in Industry.* New York: Wiley, 1956.

Benne, K. "The Processes of Re-Education: An Assessment of Kurt Lewin's Views." *Group & Organization Studies*, Mar. 1976, *1* (1), 26–42. (Presented June 28, 1971, at Central Connecticut State University, New Britain, Conn.)

Bennis, W. G. *Changing Organizations.* New York: McGraw-Hill, 1966.

Bennis, W. G. "Chairman Mac in Perspective." *Harvard Business Review*, Sept.-Oct. 1972, *50* (5), 139–143.

Bennis, W. G., Benne, K. D., and Chin, R. *The Planning of Change.* (2nd ed.) New York: Holt, Rinehart & Winston, 1969.

Bennis, W. G., and Schein, E. H. (eds.). *Leadership and Motivation: Essays of Douglas McGregor*. Cambridge, Mass.: MIT Press, 1966.

Bion, W. R. *Experience in Groups and Other Papers*. London: Tavistock, 1961.

Blake, R. R., and Mouton, J. S. *The Managerial Grid*. Houston, Texas: Gulf Publishing Company, 1964.

Block, P. *Flawless Consulting*. Austin, Texas: Learning Concepts, 1981.

Block, P. *The Empowered Manager: Positive Political Skills at Work* (2nd ed.) San Francisco: Jossey-Bass, 2004.

Bowers, D. G., and Franklin, J. L. *Survey-Guided Development I: Data-Based Organizational Change*. La Jolla, Calif.: University Associates, 1977.

Bradford, D. L., and Cohen, A. R. *Managing for Excellence: The Guide to Developing High Performance in Contemporary Organizations*. New York: Wiley, 1984.

Brand, S. "The World Information Economy, An Interview with Peter Schwartz and Jay Ogilvy." *Whole Earth Review*, Winter 1986, pp. 88–97.

Braverman, H. *Labour and Monopoly Capital*. New York: Monthly Review Press, 1974.

Bridges, W. *Transitions: Making Sense of Life's Changes*. Reading, Mass.: Addison-Wesley, 1980.

Bridges, W. "How to Manage Organizational Transition." *Training*, Sept. 1985, pp. 28–32.

Bucklow, M. "A New Role for the Work Group." *Administrative Science Quarterly*, June 1966, 1 (1), 59–78.

Bunker, B. B., and Alban, B.T. *Large Group Interventions: Engaging the Whole System for Rapid Change*. San Francisco: Jossey-Bass, 1997.

Burck, G. "Union Carbide's Patient Schemers." *Fortune*, Dec. 1965, pp. 147–149.

Burke, W. W. *Organization Development: Principles and Practices*. Boston: Little, Brown, 1982.

Buzan, T. *Use Both Sides of Your Brain*. New York: Dutton, 1974.

Bylinsky, G. "What Tomorrow Holds." *Fortune*, Oct. 13, 1986, pp. 42–44.

Cartwright, D. "Kurt Lewin, 1890–1947." *International Journal of Opinion and Attitude Research*, 1947, 1, 96–99.

Caruso, D. B. "Retirees to Fight Cutoff of Benefits." *The Philadelphia Inquirer*, March 24, 2003, p. B3.

Caruso, D. B. "Bethlehem Steel Asset Sale Okd," *The Philadelphia Inquirer*, April 23, 2003, p. C3.

Castle, P. "PS Restructuring Signals Greater Opportunities for Satisfaction in Workplace." *Canberra Times*, "The Circus" column, May 10, 1986.

Chase, S. "An Authentic Genius." *The New Republic*, Oct. 8, 1924, reprinted in *Bulletin of the Taylor Society*, Feb. 1925, 10 (1), 66–68.

Clapp, N., and others. *The Selected Wisdom of New Jersey*. Plainfield, N.J.: Block-Petrella-Weisbord Designed Learning, Inc., 1975.

Clarkson, M. "Search Conferences." Paper presented at the International Quality of Working Life Conference, Toronto, Aug. 1981.

Coch, L., and French, J. R. P., Jr. "Overcoming Resistance to Change." *Human Relations*, 1948, 1, 512–533.

Cohen, A. "Too Old To Work?" *New York Times Magazine*, March 2, 2003, pp. 54–59

Cohen, M. D., and March, J. G. "Leadership in an Organized Anarchy." *Leadership and Ambiguity: The American College President*. New York: McGraw-Hill, 1974.

Collins, J. C. *Good to Great*. New York: HarperCollins, 2001.

Collins, J. C., and Porras, J. I. *Built to Last: Successful Habits of Visionary Companies*. New York: Harper, 1997.

Cooperrider, D., Whitney, D., Anderson, H., McNamee, S., Gergen, M., and Gergen, K. J. *Appreciative Organization*. Taos, N.M.: Taos Institute Publications, 2001.

Copley, F. B. *Frederick W. Taylor: Father of Scientific Management*. 2 vols. New York: Harper & Row, 1923.

Cousins, N. "What You Believe Can Have an Effect on Your Health." *U.S. News & World Report*, Jan. 23, 1984, pp. 61–62.

Dannemiller-Tyson Associates. *Whole-Scale Change: Unleashing the Magic in Organizations*. San Francisco: Berrett-Koehler, 2000.

Davis, L. E., Canter, R. R., and Hoffman, J. F "Current Job Design Criteria." *Journal of Industrial Engineering*, 1955, 6, 5–11.

Davis, L. E. "Job Design Research." *Journal of Industrial Engineering*, Nov.-Dec. 1957.

Davis, L. E., and Sullivan, C. S. "A Labor-Management Contract and the Quality of Working Life." *Journal of Occupational Behavior*, 1980, 1, 29–41.

de Geus, A. *The Living Company*. London: Nicholas Brealy, 1997.

de Renzy-Martin, P. Executive Vice President, Shell Solar, www.shell.com, News Release, October 24, 2002.

Deming, W. E. *Quality, Productivity and Competitive Position*. Cambridge, Mass.: MIT Press, 1982.

Drucker, P. F. *Management: Tasks, Responsibilities, Practices*. New York: Harper & Row, 1974.

Drucker, P. F. "The Coming Rediscovery of Scientific Management." *The Conference Board Record*, June 1976, pp. 23–27.

Drury, H. B. *Scientific Management: A History and Criticism*. New York: Columbia University Press, 1915.

Dunn, W. N., and Swierzek, F. W. "Planned Organizational Change: Toward Grounded Theory." *Journal of Applied Behavioral Science*, 1977, 2 (13), 135–157.

Dunnette, M. D. "People Feeling: Joy, More Joy, and the Slough of Despond." *Journal of Applied Behavioral Science*, 1969, 5, 25–44.

Ebbin, R. "Turnover Takes a Turn for the Better," *Restaurants USA*, March 1999.

Egon Zehnder International. Report of survey noted in *Forbes*, June 30, 1986, p. 9.

Elden, M. "Three Generations of Work Democracy Experiments in Norway: Beyond Classical Socio-Technical Analysis." Institute for Industrial Social Research, Technical University of Trondheim, Norway, 1978.

Elden, M. "Client as Consultant: Work Reform through Participative Research." *National Productivity Review*, Spring 1983a, pp. 136–147.

Elden, M. "Democratization and Participative Research in Developing Local Theory." *Journal of Occupational Behavior*, 1983b, *4*, 21–33.

Emery, F. E. "Characteristics of Socio-Technical Systems." London: Tavistock Documents #527. Abridged in E. E. Emery, *The Emergence of a New Paradigm of Work*. Canberra: Centre for Continuing Education, 1959.

Emery, F. E. *Report on the Hunsfoss Project*. London: Tavistock Documents Series, 1964.

Emery, F. E. "The Next Thirty Years: Concepts, Methods, and Anticipations." *Human Relations*, 1967, *20*, 199–237.

Emery, F. E. *The Emergence of a New Paradigm of Work*. Canberra: Centre for Continuing Education, Australian National University, 1978.

Emery, F. E. "Designing Socio-Technical Systems for 'Greenfield' Sites." *Journal of Occupational Behavior*, 1980, *1*, 19–27.

Emery, F. E., and Trist, E. L. "Socio-Technical Systems." In C. W. Churchman and others (eds.), *Management Sciences, Models and Techniques*. London: Pergamon, 1960.

Emery, F. E., and Trist, E. L. "The Causal Texture of Organizational Environments." Paper presented to the International Psychology Congress, Washington, D.C., 1963. Reprinted in *Human Relations*, 1964, *18* (1), 21–32.

Emery, F. E., and Trist, E. L. *Toward a Social Ecology*. New York: Plenum, 1973.

Emery, M. *Searching: For New Directions, in New Ways for New Times*. Canberra: Centre for Continuing Education, Australian National University, 1982.

Emery, M. "Learning and the Quality of Working Life." *QWL Focus*, Feb. 1983, *3* (1), 1–7.

Fisher, I. "Scientific Management Made Clear." *Bulletin of the Taylor Society*, Feb. 1925, *10* (1), 41–61.

Flax, S. "Did GM Give Away the Store?" *Fortune*, Oct. 15, 1984, pp. 223–228.

Flint, J. "The Fireproof Man." *Forbes*, Oct. 22, 1984, pp. 94–98.

Fox, R. E, Lippitt, R., and Schindler-Rainman, E. *The Humanized Future: Some New Images*. La Jolla, Calif.: University Associates, 1973.

French, W. L. "Organization Development: Objectives, Assumptions and Strategies." *California Management Review*, Winter 1969, *12* (2), 23–39.

French, W. L., and Bell, C. H., Jr. *Organization Development: Behavioral Science Interventions for Organization Improvement*. Englewood Cliffs, N. J.: Prentice-Hall, 1973.

Galbraith, J. R. *Organization Design*. Reading, Mass.: Addison-Wesley, 1977.

Gantt, H. L. *Work, Wages, and Profits*. (2nd ed.) New York: Engineering Magazine Company, 1916.

Gantt, H. L. *Organizing for Work*. New York: Harcourt Brace Jovanovich, 1919.

Garfield, C. *Peak Performers: The New Heroes of American Business*. New York: William Morrow, 1986.

Garson, B. *The Electronic Sweatshop: How Computers Are Transforming the Office of the Future into the Factory of the Past*. New York: Penguin 1989.

Geertz, C. *The Interpretation of Cultures*. New York: Basic Books, 1973.

Georgopoulos, B. S., and Mann, F. C. *The Community General Hospital*. New York: Macmillan, 1962.

Gibb, J. R. *Trust: A New View of Personal and Organizational Development*. Los Angeles: Guild of Tutors Press, 1978.

Gilmore, T. N. "Overcoming Crisis and Uncertainty: The Search Conference." In L. Hirschhorn and Associates, *Cutting Back: Retrenchment and Redevelopment in Human and Community Services*. San Francisco: Jossey-Bass, 1983.

Gilmore, T., and Krantz, J. *Projective Identification in the Consulting Relationship: Exploring the Unconscious Dimensions of a Client System*. Philadelphia: University of Pennsylvania, Management and Behavioral Science Center, the Wharton School, April 1985.

Goldratt, E., and Cox, J. *The Goal*. Great Barrington, Mass.: North River Press, 1985.

Gray, S. G. "The Tavistock Institute of Human Relations." In H. V. Dicks, *50 Years of the Tavistock Clinic*. London: Routledge & Kegan Paul, 1970.

Greiner, L. E., and Metzger, R. O. *Consulting to Management*. Englewood Cliffs, N.J.: Prentice-Hall, 1983.

Gustavsen, B. "Workplace Reform and Industrial Democratic Dialogue." *Economic and Industrial Democracy*, 1985, 6, 461–479.

Gutchess, J. *Employment Security in Action: Strategies That Work*. New York: Pergamon Press, 1984.

Hackman, R. J., and Oldham, G. R. *Work Redesign*. Reading, Mass.: Addison-Wesley, 1980.

Halpern, N. "Sustaining Change in the Shell Sarnia Chemical Plant." *QWL Focus*, May 1982, 2 (1), 5–11.

Hamilton, A., Madison, J., and Jay, J. *The Federalist Papers*, introduction by Clinton Rossiter. New York: New American Library, 1961.

Harrison, R. "Role Negotiation: A Tough-Minded Approach to Team Development." In W. W. Burke and H. A. Hornstein (eds.), *The Social Technology of Organization Development*. La Jolla, Calif.: University Associates, 1972.

Heidorn, R., Jr., and Raghavan, S. "Bethlehem Steel to Close the Last Plant in Its Hometown," *Philadelphia Inquirer*, December 30, 1997, pp. A1, A9.

Herbst, P. G. *Socio-Technical Design*. London: Tavistock, 1974.

Herzberg, F., Mausner, B., and Snyderman, B. *The Motivation to Work*. (2nd ed.) New York: Wiley, 1959.

Hickey, J. W. "Productivity Gain Seen in Labor-Management Reversal." *World of Work Report*, April 1986, *11* (4), 3–4.

Hirschhorn, L. *Beyond Mechanization: Work and Technology in a Postindustrial Age.* Cambridge, Mass.: MIT Press, 1984.

Hirschhorn, L., and Associates. *Cutting Back: Retrenchment and Redevelopment in Human and Community Services.* San Francisco: Jossey-Bass, 1983.

Hjelholt, G. "Training for Reality" and a supplement, "Some Results of Ship's Crew Training," working papers nos. 5 and 5A. Leeds: University of Leeds, Department of Management Studies, Sept. 1968.

Holman, P., and Devane, T. (eds.). *The Change Handbook: Group Methods for Shaping the Future*. San Francisco: Berrett-Koehler, 2001.

Jacques, E. *The Changing Culture of a Factory*. London: Tavistock, 1951.

Janoff, S., and Weisbord, M. "Facilitating the Whole System in the Room." Seminar on a Philosophy and Method for Transforming Work Groups. Philadelphia: Future Search Network, 2001.

Janssen, C. *Personlig Dialektik*. (2nd ed.) Stockholm: Liber, 1982.

Johnson, M. J. "Fred Taylor '83: Giant of Non-Repute." *The Stevens Indicator*, Spring 1980, *97* (2), 4–8.

Kakar, S. *Frederick Taylor: A Study in Personality and Innovation*. Cambridge, Mass.: MIT Press, 1970.

Kast, F. E., and Rosenzweig, J. E. *Organization and Management: A Systems Approach*. New York: McGraw-Hill, 1970.

Kelly, F. C. *The Wright Brothers*. New York: Ballantine Books, 1943.

Kleiner, A. *Fast Company*, *3*, June 1996, p. 44.

Knickerbocker, I., and McGregor, D. "Industrial Relations and National Defense: A Change to Management." *Personnel*, July 1941, *18* (1), 49–63.

Knickerbocker, I., and McGregor, D. "Union-Management Cooperation: A Psychological Analysis." *Personnel*, Nov. 1942, *19* (3), 520–539.

Kotter, J. P., with Heskett, J. L. *Corporate Culture and Performance*. New York: Free Press, 1992.

Kristofferson, K., and Foster, F. "Me and Bobby McGee" (© Combine Music Corp.) From "Kristofferson," © 1970, Columbia/Legacy.

Langewiesche, W. *Stick and Rudder*. New York: McGraw-Hill, 1944.

Lawler, E. E., III. *High-Involvement Management: Participative Strategies for Improving Organizational Performance*. San Francisco: Jossey-Bass, 1986.

Lawrence, P. R., and Lorsch, J. W. *Organization and Environment*. Boston: Harvard University Press, 1967.

Lawrence, P. R., and Nohria, N. *Driven: How Human Nature Shapes Our Choices*. San Francisco: Jossey-Bass, 2002.

Levering, R., Moskowitz, M., and Katz, M. *The 100 Best Companies to Work for in America*. New York: New American Library, 1985.

Lewin, K. "Die Sozialisierung des Taylor systems" [Humanization of the Taylor system]. *Praktischer Sozialismus*, 1920, (4), 5–36.

Lewin, K. *Dynamic Theory of Personality*. New York: McGraw-Hill, 1935.

Lewin, K. "Research on Minority Problems." *The Technology Review*, Jan. 1946, 48 (3).

Lewin, K. "Frontiers in Group Dynamics, part 1: Concept, Method and Reality in Social Science: Social Equilibria and Social Change." *Human Relations*, 1947a, 1, 5–41.

Lewin, K. "Frontiers in Group Dynamics, part 2: Channels of Group Life: Social Planning and Action Research." *Human Relations*, 1947b, *1*, 143–153.

Lewin, K. *Resolving Social Conflicts: Selected Papers on Group Dynamics*. Edited by G. W. Lewin. New York: Harper & Row, 1948.

Lewin, K. *Field Theory in Social Science: Selected Theoretical Papers*. Edited by D. Cartwright. New York: Harper & Row, 1951.

Lewin, K., and others. "The Practicality of Democracy." In G. Murphy (ed.), *Human Nature and Enduring Peace*. Boston: Houghton-Mifflin, 1945.

Likert, R. *New Patterns of Management*. New York: McGraw-Hill, 1961.

Likert, R. *The Human Organization: Its Management and Value*. New York: McGraw-Hill, 1967.

Likert, R., and Likert, J. G. *New Ways of Managing Conflict*. New York: McGraw-Hill, 1976.

Lindaman, E. *Thinking in the Future Tense*. Nashville, Tenn.: Broadman Press, 1978.

Lindaman, E., and Lippitt, R. *Choosing the Future You Prefer*. Washington: Development Publications, 1979.

Lippitt, R. "Kurt Lewin, 1890–1947: Adventures in the Exploration of Interdependence." *Sociometry*, 1947, *10*, 87–97.

Lippitt, R. "Future Before You Plan." In *NTL Managers' Handbook*. Arlington, Va.: NTL Institute, 1983.

Lippitt, R., Watson, J., and Westley, B. *The Dynamics of Planned Change*. New York: Harcourt Brace Jovanovich, 1958.

Locke, E. A. "The Ideas of Frederick W. Taylor: An Evaluation." *Academy of Management Review*, 1982, *7* (1), 14–24.

Locke, E. A. "Participation in Decision Making: When Should It Be Used?" *Organizational Dynamics*, Winter 1986, pp. 65–79.

Lytle, W. O. *Starting an Organization Design Effort: A Planning and Preparation Guide* (rev. ed.). Englishtown, N.J.: BPW Publishing, 1997.

Lytle, W. O. *Designing a High-Performance Organization: A Guide to the Whole-Systems Approach*. Englishtown, N.J.: BPW Publishing, 1998.

Lytle, W. O. "Accelerating the Organization Design Process," *Reflections: The SoL Journal*, Winter 2002, MIT Press.

McFarland, M. W. (ed.). *The Papers of Wilbur and Orville Wright*. 2 vols. New York: McGraw-Hill, 1953.

McFletcher Associates. The Work-Style Preference Inventory. Scottsdale, Ariz., 1983.

McGregor, D. "A Year at Antioch." Yellow Springs, Ohio: Antioch College, June 1949.

McGregor, D. "Human Organization and Education." Talk delivered at the University of Michigan, March 23, 1950.

McGregor, D. "On Leadership." *Antioch Notes*, May 1954, pp. 2–3.

McGregor, D. *The Human Side of Enterprise*. New York: McGraw-Hill, 1960.

McGregor, D., Bennis, W. G., and McGregor, C. (eds.). *The Professional Manager*. New York: McGraw-Hill, 1967.

McGregor, D., and Scanlon, J. N. "The Dewey and Almy Chemical Company and the International Chemical Workers Union." Case Study no. 3. Washington: National Planning Association, 1948.

McKibbon, J. "A Labour Perspective on QWL." *QWL Focus, The News Journal of the Ontario Quality of Working Life Centre*. Ontario Ministry of Labour, Spring 1984, 4 (1).

Main, J. "Under the Spell of the Quality Gurus." *Fortune*, Aug. 18, 1986, pp. 30–34.

Mann, F. C. "Studying and Creating Change: A Means to Understanding Social Organization." In C. M. Arensbert and others (eds.), *Research in Industrial Human Relations: A Critical Appraisal*. New York: Harper & Row, 1957.

Marrow, A. F. *The Practical Theorist*. New York: Basic Books, 1969.

Maslow, A. H. *Eupsychian Management*. Homewood, Ill.: Irwin, 1965.

Maslow, A. H., and Murphy, G. (eds.). *Motivation and Personality*. New York: Harper & Row, 1954.

Mathewson, S. B. *Restriction of Output Among Unorganized Workers*. New York: Viking Penguin, 1931.

Mayo, E. *The Social Problems of an Industrial Civilization*. Boston: School of Business Administration, Harvard University, 1945.

Mead, M. "Cultural Discontinuities and Personality Transformation." *Journal of Social Issues*, 1983, 39 (4), 161–177; reprinted from *JSI Supplement*, 1954 (8), 3–16.

"Memorial to Douglas McGregor." Cambridge, Mass.: MIT, Oct. 16, 1964.

Metcalf, H. C., and Urwick, L. (eds.). *Dynamic Administration: The Collected Works of Mary Parker Follett*. New York: Harper & Row, 1940.

Miller, E. J. "The Open System Approach to Organizational Analysis, with Specific Reference to the Work of A. K. Rice." In Hofstede and Kassem (eds.), *European Contributions to Organization Theory*. Assen, 1975.

Miller, R. S. Quoted in Bethlehem Steel news release, Public Affairs Department, July 9, 2002.

Mintzberg, H. "Planning on the Left Side and Managing on the Right." *Harvard Business Review*, Jul.-Aug. 1976, 54 (4), 49–58.

Mohrman, S. A., Cohen, S. G., and Mohrman, A., Jr. *Designing Team-Based Organizations*. San Francisco: Jossey-Bass, 1995.

Moore, B. E., and Ross, T. L. *The Scanlon Way to Improved Productivity: A Practical Guide*. New York: Wiley, 1978.

Nadworny, M. J. *Scientific Management and the Unions: 1900–1923*. Cambridge, Mass.: Harvard University Press, 1955.

Naisbitt, J. *Megatrends*. New York: Warner Books, 1982.

Neilsen, E. H. *Becoming an OD Practitioner*. Englewood Cliffs, N.J.: Prentice-Hall, 1984.

Nelson, B. "Bosses Face Less Risk Than Bossed." *New York Times*, April 1983.

Nelson, D. *Frederick W. Taylor and the Rise of Scientific Management*. Madison: University of Wisconsin Press, 1980.

Nord, W. "Theory Y Assumptions in a Non-Theory Y World." *Interfaces*, Feb. 1978, 8 (2), 61–66.

Oshry, B. *Seeing Systems: Unlocking the Mysteries of Organizational Life*. San Francisco: Berrett-Koehler, 1996.

Ouchi, W. *Theory Z*. Reading, Mass.: Addison-Wesley, 1981.

Owen, H. "Let the Spirit Soar." Unpublished manuscript, 1984.

Owen, H. *Open Space Technology: A User's Guide*. San Francisco: Berrett-Koehler, 1997.

Papanek, M. L. "Kurt Lewin and His Contributions to Modern Management Theory." *Academy of Management Proceedings*, Aug. 1973, pp. 317–321.

Pasmore, W., and others. "Sociotechnical Systems: A North American Reflection on Empirical Studies of the Seventies." *Human Relations*, 1982, 35 (12).

Patterson, D. "A Labour Perspective on QWL." *QWL Focus, The News Journal of the Ontario Quality of Working Life Centre*. Ontario Ministry of Labour, Spring 1984, 4 (1).

Pava, C. H. P. *Managing New Age Technology: An Organizational Strategy*. New York: Free Press, 1983.

Paxton, T. "I Can't Help But Wonder (Where I'm Bound)" © 1963; Renewed 1991 Cherry Lane Music Publishing Company, Inc. (ASCAP) and DreamWorks Songs (ASCAP).

Pearce, J. C. *The Crack in the Cosmic Egg*. New York: Julian Press, 1971.

Perls, F., Hefferline, R., and Goodman, F. *Gestalt Therapy*. New York: Julian Press, 1951.

Perrow, C. *Complex Organizations: A Critical Essay* (2nd ed.). New York: Random House, 1979.

Peters, T. J., and Waterman, R. H. *In Search of Excellence*. New York: Harper & Row, 1982.

Petrella, T. "Managing with Teams." Plainfield, N.J.: Block Petrella Associates, 1974.

Picker, W. J. "Douglas McGregor (A Study Guide)." Unpublished manuscript, Dec. 1967, rev. June 1968.

Renier, J. J. "'Ethical Infrastructure' Vital to Productivity Gains." *World of Work Report*, Jan. 1986, *11* (1), 4–5.

Revans, R. W. *The Origins and Development of Action Learning*. England: Brookfield Publishing, 1982.

Rice, A. K. *Productivity and Social Organization: The Ahmedabad Experiment*. London: Tavistock, 1958.

Richman, T. "Peering into Tomorrow." *INC.*, Oct. 1982, pp. 45–48.

Roethlisberger, E J., and Dickson, W. J. *Management and the Worker*. Cambridge, Mass.: Harvard University Press, 1939.

Sashkin, M. "Interview [with] Eric Trist, British Interdisciplinarian." *Group & Organization Studies*, June 1980, 5 (2), 144–166.

Sashkin, M. "Participative Management Is an Ethical Imperative." *Organizational Dynamics*, Spring 1984, pp. 4–22.

Schindler-Rainmann, E., and Lippitt, R. *Building the Collaborative Community: Mobilizing Citizens for Action*. Riverside, Calif.: University of California, 1980.

Schön, D. *Beyond the Stable State*. New York: Random House, 1971.

Sheldrake, R. *The Presence of the Past: Morphic Resonance and the Habits of Nature*. New York: Vintage Books, 1989.

Simmons, J., and Mares, W. *Working Together*. New York: Knopf, 1983.

Sisan, C., and Sisan, K. (eds.). *The Oxford Book of 20th Century Verse*. London: Oxford University Press, 1973.

Sorensen, K. H. "Technology and Industrial Democracy: An Inquiry into Some Theoretical Issues and Their Social Basis." *Organization Studies*, 1986, 2 (6), 139–160.

Stark, C. "U.S. Judge Gives Green Light to Allegheny Racketeering Lawsuit," *Philadelphia Inquirer*, December 24, 1999, p. C1.

Tannenbaum, R., and Hanna, R. W. "Holding On, Letting Go, and Moving On: Understanding a Neglected Perspective on Change." In R. Tannenbaum, N. Margulies, E. Massarik, and Associates, *Human Systems Development: New Perspectives on People and Organizations*. San Francisco: Jossey-Bass, 1985.

Tarbell, I. "Making the Most of Men." *Saturday Review of Literature*, Oct. 25, 1924, reprinted in *Bulletin of the Taylor Society*, Feb. 1925, 10 (1), 80–81.

Taylor, F. W. *A Piece Rate System: A Step Toward Partial Solution of the Labor Problem*. Paper for the American Society of Mechanical Engineers, 1895.

Taylor, F. W. *Shop Management*. New York: Harper & Row, 1911.

Taylor, F. W. *The Principles of Scientific Management*. New York: Harper & Row, 1915.

Tead, O. "Taylor's Intellectual Contribution." *American Review*, July-Aug. 1924, reprinted in *Bulletin of the Taylor Society*, Feb. 1925, 10 (1), 62–65.

Thorsrud, E. "The Scandinavian Model: Strategies of Organizational Democratization in Norway." In B. Wilpert and A. Sorge (eds.), *International Perspectives on Organizational Democracy*. New York: Wiley, 1984.

Tocqueville, A. de. *Democracy in America*. 2 vols. (J. P. Mayer and A. P. Kerr, eds.) New York: Doubleday, 1969. (Originally published 1835.)

Toffler, A. *The Third Wave*. New York: McGraw-Hill, 1980.

Toffler, A. *The Adaptive Corporation*. New York: McGraw-Hill, 1984.

Tolstoy, L. *Anna Karenina*. Translated by David Magarshack. New York: New American Library, 1961. (Originally published 1877.)

Trist, E. L. Speech presented at the European Economic Community Conference, Brussels, 1974.

Trist, E. L. "Critique of Scientific Management in Terms of Socio-Technical Theory." In M. Weir (ed.), *Job Satisfaction*. Glasgow: Fontana/Collins, 1976. Reprinted from *Prakseologia*, 1971, 39–40, 159–174.

Trist, E. L., with J. Eldred and R. Keidel. "A New Approach to Economic Development." *Human Futures*, 1977 (1), 8–12.

Trist, E. L. "Adapting to a Changing World," in *Readings in Quality of Working Life*. George E. Sanderson, ed. Ottawa: Labour Canada, 1978, pp. 10–20.

Trist, E. L. *The Evolution of Socio-Technical Systems: A Conceptual Framework and an Action Research Program*. Occasional paper no. 2. Ontario Quality of Working Life Centre, June 1981.

Trist, E. L. "Intervention Strategies for Inter-organizational Domains." In R. Tannenbaum and others (eds.), *Human Systems Development: New Perspectives on People and Organizations*. San Francisco: Jossey-Bass, 1985a.

Trist, E. L. "Working with Bion in the 1940s: The Group Decade." In M. Pines (ed.), *Bion and Group Psychotherapy*. London: Routledge & Kegan Paul, 1985b.

Trist, E. L., and Dwyer, C. "The Limits of Laissez-Faire as a Sociotechnical Strategy." In R. Zager and M. F. Rosow (eds.), *The Innovative Organization*. New York: Pergamon Press, 1982.

Trist, E. L., and Emery, F. E. "Report on the Barford Conference for Bristol/Siddeley, Aero-Engine Corp." Document no. 598, July 10–16, 1960. London: Tavistock.

Trist, E. L., Higgin, G. W., Murray, H., and Pollock, A. B. *Organizational Choice*. London: Tavistock, 1963.

Trist, E. L., with Murray, H. *The Social Engagement of Social Science: A Tavistock Anthology* (Vol. I: The Socio-Psychological Perspective). Philadelphia: The University of Pennsylvania Press, 1990.

Trist, E. L., with Murray, H. *The Social Engagement of Social Science: A Tavistock Anthology* (Vol. II: The Socio-Technical Perspective). Philadelphia: The University of Pennsylvania Press, 1993.

Trist, E. L., with Emery, F., and Murray, H. *The Social Engagement of Social Science: A Tavistock Anthology* (Vol. III: The Socio-Ecological Perspective). Philadelphia: The University of Pennsylvania Press, 1997.

United Steel Workers of America. "Summary: Proposed Agreement with National Steel Corporation." Pittsburgh, April 9, 1986.

Vaill, P. B. "Cook Book Auction and Clap Trap Cocoons." *Exchange: The Organizational Behavior Teaching Journal*, 1979, 4 (1), 4.

Vaill, P. B. "The Purposing of High-Performing Systems." *Organizational Dynamics*, Autumn 1982, pp. 23–39.

Vaill, P. B. *Learning as a Way of Being: Strategies for Survival in a World of Permanent White Water*. San Francisco: Jossey-Bass, 1996.

van Beinum, H. Speech introducing Emery at "Explorations in Human Features" Conference, 1985.

Van De Ven, A. H., and Ferry, D. L. *Measuring and Assessing Organizations*. New York: Wiley, 1980.

Vickers, G. *The Art of Judgment*. London: Chapman and Hall; New York: Basic Books, 1966.

von Bertalanffy, L. "The Theory of Open Systems in Physics and Biology." *Science*, 1950 (3), 23–29.

von Bertalanffy, L. *Problems of Life*. New York: Wiley, 1952.

Walton, R. E. "The Diffusion of New Work Structures: Explaining Why Success Didn't Take." *Organizational Dynamics*, 1975, 3 (3), 2–22.

Walton, R. E. "The Topeka Work System: Optimistic Vision, Pessimistic Hypotheses, and Reality." In R. Zager and M. P. Rosow (eds.), *The Innovative Organization*. New York: Pergamon Press, 1982.

Weisbord, M. R. "Management in Crisis: Must You Liquidate People?" An interview with Dr. Rensis Likert. *The Conference Board Record*, Feb. 1970.

Weisbord, M. R. "A Mixed Model for Medical Centers: Changing Structure and Behavior." In *Theory and Method in Organization Development: An Evolutionary Process*. Washington: NTL Institute, 1974.

Weisbord, M. R. "Why Organization Development Hasn't Worked (So Far) in Medical Centers." *Health Care Management Review*, Spring 1976, 1 (2), 17–28.

Weisbord, M. R. "How Do You Know It Works If You Don't Know What It Is?" *OD Practitioner*, Oct. 1977, 9 (3), 1–80.

Weisbord, M. R. "Input Versus Output-Focused Organizations: Notes on a Contingency Theory of Practice." In W. Burke, ed., *The Cutting Edge: Current Theory and Practice in Organization Development*. La Jolla, Calif.: University Associates, 1978a.

Weisbord, M. R. *Organizational Diagnosis: A Workbook of Theory and Practice*. Reading, Mass.: Addison-Wesley, 1978b.

Weisbord, M. R. "Some Reflections on OD's Identity Crisis." *Group & Organizational Studies*, June 1981, 6 (2), 161–175.

Weisbord, M. R. "Future Search: Innovative Business Conference." *Planning Review*, July 1984, *12* (4), 16–20.

Weisbord, M. R. "Participative Work Design: A Personal Odyssey." *Organizational Dynamics*, Spring 1985, pp. 4–20.

Weisbord, M. R. "Future Search: A 'New Paradigm'? Maybe Not." *SearchNEWS*, 6, Winter 1996.

Weisbord, M. R. "Resolving a New Paradox with Old Wisdom." In P. Block and 30 Flawless Consultants, *The Flawless Consulting Fieldbook and Companion*. San Francisco: Pfeiffer, 2001.

Weisbord, M. R., and Janoff, S. *Future Search: An Action Guide to Finding Common Ground in Organizations and Communities* (2nd ed.). San Francisco: Berrett-Koehler, 2000.

Weisbord, M. R., Lamb, H., and Drexler, A. *Improving Police Department Management Through Problem-Solving Task Forces*. Reading, Mass.: Addison-Wesley, 1974.

Weisbord, M. R., Lawrence, E. R., and Charns, M. E ."Three Dilemmas of Academic Medical Centers." *The Journal of Applied Behavioral Science*, 1978, *14* (3), 284–304.

Weisbord, M. R., and Maselko, J. C. "Learning How to Influence Others." *Supervisory Management*, May 1981, *26* (5), 2–10.

Weisbord, M. R., and Stoelwinder, J. "Linking Physicians, Hospital Management, Cost Containment, and Better Medical Care," *Health Care Management Review*, Spring 1979, 7–13.

Weisbord, M. R., and 35 International Authors. *Discovering Common Ground*. San Francisco: Berrett-Koehler, 1992.

Westcott, L., and Degen, P. *Wind and Sand: The Story of the Wright Brothers at Kitty Hawk*. New York: Abrams, 1983.

Wheatley, M. J. *Leadership and the New Science Revised: Discovering Order in a Chaotic World*. San Francisco: Berrett-Koehler, 1992.

Whitfield, E., and McGregor, D. *As We See It: Antioch, 1950*. Yellow Springs, Ohio: Antioch College, 1950.

Whyte, W. F. *Money and Motivation*. New York: Harper & Row, 1955.

Whyte, W. F., with Whyte, K. K. *Learning from the Field: A Guide from Experience*. Chapter 10, "Types of Applied Social Research." Beverly Hills, Calif.: Sage Publications, 1984.

Wilenski, P. "The SES Manager of the Future." Address to the Australian Government Senior Executives Association, Victorian Branch, July 25, 1986.

Wilson, A. T. M. "Some Aspects of Social Process." *Journal of Social Issues*, 1983, 39 (4), 91–107 (1951 Kurt Lewin Memorial Lecture).

Wolf, W. B. "The Impact of Kurt Lewin on Management Thought." *Academy of Management Proceedings*, August 1973, pp. 322–325.

Wolfe, T. *The Right Stuff*. New York: Bantam, 1980.

Wrege, C. D., and Perroni, A. G. "Taylor's Pig-Tale: A Historical Analysis of Frederick W. Taylor's Pig-Iron Experiments." *Academy of Management Journal*, March 1974, *17* (1), 6–27.

Wrege, C. D., and Stotka, A. M. "Cooke Creates a Classic: The Story Behind F. W. Taylor's Principles of Scientific Management." *Academy of Management Review*, Oct. 1978, *3* (4), 736–749.

Wren, D. A. *The Evolution of Management Thought*. (2nd ed.) New York: Wiley, 1979.

Zager, R., and Rosow, M. P. *The Innovative Organization: Productivity Programs in Action*. New York: Pergamon Press, 1982.

Zaleznik, A. "Management of Disappointment." *Harvard Business Review*, Nov.-Dec. 1967, pp. 59–70.

Zand, D. E., Miles, M. B., and Lytle, W. O., Jr. "Enlarging Organizational Choice Through Use of a Temporary Problem-Solving System" (unpublished paper, 1970).

Index